I object to the title a
W's memoirs upon which book
more novelistic than reportorial — "A Memoir
of Imperial Russia" would have been better.
W. subtitled his Memoir, paperback, perhaps because
he was dictating them.

A study in gender history? A Victorian man,
↳ "would have"
Was W writing a hybrid ~~auto~~ biography?

    Lots of quotes from various primary sources so
difficult to get a feel of W's memoirs
    Really, parsing the memoirs.

Bk is a bit fanciful

✓Translations??

    Does A ever look to an ideal past à la
                                    Solotsev
Prichford: a monarchist, staunch & true
"Tales" & "dreams" have a utopian, fictional
            aspect to them that W doesn't.
✓Keeps calling W, a Victorian, but what does he
        mean?
    Seems to be fleshing out the Memoir
    Get to his real contrib only mid-way
            through the book

"dreams"   "tales"

chronology goes back + forth : confusing

also confusing : what is background + what is
memoir

treatment of 1905 sketchy

? Conversion from monarchist to const'l monarchist

people
population
markets
problems

TALES OF IMPERIAL RUSSIA: THE LIFE AND TIMES OF SERGEI WITTE, 1849–1915

TALES

OF

IMPERIAL

RUSSIA

THE LIFE AND TIMES OF
SERGEI WITTE,
1849–1915

FRANCIS W. WCISLO

OXFORD
UNIVERSITY PRESS

OXFORD
UNIVERSITY PRESS

Great Clarendon Street, Oxford OX2 6DP

Oxford University Press is a department of the University of Oxford.
It furthers the University's objective of excellence in research, scholarship,
and education by publishing worldwide in

Oxford New York

Auckland Cape Town Dar es Salaam Hong Kong Karachi
Kuala Lumpur Madrid Melbourne Mexico City Nairobi
New Delhi Shanghai Taipei Toronto

With offices in

Argentina Austria Brazil Chile Czech Republic France Greece
Guatemala Hungary Italy Japan Poland Portugal Singapore
South Korea Switzerland Thailand Turkey Ukraine Vietnam

Oxford is a registered trade mark of Oxford University Press
in the UK and in certain other countries

Published in the United States
by Oxford University Press Inc., New York

© Francis W. Wcislo 2011

British Library Cataloguing in Publication Data

Data available

Library of Congress Cataloging in Publication Data

Data available

Typeset by SPI Publisher Services, Pondicherry, India
Printed in Great Britain
on acid-free paper by
MPG Biddles Ltd, Bodmin and Kings Lynn

ISBN 978-0-19-954356-4

1 3 5 7 9 10 8 6 4 2

For Katherine, Daniel, Emily, and Julia
Our gold.

Acknowledgments

The nicest thing about finishing a book is the opportunity to thank those who contributed to it. I have accumulated more debts than I have space to acknowledge. The financial support of the following institutions made research possible at various stages of the project: the International Research and Exchanges Board, the Kennan Institute of the Woodrow Wilson International Center for Scholars, the Vanderbilt University Research Council and Research Scholar's Program, the Robert Penn Warren Center for the Humanities of Vanderbilt University, and The Harriman Institute of Columbia University. Librarians and archivists of the following repositories have supplied invaluable help: the Russian State Historical Archive, St Petersburg; the Russian National Library and its Manuscript Division, St Petersburg; the Hoover Institution of Stanford University; the Jean and Alexander Heard Library of Vanderbilt University; the Leeds University Library; the Library of Congress; the New York Public Library; and the Columbia University Library. Special thanks are due the Bakhmeteff Archive of Russian and East European Culture, Columbia University, for permitting the reproduction of paper copies of the Witte memoir manuscripts.

Many colleagues and friends have contributed their critiques and ideas to this work. I especially want to acknowledge Heather Hogan, Bill Rosenberg, David McDonald, Mark Von Hagen, Yanni Kotsonis, Peter Holquist, Willard Sunderland, Ron Suny, Bob Thurston, Sean Pollock, John Le-Donne, Abby Schrader, Melissa Stockdale, Andrew Verner, David Darrow, Steven Hoch, John Morison, Dominic Lieven, Anthony Heywood, Jack Hausen, Peter Gatrell, Rosalind Marsh, Susan McCaffrey, Gary Marker, Don Wright, and Rochelle Ruthchild. Boris Anan'ich and Rafael Ganelin were unendingly generous with their time, scholarship, knowledge, and patience. Leopold Haimson supplied early encouragement and intellectual mentorship. Marc Raeff, before his death, set down a challenge to be better.

At Vanderbilt University, I have been extraordinarily fortunate to be a member of a department of historians whose intellectual rigor and creativity are matched by their compassion and camaraderie. Thanks in particular to Helmut Smith, Arleen Tuchman, Michael Bess, James Epstein, Elizabeth Lunbeck, Marshall Eakin, Joel Harrington, Jane Landers, Katherine Crawford, Richard Blackett, and Tom Schwartz. Undergraduates in lecture courses and seminars at Vanderbilt and Leeds University have heard more about Witte than they ever wanted to know, but their contributions to this work are present on every page. Special thanks to Reanne Zheng, who provided the first draft of the bibliography; Bryan McGraw, for his undergraduate research project on the American press in 1905, and my graduate teaching assistant, Joanna Mazurska, who shared her insights over four semesters of teaching and readings. Three years ago I had the good fortune of moving into the Dean's Residence on The Vanderbilt University Commons, where I serve as its dean. Thanks to Vanderbilt University for affording me this opportunity to live and learn with extraordinary undergraduates.

At Oxford University Press, Christopher Wheeler and Matthew Cotton have supplied recognition, encouragement, tolerance, and spine, each in the proper amount at the appropriate moment. Thanks as well to Barbara Ball for superb copyediting. Joseph Hills designed the map.

Finally, friends and family. The Brusovani family gave me a home in St Petersburg and tolerated their curious American friend's obsession with Sergei Iul'evich. The Nielson family was a source of undying friendship, camaraderie, and sunshine. My father, brothers, and sisters have always been my cocoon. I wish our mother were here to see this. My wife and love, Jane, cannot believe this is over. She never once allowed me to think it was. Our children Katherine, Daniel, Emily, and Julia for the longest time thought Sergei and Mathil'da were cats. Then they discovered they were 'in Dad's book'. Each of my four children has enriched my life and together they have made me incomparably richer. They are, Russian friends say, our gold. I dedicate this book, at long last, to them.

Dean's Residence
The Commons, Vanderbilt University

1 July 2010

Contents

List of Abbreviations

BAR Witte	Bakhmeteff Archive Witte Collection, Special Collections, Columbia University
BE	Bol'shaia entsiklopediia
RGIA	Russkii Gosudarstvennyi Istoricheskii Arkhiv
SZ	Vospominaniia [razskazy v stenograficheskoi zapisi] Grafa Sergeia Iul'evicha Vitte (1911–1912)
VAMF RA	Vospominaniia Andreia Mikhailovicha Fadeeva
VD ministra	fond 560 (General Chancellery of the Minister of Finances), vsepoddanneishie dokladnye zapiski ministra finansov, 1888–1903
ZGV	Zapisi Grafa Vitte, 1907–1912

Dissonance between dream and reality is not harmful at all, so long as the person who is dreaming believes in his dream seriously, and, attentively looking to life, compares his observations (of it) with the castles he has built in the air, and generally works honestly to bring his fantasy (*fantaziia*) to reality.[1]

Dmitrii Pisarev, as transcribed by V. Lenin, What Is To Be Done?

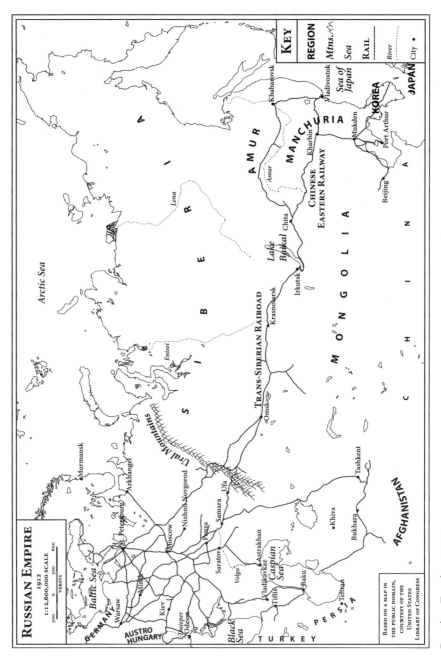

Russian Empire, 1912

Aim of this chapter to explain weird Hitler

Introduction: The Storyteller and His Story

In my younger days perhaps eight hundred of every thousand intelligent youths dreamed of becoming poets. Nowadays it is quite different. I have just been playing with my grandson. He is four years old. He does not like storybooks as the children of our days did. He is interested in automobiles and all sorts of mechanical devices. I can remember—when I was a child in Caucasia—the emotion I experienced when I saw the first telegraph erected there.

Count Sergei Witte, interview with Herman Bernstein, 1908[1]

Hence in my stenographic memoirs I have come to the year 1912. For the moment I am ending this work. As the preceding has made evident, in these tales (*razskazy*) I have left out the entire period relating to my chairmanship of the Council of Ministers, because the events of this period I myself am outlining (*izlagat'*) in the form of written drafts and commentaries (*nabroski i zametki*). Usually I carry out this labor (*trud*) when I am residing abroad.

Count Sergei Iul'evich Witte, Tales in stenographic recording
(Razskazy v stenograficheskoi zapisi), March 1912, p. 2438
(Bakhmeteff Archive, Columbia University in
the City of New York: BAR Witte).[2]

When soul-searching our past, don't we all hopscotch back and forth trying to encompass in a single glance the stretch allotted each person, along with a few points in a life that is still in motion? Don't our thoughts return to events, friends, enemies, ourselves, and to dreams that are always new yet always addressed in the same person? . . . Though not promising a linear and consecutive narrative, I will all the same attempt not to deviate one iota from the actual pattern made by the events and collisions that reality bestowed upon me.

Abram Tertz (Andrei Sinyavsky),
Goodnight! A Novel by Abrahm Tertz (Andrei Sinyavsky)[3]

A man is an extremely complex phenomenon, difficult to define in many pages, much less a phrase. First, there is not one louse that has considered or done something good. And there is not some most honorable and most noble fellow (of course, not a saint), who has at least once thought up something evil and even in a given set of circumstances committed some foul deed. . . . In order to describe a person, you have to write the novel of his life.

Notes of Count Witte (Zapisi Grafa Vitte), Biarritz, August 1907[4]

This is a story about a storyteller and his story. The story is that of Sergei Witte, and he is also the storyteller. A prominent statesman of the Russian Empire during the last three decades of its existence, Witte's life began in 1849, amidst a world of Russian serfdom, in the imperial border-lands of the Caucasus. Over his lifetime, that empire expanded—in territo-rial scale, industrial and commercial wealth, international power, and modern complexity. At the end of a lifetime that had brought him to the pinnacle of Russian political and cultural power, he died in 1915 in the capital city of Petrograd, amidst the great war that had descended upon Europe's age of empire in 1914, and less than two years before the 1917 revolution that would sweep imperial Russia away. His adopted ward, his second wife Mathilda's daughter, Vera Naryshkina, writing her own story in 1922 called *Notes of a Girl*, is the extant voice closest to her father. He was a man who cried when he heard the news that his patron, Alexander III, had died. He sat at her bedside when she was ill with angina, 'beside himself... sitting around her bed for hours, drawing her little pictures in colored crayon... the one was especially pretty, a head of the Madonna with averted eyes and with cheeks, soft as pears'. His was the dining room with oak chairs from the eighteenth-century reign of Peter the Great and an enormous Persian rug, and his too was the study in which there were shelves with books or papers, leather furniture, pushed up against the wall: 'papa, when he worked, always paced back and forth around the room'. She remembered a tall man with a favored Irish Setter, Arapka, dashing with her on a city street to play a prank on her mother, and a stern 'Vulcan', unrecognizable when she accidentally walked into his office and beheld the life of a minister, a public persona that was but one of the many voices Witte had acquired over a lifetime.[5]

The central problem of any biography, much less one that aspires as well to be history, is the problem of voice. Which voice is Witte's? His contemporaries knew Witte as an extraordinary presence in St Petersburg. Scholars researching in imperial archives on topics far afield from the political or economic histories with which his name traditionally is asso-ciated come to the same conclusion when they stumble upon Witte, his eclectic interests and encyclopedic intellect having led him to opera, Push-kin centenaries, architectural designs, Arctic expeditions, world trade fairs, or international finance.[6] He read impressively. Parts of his sizeable personal library are still extant at the St Petersburg Technological University, whose founding he had authorized as part of a program to transform the technical and commercial culture of the empire. That collection of books reflects studious, and imperial, reading in geography, history, political economy, literature, and natural science.[7] He was a published writer, authoring in the 1880s two theoretical works on political economy, which tended toward the proto-technocratic, and engaged ongoing public debates over business practices, railroad technology, political economy, and the role of the state in national economic development.[8] He also was an administrative official. Much of his adult life was spent first in corporate and, following his appointment to the imperial civil service in 1888, government offices. Issuing queries to subordinate employees for information concerning a decision that loomed before him or reviewing research memoranda written for him by others, he appeared pervasively in the margins of archived government paper, in a scrawl that often puzzles even those most familiar with it.[9] He also understood the emerging power of the press, and was a practitioner of yellow-press, editorial insinuation throughout his adult life: as published essayist, anonymous financial backer, disseminator of information, and manipulator of public opinion.[10] For historians of the era, Witte, as his step-daughter once discovered accidentally, was the archetypal tsarist 'statesman (*gosudarstvennyi deiatel'*)', whose brilliance fed a career dedicated to advancement, influence, and the most valuable currency of the tsarist state—power. How he utilized that power—as careerist, minister, modernizer, industrializer, diplomat, and political reformer—is a question that remains the subject of continuing scholarly debate. Its scale and scope, however, speak to the cacophony of voices that marked Witte's life.[11]

One voice, however, did belong to Witte. It echoes in his memoirs. That Sergei Witte was archly conscious of his personal reputation is an understatement. He was a compulsive keeper of records. Shortly after he became Minister of Finances in 1892, for example, he created an archive within the minister's chancellery. Witte's curt '*v arkhiv* (to the archive)', a very familiar scrawl in the margins of ministerial documents during the 1890s, created a repository of organized knowledge and thus a powerful source of authority in his ministry's far-flung operations at the center of the imperial state's economic, civic, and political life.[12] These same sensibilities were at work when Witte turned his attention directly onto his favorite subject, himself. He organized a large personal archive of correspondence, state papers, telegrams, legislative draft projects, and various other materials—a record of his adult life. Following his dismissal by Nicholas II from his post as de facto prime minister of the Russian Empire in April 1906, Witte, in the last decade of his life, structured, cataloged, and referenced these papers, which he intended as the documentary foundation for his memoirs.[13] Eventually a sprawling manuscript of over 3,500 pages, he assembled this project over the years 1907–1912.[14] Scholars know these materials, in short-hand fashion, as 'the Witte memoirs,' although typically they have read an edited conflation of two, distinct memoir monuments Witte constructed to his memory. Avrahm Yarmolinsky, the literary scholar and former director of the New York Public Library's Slavonic Division, published an abbreviated English-language translation of these texts in 1921. The first Russian-language version of the memoirs, edited by the Witte family friend and liberal legal scholar I. V. Gessen, with an approving forward written by his widow, Mathil'da Ivanovna Witte, was published in Berlin in 1922–23. The State Publishing House of the Russian Federated Socialist Republic issued its own copy of the Berlin texts, with a forward by the Marxist historian Mikhail Pokrovsky, in 1923. During the era of the Khrushchev cultural thaw, a three-volume re-issue of this text appeared in 1960 under the auspices of the Academy of Science's Institute of History, with annotations supplied by two young historians, Boris Anan'ich and Rafael Ganelin. A half-century later, after the collapse of the USSR, these two scholars eventually oversaw the publication of the original manuscripts as Witte had written them.[15]

To judge from their very first pages, Witte began writing the memoir to tell his version of what historians often call the first Russian Revolution. This complex set of international and domestic events, the result of the entanglements of the Russian Empire in the Far East and its disastrous military defeat by Japan in 1904–5, also entailed social, political, and constitutional upheaval so profound as to threaten, for a very brief period of time in the autumn of 1905, the very existence of monarchical rule.[16] Witte was a central player in all of it. In the 1890s as Minister of Finances he oversaw the construction of the Trans-Siberian Railroad, which tied together the European and Asiatic territories of the empire and drove Russian imperial ambitions toward the Pacific. In 1905 he was the diplomatic plenipotentiary who traveled to America to negotiate the Portsmouth Peace Treaty that ended the war. For a brief six months in 1905–06, he was the de facto prime minister who wagered a career that he could preserve a unitary monarchical empire by reforming its political and social structures, the crown of which was a parliament, the State Duma. Dismissed from power peremptorily by Nicholas II in April 1906, he was living in Germany, France, and Belgium during the summer and fall of 1907 when he began writing to counter what, rumor had it, was a ~~court~~ version of these events favored at the imperial court, most of all by Nicholas II and his wife, the Empress Alexandra Fedorovna. Rather than the tragic hero he imagined himself to have been, in the court narrative he played the villain, responsible not only for military defeat and revolution, but accused as well of republican sympathies and the betrayal of monarchical rule. Witte responded in kind, fixing blame instead on palace cliques, political foes, and ultimately what he perceived to be the personal weaknesses of the autocratic sovereign he served, Nicholas II, and, as he derisively thought of her, the wife, the Empress Alexandra, that woman who, he was certain, wielded the power behind the throne.[17]

From these beginnings grew an enormous tale, the lifetime of an imperial Russian. The first 250 pages of manuscript, which he laboriously scrawled over the six months of June–November 1907, by 1912 came to fill almost 700 copybook pages in nine mottled green, hard-covered notebooks. Evocative and memory laden, often vindictive, cynical, and score-settling, what he entitled *The Notes of Count Witte (Zapisi Grafa Vitte)* was one, richly embellished version of the high politics of the Russian Empire during the Revolution of 1905. It began with his dismissal in August 1903 from his post of Finance Minister, and really was concerned to shift all responsibility for the onset of the Japanese war, and what public opinion deemed the shameful military defeat and unsettling domestic upheaval that ensued in 1905, squarely upon Nicholas II. It also detailed the bureaucratic politics that swirled in 1905–06 when he became the prime minister of the Russian Empire and, handed the power that he had demanded as a condition of his service, tried to extricate the monarchy from crisis by building the legislative edifice of a reformed central state, partially adapted to the patterns of early twentieth-century parliamentary politics and popular male suffrage. In the main, he wrote in the spa towns of France and Germany, where Witte went to tend his deteriorating health and escape the notoriously prying eyes of his willful royal master and former protégé, Nicholas II. These notes—in a preface Witte wrote of hating the task and forcing himself to write for hour-long stretches—followed, in all their Byzantine complexity, the pathways that had led to his resignation as Russia's first premier on the eve of his crowning achievement, the convocation of a State Duma in April 1906.

The last essay in these notebooks was written in autumn 1912, less than three years before he died. In 1911, however, he already had taken up a second, even larger undertaking, his autobiographical opus, *Memoirs (Tales*

in Stennographic Recording) [*Vospominaniia (razskazy v stenograficheskoi zapisi)*].
Seventeen bound, typewritten volumes, they revealed much of Witte's
times, and even more of the mercurial personality of its author, his often
scandalous and venomous commentaries about the personages and mores of
turn-of-the-century Petersburg—some hint of what must have resonated
from Witte in the salons and dining rooms of high society. He dictated the
first thousand pages of *Memoirs* between January and May 1911. Dating and
paginating the dictation sessions he conducted each week, he talked of his
family heritage and its traditions of military and civil service to the imperial
crown, his upbringing in the Caucasus and university years in Odessa, as
well as a public life that led him from the obscurity of railway offices in New
Russia and Ukraine to the Moika Canal edifice of the Ministry of Finances
in central St Petersburg. He resumed the task the following December, and
for three more months, until March 1912, dictated an even larger mound of
typescript, almost 1,500 pages that ranged across the reign of Nicholas II, his
own role in its high politics, and his ever-present fascination for the
personalities and mores of *fin-de-siècle* Russia.

The idea of Witte as a storyteller of his story he long ago buried in a title
of a manuscript filled with narrative tales (*razskazy*). They were stories that
he remembered, a story that, in some sense, he had told before, not only as
he created it over the course of a lifetime, but as he repeatedly returned to it,
reconsidered it, burnished it, and fashioned it across a lifetime. His memoirs
were dictated to a stenographer, spoken rather than written, and, it seems
likely, as he stalked and paced around the room. He intended them to be a
chronological rendering of his life, from his birth in 1849. These dictated
memoirs, he claimed, left largely without comment the years of war and
revolution of which he had written in his notes, although the selective, hop-
scotching patterns imposed upon the past by memory ensured that the
ageing statesman never could entirely maintain such an artificial distinction.
Although they were a chronological narrative of sorts, Witte, as he wrote his
Notes and even more as he mused and dictated his memoirs, was prone,
seemingly at times eager, to pursue a line of thinking tangential to his
theme, always ready to examine some thread of his lifetime—some personality, event, institution, or cultural moment—and whatever fabric it might
have helped weave.[18]

Reviewing the first published edition of these manuscripts in the
literary journal *Books and Revolution* in 1923, a young Soviet historian,
B. A. Romanov, was stunned by the glimpses of the man and his times

that they afforded. Presaging an interest in the Witte manuscripts that he eventually passed to his own students, the Leningrad historians Boris Ana-n'ich and Rafael Ganelin, Romanov deemed the memoirs an 'invaluable book (*vechnaia kniga*)' for future biographers, but recognized that the self-serving nature of a memoir would require 'the critical corroboration and evaluation' of many historians before a political history of Witte's times could be constructed from the foundation of this autobiographical narra-tive.[19] Interwoven into this scholarly appraisal, however, was the young scholar's personal reaction as he read Witte's memoirs, his dawning sense of discovery as he encountered the imperial Russian. In the published volumes, he wrote, the reader encountered 'an enormous heap (*vorokh*) of photo-graphic images of the great personae of the era, through which Witte, in all these stories of the political regime, lets himself come to life as if to study himself—with an astounding frankness, leaving both himself and all these personalities undefended even by the usual literary devices'. An individual he personally had regarded as the most enigmatic of tsarist officials, Roma-nov continued, a man who was 'in life somehow constantly present but always partly concealed, now rises before the reader whole and complete, entirely alive, embedded in the circumstances and milieu that surrounded him'.[20] Witte's bent for the role of storyteller; his modern preoccupation with self; the complex fashioning of personality; the layers of public, private, and personal that constructed identity: all were very much in evidence in these pages.

That Witte told stories ought not to be surprising. He lived in a nine-teenth-century passionate for the narrated story, a mode of cultural expres-sion that manifested itself in serialized novels, poetry readings, operatic arias, salon conversation, theater performance, diary confessions—and memoirs. Each allowed individuals to imagine themselves in settings, circumstances, and communities beyond the objective realities in which they lived their daily lives.[21] Witte came of age in an extended family that luxuriated in this passion. His mother's father, Andrei Mikhailovich Fadeev, was born in the first year of the French Revolution, 1789, and bequeathed at his death in 1866 a combination of memoir and diary that represented his life and that of his family from the time of Napoleon's invasion of Russia to the old general's death in Russian-colonized Georgia. His wife, Witte's grandmother, Elena Pavlovna Dolgorukaia, a daughter of Russia's late eighteenth-century Catherinian enlightenment, left fragments of a young woman's autobiography in her husband's manuscript. They described episodes before and after her marriage at the end of the Napoleonic Wars.[22] These autobiographical writings also glimpsed the lively salon, an oral milieu of intermingled conversation and performance in Tiflis (Tblisi, the capital of Georgia), over which the two grandparents presided as late as the 1860s, in the house where Witte was raised as a boy.[23] The youngest of their four children, Witte's aunt Nadezhda Fadeeva, edited the memoirs of her parents when they appeared in 1891 in the national history journal *Russian Archive*, and attended as well, as an editor of his writings, to the historical reputation of her brother, the panslavist polemicist Rostislav Fadeev.[24] The role she may have played in either inspiring or shaping her own nephew's memoirs remains unexplored, although she was alive when Witte wrote them. His eldest aunt, Elena Gan, was a novelist of some repute in the 1830s, although she wrote under the pseudonym Zinaida R. Her so-called society tales, which portrayed the dilemmas of autonomous women constrained by their times, were set in the imperial borderlands of the Caucasus where she had been raised and apparently experienced, or dreamed about, the themes of love, sexuality, and suppressed eroticism that lurked in her novels. Gan's two daughters, Witte's cousins, were also storytellers. The younger, Vera Zhelikhovskaia, was a writer of children's storybooks. The older was the internationally acclaimed theosophist Helene Blavatsky (Elena Blavatskaia), a mystic and a teller of fortunes when she was still a young woman, and a prominent Victorian-era celebrity of a new-age religion as an adult.[25] His only uncle, the military officer and public commentator Rostislav Fadeev, is usually labeled a Pan-Slavist to characterize his views of Russian imperial destiny in Europe, but his essays ranged widely across military policy, geopolitical standing, and the cultural dilemmas of the Russian imperial experience. Alone among the four children of Mikhail and Elena Fadeev, the middle sister, Witte's mother Ekaterina, failed to indulge this family penchant for narrative. It appears, however, that she passed this acquired family trait to her son.

The storyteller told stories, but what use are they to historians generally, and historians of the pre-revolutionary Russian Empire in particular? To allow the biographer's voice to intrude for what will not be the last time in the chapters that follow. When first conceived in 1988, a biography of Sergei Witte aimed to study a critical figure in the political history of the tsarist old regime. Witte was one of the last great architects of its economic and political modernization, and a paragon of both the promise and limits of state-sponsored reform. The industrialization strategies he facilitated as

Minister of Finances in the 1890s, and the political reforms he sponsored after the turn of the century were considered to be causal factors by a historical consensus in the West that explained the 1917 Revolution as a crisis of rapid modernization created in part by these very policies. His life thus could be said to illuminate not only the causes of the 1917 Russian Revolution, which gave birth to the world's first communist state, but also the reformist possibilities of the late twentieth-century Soviet polity—concerns of continuing scholarly and ideological debate even as a half-century of superpower cold war was ending. Still valid, their exploration constitutes one of the central underpinnings of this work.

Yet, both history and scholarship conspired to undermine the cold war paradigm that had provoked and legitimated such analytical concerns. The disintegration of the Eastern Bloc and the Soviet Union rendered these issues increasingly less relevant to scholarly audiences and reading publics alike. Influenced by post-modernist advances in the humanities and social sciences generally, the historical scholarship investigating modern Russia became more comparative, interdisciplinary, trans-national, and global in character. Chronological boundaries, research questions, and thematic concerns all shifted, as historians took up or intensified their study of empire and colonialism, modernity and human subjectivity, narrative and memory, knowledge and power, religiosity and illiberalism, the state and modernity.[26] Rather than apocalyptic, the demise of a paradigm was emancipating. To study Witte's life and times no longer required detailing his political narrative of the old regime's last decades, but became instead an opportunity to listen to his tales of imperial Russia. Witte, as was true of most of his contemporaries, possessed but the most vague premonitions of what awaited Russia in 1917, and certainly no knowledge of the revolutionary upheaval that inevitably shaped how historians narrated the imperial age. Instead, he knew and experienced the long nineteenth century that preceded the apocalypse of war and revolution imposed by history's fiat in 1917. Witte's memoirs, what the memoirist-storyteller himself called stories or tales, provide the historian access to the late imperial era that existed before revolution destroyed it. A biography using autobiographical memories provides a foundation to interrogate and examine the social and cultural terrain of the late Russian Empire as Witte remembered it to have been.

What stands out when reading Witte's memoirs was the imperial Russian, the man living, and dreaming, in a nineteenth-century imperial world, his life a reflection of its shifting, carnivalesque society and culture, where borders and boundaries of all kinds were repeatedly being contested and renegotiated.[27] Witte naturally regarded himself as a subject (*poddannyi*) of an empire, an imperial Russian in an imperial era that assumed the historical legitimacy and modern viability of empire in individual, communal, and public life. These assumptions shaped his behavior, as well as his imagination and dreams, pathways by which he envisioned imperial polity, society, and culture in a nineteenth-century Age of Empire. Few imperial Russians left historians a life richer in grand dreams and imagined futures than did Sergei Witte. As the British historian Eric Hobsbawm once reminded us, however, this was not a moment peculiar only to Witte. In Europe generally, the decades of the long nineteenth century constituted an age of grand illusions and dreams. Europe's was a civilization whose technological prowess and Christian morality would spur evolution beyond the boundaries of Europe; produce imperial splendor, adventuresome travel, and colonial exotica; generate technologies transforming time and space; create national communities and powerfully triumphant national states. This was also an era in which dreams were already shading into nightmares, as nationalism blended into racism, imperial splendor into imperialist ambition, and civilization into the irrational, the violent, and the mass.[28] A biography of an imperial Russian thus examines not only a history of empire, but also a history of imperial imagination and dreams.

A rich scholarly literature has arisen in recent decades to study the historical experience of European empires generally.[29] The passing of the Soviet empire in 1989–91 only accelerated that shift for historians of the Russian (*rossiiskaia*) Empire, who have generated an area of scholarship that has deepened and expanded our understanding of its multi-ethnic character, the histories of the ethnic and national communities subjected to imperial rule, the dynamics of the imperial state that resulted from this interaction, and the kaleidoscopic influence of purportedly colonized and subjected societies upon the European-styled metropolitan world that claimed to civilize them.[30] Within that literature, a series of writers have directed attention to the ways in which elites experienced and conceptualized imperial polity and society. Benedict Anderson, in interrogating the cultural roots of nationhood and leading a generation of scholars to think of nations as 'imagined communities', found as well an imagining of imperial polity, where dynastic states organized 'everything around a high center', borders were porous and indistinct, and the populations and lands they encompassed heterogeneous and ill-defined.[31]

Richard Wortman suggests one scenario by which the Romanov dynasty imagined itself to be imperial, and delineates how, rooting itself in historical constructs of medieval *Rus'*, this 'Russian ethnic heartland' became a part of '*Rossiia*, or greater Russia', which had emerged in the sixteenth and seventeenth centuries as an imperial state that engulfed *Rus'*. *Rossiia* was a multinational empire ruled by a westernized sovereign, through a westernized bureaucracy, and dominated by a cosmopolitan nobility united by a common European culture. The antithesis of this monologic world of myth, Wortman warns, is the modern politics of organized groups, a world of bitter contestation over important policies and compromises that percolated just beneath the surface of absolutist imperial ideals, with increasing pressure, as empire encountered the powerful alternatives of modernity and nationalism.[32] Dominic Lieven portrays the Russian Empire geopolitically: a tenuous dominion over its east central European borderlands in the west; a Ukraine essential to the imperial economy for its immense waves of exported cereal products, people, and wealth; and a Siberia akin at its beginnings to the eighteenth-century 'French Empire in Canada...an empire of the wandering trapper, whose *raison d'être* was harvesting furs' that later, after Russian frontier colonization, became a major twentieth-century source of petroleum and natural gas. Place of primacy, however, Lieven accords to the vast inland sea of the steppe, and horizons that lead imperceptibly away from Europe, into both Eurasia and Asia. It was there in the fifteenth century, in this rendering, that Russian elites, themselves bearing a history of subordination to the steppe empire of the Mongols, first began to rule. There too by the death of Catherine the Great in 1796, an apogee of Russian imperial power, did they acquire an 'imperial mentality'. Underpinned by a shared orthodox Christian cosmology, it assumed the mission to civilize an inferior Asian and Islamic world, to render valuable natural resources that were otherwise useless, to enjoy even exotic adventures as explorers, entrepreneurs, or personalities, and, as Lieven quotes Dostoyevsky, famously, to write about an emerging eurasianism in late imperial Russian discourse: 'In Europe we were hangers-on and slaves, whereas in Asia we shall go as masters.'[33]

Alfred Rieber writes of the Russian Empire (*rossiiskaia imperiia*) as an 'imperial idea' rooted in historical experience. Already a multicultural empire when the early modern Muscovite state first created it, the inheritance of *Rossiia* included an even more complex and aged Eurasian steppe politics that had produced the struggle for succession over the medieval

[margin handwritten note: Concepts of Empire]

Mongol Empire. He emphasizes as well what, closer to our story, historians call the Petrine Empire, the creation in early eighteenth-century north-eastern Europe of its namesake, Peter the Great. His reign saw discourse coupled with experience—nothing better captures that experience more than the city of St Petersburg itself. His era produced a language of empire to make that experience broadly available among elites. Imperial power understood historically was, Rieber argues, multicultural, and that axiom, by the early nineteenth century at the latest, had come to be applied to a long, ill-defined, and porous border zone that had slowly grown away from the great Russian ethnic heartland toward the south and east into the great inland sea of the Eurasian steppe. Rieber's imperial idea reached its apogee in an essentialist mission to civilize Asia, a scenario which accorded the lead role to Russians because they were more willing than Europeans to tolerate the mingling of racial, religious, and ethnic categories that swirled in these borderlands, and more intellectually capable, given the common citizenship that Christian orthodoxy extended, however grudgingly to Islam, Protestant and Roman Christianity, and Judaism.[34]

Empires dreamed or imagined. Experiences remembered. Stories told. Identities explored. Historians especially may pause here to ask: is there not a danger that these tales of imperial Russia told by our storyteller are fiction? In the ever more intensely postmodern age in which we live, no author could possibly avoid, at the least, considering the dangers of being seduced by her subject. That view might apply even more to an historian writing biography, especially one that privileges the autobiographical musings and lifetime of one man from the most elite stratum of Russian imperial society. One answer is apparent in the historical literature. If well buttressed by other, judiciously researched primary and secondary sources, biographical narrative in the hands of the historian, given its focus upon the individual, can address otherwise inaccessible issues of human identity and subjectivity, the multi-tiered complexity of human personhood that any one individual life encapsulates.[35] Biographical narrative can be a historical methodology that allows what the anthropologist Clifford Geertz classically called a 'thick description' of an individual life, one that understands the complexity of the individual embedded within the human topography of society and culture in which he was both subject and object.[36] Biography accesses individual emotion, psychology, values, identity, behavior, and experience in ways simply unavailable to scholars studying at more generalized, macro-levels of human ideas and experience. How and why did Witte aspire, dream, fear, love, hate, believe, or sympathize? How and why did he understand the identity, the being of a man or a woman? How did he comprehend time and space, past and future, life and death? Finally, of particular significance in a biography that privileges autobiographical memoirs, what of the past did he choose to remember—and forget?

Whether professional scholars or generalist readers, skeptics nevertheless will remain doubtful about this work. They are more certain than the biographer-historian can be, convinced that the historian goes too far in embracing artifacts as unreliable as the autobiographical memoir, particularly one as meticulously and obsessively organized as the archive and master narrative that Sergei Witte produced at the end of his life. For these, there is a second answer: the rewards are worth the risk. The former Soviet-era dissident Andrei Sinyavsky, who wrote under the pseudonym Avrahm Tertz, asked in his own fictionalized memoir *Goodnight! A Novel*, at the end of the 1980s: 'When soul-searching our past, don't we all hopscotch back and forth trying to encompass in a single glance the stretch allotted each person, along with a few points in a life that is still in motion? Don't our thoughts return to events, friends, enemies, ourselves, and to dreams that are always new yet always addressed in the same person . . . ?' For both their readers and their authors, Sinyavsky cautioned, memoirs are a siren's song, their logical chronological narration of a life constructed from the kaleidoscopic rendering of events that remembering resurrects.[37] Accessing that kaleidoscopic experience as history is a reward for which the biographer is willing to take this risk. Yosef Yerushalmi offers a second argument. Writing during the early 1980s in *Zakhor. Jewish History and Jewish Memory*, Yerushalmi explored this space between narrative and memory and identified it as the modern dilemma of the historian. The historian of Jewish history, Yerushalmi contends, confronts the dilemma that a people so dependent on a collective memory for its very identity rely least of all on the historian's narrative to recollect or represent it. Among a welter of pasts available to the present (in literature, film, or collective tradition), historians must struggle to make their version of the past memorable. Witte surely was not a historian, but he sought to explore and explain his past, obsessively soul-searching and hop-scotching across the stories of his life, drawing willingly and eagerly on his memories of that past, and pouring them across the landscape of his memoirs. Typically, historians do warn that the Witte memoirs are unreliable, that Witte is not to be trusted as a primary source that objectively can explicate, because it so subjectively represents his

vociferously burnished version of events. All of these complaints are quite
true. Yet, the Witte manuscripts are texts whose opportunities are less
explanatory and more evocative, which sacrifice an 'objective' narrative
to the more tantalizing past that Witte chose from among the welter of those
available to him. Can one tell the story of a life as the subject understood it,
particularly if the objective in telling the story is, at least in part, the
illumination of the historical context, not as it objectively existed, but as it
was preserved in the collective memory, as people dreamed it, as they were
seduced by it? *Tales of Imperial Russia* relates how the storyteller told this
particular story of his life.[38]

We return to biography and history. Truth be told, his memoirs are, quite
simply, stories: narrated tales and remembered impressions of a life in
imperial Russia that allow the historian access to the cultural values,
human identities, and patterns of life experience, which constituted its
rhythms. Chapter 1 is a story of a boyhood spent in a family of memoirists
and storytellers in Russia's India, the Caucasus. The third son of a family of
middling colonial officials, who in the Russian tradition had earned hereditary ennoblement through civil service on the southern and eventually so-
called trans-Caucasian frontiers of the empire, Witte was born in 1849. He
spent his childhood and adolescence far from the metropolitan centers of
St Petersburg and Moscow on a distant imperial border across the Caucasus
Mountains in Georgia, where in the Russian mind Europe met Asia.
He bore the Baltic German surname of a converted Lutheran father, was
baptized an Orthodox Christian, but as an adult repeatedly proclaimed
his maternal lineage, and claimed his Russian ethnicity, through his grandmother, the daughter of a déclassé branch of an early modern Muscovite
aristocratic clan.

Chapter 2 details how a young man, by heritage and family upbringing a
hereditary nobleman of the late eighteenth to early nineteenth century,
encountered a complex, contradictory, and kaleidoscopic adult life that was
becoming ever more intensely modern. It speaks of 1860s Odessa, the
empire's Marseilles, the international commercial port on the northern
shore of the Black Sea, which served as the capital city of an administrative
territory called New Russia (*Novorossiia*), the city and region themselves
both markers of a process by which the Eurasian grassland steppe, and the
peoples who populated it, were being reconstructed in the imperial imagination as a new Russia, whose civilization legitimated imperial hegemony.[39]
Witte entered New Russia University in the 1860s, a decade classically

portrayed by historians as one of student nihilism and the emergence of intelligentsia radicalism. He dabbled in both, but distinguished himself as well as a monarchist, a mathematician, and a gay blade among the young men of his fast-paced, carousing social circle. His Victorian and European masculinity was complex enough that it saddled upon him military valor, the male gaze that he directed at the bodies of actresses, prima ballerinas, and opera sopranos, male friendship that hinted at the homoerotic and explicitly extended to a mentoring relationship, from which his career benefited, with one of the most openly homosexual men of late imperial high society, and finally marriage to women whose divorces from their estranged husbands he arranged.

Chapter 3 tells of a railroad executive in Ukraine's capital city Kiev, who rose to prominence in the railroad business and dreamt of technology, geographical expanse, and imperial grandeur. Amidst a public life that mixed a potent brew of managerial expertise and proto-technocratic power, Witte experienced career in a Victorian frame, a world where increasingly intellect, talent, business, and technology bred male profession-al expertise in the ever larger corporate and governmental organizations that marked the later nineteenth century. Critical in his life's story was the railroad, that most revolutionary of nineteenth-century communications technologies that constricted space and abbreviated time. By the 1880s, the chief operations officer of the Southwestern Railroad, a privately owned but government subsidized joint stock company, Witte oversaw a freight and passenger network that directed the agricultural, mineral, and human resources of New Russia and Ukraine southwards toward the Black Sea, westwards toward the east-central European Danube river valley, north-wards toward east central Europe and Great Russia, and eastwards toward the Volga River valley, and the vast spaces of Central Asia and Siberia beyond. That expansive space provided him visions of empire.

Chapter 4 examines that vision. Appointed to the ministerial state in 1888 and by 1892 Minister of Finances to Tsar Alexander III, Witte reached the height of his personal and public powers in the equally triumphant gilded age of the 1890s. He oversaw the construction of a Eurasian transcontinental railroad across Siberia to the Pacific, began to effect the renovation of imperial commercial-industrial life, expanded Russian industrial investment significantly, and brought his modernizing influence to bear throughout the imperial state. For a brief period in Russia at the *fin-de-siècle*, Witte com-bined his technocratic sensibilities with concentrations of ministerial power

so sweeping that he indeed did, to borrow from James Scott, see like a
state.[40] What he saw was a dream, like all dreams to some degree a utopian
vision, of a modern Russian empire. It was an imperial polity rooted in
commercial-industrial prosperity throughout its Eurasian expanse, international capital investment, Russian state power, and the European cultural
civilization that Russian political hegemony assured. His was a vision
grounded in the objective economic reality of international capitalism.
Economic historians both old and new share the view that Russia's gilded
age saw a commercial and industrial expansion of the imperial economy that
became self-sustaining.[41] Its motive power, in Witte's always somehow
neo-mercantilist mind, derived from the international capitalist order of
which the empire was a constituent element, the international circulation of
capital, commodities, and labor that coursed through it, and finally, through
the instrument of the state, the attraction of capital investment to the
imperial economy, and thus the intensification of the movement of
goods, capital, and labor that created wealth and power within it. The
signifier of this future was the gold ruble, the *Imperial'*.

Chapter 5 tells of a senior statesman in the Age of Empire, confronting in
Russia what perhaps was the first of a series of twentieth-century national
and social revolutions. Following Russian military defeat in the Russo-
Japanese War, and confronted by explosions of political and social protests
as its aftermath, Witte sought to salvage, reform, and thus preserve the
Russian Empire for the twentieth century. It also examines the story of an
aged memoirist, in his last years before he died during World War I,
pondering, occasionally, the loss of his Victorian faith in the empire's
longevity, even legitimacy in a twentieth century where ethnicity, ideology, social movements, the nation-state, and the modern diversity of cultural
experience challenged the imperial narrative that his life had constructed
and his memoirs conveyed. He died suddenly in February 1915, a half-year
after the outbreak of what was becoming the Great War. He was buried in a
place, fittingly, where Petersburgers honored themselves, the Cemetery of
the Alexander Nevsky Monastery, at the far end of Nevskii Prospekt from
the Winter Palace, where he had often held forth in what was not the only,
or perhaps even the most important part of his life. There, tucked in a small,
enclosed courtyard expanse, is to be found a large, granite grey tombstone,
the length of his large frame, surrounded by a black wrought-iron fence,
bearing the inscription 'S. Iu. Vitte'. Here, with the storyteller, his story
ended.

Having begun with Witte lamenting his Petersburg grandson's inability to imagine through poetry, justice demands that the final note should belong to a Petersburg poet. Joseph Brodsky, a bard from that city after it had survived the siege of Leningrad, wrote in his own autobiographical essay, *Less Than One*, that 'memory contains precisely details, not the whole picture; highlights, if you will, not the entire show'. The idea, Brodsky continued, that any such exercise could succeed in 'somehow remembering the whole thing in blanket fashion, the very conviction that allows the species to go on with its life, is groundless'. Fully aware of risks involved in probing memory, which resembled 'a library in alphabetical disorder, and with no collected works by anyone', Brodsky nevertheless plunged ahead, content to tell the one story about himself that he knew.[42] Be mindful in that regard that this is only one telling of Sergei Witte's life.

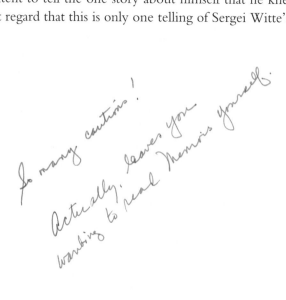

So many cautions! Actually, leaves you wanting to read Memoirs yourself.

I

Transcaucasia: Boyhood and Family on an Imperial Frontier, 1849–1865

I am 62 years-old, I was born in Tiflis in 1849. My father, Iulii Fedorovich Witte, was director of the Department of State Properties in the Caucasus. My mother was Ekaterina Andreevna Fadeeva, daughter of the Fadeev who was a member of the Main Administration of the Viceroy of the Caucasus. Fadeev was married to the princess Elena Pavlovna Dolgorukaia, who was the last of the senior branch of the princes Dolgorukii, descending from Grigorii Fedorovich Dolgorukov, a senator under Peter I and brother of the renowned Iakov Fedorovich Dolgorukov. My grandfather came to the Caucasus with the Viceroy, His Highness Prince Vorontsov, who established a stable civil foundation for the administration of the Caucasus.

Count Sergei Iul'evich Witte, Memoirs
(*Tales in stenographic recording*), p. 1[1]

I set out on 5 April to inspect the state properties of Shemansk province. My wife and daughter accompanied me for us to meet my older daughter Ekaterina and my grandsons in Baku. They were moving (from Saratov) to live with us, given the pending transfer of my son-in-law Witte to the service in Transcaucasia.

Andrei Mikhailovich Fadeev, Memoirs, 1847[2]

In the winter the library of her scholarly grandmother was a most interesting place, firing even the less well-endowed imagination. There was much that was amazing in this library: stuffed animals—the snarling heads of bears and tigers, as well as elegant little humming-birds, owls, hawks, and falcons, and over them all near the ceiling an enormous eagle spread its majestic wings. But the most impressive was the white flamingo, extending its long neck as if it were alive. When the children came into the study of their grandmother, they rode it, as if a horse, seated on a white sealskin, and at twilight it began to seem to them that the stuffed animals came alive and began to move . . .

E. F. Pisareva, *Theosophist*, January 1913[3]

1854 was the most alarming year for Transcaucasia since the time it was united to Russia. The Turks, besieging our borders, had many troops, and we, in the beginning (of the Crimean War), too few, so few that there

could be no certainty of the future. . . . And right here up in the mountains
sat at the ready Shamil, like a bird of prey over his spoils, impatiently
awaiting the first hint of victory to bring all his forces swooping down to
aid the Turks. . . . On the streets often Russians had to hear exclamations of
this sort: 'It won't be much longer that you'll reign here, soon they'll drive
you out, soon it will be the end of you!' . . . Everyone who could left Tiflis
for Russia.'[4]

Andrei Mikhailovich Fadeev, Memoirs, 1854

(O)ne must imagine them as they lived, in the world that surrounded
them, with certain social and ethical codes, service duties, customs, dress,
the reasons why they acted as they did.

Iurii Lotman, The Daily Life and Traditions of the Russian Dvorianstvo (XVIII–Early XIX
Centuries). Conversations on Russian Culture[5]

A dults remember childhood but vaguely. It is a place and time that they
use to bring some sense of order to their jumbled present. What
follows, in the narrowest sense, is the fleeting memories of a boyhood,
spent in Georgia, in a noble family on a colonial frontier. Historians of the
Russian imperial experience pay surprisingly slight attention to these first
years of life, when the men and women closest to an individual shape
human identity and instill the values that figure prominently later in adult
life. Witte, however, began his life's story with these subjects. In the fashion
typical of both the memoir genre and the era from which it came, he
reminisced at length about his family, extended clan, and ancestral lineage.[6]
He recalled his father, a civil servant, whose education, loyal service, and
marriage had won him promotion in the imperial bureaucracy, and his
mother, her status defined less by marriage than birth, aristocratic genealogy, and her still living father, in whose household she, with her husband and
children, resided. With a nod to the public viceregal reputation of that
Fadeev, Witte remembered this man, his grandfather, whose connections to
an aristocratic counselor of the emperor had led the family to the Caucasus.
Here too was the wife of Andrei Mikhailovich, Witte's babushka-grand-
mother, Elena Pavlovna Dolgorukaia. Her genealogical connection to one
of the ancient, princely clans of Rus', as well as its involvement with the
imperial state that Peter the Great had created in the early eighteenth
century were not the only sources of her influence on Sergei Witte's life.

Telling this story, Witte also opened a window onto the history of the daily life (*bytovaia istoriia*) of the colonial service nobility that defined the status of this family. The cultural historian Iurii Lotman wrote that such 'lives of insignificant people' shed light upon the complexly intertwined networks of personal, experiential, linguistic, symbolic, and historical ties that constitute cultural heritage.[7] Witte remembered his early life among men and women, subjects and servants of an empire, who had rooted much of their lives on a borderland where, in the imperial imagination, Europeans encountered Asia.[8]

Tblisi was the capital city of the medieval kingdom of Georgia, which had come under Russian dominion at the end of the eighteenth century. On the southern slopes of the Caucasus mountain range was an outpost of imperial rule which the Russians called Tiflis, their administrative center in Transcaucasia—*Zakavkazia*. From it, the empire had engaged in what at the time of Witte's birth was a half-century's diplomatic and military campaign to subjugate this strategic isthmus between the Black and Caspian Seas, establish its sovereignty over the Christian and Islamic ethnic communities that populated the region, and confront the Ottoman Empire to the south. That effort brought Witte's grandfather to the region in 1847. A middling noble who had made his career in the state service, Andrei Fadeev was a colonial commissioner, whose civil administrative obligations required him to ride circuit through much of present-day Georgia, Armenia, and Azerbaijan. He and his family encountered the cauldron of ethnic, religious, and dawning nationalist sentiments found among the mountaineer and Islamic tribal communities of the Great Caucasus Mountains, as well as the potent brew of military violence, despotism, and civilizing zeal that was the Russian response to them. Distant geographically and culturally from Russia, Tblisi was joined to European Russia by the Georgian Military Highway, a circuitous route from Vladikavkaz in New Russia that Fadeev compared to traveling along a 'narrow road hanging over bottomless chasms'. He, and even more his scholarly naturalist wife, Elena Pavlovna Dolgorukaia, were stunned 'by the beauty of the wild, magical greatness' encountered in the mountains, and 'the fantastic grandiosity of the view, with its unending diversity.'[9] Founded as early as the fifth century, the ancient Georgian capital was itself dominated by the ruins of two citadels perched above mountain cliffs, below which cascaded a town whose flat-roofed housing was piled densely on a terraced landscape.

Fadeev paid some attention to the old quarter of the town in his diary-memoir—the transplanted Russian always quick to remark the strange, exotic, and less civilized Asian world over which he ruled. His memoir included observant commentaries on urban price riots, multi-ethnic and decidedly non-Russian street crowds that could quickly turn violent, or the Caucasus front of the Crimean War in 1854–56, where Russian imperial arms were victorious against the Ottoman Empire. He remembered the city's sounds, although only in contrast to the 'sonorous, ceremonious, powerful, often deafening sound' of Russian Orthodox church bells that was so noticeably absent from its daily background din, '(s)ome sort of discombobulated clashing of sounds (*brianchanie*) that assaulted the ears, as if something unpleasant, alien, even burdensome (*tiagostnyi*)', Fadeev wrote, hinting at the otherness of the experience. The family certainly knew of Tblisi's narrow, crooked alleys and bazaars, which historically had served as termini for commercial routes between Europe and the Near East, and echoed with a polyglot of Asian and European languages that Fadeev apparently disliked but heard. In his eyes, they bred both ethnic hostility, perhaps well deserved, directed at Russians by 'locals', especially 'Tatars' and 'Musselmen', and epidemics, like the cholera that periodically struck during hot, dry summers. Andrei in his memoirs, and his grandson Sergei much later in his own, remembered family lore of escaping the city in summer to seek a family 'summer refuge' in the heights of the Kura River gorge, 'a beautiful place to be, pure mountain air and mineral waters'. Much of the Fadeev family's daily life, however, was segregated in the new district, constructed largely in the Russian classical style, which grew on the edge of the old town in this first half-century of Russian sovereignty. Here were located the instruments of imperial rule: the residences and offices of the viceroy, the headquarters of the army general staff, the cathedral, the opera house, and the state gymnasium. The Fadeev clan moved to the outskirts of this area in 1847, taking up residence in a townhouse with 'a great oval hall (surrounded) by a balcony', near a hilltop where, Fadeev would remember, public ritual and entertainment were centered, whether carnival or public execution. In this place, Sergei Witte was born.[10]

'On Ancestors [O predkakh]': Men and Masculinity

Chapter headings litter Witte's memoir narratives. He used them to mark the subject with which he began, but did not necessarily conclude his peripatetic sessions of dictation and storytelling. The very first of these titles is 'on ancestors'. What he remembered reflected, in the first instance, the experience of men of the Russian hereditary service nobility (*potomstvennoe dvorianstvo*), which historically had supplied the Crown with its officers, civil officials, courtiers, and cultural elite. Their traditions of military and civil service were a taproot of the imperial power that first Muscovite and then Romanov tsars had created in eastern Europe and the Eurasian steppe. At the time of Witte's birth, the hereditary service nobility numbered no more than 1 per cent of an imperial population of some 56 million subjects, and represented perhaps 100,000 families ranging in economic wealth and social standing from a thin elite stratum of great aristocratic clans to poverty-stricken servitors noble in name only.[11] The Witte family stood in the middle of this continuum. Three generations of noblemen loomed in Witte's retelling of his childhood. They were all military officers or civilian officials, and all were distinguished by that combination of persistence, talent, bravery, and intelligence that typically assured success in the Crown's service. They all modeled masculinity, having created patterns of human experience for a boy seeking to understand manhood, to which the aged memoirist inevitably returned as he rummaged in memories of these years. His grandfather Fadeev and his father, Iulii Witte, capped a lifetime pursuing career advancement in a bureaucratic hierarchy known for both its power and pettiness, their success publicly crowned by propelling their family into the social circle of the viceroys who represented Russian imperial power in mid nineteenth-century Transcaucasia. His oldest brother, Alexander Witte, and his uncle Rostislav Fadeev were army officers. Their martial bravery, prowess, and valor also distinguished the Witte clan. To judge from the old man's memories, the boy valued their martial path to adulthood more than the ascendant official careers of his father and grandfather. Finally, Rostislav Fadeev was a self-educated intellectual and public personality, defined by both the breadth of his knowledge and the acuity of his imagination. He too was a critical influence in his young nephew's world.

He began with his mother's father, a critical bond in any Russian family. 'My grandfather', Witte recalled about Andrei Mikhailovich Fadeev (1789–1867), served long and loyally in a succession of provincial outposts, eventually winning the attention of M. S. Vorontsov, the governor-general of New Russia and from 1844 imperial viceroy in the Caucasus. That 'His Highness the Prince (*svetleishii kniaz'*)', the English-educated, aristocratic son of a Russian ambassador, had commanded the Russian military occupation of Paris after Napoleon's defeat in 1815, required no explanation for readers still conversant, in 1912, with the rhythms of the Russian service nobility, a world where loyalty fostered patronage and created career.[12] Writing in his own memoir a half-century earlier, Fadeev instead emphasized a family tradition of military service, which he proudly traced to a great-grandfather who had fought with Peter the Great at the decisive battle of Poltava in 1709. The seventh of eight sons, Fadeev entered the civil service at age 12, effectively apprenticed to his father, whose own public life moved from retired dragoons officer to civilian supervisor on the Baltic Sea–Volga River canal. By this not unusual means a family of the middling eighteenth-century nobility assured its livelihood and future. Tutors hired to teach him German and French, and the rudimentary clerk's skills learned in his father's office, constituted the limits of Fadeev's formal education. By his own testimony he survived this drudgery by 'reading greedily everything I could lay my hands on' from a local nobleman's library.[13]   *grandfather*

His subsequent career trod a path familiar to many tsarist officials of the nineteenth century. To read his memoir was to encounter a tale of duties performed, superiors more often disdained than admired, and status established through salary, honors, and influence. An almost nomadic life led him and a growing family from one bureaucratic post to another. Occasionally journeying to St Petersburg, where he utilized introductions culled from family or work to frequent ministerial offices or society salons, he spent most of his adult life outside the capital in imperial borderlands, first in Belorussia and Ukraine, and for the bulk of his career in southern Russia and the Caucasus. Posts in Ekaterinoslav, Astrakhan, Odessa, and Saratov, where he served almost five years as governor, preceded his transfer to Tiflis in 1846–47. Much of this work entailed administrative oversight of the panoply of non-Russian Orthodox populations—European colonists, Cossacks, Kalmyk nomads, Russian religious sectarians, Tatars, Armenians, Georgians, Muslims—who lived across the band of territory stretching from the northern reaches of the Black Sea into the steppe lands east of the Caspian. There Fadeev upheld the law—and mediated the often arbitrary decision-making of the officialdom charged to uphold it. He remembered physically displaying the Code of Laws to a Kalmyk Buddhist lama, the steppe wind howling and tearing its pages away. He recalled interpreting, often while riding circuit or on inspection, the administrative regulations applying to the properties and populations of the imperial state in the lands he was charged to oversee. He repeatedly reflected in his writing a royal and imperial official negotiating on horseback the territory he administered, displaying by his presence in a place the sovereignty of Russian imperial power.[14]

Andrei Fadeev's example of long service must have been instructive for Witte, who claimed that he had been his grandfather's 'favorite'.[15] 'Sergei' appeared rarely in his grandfather's memoir, the first such mention a long reminiscence about the summer mountain fete provided for his family and its circle of acquaintances by a local Tatar, Toshtamur, a companion and language teacher of his son Rostislav. Holding the rank of lieutenant of militia, this alien (*inorodets*), the term used to classify such non-Russian subjects of the Crown, perhaps not coincidentally moved back and forth between Russian society and what Fadeev merely termed 'a world of banditry (*razboinichii sfer*)'. That he managed to mount an extravagant carnival at his own summer camp, its food and entertainment 'attention-grabbing and wondrous (*zanimatel'noe i zabavnoe*), especially for my grand-sons', was only one of a series of such episodes through which Witte might have glimpsed or experienced this borderland in his early childhood.[16]

His arrival for a summer mountain holiday after a first year at university around 1865 represented the last mention of Sergei the dying man made. Nadezhda Fadeeva, his daughter and editor, noted Witte's presence at the deathbed and funeral in Tiflis.[17] Witte recalled the moment—'as far as I remember it was in '67'—when 'the old man (*starik*)' died: 'his death made a huge impression on me, because...I loved him terribly.'[18] He too remembered the Fadeev residence, and how his grandfather 'lived as they had lived in the old days, the times of serfs (and) great lords.... (W)e had some 84 house servants alone,' he exclaimed. A European contemporary who visited the family in Tiflis in the last years of Fadeev's life remarked how, even after the abolition of serfdom, 'the daily life' of the family 'proceeded as it always had—on the lavish scale to which they were accustomed'. Receiving guests in his apartments as he once likely had greeted petitioners, an aged Fadeev still presided over that animated salon where his now deceased wife, Elena Pavlovna Dolgorukaia, once had held sway.[19] By the end of his life, Witte's persistent and talented grandfather had dutifully served, and come to know, three different imperial viceroys in the Caucasus, built solid positions for his children and their families, and become a figure of some distinction and standing in the Russian community of Tiflis.[20]

If a lifetime of duty and service was one factor shaping Witte's under-standing of masculinity, the distinctions earned in service by education and

BOYHOOD AND FAMILY IN TRANSCAUCASIA, 1849–1865   25

expertise were a second. As in central and western Europe, to which since the seventeenth century relative handfuls of the empire's men had traveled to seek university degrees, the knowledge, ability, and expertise that those diplomas conveyed loomed as markers of cultural status in the early nineteenth-century empire. That was especially true for its growing officialdom, which not only generated the legendary corruption lampooned by Russian satirists such as Saltykov-Shchedrin and Gogol, but also created demand for what the historian Bruce Lincoln called enlightened bureaucrats, administrators in key government posts trained at university in law, natural philosophy, and science.[21] Alone among those male relatives whose influence he acknowledged, that distinction belonged to Iulii Fedorovich Witte (1814–186?), laconically introduced in his son's memoir as 'my father, the nobleman (*dvorianin*) Witte'.[22]

Witte's relationship with his father, to the extent that it can be uncovered at all, appeared to have been distant, perhaps even problematic. Born in 1849, Witte was the youngest of three sons. His brother Alexander, the family's first child, had been born in 1846. A second son, Boris, followed in 1848, twelve months before Sergei. Two sisters, Olga and Sofia, came after him. 'I was the favorite of my grandfather and in the family as a whole they treated me lovingly but generally quite indifferently,' he wrote in one of the few passages characterizing the emotional content of a childhood played out in the nursery, where a series of household servants and tutors replaced parents caught up in a swirl of service and social life. 'I tell all these stories', he wrote elsewhere in detailing the sometimes negligent care given children, and the glimpses of sexuality among these servants afforded young boys, 'in order to show how hard it is to protect children, even in families with material means, from things that demoralize them, when their parents do not strictly tend to their upbringing'.[23] Commentators also have speculated why the adult Witte, whether in the salons of St Petersburg high society or the pages of his memoirs, never missed an opportunity to emphasize his maternal lineage. Although only by custom did the maternal line create status, he was descended from the aristocratic Dolgorukii clan through his mother and grandmother. If not concealing, he was attempting to compensate, they argued, for a non-Russian father whose social standing derived entirely from his bureaucratic career.[24]

Christopher Heinrich Georg Iulius Witte had been born a Lutheran Protestant in the Baltic province of Courland (modern Latvia) in 1814. In 1856, however, he and his five brothers passed the most significant

Odd as the ultimat Petria official

milestone on the well-worn path by which the Russian hereditary nobility, at least as shaped by the Petrine state, had filled its ranks from the eighteenth century onwards. Their vitae (*formuliarnyi spisok*), as required with maddening attention in the law, stipulated that the six men produced the official records necessary to establish that they, and hence their wives and children, had earned ennoblement through the thirty-five year civil service of their father, Friedrich, a Russian subject who joined the imperial civil service as a forest surveyor in Courland shortly after its annexation into the empire in 1795. These records also revealed how centrally education figured in the careers of Friedrich's sons. The eldest, a military surgeon, studied medicine at Dorpat University, while the youngest, an inspector in the elite Imperial School of Jurisprudence, graduated from the Main Pedagogical Institute. Two others had studied military engineering and forestry at specialized technical schools. Iulii Witte (it is unclear when he russianized his name) graduated from an agricultural technical school in Mogilev, took a degree in agriculture and mining at Dorpat University, and subsequently, his son claimed, went abroad to study in Prussia. Witte's own scattered recollections of his father recognized the centrality of education to his life. A young 'specialist in agriculture' arrived in Saratov province, where he soon 'fell in love with my mother and married her', Witte noted, intermingling public persona with what little he knew of the man's private life.[25]

Witte also knew that education fostered, but could not alone define status. It provided access to position and rank. With them, marriage and family could provide the foundation for position, influence, and power. Education and marriage had been a successful combination for his father. Andrei Fadeev's memoir first mentioned Iulii Witte in recollections of the year 1841. Working in Saratov province for the newly created Ministry of State Properties, Fadeev then was a protégé of its chief, the reform-minded councilor of Nicholas I, P. D. Kiselev. Known for mentoring educated, talented officials, Kiselev was equally renowned among his contemporaries for dispatching well-qualified but jesuitical auditors from St Petersburg to root out corruption and sloth in provincial government—a practice in Fadeev's eyes productive of little more than 'complaints and distractions from business'. Accompanying the 'intelligent, efficient, and well-intentioned' investigator who visited Saratov were two young officials, one of whom was his 'future son-in-law'.[26] Within four years, in 1844, that anonymous man had become the husband of Fadeev's second daughter, Ekaterina. He wrote with pride how 'God blessed this marriage with familial bliss (*semeinnoe schast'e*)', but at the same time figured the groom's official reputation as a valuable possessed by the Fadeev family: 'he held the office of manager of a model farm in the Ministry of State Properties ... one of the best institutions of its kind, in the opinion of experienced and unbiased individuals.'[27] In 1847, Fadeev arranged Witte's transfer to the Caucasus, and of equal importance, that of 'my daughter Ekaterina and my grandsons'. By the early 1850s, the now prized son-in-law, who accompanied Fadeev and his son Rostislav on summer journeys into the Asian mountains to hunt exotic tigers, had become his de facto 'diligent, trusted aide', a position made official in 1857 when, 'to our great pleasure', Witte's 'place in the service was guaranteed with his appointment as my assistant'. At the very end of his life, a semi-retired Fadeev, summering in the Russian garrison settlement of Belyi Kliuch, warmed himself in the knowledge that 'my daughter and her husband ... appeared often at dinners, evening parties, and balls given by the (viceroy) Grand Duke (Mikhail Nikolaevich, a brother of the tsar) or the garrison commander'.[28] Education, talent, and marriage allowed a young official to construct a version of manhood that encompassed the career success of the bureaucrat, the social prominence of the husband and father, and the cultural influence of the well-positioned, proper man.

Witte, to reiterate, knew less of this history. His scattered memories of boyhood and adolescence, the shards of a lost mosaic, reveal a father with position and influence, who supplied his sons formal education, but attended less to its intellectual content. 'Tutors (*guvernery*)', both imported from Europe and hired locally, prepared Witte to enter the Russian gymnaziium in Tiflis. His recollections of them, strewn with the 'amorous relations' of adult men and women observed surreptitiously by bored but eager boys, suggested that he learned as much about the sexual and erotic as 'various subjects like history, geography, and German language'. Entering the gymnaziium at age 12, where he and his brother Boris spent the next four years, Witte wrote, 'I studied very poorly, and ordinarily never went to lessons ... But given that we were auditors (*vol'noslushateli*) and in view of the special position, known to all, occupied by our parents, the teachers paid us no attention because they were responsible neither for our studies nor our conduct.' He passed the crucial examinations required for entry into university thanks only to his father paying 'the required compensation' for tutoring from gymnaziium teachers who also likely were his examiners. The journey to university also revolved around the senior Witte, who tried, ultimately without success, to use family connections to place his poorly prepared sons at the prestigious St Vladimir University in Kiev.[29]

The starkest memory of his father, however, was also the darkest lesson about the experience of manhood. In 1868, amidst business dealings requiring investment of the family's savings, Iulii Witte died—'little more than 50 years old,' his son wrote.[30] Whatever the psychological impact of parental death, its traumatic economic consequences, as well as the limits to masculine talent it drew, registered explicitly in Witte's recollections. At length, he described how his father had become enmeshed in a scheme to develop cast-iron production in colonial Georgia. His was a classic tale of nineteenth-century Russian commercial–industrial enterprise, which melded officialdom, entrepreneurial initiative, and cronyism, a narrative with which, as we shall see, Witte was quite familiar at the end of his own life. Because they had been granted a state concession to mine ore deposits near Tiflis, German entrepreneurs came under the purview of Iulii Witte's office. 'I remember that my father traveled more than once to inspect these factories (sic) and took me and my older brother Boris with him,' he wrote, detailing the boys' refusal to eat the unpalatable German delicacies served to honor their dignitary father. The concessionaire, however, suddenly died. The viceroy I. Ia. Bariatinskii, a confidant of Alexander II and another patron of the Witte clan, intervened, insisting that Iulii Witte, given his technical education in mining, assume management of the enterprise. The financial entanglement itself unexamined in his memoir, Witte's story merely noted that, despite the losses he anticipated, the father nevertheless 'agreed, or more accurately, submitted to the desires of the viceroy... (who) promised with time to arrange everything'. Contracting 'enormous debts', his father used as collateral that which he had earned through education and marriage—lands in southern Stavropol province awarded him for his service in Georgia and 'the quite large dowry from his wife, my mother', which she had brought to their marriage. The Grand Duke Mikhail Nikolaevich replaced Bariatinskii in 1862. This even more august personage assured Witte that 'he would write the Sovereign about all of this and then the matter would be resolved and the monies returned to him'. But six years later, in 1868, the father's sudden death left a mountain of debt so steep that his son estimated his own share to have been a huge sum of over 200,000 rubles. Although finally rescinded by royal decree in the early 1880s, family debt was Witte's legacy from his educated, expert, and influential father. His was a memory of 'the utter ruin of our entire family;

from wealthy people, thanks to this, we became people of extremely limited means'. Living from pensions, stipends, and the generosity and influence of his uncle Rostislav Fadeev, the family moved to 'a modest life in Odessa', one, Witte remembered in conclusion, which his mother found 'terribly hard'.[31] Much later, in his early years as a minister in the 1890s, Witte's files would contain letters of supplication from other widows, who perhaps had touched this memory as well.[32] Like his father, Witte would use education and expertise to achieve status and influence. But he would draw as well on other attributes of manhood to avoid the fate that had befallen the 'noble-man Witte'.

If civil officials shaped the boy's understanding of masculinity, in these reminiscences of his earliest years Witte also dwelled on a third man, an older brother, who served in the army and plainly also shaped his ideas of manhood. 'My oldest brother Alexander died after the last Turkish war' (the great Eastern War of 1878–80), Witte remarked when he first remembered a man, three years his elder, whose entire life had been spent in the Caucasus. A career cavalry officer, Alexander received more attention in Witte's memoirs than either his civil servant father or grandfather, and appeared to be more emotionally important than either. What brother might have felt for brother—'Of my family I loved him more fiercely than anyone else'—can only be judged from one rumination, a remembrance of an intimate male relationship startling because, good Victorian that he was, Witte so rarely revealed one.[33] The frontier region in which Witte came of age was a world at war, to which Russian men for a half-century had streamed, seeking to escape the strict hierarchies of metropolitan society and prove themselves to be, somehow, men: valorous, honorable, comradely, and fearless.[34] As he had looked to his long-serving grandfather and talented father, so too did Witte look to his brother, a military officer, to understand manhood.

That Alexander was a shining light in the Witte family seemed clear. His grandfather doted on this 'fine (slavnyi) young man, this exemplary officer', as Fadeev called him when remembering his birth. His aunt, Nadezhda Fadeeva, remarked her nephew's 'heroic exploits' in the Russo-Turkish War, and his tragic death in 1884, most likely from shellshock suffered in battle.[35] Marking his brother as a graduate of a Moscow military academy and a warrior still honored in regimental marching songs as 'the valiant (khrabryi) Major Witte'. Sergei dwelled on his brother's emotional charac-teristics—a perspective that would reappear again and again when this most

emotional of men regarded other men. 'Alexander was of average intellectual abilities, average education, but was a most kind-hearted soul (*prekras-
neishei dushi chelovek*)', one whom 'all his comrades loved', Witte wrote. As
standing physically before him, Witte remembered a man 'of middling
height, very stout, unattractive, a loutish sort (*sovershennyi vakhlak*), but
quite the sympathetic and genial man from whose eyes shone only goodness'.[36] So unlike the staid bureaucratic councilors who had filled his adult
public world, Witte's brother was compassionate, robust, even hearty.

Witte remembered as well his brother's gallantry, captured in tales of the
nineteenth-century male death sport of dueling. Here was the undoubtedly
romanticized memory of the valorous, cool-headed brother entangled with
'a very handsome, gallant officer' over public displays of attention to 'one
lady (*baryshnia*)' and a single utterance, 'scoundrel (*podlets*) . . . to summon
forth all the consequences following from that word'. Alexander shot and
killed his jealous opponent only after surviving the duel's ritualized male

flirtation with death, which Witte, having heard the story from his brother,
remembered still with evident fascination. Three times the combatants
exchanged shots; each time they paused to send emissaries and inquire
whether the other would submit. 'Alexander told me how, at the first
signal, he fired into the air, and (his opponent) fired in such a way that
the bullet rushed by my brother's ear and he felt the contusion.' A second
shot into the air, and his brother felt a second bullet 'fly past his other ear'.
Only then, 'very much enraged', but waiting a final time for his opponent
to withdraw the insulting word, 'did he shoot taking aim'. Although it cost
him a six-month sentence of imprisonment from a military court, the
duel—its display of foolhardiness, honor, and gallantry—distinguished his
brother as a man.[37]

Even more, Witte was drawn to his brother's bravery, martial valor, and
élan. 'Alexander did not serve more than two months of his time' before
war with Turkey broke out in 1878, Witte continued, focusing upon a long
reminiscence about a man who 'went to war with his regiment' and 'many
times distinguished himself, but was never once wounded'. He fought in a
legendary Russian victory, the second storming of the Turkish fortress of
Kars in southern Armenia, and received a St George's Cross for bravery,
awarded personally by the Emperor Alexander II. Witte honored Alexander's 'most renowned exploit', a cavalry reconnaissance across mountainous
terrain and large concentrations of Ottoman infantry, combat, and death
that he detailed.[38] The two brothers must have conversed about the war;

they certainly shared the experience of early years spent in the war-besotted Caucasus. Whatever their source, Witte peppered these earliest recollections with tales of soldierly exploits. Never did he mention the violent, often merciless, scorched-earth campaign that the Russians waged against the region, which was evident, for example, in the writing of his uncle, R. A. Fadeev. Where Fadeev recalled burned-out villages, trampled grain fields, and destroyed homes, Witte, a generation removed from the combat, remembered only iconographic figures. The 'valorous general' Baron Nikolai fought against Muslim mountaineers and late in life, remarkably converted to Catholicism to become a French monk. General N. I. Evdokimov, 'remembered... as an utterly brilliant military commander,' visited his boyhood home; Evdokimov led Russian forces in Chechnya during the late 1850s and deforested swaths of the region to deny guerilla fighters cover and refuge. 'Of the military men of that time I remember Chevchevadze', Witte wrote of a native Georgian officer, whom he admired for more than his valor, as 'an extremely tall man with broad shoulders and a waist that any young lady might envy'. An officer 'distinguished by enormous strength and extraordinary valor (*khrabrost'*)', he was 'seemingly forged from steel'. Alexander 'laughingly assured me', Witte wrote, 'that he himself had seen bullets ricochet' off the brave Georgian, who simply paid them no mind.[39] That such typecasts were one of the fuller expressions of his boyhood memories of Georgians underscores how little Witte's experience was rooted in the ethnic communities that populated the region.

If manhood connoted valor, bravado or courage, in the end it also meant stoicism in the face of fear and death. Witte learned this from his brother as well. 'I often talked... with my deceased brother... about the sensations that he experienced in war,' he wrote.

> Aleksander said: if anyone ever tells you that he is not afraid going into battle, don't believe him. Before battle everyone is afraid, but when the battle has been joined, people, in actuality, forget, and forgetting, they no longer fear anything. He said that he well remembered how often... he cut down the enemy with less regret than if he were slaughtering cattle. The blood, which splattered and flowed around my brother, made no impression on him and, nevertheless, before the battle... he was always agitated.

'I personally was forced to experience just such a feeling,' Witte immediately added, pausing as he frequently would to reflect on his more recent adult political life. 'At the very height of the revolution,' he wrote about the turbulent, haunting months of revolutionary violence that wracked the empire in 1905–06, officials repeatedly warned him against appearing in public. Often, late at night 'alone, when I lay down to sleep . . . I was always horribly afraid'. Leaving the safety of his home in the morning, 'every time I cowered horribly'. Yet, once seated in his carriage, negotiating the streets—one is tempted to say once he put on his public face—'the fear passed and I moved about, feeling just as calm as I do now, dictating these lines.'[40] Like his brother, whom he had claimed as a model for such behavior, Witte too had learned that masculinity demanded the stoic control of fear and emotion.

Dutiful and loyal, talented and educated, gallant and stoic: during the years of his boyhood and adolescence, the men of Sergei Witte's family delicately sculpted an understanding of masculinity for their most prestigious descendant. Yet, none of them influenced the young Witte more profoundly than his uncle, the gadfly publicist, pan-slav nationalist, and military officer Rostislav Andreevich Fadeev (1824–1883). Nadezhda Fadeeva asserted that her bachelor brother, who 'loved his sister's children as if they were his own, was entirely like a father to them' after Iulii Witte died when his son was already attending university.[41] Witte insisted he remembered his uncle bundling him out of a baby cradle and carrying him from a fever-ridden Tiflis on horseback. The family's women scoffed at a memory they reasoned originated later from stories told by his nurse, but Witte swore it was not 'my fantasy'. Certainly, the memory evinced the strong emotional bond between uncle and nephew.[42] Apparent as well was Fadeev's intellectual influence. 'From the following account it will be apparent', Witte wrote, 'that Fadeev exerted an enormous influence on my education and my intellectual psychology (umstvennaia psikhologiia). I was very close to him,' he continued, 'especially after graduating university and thus living the fully conscious (soznatel'naia) life' of a young adult man. It was then that he began to read the essays and polemical tracts that poured from his uncle's pen in the 1860s and 1870s. Fadeev's peripatetic writings— on Russia and Asia, imperial destiny, Russian national identity—would all place their mark on Witte's mentality.[43] Judging from his reminiscence about Fadeev, the longest about any family member, his uncle still fascinated the old memoirist. Judging from its contents, that influence began well before he reached intellectual maturity. Fadeev provided Witte with a first example of the man he would be: a man of intellect and imagination.

In a biographical essay she wrote for a posthumously published collection of his writings, the family editor and biographer Nadezhda Fadeeva lionized her brilliant yet quixotic brother—'an intelligent man, but an idealist', she wrote.[44] Born in 1824, ten years after imperial Russia had vanquished Napoleon and established its sway across the European continent, the impressionable young boy, Fadeeva related, relished 'historical tales, the lives of great people, military events'. In provincial Ekaterinoslav, his home through age 10, his 'dreams were drawn to the East. He thought about Persia, about India and already was making plans for their conquest,' Fadeeva added, knowing how her brother later had gazed into Asia from the crests of the Caucasus Mountains and indulged imperial visions of Russian control over Central Asia. Schooled in classical Latin and mathematics, familiar with French and Russian literature, thrilled by the poetry of Pushkin, Fadeev reveled in his 'beloved history reading' and 'with his powerful imagination rendered himself a hero', like the Cossack military commander Ermak and his legendary, marauding conquest of Siberia. Later, in the 'broad steppe of Astrakhan province', where the civil service led his father in 1836, Fadeev hunted, fished, and rode a prairie wilderness, shielded by Kalmyk and Kirghiz chieftains whose relationship with his father, their supervisory Russian official, required attention to his son as well.[45]

Raised on the periphery of the empire, Fadeev was taken to its center, albeit but briefly, a year later, when he was 14. Resigned to their son's demand to begin a military career, his parents used family connections to obtain a place for him in an elite cadet academy in Moscow. Within eighteen months, he had avoided expulsion for insubordination only by again using family influence to gain appointment as a junior officer in an artillery regiment quartered in the provinces. In 1841, at the age of 17, he 'retired' to live with his parents in Saratov. He spent parts of the next eight years educating himself. According to his sister, he read 'thousands of volumes' and wrote 'masterfully produced summations and commentaries' on whole academic fields. Here too, however, in a frontier provincial center like Saratov, a young man in his twenties, whose 'imagination worked tirelessly and demanded lively action', found little to satisfy his 'thirst for activity'. She wrote: '... naturally, the power of fantasy (*sila fantazii*) sometimes drew the young man into eccentricities, about which among his acquaintances entire legends were preserved over the years.' What these might have been she did not say.[46]

Fadeev first traveled to the Caucuses in 1844. For more than a year he explored the region and volunteered in Russian military expeditions, twice suffering minor wounds. His parents' transfer to Tiflis followed in 1846. His transit complicated by suspicions raised in the Third Section, the central government's political police, about the young man's ideological sympathies during the European revolutions of 1848, Fadeev only arrived in Tiflis in 1849, and, like so many Russians of his era, found this borderland of empire a place where he could reimagine his life. Studying the Tatar language, reading, journeying with his father on official circuit, Fadeev found this country 'utterly interesting'. 'He loved nature terribly,' his sister wrote, 'and his lively soul greedily took in the impressions abundantly supplied it by this poetic country, with its magnificent, wild surroundings and recollections of a historic past.'[47] A year later he rejoined the army and began what she called his 'fighting life (*boevaia zhizn'*)'. Shaped by Russia's war of imperial conquest in the Caucasus, these years saw him rise from the obscurity of a junior officer serving in southern Dagestan to become a trusted adjutant of the viceroy, Prince I. A. Bariatinskii, and in 1864, at age 40, attain the rank of general.

Fadeev first gained public attention in the 1860s, when he published a series of articles about this half-century long campaign of subjugation, which he characterized as an inevitable and legitimate triumph of Europe over Asia.[48] These writings, as did family correspondence reproduced by his sister, testified to the bloody violence of the fifteen years Fadeev spent fighting against the Muslim mountaineers of Chechnya and Dagestan, lands whose ethnic and tribal clans sheltered resistance to Russian power that grew from Islamic Sufism and the calls for holy war that it generated from a succession of imams. The historian Geoffrey Hosking uses the word 'genocide' to describe a war in which the Russians employed a strategy that rested on clear-cutting forests, constructing roads, and destroying housing and agriculture in communities that refused to acknowledge Russian suzerainty.[49] A culminating moment in this conflict, and a pivotal one in Fadeev's own life, was the subsequently much glorified Russian campaign in 1858–59 to capture the imam Shamil. Fadeev, who detailed the campaign in his writing, participated in its final, often dramatized episode, Shamil's surrender to the viceroy, Bariatinskii, in his mountain redoubt village of Gunib in summer 1859. 'In Tiflis, on 30 August a 101-gun salute announced the taking of Shamil and the subjugation of the Caucasus,' Nadezhda Fadeeva many years later wrote. 'As a mark to remember Gunib, Prince

Bariatinskii presented Fadeev a banner taken from Shamil,' she added, a memento which, when Fadeeva wrote in the late 1880s, she already had inherited from her deceased brother.[50]

Of course, Witte was only a 10-year-old in 1859. Yet, in 1911, it bears noting, that banner, bequeathed in turn to Witte, hung in the private library of his 'White House' on Kamenoostrovskii Prospect in St Petersburg,[51] perhaps even facing him as he dictated these memoirs and reflected on the uncle who, by his own admission, had so shaped his 'mental outlook'. More sparse than his aunt's had been, Witte's reminiscences sometimes mimicked what she had written. He found in his uncle's life examples of dutiful service, educational achievement, and martial bravery. Yet, more so than any of these attributes, Fadeev's imaginative intellect, and the powerful impetus it supplied him in life, captivated Witte. In Witte's telling of family legend, Fadeev appeared first not as a brilliant boy, but an insubordinate military cadet, who at an early age already had 'returned to his father in Saratov, a nobleman without any kind of purpose (*dvorianin bez vsiakikh zaniatii*)'. Yet, rather than provincial anomie, Fadeev, especially 'thanks to the influence of his mother, a quite educated woman, became engrossed in reading and the study of the sciences', Witte wrote. Noting his grand-mother's looming intellectual influence not for the last time, Witte continued that Fadeev 'became an altogether educated man (*obrazovannyi chelovek*)', distinguished more by his intellect than the formal perquisites of the university education earned by both his father and himself. 'He was full of knowledge, and talent, and in general spiritual power', Witte remem-bered, adding that he 'was somewhat inclined to mysticism and even to spiritualism'. The imaginative power of Fadeev's intellect was so pro-nounced in his mind that Witte, explaining why a man so 'educated and talented' had never achieved 'the huge career' his gifts had promised, cited his 'one shortcoming . . . in that he readily indulged the fantasy-like charac-ter of his personality (*legko poddavalsia uvlecheniiam po fantastichnosti svoei natury*)'.[52] He was, as Nadezhda Fadeeva had observed as well, a man of intellect, imagination—and dreams.

Even though it cost Fadeev his career, a never inconsequential price in Witte's eyes, he recognized and admired his uncle's imagination and intel-lect precisely because, through them, he was able to remake himself. As Witte continued Fadeev's story, he recalled a young man who, despite his 'passion' for study, was still a stifled 'do-nothing nobleman (*nichego nede-laiushchii dvorianin'*)' prone to 'scandalous escapades' on the streets of

Saratov. Yet, resolving to abandon his settled, provincial life, together with its constraining hierarchies, expectations, and cultural mores, 'Fadeev left as a volunteer for the Caucasus. He went there', his nephew explained, 'because at that time the Caucasus lured everyone who preferred to live amidst war, rather than in a civilized and peaceful society (*mirnoe obshchestvo*).' In this distant borderland, when 'tribes unfriendly to us' separated the region from Russia and 'the entire Caucasus blazed with uprisings and military action against the Turks', the young Fadeev transformed himself, becoming an officer and serving ever more prominently under four different imperial viceroys. Witte described this history at some length, interspersing his own observations about these prominent personalities with tales chiefly of Fadeev's military exploits.[53] But repeatedly he came back to the dramatic changes of personality that marked the lifetime of this man.

Two episodes in particular stood out for Witte. The first involved Fadeev's discovery of religious belief. This aspect of imagination and intellect intrigued Witte as well. As a young man he had read, at the urging of his uncle, essays on orthodox religiosity and belief by the prominent Slavophil writer Aleksei Khomiakov.[54] As a regimental officer during the Crimean War, Fadeev had served at the long and bloody siege of the Ottoman fortress at Kars, in Armenia, and told Witte how, abandoning atheism and instead embracing faith during that combat, 'he became a religious man'. Echoing a criticism of the materialist non-belief that had swept Russian intellectual life as he came of age and that he likely had taken from Fadeev as well, Witte remembered his uncle's apparently genuine conversion, a tale of a Gethsemane-like night spent before the climactic battle. Knowing the likely fate awaiting them, 'many officers, as was the custom of that time, caroused through the night'. Fadeev, following the example of a senior officer, instead 'spent the entire night in prayer and in preparing himself for death'. From that time onward, Witte continued, Fadeev 'ceased being an atheist, believed in God, in life beyond the grave and became a strong adherent of our holy orthodox church, into which, of course, he had been born.'[55]

If that episode reminded Witte that a man's personality could change, a second distant memory, one that plainly sparked his own imagination, conveyed the rewards that such psychological flexibility might afford a young man. Witte wrote at length about his uncle's service as an adjutant to the imperial viceroy A. I. Bariatinskii, who later assisted Witte in the early stages of his own career—and from whose hands Fadeev had received

Shamil's banner. 'Bariatinskii was a bachelor,' Witte wrote, 'and lived in the viceroy's palace (in Tiflis) and I remember how, still as a boy, I was present at his great balls, in the choir balcony.' The clarity of the memory was striking, as the old man recalled a youth's awe, how he peered from behind balustrades not only at the viceroy, who 'carried himself so majestically', but also at his adjutants, 'many of whom were from the Petersburg gilded youth (*jeunesse dorée*)':

> they entirely bedecked his balls. Besides that, at that time in Tiflis there were many young people, who arrived here [sic] from Russia for sport: some went to serve in the military service, desiring to experience the sensations of war; others went to the civil service, mindful that life in the Caucasus generally was very gay (*veselaia*).[56]

Presumably, somewhere in this throng stood Fadeev, a once useless provincial nobleman transformed into a glittering adjutant, a man favored with access at the heights of the society in which he lived. Of course, all the men who influenced Witte in his early years were members of this elite. Whether through duty, talent, bravery, or intellect, each, in his own way, had established a pathway by which male identity and status, the two often inseparable, were created. Witte would be dutiful, talented, brave, and intelligent. Yet, the testimony of his memoir suggests Witte emulated Fadeev, a man of intelligence, imagination, and, most of all, dreams.

Frontier Women and Imperial Imagination

Witte's autobiographical ruminations were crowded with female personalities as well, and they suggest that the women who guided his upbringing (*vospitanie*) also shaped his identity as a man—perhaps even more so than had the men in his life.[57] His memoirs confirm much of what scholars have written about the nineteenth-century Russian noble family and its ideals of female domesticity.[58] The roles women played inside the family shaped elite cultural understanding of womanhood. Women moved through adult life as wives, household managers, and moral exemplars. They influenced the boyhoods of men deeply, guiding their upbringing (*vospitanie*) either directly or by supervising the domestics and governesses given that charge. Women were literate, often well read, raised properly, and typically educated at home. To the extent that the sexual and erotic skittishly came into public view at all, women were objects of male admiration, affection, love, and desire. They played subordinate roles in a public and civic world that men dominated. What would prove most striking about the Fadeev women, however, was their life experience as frontier women, through whom Witte was nurtured in what they imagined to be the civilizing culture that European Russians brought to the modern world. Scholars studying the nineteenth-century imperial experience have shown how European understandings of womanhood became more fluid and transitional on frontiers, where established gender identities were tested along the new racial, ethno-national, and biological boundaries of colonial environments.[59] European women's experience on frontiers thus often challenged and reshaped cultural understandings of womanhood existing in the metropolis. To apply these general observations to Witte is to note that his reminiscences, while dwelling on the images of domesticity and femininity that so influenced the lives of ninetenth-century Russian women, also reflected a captivation with the autonomy of women challenged by life on the frontiers of empire. These Russian women were agents of order and cultural enlightenment: the sinews of an imperial civilization.

Witte's mother, Ekaterina Mikhailovna Fadeeva (1819–1898), spent a lifetime following both father and husband as they served in southern Russia and the Caucasus.[60] In the richly detailed travelogues that filled his memoir, Andrei Fadeev mentioned his daughter in the 1840s sailing with him by steamer along the Crimean coast, bringing her two sons (two years before Witte's birth) from Saratov to the Caspian seaport of Baku, or making a harrowing trip by carriage across the Caucasus Mountains on the narrow track of the Georgian Military Highway.[61] Witte, who acknowledged nothing of this history beyond the tenacity that it might partially have created, idealized his mother more than any other woman in his family. We already have had opportunity to see how he pitied the widow, victimized by the chicanery of business and bureaucracy. For her son, Ekaterina Fadeeva was a young woman, who fell in love with and married his father. She was a mother, who gave birth to three sons and two daughters. She was a wife, who supervised the enserfed servants and hired tutors that worked the family household, while she accompanied her nobleman husband in public life. As was her husband, she largely was absent from the childhood of her son—or so the distant, scattered memories of his mother would suggest. Indeed, all that can be judged about Ekaterina Witte is that which her son, as an old man, remembered her ideally to have been. His testimony suggests that in the Tiflis household where Witte was raised to become a man, she was an agent of order.

In the first instance, upholding codes of noble behavior, she was a source of moral order and decorum in her family. The daughter of a Fadeev clan 'not at all unfamiliar with a certain kind of noble, even aristocratic pride (*boiarskoe chvanstvo*)', she refused to receive in her home nieces of whose marriages she disapproved, and, of much more direct import for Witte, 'looked askance at my intention to be a professor' when he was a university student, arguing against a career that properly 'was not a nobleman's affair (*dvorianskoe delo*)'.[62] If order and decorum in the family were her affair, so too was her protection of the family's political order, the personal bonds of monarchical loyalty tying noble families to the imperial throne. Witte claimed to remember how, in 1854 when he was some 5 years old, his family reacted to 'news of the death of the Emperor' Nicholas I. 'I remember... being in my room with my nurse (this was in Tiflis), when my mother entered, sobbing....' Soon 'everyone was tearfully sobbing', he recalled, remembering a scene that had left a 'powerful impression', because such grief normally was expressed only at the death of 'a very close intimate'. A boy would not have known that this second year of the Crimean War, with Ottoman armies looming on nearby borders, had been, as remembered by Andrei Fadeev, 'the most alarming year for Transcaucasia since the time it was joined to Russia'. Within the Russian community of Tiflis, it was 'widely held that the entire Muslim population of the region would rise up at once, greet the Turks with open embrace and join them,' he wrote. 'Constant emotional alarms and fears,' he continued, 'an uncertainty about tomorrow, could not but weigh overwhelmingly on the mood of society and family alike (*na obshchestvennom i domashnem nastroenii*)'. Witte only remembered his sobbing mother, then added: 'In general my entire family was to a very high degree a monarchical family and I inherited this characteristic from them.'[63]

Finally, together with moral and political order, his mother symbolized an ethno-religious order, acknowledged even late in life by this bearer of a most un-Russian surname, who insisted upon acknowledging his maternal lineage as a Russian Orthodox Christian man. 'Witte loved to insist on his fealty (*priviazannost'*) to the Orthodox Church,' the legal scholar Maksim Kovalevskii wrote about a man with whom he worked and socialized. He 'prided himself on belonging to a family, to be sure via the maternal line,' Kovalevskii explained concerning Ekaterina Fadeeva's pedigree through her mother, 'which in its turn was related to the renowned prince (Iakov) Dolgorukov, known for having spoken the truth (*skazavshii pravdu*) before Peter the Great himself.' A portrait of this early eighteenth-century Russian statesman, an uncle six generations removed, hung at home in Witte's private study on one wall almost entirely covered with pictures of these ancestors.[64] Observers of imperial Russia long have been accustomed to think of its patriarchal structures. Yet Witte, it bears emphasizing, framed the marriage of his father, Iulius Witte, to Ekaterina Fadeeva as not only his Protestant father's religious conversion to Russian Orthodoxy, but his spiritual and psychological transformation as well. 'I know that my father, when he came to Saratov, was a Lutheran... (and) a nobleman of Pskov province, although of Baltic origins,' Witte recalled. 'His ancestors were Dutchmen who emigrated to the Baltic provinces when they still belonged to the Swedes,' noting here almost nothing about his father's large extended family. He mused, in memoirs first dictated and thus spoken, about his mother, father, and himself:

> The Fadeev family was so ultra-orthodox... truly orthodox that, of course, no matter how deep my mother's love for the young Witte, this marriage could not take place as long as my father had not become orthodox. Hence, before the marriage, or in any case in the first years of the marriage, before my birth, my father already was orthodox and because he entered completely (*voshel sovershenno*) into the Fadeev family, and with the Witte family had no close relations whatsoever, then, of course, having lived for many decades in matrimonial harmony (*schastlivoe supruzhestvo*) with my mother, he became in spirit entirely orthodox. They had three sons: Aleksandr, Boris, and the third was I, Sergei, and then two daughters who were younger than I, the one, Olga, and the other, Sofia. [sic][65]

If a pillar of cultural order in his memories, Witte's mother lacked the patina of education that had shone so brightly when he pondered the men of his clan. She was, however, an exception in an extended family in which education and the intellectual life it germinated were central to the femininity that Witte had experienced as a boy. With the exception of his mother and two sisters, all the other women of the Witte clan in some fashion were writers and intellectuals. Nadezhda Fadeeva, for example, brought her not inconsequential skills as author and editor to the task of chronicling her family's experience in Transcaucasia. About her endeavours Witte remained silent. His adopted daughter Vera recalled the family visiting her in Odessa at the time of his mother's death—and her study with its 'enormous library and portraits of all her ancestors in identical, plain gold frames'. Witte merely noted that she 'remained a maiden', and was still alive in Odessa, nursing Sofia, the younger of his two sisters, who had contracted tuberculosis from the deceased elder sister, Olga.[66] His mother's older aunt was the novelist Elena Gan. Witte knew her only as 'a quite well-known female writer of Belinsky's time', published beginning in the 1830s under the pseudonym Zinaida R, and renowned enough to have won the acclaim of the mid-century's ruling Russian literary critic, Vissarion Belinsky, before she died in her third childbirth at age 28. Gan's two daughters, Witte's cousins and contemporaries, were the children's writer Vera Zhelikhovskaia and the international spiritualist, Helene Blavatsky. Looming over them all was his grandmother, the amateur naturalist Elena Pavlovna Fadeeva. All women of the frontier, they were agents of an imperial Russian (*rossisskii*) culture—writers, scholars, and public persons who never questioned that the ascendancy of Russian language, enlightenment, and power begun in the eighteenth century was creating a Russian civilization in the nineteenth.

An author of some public repute whom Vissarion Belinsky had called a Russian Georges Sand, Elena Gan grew up in the New Russia, southern border capital of Ekaterinoslav. She was married at age 16, to an artillery officer twice her age who had graduated from the aristocratic Corps of Pages, the son of yet another family in the imperial service elite. Literary historians classify her so-called society tales as portrayals of autonomous women constrained by their times. Living with her husband in a succession of dull, provincial border towns, Gan also had the opportunity to discover and circulate in the bright salon society of St Petersburg. The contrast between the two released her imagination. She began to write fiction that she set within the exotic cultures populating the borderlands where service had led her family: the lower Volga and Caspian steppe, the Crimea, the Black Sea littoral, and the Caucasus.[67] In one of them, 'The Reminiscence of Zheleznovodsk', Gan described a young, unmarried Russian woman of that same Petersburg salon society, who, having first read a novel, dreamt about her capture and possession by Circassian 'savages'. At the story's center were erotic hints about a 'young Circassian' prince, distinguished by 'the signs of respect . . . (as) his fellow natives honored him.' Describing that young woman awakening from her reveries, Gan questioned what she assumed would be the reader's unwillingness to believe such a scenario possible and wondered about the origins of this 'urge to contest my dream'.

'If you do not have such dreams, it is not really my fault,' Gan, in richly textured metaphors, explained. 'In my soul there is more gunpowder than in yours,' she wrote. 'In mine there are great quantities of flammable substances, so it is no wonder that loaded with imagination it hit harder, and that my imagination, fired by our conversations yesterday and by this terrible novel, swept off with an unbelievable speed over days and weeks.'[68]

Gan's two daughters also drew Witte's attention. Vera Zhelikhovskaia (1835–1898), a cousin fifteen years older than Witte, was 'well known in Petersburg and generally in large imperial Russian towns (*Rossiiskie goroda*), thanks to her books.' Zheilkhovskaia's work as an essayist and journalist, in the 1880s and 1890s, as well as her authorship of some ten storybooks for younger and middle grade children, earned her public repute significant enough for mention in a major encyclopedia of the day.[69] She too was a memoirist, and left remarkable commentaries about her childhood in the Fadeev clan when it still lived in Saratov, another imperial town on the frontier. An 'old nurse' who served the Fadeev family, Zhelikhovskaia later wrote in these texts, 'received praise for her fairy tales, the number of which was endless'. Such stories 'excited us all very much'. She remembered 'a holy man (*starets*) "Baranik Buriak"', who lived in the forest and claimed to speak the languages of birds, animals, and insects. She recalled at length her sister, the spiritualist guru Elena Blavatsky, a girl for whom, when they lived in Saratov province in the 1840s, 'all nature was enchanted (*odushevlennoi*)'. She 'heard the voice of every thing and attributed consciousness to things, the existence in them of hidden powers, which she alone saw and heard'. And Zhelikhovskaia more than once mentioned what was a central place for the family, 'grandmother's zoological museum of prehistoric artifacts, birds and animals'.[70]

A microcosm of an imperial civilization's fascination with the world it was encountering and attempting to categorize, so as to comprehend and control it, her rooms, in the words of one family intimate, were something to be found 'among the most remarkable private museums. Gathered there were coats of arms and weapons from all countries of the world, antique dishes, statues of Chinese and Japanese idols, Byzantine mosaics, Persian and Turkish carpets, paintings, portraits, and a very rare and large library'.[71] Another, close to the family in the 1840s, described this 'most interesting place, able to spark even the less developed imagination (*razzhigaiushchee dazhe menee bogatoe voobrazhenie*)', in which were to be found 'various stuffed animals—the snarling visages of bears and tigers, and elegant little humming birds, owls, falcons, hawks, and over them all, near the ceiling, an enormous eagle spread its majestic (*velichestvennye*) wings'. Scholars will be most taken by this metaphor for Russian imperial rule, but the woman writing these remarks offered instead something more akin to the child's view that what was 'most memorable was a white flamingo, extending its long neck as if it were alive. When children came into their grandmother's study, they would mount it, as if a horse', appropriate enough behavior for youth wrestling with the strange and exotic colonial world they inhabited.[72]

Zhelikhovskaya described how her sister Elena loved at sunset to gather children in grandmother's 'museum' and 'there fire their imagination with supernatural stories, with unheard-of twists, in which she herself was the main heroine'. She was Gan's second and older daughter, the internationally acclaimed spiritualist and theosophist E. P. Blavatskaia (1831–1891). Another frontier woman, Blavatskaia eventually acquired international stature through her explorations of Eastern religions and spiritualism, as well as a mystic's taste for séances and public masking. She fascinated educated Europeans and Americans in the age of empire.[73] Witte lavished attention on her life story, which he recollected at the very beginning of his dictated memoirs; indeed, Blavatsky's story was the very first genuine 'tale' he told.[74] All of Witte's narrative devices were here for the first time on display. Mentioning the author of the acclaimed 'In the Wilds of Hindustan', which Mikhail Katkov had serialized in *The Russian Herald* in 1880, accentuated the patronage he had received from this conservative nationalist tribune in the years of his own public ascendancy. It allowed him to bemoan the imperial elite's penchant for mysticism and new-age spiritualism, on display, as he dictated the text in 1911, in St Petersburg high society, most infamously in those circles close to the royal family frequented by Rasputin. Mentioning Blavatsky also provided a dash of sensationalism, perhaps even a commercial ploy to net him the market price he envisioned for his manuscript. Yet, the story of Elena Blavatsky, a Russian woman who commanded international attention and cultural power, was the first memory of his childhood he chose to explore: some mark of the impact her memory provoked.

Without doubt, Witte was most taken by the insights afforded him through the psychological, a perspective he understood and sometimes named. As he continued to think about Blavatsky, Rostislav Fadeev, another fantasy-like personality, reappeared in his thoughts. Although Fadeev was somehow 'purer, in a moral sense' and 'much more educated' than Blavatsky, the two were 'proof that certain characteristics of nature are passed on via birth (by inheritance) from generation to generation'. What Witte knew of Blavatsky's debut in the 1850s was mainly family lore, buttressed by both his belief she possessed 'some sort of supernatural talent' and his own few boyhood memories of her. In that sense he constructed Blavatsky. There was Blavatsky the orphan, raised by his grandparents after Elena Gan's early death. Blavatsky was a young, harried woman, married off to a much older civil official in Armenia when she was 17, who within months had fled home to her grandparents. She was the runaway. Returned to Tiflis, Blavatsky was dispatched to her father in Russia, but, arriving in the Black Sea steamship depot of Poti, she 'took the scent (*sniukhat'sia*)' of an English steamship captain and sailed off with him to the capital city of the Ottomans, which Witte in Greek and Slavic fashion called Constantinople. There she became … a circus bareback rider, lover of the European opera bass Mitrovich, companion of a London man on business in America, follower of the mid-century's 'greatest spiritualist', concert pianist and choirmaster of the Serbian king. This bewildering array of identities for the illicit woman was very much Witte's own concoction. They all bore little facsimile to the historical record, none more so than his own memory of a chastened Blavatsky, returned in 1860 to Tiflis and a respectable life, when Witte would have been 12.[75]

In fact, by Blavatsky's own testimony in a letter of 1885, she agreed to a marriage promising so much unhappiness only after yielding to family pressure, some of it by 'my aunt', Witte's mother 'Madame Witte' who, as we have seen, played this family role. Credible evidence suggests that the family legend about Blavatsky's amorous affair with an English ship captain was apocryphal, masking the fact that she very well may have arranged her own disappearance.[76] Finally, she hardly returned to Tiflis chastened. Even Witte knew this, because he 'remembered her at that time'. He described 'a middle-aged woman', her 'face extremely expressive', once 'very beautiful but with time all rounded-out', who went about in shapeless clothing and thus 'lacked all appeal (*privlekatel'nost'*)'. He also remembered accurately enough to recall how Russian colonial society in Tiflis was swept up in séances at the Fadeev home, with Blavatsky presiding, his mother, aunt, and uncle Fadeev all believers, his grandparents and father, skeptics. A contemporary of that time described the well-known Fadeev salon:

Occasionally 'Radda-Bai—E. P. Blavatskaia, the granddaughter of general Fadeev, told of some incredible episode from her life and her travels through

America . . . Often, the conversation took on a mystical hue, and she would begin to 'summon the spirits'. At these evenings, long candles would burn down to nothing; in their flickering light human figures on the wall tapestries, it seemed, came alive and shook, and we involuntarily felt the motion.[77]

Witte remembered the time less dramatically, but even over the years a sense still remained of how he had been 'stunned by her most enormous talent to comprehend everything so quickly (*vse skhvatyvat'*)'—music, foreign languages, lyrical poetry, writing. 'She had these enormous blue eyes, which afterwards I never again saw in my entire life, and when she began to tell stories, especially something improbable, untruth, these eyes the entire time sparkled horribly (*strashno*) and thus it does not surprise me that she had enormous influence on many people prone to crude mysticism, to all that is unusual,' to all, Witte added, that left them unable to accept inevitable death and need instead 'a falsification of life beyond the grave'. Blavatsky's intellect, and her imagination, remained Witte's key memory of this truly imperial figure, whose theosophist teachings, societies, and journal were to be found 'in many places of the world'. 'In the end', Witte concluded, Blavatsky only solidified his anti-Darwinian insistence 'that a human is not an animal, that there is in him a spirit which cannot be explained through material origins . . . ; unquestionably there was in her a spirit entirely independent of her physical or physiological existence'. Whether serious, or indulging the kind of wicked banter that he himself dispensed in society, Witte concluded: 'The only question was: what kind of spirit. If one takes the view of an afterlife divided among hell, purgatory, and paradise, then from whence came the spirit that settled in Blavatsky during the time of her earthly existence?'[78]

A final woman remained. At the center of the Fadeev clan, repeatedly acknowledged as its members' intellectual wellspring, stood Witte's grandmother, the amateur naturalist Elena Pavlovna Fadeeva-Dolgorukaia (1789–1860). In the eyes of her intimates extending enlightenment and civilization on all its frontiers, she was a true daughter of the eighteenth-century Russian Empire. Witte perhaps had read her entry in the Russian Biographical Encyclopedia, a turn-of-the-century barometer of public standing. It openly admired a woman of distinguished intellectual stature, and noted her study of natural science, encompassing botany, ornithology, geology, and paleontology, as well as the fifty-volume, annotated collection of sketched flora she had classified while living in Saratov and the Caucasus.

The heir to what, by all accounts, was a most impressive family library, de facto curator of the private natural science museum she had created, Elena Pavlovna was well read in history, archeology, and numismatics, and fluent in five languages. She corresponded with a number of prominent European academics.[79] Only a boy 'some 10 or 12 years old' when his grandmother died in 1860, Witte did 'not remember her other than sitting in a chair, as a result of being partly paralyzed', the result, some evidence suggests, of a congenital rheumatoid condition that began afflicting her in childbearing years. What Witte remembered about her, as distinguished from what he had heard about her, was thin, but unusually concise. 'The first years' upbringing and education in childhood we all three boys received from our babushka—Elena Pavlovna Fadeeva, born Dolgorukaia,' Witte wrote. 'Elena Pavlovna was utterly an extraordinarily gifted (*sovershenno iz riada von vykhodiashchaia*) woman of that era, in the sense of her education; she quite loved nature and studied botany quite enthusiastically.' He added that he had gifted his alma mater, New Russia University, her 'enormous collection of flora of the Caucasus'. Good Victorian, Witte hastened to note that 'grandmother taught us to read and write, instilled in us the principles of religiosity and the dogmas of our orthodox church'—and, as grand matriarch, guarded the family's moral well-being, enough, Witte continued, that she held her husband 'under her moral sway (*nravstvennoe obaianie*), so that the head of the family (*glava semesitva*) was always Fadeeva-Dolgorukaia'.[80]

Beyond that, Witte knew only that his grandparents had married while young, and that Elena Pavlovna's parents had been provincial nobles in Penza province. This knowledge flowed from his possession of a second Fadeev clan artifact. Couple an 'ancient cross' with Shamil's banner, inherited from his uncle Rostislav, and behold the prying biographer–historian's opportunity to remark coincidence. Witte prized, those who were his contemporaries agreed, an 'ancient cross' used by Elena Pavlovna's father '—Pavel Vasilievich Dolgorukii—' to bless their marriage. '(F)amily legend' held that the bejeweled cross had been bequeathed by the thirteenth-century founder of the Dolgorukov house, the martyred and canonized medieval Prince Mikhail of Chernigov. It was passed to loyal boyars as he went to his execution, sentenced by the Mongol Golden Horde for his refusal, Witte maintained, 'to bow to their idols'. Whether these were gods of suzerainty or faith he did not say. 'This cross passed gradually from father to son, across the generations that followed Mikhail of Chernigov,' he continued. Unable to ascertain through research the veracity of the legend, he did nevertheless determine the 'most ancient origins' of the cross, which mattered just as much. From his grandmother, whose life marked 'the demise of the senior Dolgorukii line', the cross made its way to his childless uncle, then his mother, again his aunt Nadezhda Fadeeva, and finally, in 1909, to him.[81]

Elena Pavlovna—'the last of the senior branch of the princes Dolgorukii' had been emblazoned in the first lines of his autobiography—did provide Witte genealogical *gravitas*. The Dolgorukiis, a great aristocratic clan of eastern Europe, rooted its gnarled genealogical tree in the history of medieval Rus'. Witte dated the history of his branch of the family to 'Grigorii Fedorovich Dolgorukov (1656–1723), a senator under Peter I and brother of the renowned Iakov Fedorovich Dolgorukov (1659–1720).'[82] It went without saying that these two late seventeenth-century aristocratic sons served at the founding of the Petrine imperial state. Iakov Dolgorukov had been a boyhood courtier (*komnatnyi stolnik*) of the future Peter the Great, and used eleven years of Swedish captivity after the young tsar's humiliating defeat at Narva in 1700 to learn the technology of statecraft. His was the authorship of the so-called Twelve Colleges, the collegial institutions of an enlightened absolutist state whose government buildings Peter constructed on the north bank of the Neva River (the present St Petersburg University). The less well-known Grigorii, Witte's great grandparent, fought at the celebrated victory of imperial arms over Sweden at Poltava in 1709, represented the tsar to The Polish-Lithuanian Commonwealth and to Ukraine, and became a senator of the emperor near the end of his life. His sons, whom Witte ignored, were aristocratic *frondeurs* at the 'Constitutional Crisis of 1730', one episode in a grander eighteenth-century imperial Russian politics of great clans jostling for influence around the Romanov dynastic throne. These Dolgorukiis played the wrong card. Their plotting around the 11-year old boy tsar, Peter Alekseevich, grandson of Peter the Great, eventually produced the boy's betrothal with one of their daughters, the clan's attempt to forge a dying Peter's last will ceding the throne to his fiancée, and disaster when instead Anna Ionnovna, supported by her own coterie of favorites and Guards officers, assumed the throne in 1730. S. G. Dolgorukov lost his substantial holdings in property and serfs, and his life. Although the family's status and some of its lands were restored in 1740, it never recovered its former splendor. Elena Pavlovna's father and grandfather bore princely titles, but they were hereditary noblemen and regimental officers, nothing more.[83]

lots of background

Then why dwell on it?

Hence, what Witte took from his grandmother, his matrilineal lineage, was a genealogy that in a very literal sense made him Russian and imperial: the ethnic fabric of seventeenth-century Muscovite Russia consistently interstitched with service to the eightenth-century Petrine empire. One of a family of Russian service nobles, what Marc Raeff has described as noble *Kulturträger*, Witte inherited a tradition that equated empire with civilization and enlightenment.[84] No better example of this conjuncture existed than his grandmother, in a sense already a frontier woman when she first met Andrei Fadeev in 1812. Geographical expanse and knowledge of that space were two dimensions through which the imperial experience of Europeans evolved.[85] Certainly Elena Pavlovna, in her lifetime's travels, came to know the imperial borderlands as her life circumscribed an arc that led from Ukraine, to north-eastern Russia, down the Volga to the Astrakhan steppe, the Caspian and Black Seas, and Transcaucasia. As she went, she catalogued and named natural phenomena; we have already heard tell about the natural history museum she had assembled by 1840. Was Sergei one of the children who played in it? Had she taught him to imagine the imperial world?

Witte himself, of course, only admitted to knowing her when she was an old woman, when she was responsible, he had remembered, for teaching all three grandsons to read and write, and the religious precepts by which to believe. The reader should heed where historians will not tread. There is no way to define a relationship as subjective and private as that between grandmother and grandson, although its centrality in twenty-first-century Russian life suggests the necessity of historicizing this critical cultural linkage. That answer biography leaves to its readers—and a final tale of empire that Elena Pavlovna wrote. Whether she ever spoke it to the children who surrounded her is unknown.

Conclusion: A Grandmother's Tale

'On the 12th of August, in the fourth hour of the morning, my good wife is no more!' Andrei Fadeev grieved the words, palpably, in his memoir–diary for 1860, the year of Elena Pavlovna Fadeeva's death. Appended to that text, and of course edited by Nadezhda Fadeeva, was a memorial written by Fadeev. Its opening lines offered an obituary of his wife for posterity, an identity rippling with the sentimental romanticism of the post-revolutionary world that preceded the Victorians, and the commitment to rationalism, and enlightenment enchantment, that had been drawn from a family with roots in the splendor and power of the eighteenth-century Russian Empire:

> To a deep and serious intellect, a remarkable education, (and) knowledge so extensive and varied as to attract the attention of European scholars, Elena Pavlovna added a true, noble heart; she loved the blissful life amidst her family and studies, which were the chief comfort and diversion of her life. She loved nature, learned it, and especially studied botany in those hours when she was not preoccupied with children or the household, which she oversaw herself and ran admirably.'[86]

Fadeev's memorial continued, a final glimpse at the woman whom he had known for a half-century. He had prized her intellect, as had the family, which often also noted her collection of annotated scientific sketches, researched in 'a library of the best works on this subject', a place that the family had prized. Andrei praised as well Elena's thorough mastery of academic fields, an intellectual habit, which resulted, he explained, from the fact that 'her versatile intellect demanded such varied food'. That intellect had grounded the Fadeev clan, and she plainly encouraged this frame of mind in her daughters, her son Rostislav, and her grandchildren, a remarkable and talented group of writers, thinkers, and performers. Even the son-in-law, Iulius Witte, tied his career to intellectual advancement, his psyche, if his son were to be believed, tied to Orthodoxy and Russia. Yet, Andrei the husband found beyond intellect something womanly, something that made her, in the term that has been applied here to the frontier women of the Fadeev clan, autonomous.

'The breadth of what she knew', Fadeev wrote, 'was united within her with such a truly-womanly modesty (*istinno-zhenskoi skromnost'*), that a person not interested in scientific subjects could be acquainted with her for a year, every day enjoying the warmth of her conversation, and never suspect her knowledge.' He tried to explain this characteristic; whether he was describing his wife or constructing her can never be known, but he did portray the formidable armature of intellect, memory, and . . . story-telling, even masking, which Elena Pavlovna possessed and used to great advantage during an adult life preoccupied with boundaries:

> A broad set of acquaintances from the first half of her life, bonds of friendship with many remarkable people, whom her personality attracted to her, left in her memory a complete chronicle of events and personae, which made conversation with her an unusual pleasure. Of special import is to note that

E. P. Fadeeva, when she was engaged in conversations with individuals who stood far below her in education, knew how not to give them to understand this difference, and conversation with her always held interests for individuals of all ages, all characters, and almost all specializations . . . Elena Pavlovna raised her own children with that same loving concern, in the main replacing the teachers. All her children, and subsequently her grandsons, sitting at her knees, learned to read Russian and French and much more.

Hence, Andrei concluded, was supplied 'the foundation' from which had come the likes of his own children, the still mourned, 'talented *belletristka* Elena Andreevna Gan' or 'our well-known' R. A. Fadeev.[87]

Witte, of course, was one of the grandsons. None will dispute how significantly his adult life was influenced by the male-oriented considerations of power, career, and politics that his contemporaries, and thus historians, traditionally have brought to bear in their attempts to understand him. Perhaps for that reason it is of special import to note that E. P. Fadeeva taught him to read, and talked to him about much more, for the first years of his formal upbringing. Here, for a final time, the reader is asked to leap beyond the historian, and weigh what little remaining historical evidence the record contains. Among the few stories remaining, told not by, but about, Elena Pavlovna, is the one written by Andrei. His memoir, as it came toward its own ending, became as much a testimonial to her, to their long life together, their genuine love, and the personality he would no longer know. Her world did flicker, however, in the memoirs of her husband, who shared with his grandson a passion for detail and personality. Fadeev's memoirs tell of the imperial Russia he and Elena Pavlovna inhabited during the post revolutionary decades of the early nineteenth century. Both born in 1789, the last for absolutist and the first for democratic France, Andrei and Elena lived in an era when the Russian Empire was at the apex of its power and influence.[88] Andrei's tale of his life with Elena excavates the cultural environment in which a young boy was raised and acculturated. Fadeev's memoir can be read as a grandmother's tale.

Andrei and Elena first met in 1812, when they were 23, and the Russian Empire was enmeshed in world war with France. An apprenticed clerk in his father's provincial canal division of the Department of Communications, Andrei had been evacuated into Ukraine, from Minsk, with his parents and large family, as Napoleon's Grand Army made for Moscow. Living in Rzhishche, a small village south of Kiev, with her widowed and impoverished grandmother, Elena must have seemed an exotic figure to the well-read, curious, but utterly bored clerk. 'We became close to one another through a shared inclination to reading, to literary work (*literaturnye zaniatiia*),' Fadeev recalled. '(W)e read together, translated, and finally fell truly in love with each other (sic).' European and imperial pulses coursed through her family background. Elena's grandfather, Lieutenant-General Adolf Frantsovich de Bandre du Plessy, was descended from sixteenth-century French Huguenot nobles who had emigrated to Saxony, joined the Russian service in the 1760s, and followed military honor in Crimea with diplomatic status as a protégé of the statesman Nikita Panin. A not unfamiliar male pathology of this elite, du Plessy's career collapsed with his health around 1790. He retired to his estate, settled land in Belorussia distributed as an imperial bequest to a worthy servitor, confiscated shamelessly from Polish owners. After his death, the expropriated Poles launched legal proceedings against his widow, who, all the while blaming local graft and corrupt courts, eventually lost the property and was forced to move with her now impoverished family to Ukraine. Elena's largely absent mother Henrietta, was a woman who, 'remarked for her beauty and somewhat frivolous and idiosyncratic character, loved society and its pleasures'. Her marriage in 1787 to Elena's father, a 'serious man', doomed her to a lifetime of 'enmity' with her husband, but provided the tie that would make Elena Pavlovna the last of the senior Dolgorukiis.[89]

We have seen how service and its twisting currents figured centrally in the sculpting of Witte's masculinity. Andrei, who provided the foundation for Witte's own career, described the minuets he danced to obtain an appointment as a low-ranking assessor in the provincial capital administration of Nizhnii Novgorod, at the confluence of the Oka, which flowed from the Muscovite heartland, and the Volga, along whose waters had flowed the history of imperial Russia from the time of Ivan the Terrible. Testimony to daily life in an imperial town, Fadeev bemoaned the appointment, but knew it to be one that located Elena closer to her father and other Dolgorukii relatives living deeper in south-central Russia, in Penza province. Describing their travel, via 'Belorussian Mogiliev', Moscow, and Vladimir, into the Russian interior toward Nizhnii, Andrei remembered that 'Elena Pavlovna up until that time had never yet spent time within Russia, and therefore all the places, through which we traveled, interested her enormously.'[90] No evidence exists to show what sparked her imagination, but certainly smoldering here as she journeyed eastwards from her native Ukraine was her impulse to explore boundaries, which she would have ample opportunity to encourage as service drew her family southward, toward the frontier of the Caucasus, in the following thirty years.

Settling in Nizhnii, the story continued, the couple soon traveled overland to their 'blood relatives (*rodnye*)', who 'lived on the remains (*otstatki*) of their formerly great lands in Znamenskii', a rural village close to the provincial capital city. The members of the household were, in a fashion, also remnants, survivors, first, of the royal wrath visited on their clan in the 1730s, and, second, of the eighteenth century as a cultural experience. They bore what Sergei Witte had labeled 'boyar pretension', a Muscovite coloration to their Petrine imperial standards. Andrei and Elena stayed four months on an estate where early modern Muscovite and eighteenth-century imperial rhythms intermingled. 'In everything there was as if a confusion of clannish pride (*rodovaia gordost'*) and innocence,' Fadeev wrote of the family, 'the remnants of past glory and wealth with the absence of the most elementary comforts of life.' He recalled the eighteenth-century Russian manor house, 'the most enormous wooden home of forty rooms', with its baroque, heavily framed family portraits, faded tapestries, and gilded, ornate, yet worn furniture all silently acknowledging how the family had navigated the temporal boundary that had come to separate the Tsardom of Russe and the Russian Empire during the reign of the first emperor, Peter the Great. Andrei's attention was drawn as well to another boundary, this at the base of imperial society. He touched on serfdom only briefly and fleetingly, however, as always seemed true in the sources relating to the earliest years of Witte's life. Fadeev commented on 'the numberless house servants, who made up almost a quarter of all the souls (serfs) on the estate, and among these were more than one joker, fool, and ass'. He feigned distaste for the 'quite unenviable orchestra of musicians from amongst the people of the household (*dvorovye liudi*), and a choir of singers, still more not to be envied', even though it was just as likely that he was entertained by what was probably lively, if not locally renowned, popular talent. The peasant village—native, uneducated, and uncivilized—marked out another frontier that imperial Russia barely had colonized. Readers of Sergei Aksakov's *A Family Chronicle* would find familiar a noble family nest in which 'each of the members of the family had their own habits, idiosyncrasies, superstitions and fancies, although they were all intelligent, educated, and entirely enlightened people'. Elena and he 'were very much taken up with relatives' tales (*razskazy*) of the good that had been, the old time, about personages of historical significance whom they had known'.[91]

Andrei struck a very different, more rational and enlightened tone when he wrote separately about his father-in-law. P. V. Dolgorukii lived, an officer, as had his father before him, on a neighboring 'small estate', ownership of 100 serfs a mark of how far the family's wealth had declined in two generations. Yet, economic decline could not undermine the intellectual achievement that had made the Dolgorukiis cultural standard bearers for the state and empire their ancestors had helped to create in the eighteenth century. 'He was,' his son-in-law wrote of this Franklinesque bibliophile whose library enlightened his family and its service to the empire:

> a fellow far from ordinary, distinguished by his highly enlightened (*prosvesh-chennyi*) intellect and his detailed technical knowledge, enjoying great respect among people who knew him. All his free time went to serious study in his enormous library, which primarily had been assembled from books of foreign contents, in all branches of knowledge and all languages. . . . Life in the village (*derevenskaia zhizn'*) did not hinder his relations with high society: the ties of confidant, relative, and friend were sustained by constant intercourse and correspondence with the greatest houses of both capitals.

'We learned much that was new and interesting, and the time spent was pleasant and entertaining,' Andrei Mikhailovich concluded as he ended this rumination on his wife's family, his attention turning, as had the text of his story, away from these memories and instead southwards, down the Volga, toward New Russia and the Caucasus.[92]

Appended in a footnote, however, most likely by the ubiquitous editor Nadezhda Fadeeva, remained one last voice. It is of greatest interest to this discussion, because it was Elena Pavlovna's, the one that had been audible to Sergei Witte when he was a boy. Elena 'speaks' in a fragment of a no-longer extant text, called 'the written tales (*zapisannye razskasy*) of Elena Pavlovna Dolgorukova'. Why they survive is impossible to say, although most likely they were included because they revolved about the most prestigious personage that the Fadeev family could claim, Elena's godmother, the Countess Anna Rodionovna Chernyshova, also godmother to the Emperor Alexander I. She and Andrei, as well as her 6-month-old daughter Elena, and her own grandmother, while they had been in Penza in 1816, paid a formal visit to Chernyshova at her ancestral estate, Chechersk. The visit yielded three tales about a salon world that was closed to adult men, and that, through the lifetimes of the women and children who flitted through it, dated to the 1740s. Whether these might also have been tales told by a grandmother to a grandson about this imperial universe is a question again left to the reader to answer.[93]

Of the three, the first entailed 'a strange episode' in 1805, of which she had heard first as a 16-year-old girl visiting Chernyshova. An adolescent torn between enchantment and faith, on the one hand, and adult skepticism, on the other, Elena Pavlovna accompanied her grandmother to visit the estate of their great relative. At an evening gathering of women in Chernyshova's chambers, the 16-year-old, singled out as the youngest woman in the company that night, was told to read aloud from 'an old letter, yellowing with age', which helped 'Anna Rodionovna' tell of the 'apparition of the Virgin Mother'. A performance undoubtedly demanded from more than one young girl, the reading of the letter detailed what to the rational mind was improbable. Rendered at length, the tale spoke of Chernyshova's already ailing mother, on a pilgrimage to the Akhtyrsk Mother of God icon in Khar'kov province, and how she experienced a vision of the Virgin, who prophesied her death, but promised her soon-to-be orphaned daughters divine protection should their mother contribute her wealth to the poor—'I will make the strong of this world care for them,' Elena read. The money distributed, the mother died. Thanks to yet another Marian apparition, their father, for good measure, himself converted to Orthodoxy from Lutheranism. Shortly before he died, Chernyshova and her sister were presented at the court of Elizabeth I, made wards of the empress who lived at her court, and eventually married into powerful aristocratic families. 'See what fate sent us as part of our inheritance! (*Vot kakaia sud'ba vyshla nam v udel!*),' Elena Pavlovna remembered, a fatalistic colloquialism that still echoed with Muscovite tones, as she concluded a story rife with faith, belief, imagination, and fantasy.[94]

The second tale, this perhaps Elena Pavlovna's most cherished memory, portrayed her own mother, when still a young girl of 12. Sometime in the 1780s, appearing in high society for the first time on Chernyshova's estate, the young woman performed an illuminated dramatic portrayal, where by the light of flares and fireworks she appeared as 'an enchantress' (*vol'shebnitsa)*', who with a wave of her wand made the seasons change. Her 'great success' occurred before the heir to the throne, Paul Petrovich, and his wife, Marie Fedorovna. The girl 'was very stunning and everyone liked her extremely well,' Elena recorded, proceeding to tell that within five years her mother would already be married and, as a Dolgorukii bride, again presented at the court of Marie Fedorovna, which, judging from its architectural monuments in Pavlovsk outside St Petersburg, was itself a classical environment of enlightenment enchantment.[95]

The last of these grandmother's tales detailed the evening that sparked these reminiscences, which Elena Pavlovna and Andrei spent on Chernyshova's ancestral estate in 1816. By this time, a widowed Chernyshova had withdrawn from court society to live, as Russians of all classes could, in religious isolation, traveling as a pilgrim from church to church. She lived alone on her rural estate, which she had organized according to 'her own order', even maintaining a hired constable to enforce its rules. Chief among these that night was that 'entry was denied my husband, as a man'. She, her grandmother, and child daughter traversed three courtyards, the outer patrolled by men, but the inner two places 'where men would not dare to show themselves'. Elena Pavlovna entered, through the trappings of the Muscovite boyar *terem*, what, in effect, was a women's salon, its activities probably much like those over which she herself would preside in the 1840s and 1850s. Her young child was formally presented to the aged countess, allowing her to display ritual affection toward the young. 'We dined promptly at midnight, and our conversation and banter continued almost until dawn,' she wrote. 'We barely were able to convince her', Elena Pavlovna finished, 'that we needed to go.'[96]

A final story about Elena Pavlovna, and the imperial boundaries that she touched, belonged to Helen Blavatsky, as her namesake came to be known in the West. It was told of Elena Blavatskaia that once, as a young girl, she slapped her peasant nurse in the face. From any perspective, this was an act that violated human propriety; serfdom, commentators have rightfully interjected, made it all too brutally typical in Russian society. 'When the grandmother heard of this, the child was summoned, they questioned her, and she acknowledged her guilt. Then the grandmother commanded that the bell be rung to summon all the servants, and she told her granddaughter that she had struck one who was helpless, a person standing beneath her who would not dare to defend herself, that she had comported herself unworthily and that she was obligated to ask forgiveness of her nurse and to kiss her hand.' Blavatsky—no mention appeared in this source of the glittering eyes Witte had remembered so vividly—began to object, but was cut short, her grandmother insisting on an immediate choice between obedience or public shaming. She added the moral: 'the noble person does not hesitate to correct a mistake against servants, especially those who by their loyal service deserve the confidence of their lords (*svoi gospoda*).'[97]

Let us, especially those uncomfortable with an introspection born of cultural criticism, pause for a moment and take stock. What really can be said about Witte's boyhood and family life on the borders of the empire? That he ultimately knew little of 'the people' in whose name he would act at the end of the century was less surprising, given the imperial assumptions about them that he had inherited in his youth. That he was raised in a Russian family of civil servants and officers on the empire's periphery, where male talent and persistence yielded career success more rapidly than in the center, perhaps influenced later adult behavior that relied on precisely this combination of traits. That his boyhood was spent in close proximity to war and warriors, heroism and death might have shaped an adult understanding of masculinity as it did for imperial Russian writers from Lermontov and Pushkin to Tolstoy. Or, finally, that he was raised by women who, finding at the edge of imperial civilization opportunity and space to fashion identities blending arch-domesticity with unusual intellect and autonomy, must have shaped his own penchant to dream, imagine, and project as his own life's path made its way in the structured worlds of tsarist society and polity. In this sense, the imperial borderland became a place where the identity of Sergei Witte was rooted, shaped, and legitimated.

2

Imperial Identity: Coming of Age in New Russia, 1865-1881

...my brother and I were utter ignoramuses (*polnye nevezhdy*), knew absolutely nothing, because we had never studied anything seriously, and only knew how to banter (*boltat'*) well in French.

Memoirs /Tales in stenographic record/ of Count Sergei Iul'evich Witte[1]

When I matriculated to the juridical faculty (of New Russia University), Sergei Iul'evich already had moved from the second to the third year of the mathematics faculty. Back then there were few of us students, in all some 400, so we all knew each other, more or less. But Witte, you couldn't but know him, because he stood out with his tall frame and riotous life (*razgul'naia zhizn'*) in a company of well-off students, where he presided.

V. V. Kirkhner, *Volny*, April 1915[2]

I have heard that the capable Witte finished first at University and consider it my obligation to his family to turn your attention toward this young man and ask You to advance him in the service (*dat' emu khod po sluzhbe*), if he proves worthy, as one would hope.

Letter of Prince A. I. Bariatinskii to N. M. Chikhachev. Director. Russian Steamship, Commerce, and Odessa Railroad Company, 28 January 1871[3]

... the fortress that is our state allows us a period of transition, during the course of which we can grow into a society; yet, this period, certainly not unending, will see resolved the future that awaits us. Will we be a vital people (*zhivoi narod*), or a political aggregation (*politicheskii sbor*) of disconnected entities? On the order of the day, when it is framed in this way, lies the key to our future.

Rostislav Fadeev, chapter I, 'Our Contemporary Society', in *Russian Society in the Present and the Future (What Will We Be?) (Chem nam byt ')?* (1874)[4]

Witte, with his older brother Boris, arrived in Odessa, in New Russia, in 1865. Isaac Babel had not yet written the tales that revealed this city to the world, but Russian Odessa was the quintessential imperial city. An anchorage sheltered by the delta of the Dnieper River to its east, the site had served Greeks, Romans, Italians, Mongols and Tatars, Ottomans, Poles, and Lithuanians, and, from the late eighteenth century, latecomer imperial Russians. The Russian military destruction of the Ottoman fortress Khadz-hibei in 1791, a key moment in the two empires' conflict to control the Black Sea, led two years later to the founding of Odessa. An imperial rescript of Catherine the Great ordered a military harbor, 'equipped with merchantry (*kupno s kupecheskoiu*)', to be built on the site. Within a half-century, a city of some 116,000 had blossomed, chiefly because the trade and commerce that moved through the tariff-free port declared there in 1817 grew significantly. Located not far from the waterfront, the university was one of the accoutrements of imperial rule sported in a city with its European architecture, harbor, churches, synagogues, mosques, its opera house and broad boulevards framing a classically geometrical city center. Already served by steamship companies that radiated outwards from its port into the Black and Mediterranean Seas, the city was a natural railroad terminus for overland domestic and foreign commerce. A crown railroad line, financed by the treasury and constructed by army penal companies, was being built toward Kishinev and the Danube River valley. A group of private concessionaires was constructing a railroad between Kiev and Odessa. Aiming toward Ottoman and Austrian imperial frontiers, and seeking direct rail links with a system that linked Moscow, St Petersburg, and Warsaw, these projects, and others like them, would intensify further than ever before imagined the possibilities for commerce, strategic confron-tation, and human intercourse in the great upland expanse that reached, across the Black Sea, from the Danube toward the Caucasus and the Caspian Sea.[5]

In contrast, Boris and Sergei, escorted by both their mother and father, had been journeying by land and sea for days when they arrived in Odessa. As Witte remembered his first trip into Russia, the family had left Tiflis and the Caucasus bound for Kiev and its prestigious St Vladimir University.[6] The journey brought them across the Black Sea to Crimea, where they learned that the Education Ministry had transferred their father's brother from Kiev to Warsaw, and thereby eliminated any possibility that family connections might influence admissions decisions for his nephews. The uncle urged them instead to go to Odessa, where the New Russia University (*Novorossiiskii universitet*) was opening for its first year. Soon discovering that his sons' gymnaziium preparation was so poor neither of them could gain admission, Iulii Witte boarded them in the city, and arranged for them to retake the entrance examinations that year. His business finished, 'he traveled again back to the place of his service in the Caucasus'.

'My brother and I the two of us remained, utterly alone,' Witte wrote. His gymnaziium education was poor, in part because a privileged son in colonial Georgia had neglected study, in part because the only passions in Tiflis that stirred him, by his own admission, were the flute and opera.[7] Although there is no record of the quality of the staff or its school, other contemporary portrayals of the later nineteenth-century gymnaziium could be dark, filled with ridicule by the students who survived it. One remarked the typical class to begin with the teacher writing in chalk what needed to be prepared for the next lesson, and then examining the students on the results of their previous day's study, a task that at times necessitated 'dragging nearly every word out of them'. Pushkin's 'renowned' aphorism, this source continued, more often than not applied: 'We all studied somewhat, something and somehow.'[8] Whatever its cause, the obstacle of his academic background nevertheless blocked any chance Witte could pass the state examinations required to gain a place in the university. Deciding to overcome it, Witte remembered, he experienced what amounted to a conversion, the moment of his intellectual epiphany:

> When we were left alone, it occurred to us, in essence to me, that I never had studied anything, and only had indulged myself, and that, therefore, my brother and I were going to perish. For the first time intellectual consciousness dawned on me (*soznanie poiavilos'*) and together with it emerged my character (*sobstvennyi kharakter*), which has guided me my entire life, so that even up until today I never follow another's advice or direction, and always rely on my own judgment, and especially, on my own character.[9]

In what is an otherwise uncorroborated story, and thus possibly a Horatio Alger tale that Victorians indulged as intellectual fashion, Witte portrayed the two brothers deciding, without parental advice, to move to Kishinev. '(B)y railroad to Razdel'nyi station, and then by conveyance' to the town, he remembered, there to hire rooms from a tutor in mathematics and study for six months, 'day and night', funding eventually arranged through faraway Tiflis. Despite what proved the circumstances that eventually led to a university specialization in mathematics, these months left Witte still unable to qualify for admission without several sympathetic school officials, who both encouraged his evident talent in their field and assisted him through the entrance examinations. That year he returned home, for holiday, the same summer that his grandfather died, he recalled with grief, remembering as well how several years 'before this my grandmother Fadeeva died before my very eyes'.[10] One wonders what these two elders, whose lives had been rooted in the Russia of the eighteennth century, would have made of their grandson as he matriculated at New Russia University in 1866.

Certainly Elena Pavlovna would have understood his autonomous personality. His emergent sensibilities for the hierarchical order of a world shaped by service and patronage would have pleased both grandparents, but much else in their grandson they would have found inchoate, even incomprehensible, as, in their turn, had they their Muscovite forbears. This for good reason. Regardless of how differently scholars explain the fact, the middle decades of the European nineteenth century were years of tectonic shifts in imperial Russia. Chief among these was the abolition of serfdom, a legislative act and cultural turn whose impact and scale rivaled that of the civil war required to abolish American slavery. A host of structural changes occurred: new forms of election, courts, business investment, censorship laws, forms of public language. Here, rather than in the last decades of Soviet communism, was the origin of the word *perestroika*. What Witte experienced was a new Russia emerging from the old world of serfdom, and the broadening, popularizing, and deepening of this culture that was a hallmark of the period. A penny-press emerged, stereotypes of ethnics filled popular literature, which itself became more available, and for the very first time, mainstream. Music, dance, and song expanded their reach in social realms both high-brow and low. The novel was increasingly popularized: Russians read, for example, Dostoevsky or Tolstoy in serialized installments. The growth of readership generally meant the availability, and the capacity of individuals to imagine as they read, alternative images, themes, and realities.[11]

Witte's story of becoming an adult man was also a tale of that momentous era. This son of the Russian service nobility, sent to Russia from an avowedly monarchist household in colonial Tiflis, experimented with university mathematics, student radicalism, and male camaraderie. While still in university, he used family connections to obtain a low-ranking appointment to the civil service, the critical first rung on the service ladder his father and grandfather before him had climbed. Yet, graduated from university in 1870 and briefly oriented to a university career as a professor, the young clerk really preferred the position arranged by his uncle Fadeev on the crown-operated Odessa Railroad. Similarly, he would come to prefer the

commercial power and speed of the new railroad technology to the traditional influence of government office. Witte's tale in these years also reflected
the life of the proper, and decidedly modern, Victorian man, enticed by the
clarion of imperialist rhetoric and the fantasies glimpsed through the company of men, opera house divas, and divorcees. Like any proper Victorian
gentleman in an age of empire, Witte would regard both himself and his *Prove ?*
world with an air of confidence, optimism, and unprecedented possibility.

The University and 'Studenthood'

In autumn 1899, following student disorders that had wracked St Petersburg
University at the beginning of that semester, Witte, by this time a powerful
minister, joined a small group of officials to investigate events that had
scandalized and riveted the attention of the imperial capital. Witte was the
author of the recommendations produced for the tsar, Nicholas II. 'One
cannot but remark', the report stated in the delicate but awkward phraseol-
ogy required of those who addressed the Russian emperor, 'that the majority
of students in schools of higher education are at that transitional, youthful
age when they are easily carried away (*tak svoistvenno uvlechenie*), easily
susceptible to outside impressions, when a (young) person still fears ruining
a not yet fully articulated sense of self-worth (*dostoinstvo*) and worries to
death over his own honor (*chest'*) and that of his comrades'. He urged
leniency in dealing with disorders rooted in youthful excess, and warned
that patronizing behavior by university officials, police violence on the
streets, and uncompromising legal prosecution of those arrested was causing
public, if not political discontent. Offering against this all too familiar
bureaucratic behavior a competing view, Witte girded his arguments with
his knowledge of university student life and the power of the scientific
viewpoint a university diploma affirmed. 'The interests of our student youth
should be close to the heart of every Russian,' Witte explained, but were
especially 'dear to me because I myself am a graduate of the University
(*vospitannik Universiteta*) . . . (and) because both New Russia University and
the six other (imperial universities) consider me among their compatriots'.[12]
Some three decades removed from his years at university, the bond which
tied him to its intellectual culture and modern sensibilities remained as
strong as an entire literature, long preoccupied by Russian 'studenthood'
(*studenchestvo*), always has suggested it to have been.[13]

When Witte began his studies in 1866, New Russia University had been operating for only a year. It had been established from the existing Richelieu Lyceum, since 1822 the only institution of Russian higher education in the region. The most recently established of the empire's six universities, its founding was credited, in part, to the Crimean War surgeon and research physician N. I. Pirogov, as well as local imperialist opinion in Odessa that viewed a university there to be a portal through which Russian education, culture, and Orthodox Christianity could challenge Ottoman sway in the region. A university annual report for 1871, the year following Witte's graduation, reported a student body of more than 400 students, two of every three on the juridical faculty. Less than half received full stipends. A faculty of some forty men, half of them full professors, awaited authorization to fund existing or new positions in general literature, physical geography, technical chemistry, and three different juridical faculty posts. The university faculty council that year had approved strengthening the academic performance of its students by instituting tutorials, whose proposed topics gave some sense of the university's intellectual atmosphere. Courses on the history of philology and Slavic dialect reflected the imperial and nationalist present; studies of Machiavelli and Plato, perhaps a mirror of a more ideological future; and translations from classical Latin, a pillar of an increasingly treasured but challenged past. The faculty also had rejected a motion requiring that students, as a mark of their honor, attend all lectures. Professors were convinced that a student's 'internal conviction' rather than external compulsion should oblige his attendance. Encouraging that conviction was a responsibility of the faculty. Themselves all university graduates, they believed that their own scientific credentials validated 'the moral influence of the entire professoriate (*professorskaia korporatsiia*), which through its pedagogical experience and honor, its conscientious regard for its work, will attract students to lecture.'[14]

That thoroughly modern sentiment—an autonomous individual was one who internalized codes of behavior that rational science, rather than the absolutism of state law, rendered legitimate—was one note in the cacophony Witte encountered when he first entered the university in 1866.[15] These years, the sentimentality that surrounded them and the intellectual modernity they produced, were themselves also something of a text, judging how frequently the process was described and honored among those, mainly men, who experienced it in the later nineteenth century. The university was written about as a place that was both private and civic space, a place for the development of both the private and public person.[16] It certainly should be understood as a ground on which power and science, two influential forces in imperial public life, came together and created a range of possibilities for individual action that would have been unthinkable a century before.[17] Witte, dictating in 1911, remembered it that way. He described 'a university (that) lives through free science (*svobodnaia nauka*)', musing that 'without free science there can be created neither significant scientific works, nor scientific discoveries, nor celebrity (*znamenitost'*)'. 'Moreover,' he continued, thinking about the culture of his own student days, 'the University creates from within itself a milieu (*sreda*) for the scholarly development of young people', one where students could encounter 'all scientific categories of knowledge, which at a given moment constitute the achievement of humanity (*dostoianie chelovechestva*).' The years could not dull the excitement of intellectual empowerment he had discovered there. 'Students', he recalled, 'from morning to night find themselves in a student body; they constantly collide with different thoughts and ideas that students from other faculties have assimilated.'[18]

Rather than the choice of law and juridical theory, which provided expertise and access to the tsarist bureaucracy, Witte entered the physics–mathematics faculty, where the study of all natural sciences was concentrated. The choice itself was distinctive. Although Witte was no Bazarov, the nihilist everyman Turgenev sketched in 1862 in his novel *Fathers and Children*, his turn to the natural sciences was typical of university students in the 1860s and 1870s, when scientific materialism, utilitarianism, and the intellectual empowerment they created were very much centerpieces of Russian public discourse.[19] Found in his reminiscences of these four years were memories of not only subjects studied, but the professors who taught them: theoretical mechanics, calculus, integral functions, zoology, physiology, chemistry, botany, and physics. Courses in other faculties were audited and not subject to examination, but he chose to attend lectures in both Slavic languages and Russian law—the combination itself a pillar of imperial consciousness.[20] Looming over these, however, was what he called his 'mathematical gift, which is a gift of a very special sort', and it apparently led him to an engagement with this area of study above all others. He remembered an undistinguished—or unremarkable—mathematics faculty, excepting one 'utterly young professor of theoretical (*chistaia*) mathematics, Andreevskii, who ... for a professor was strikingly young; he was 22.'[21] That Witte genuinely assimilated this particular scientific outlook, and made it a part of his intellectual armature, is beyond question. Looking back, the aged memoirist firmly fixed himself among 'mathematician-philosophers, that is mathematicians of a higher mathematical idea, for whom figures and calculations are a craftsman's trade'. What he acquired intellectually could also be judged from a late nineteenth-century Russian encyclopedia, which explained mathematics to be a science that 'objectifies the qualitative aspects of all subjects in our consciousness (*kachestvennye svoistva vsekh predmetov nashego soznaniia*)' and studies 'quantity, magnitude, and value, as well as their measurement'. Theoretical mathematics, that same source noted, 'has no regard for the contents of phenomena.' For example, the introductory stages of the discipline classified as the study of complex arithmetic or geometry became for the theoretical mathematician the 'science of numbers' or the 'science of extended space (*protiazhenie*)'.[22] That Witte studied objective systems in space is an intriguing proposition to hold in reserve, given the role that railroads and imperial expanse would play in his career.

There is no reason to dispute his own ritualized account of academic excellence, although the seemingly stammering way in which he dictated lines of self-praise was curious. '(E)ntering the university, I studied day and night,' he declaimed, 'and thus, for all the entire time of my stay at university, I, really, was, in the sense of knowledge, the best student.' Certainly in these years he began to develop the intellectual acuity and ability to organize knowledge that later would make him such a formidable presence in business and government. Students themselves, if Witte is to be believed, recognized this talent. 'I studied so much and so knew the material', he continued, 'that I never prepared for (annual) examinations . . . but in the main read or explained to my comrades all the lectures relating to the end-of-year examination questions (*vse lektsii po biletam*).' His four years at university, which included a candidate's (undergraduate) thesis, 'On Infinitely Small Integers', won him high marks, and at their conclusion, candidacy for the gold medal awarded a class's valedictorian. That status, however, required a second dissertation, a topic in astronomy that he abandoned when he became entangled in a love affair with 'the actress Sokolova, and thus no longer had any desire to write a dissertation'. This was not the last erotic reference to be found in the recollections of these years.[23]

Witte explored his 'university life' at some length, and revealed much about the culture of the university, as well as the male students who both imbibed and created it.[24] Historians of Russia have studied copiously the distinctive university student radicalism of the 1860s.[25] Nobleman and avowed monarchist, Witte's experience of the student movement revealed how much more than political ideology was to be found in student life. He recalled university years 'dominated (by) a trend toward atheism' and by 'the idols of the young—(the publicists) Pisarev, Dobroliubov, and Cherny-shevskii', the poet, essayist, and critic respectively who together set this public tone during the heady and often discordant years of the later 1850s and 1860s. At the end of his life as untrusting of unbelief as he apparently had been as a student, Witte nevertheless was affected deeply by the underlying civic activism that swept and transformed urban public life in these years.[26] 'Being a student,' he recalled, 'I was little involved in politics (politika), because I was constantly occupied with my studies, but to the extent that I engaged in them, I was always against these tendencies, because by my upbringing I was an extreme (krainyi) monarchist...and also a religious man.' Yet, during his first year at university, Witte's intellectual 'seriousness (sereznost') and knowledge' had won him sufficient enough 'respect within the student body' to be elected to the governing board of a student-run loan fund. Levying an obligatory four-kopeck tax on students, the fund made loans to poorer classmates in need, who were then responsible for their repayment.[27]

The fund's treasurer, G. E. Afanasiev, a roommate who subsequently became a professor of general history and even later a State Bank branch director in Witte's Ministry of Finances, wrote in a 1915 obituary how assiduously 'Witte—the student' shouldered these responsibilities. Display-ing his lifelong character traits, 'a great capacity to work and integrity in performing obligations once assumed', Witte as a student, Afanasiev re-called, also acted with clerk-like punctuality at meetings, and showed diligence in collecting student taxes and debts—and always with proper loyalty to the Crown.[28] From Witte's own recollections came the ready admission that this undertaking had raised the ire of local provincial officials. Why this happened, he did not say—although the exercise of student public initiative, without administrative oversight or sanction, most likely led local authorities to close the loan fund and prepare criminal indictments against its officers. A classic confrontation between officialdom and radicalized students—such often is the framing historians give to the proliferation of these forms of conflict in the 1860s—ended when, Witte exclaimed, 'The English Club saved us from all of this!' A club for aristocratic men exercised its informal influence by deliberately denying a membership to the city prosecutor, and thus bringing both the intended insult and the matter of loyal young men wrongfully accused to the attention of the proper minister in St Petersburg. Within the year, the case had been transferred to civil court, and the students, given a much lighter monetary punishment, allowed to retain their standing.[29]

Although they went otherwise unexplained, this display of influence, the prominent individuals involved, and the ties that bound students to them all suggest how Witte's memories of university also ranged, beyond academics and civic activism, to the private life of a young man as well. V. V. Kirkhner, a younger classmate who entered the university when Witte was in his third year, detailed a side of him present, but, as here, always understated in the great statesman's reminiscences: 'It was impossible not to know Witte, because he stood out with his tall stature and rakish style of life (*razgul'naia zhizn'*) in the company of well-off students, where he presided (*v kotoroi on glavenstvoval*).'[30] It is impossible to reconstruct this life in any great detail. Odessa, like Tiflis and later both Kiev and St Petersburg, had its opera house and theaters, where he indulged what were two lifelong cultural passions. About his appetites even less can be said. Only once in reminiscences of these years did he mention a drinking bout, although it lasted a day and a night.[31] His adopted daughter, Vera Naryshkina-Witte, during a visit to Odessa with her father, met the owner of the restaurant where he had regularly dined as a student, 'on broiled beefsteak with potatoes . . . and what an appetite you had then,' she recalled the *maitre d'hotel* bluster.[32] His love affair with the 'actress Sokolova', or his claim to be acquainted, 'because I then was young and not married, of all the more or less prominent actresses . . . in Odessa,' suggested some combination of sexual love and fantasy as well.[33]

Whether Witte caroused, as Kirkhner claimed, or managed somehow to attach himself to aristocratic clubs, as he himself had hinted, much more of his private life revolved around male companionship. Afanasiev told of Witte, in the 1890s when he already was a minister in St Petersburg, traveling on Nevskii Prospect, leaping from his carriage upon spying their fellow classmate, the publicist S. N. Iuzhakov, and with loud shouts greeting an old acquaintance whom he had not seen in years.[34] Vera Naryshkina-Witte described her father in the same period, burdened with the obligations of his office, as being 'so content and joyful when his old university comrades . . . came to St Petersburg. Papa recalled with them the old days (*starina*); the stern expression on his face would soften, his smile became almost child-like.' In his own private archive, Witte saved a letter from the leftist publicist P. P. Semeniut, who had written in 1909 to mark his old friend's fiftieth birthday. Semeniut hoped that Witte too would recall 'the best of what is dear to a man—memories of youth', and reminded him of the years 1869–79, when the two 'belonged to that circle headed by our mutual friend Baron "X"', S. T. Gertso-Vinogradskii, who had attended the university, wrote in Odessa dailies under this pseudonym in the 1870s, and was employed by Witte as a secretary in the offices of the Odessa Railroad. Both Vinogradskii and Semeniut, the historian can note, suffered political exile in the early 1880s.[35]

Finally, replete with the rhetorical flourishes necessary to describe without naming, these recollections intermingled Victorian male friendship and homoeroticism. The boundaries separating male companionship and physical love, or admiration for the male physique and arousal by it were less definitively constructed by nineteenth-century society than would be the case in the twenty-first century. Nothing was more understated, both in Witte's memoirs and the late imperial memoir genre generally—and nothing until recently has been more ignored by scholars.[36] Yet, this boundary repeatedly surfaced in his recollections. He admired the male physique—the shape of a man's hips, the curve of his face. 'He was a man of enormous size, with shoulders almost a sazhen (2 meters) wide and he had a waist that any young woman would envy,' he wrote of one officer. 'I well remember his face because its extreme paleness stunned me,' Witte recalled about another man who figured into his recollections of these years; 'his face was like a statue's, absolutely correct, as if exactly sculpted from marble.'[37] Most notable were Witte's well-established ties to Prince V. P. Meshchersky, an influential conservative publisher, who was a confidant of both tsars Alexander III and Nicholas II, and a man who shepherded Witte's career when he first came to St Petersburg. Witte then spurned him during the very first years of his ministerial career.[38] Meshchersky was also one of the most prominent homosexual men in imperial high society. Judging from correspondence they conducted in the early 1890s that Witte preserved in his private papers, their relationship involved love—at least in Meshchersky's eyes. 'The dacha where I am now living and writing to you is very dear to me, for here between us was established our friendship (*nasha druzhba*),' Meshchersky wrote. 'Here with all my soul I loved you for a bit (*poliubit'*), and learned to understand you and value you, and here too I realized that you taught me not just to esteem you, but (to be) as your friend!'[39]

No evidence suggests Witte's own homosexuality. A man twice married, Witte left in his private notebooks a long soliloquy about 'Prince Mesh-cherskii', which reiterated the sobriquets the era leveled at homosexuals. Meshcherskii was 'immoral and, in addition, unnaturally immoral' and a 'dirty (*griaznyi*) man', Witte averred, but commented as well how Mesh-cherskii always surrounded himself with 'several young people', who ma-nipulated the older man in order to advance their own careers. It was, he added, a pattern to which Meshchersky eagerly contributed.[40] Witte's attention to this aspect of masculinity appeared for the first time in his reminiscences of university years. Here, the spoken character of *Memoirs* is very much in evidence. Witte, amidst retelling the tale of the student loan fund, found himself musing first about his friend Afanasiev, and then a certain Iuzefovich, a largely anonymous figure who, in one of Witte's favored sobriquets, was a police informant: first smearing Afanasiev's repu-tation in the 1880s, later appearing in similar capacities in Kiev, and finally in Paris discredited by some scandalous but unspecified behavior. He was 'a man of the lowest morality . . . (b)y the way I myself know Iuzefovich in this way,' he muttered, leaving entirely unexplained when he knew him and how. Characteristically in such moments, Witte followed a line of thought to its end, especially when it touched a personage of importance. Iuzefovich had been a boyhood friend and eventually a private secretary to P. P. Gesse, the Military Commandant of the Imperial Palace under Nicholas II. Here was a memory of asking Gesse how, given his 'extremely despicable (*dur-naia*) reputation', he could 'allow Mr. Iuzefovich close to him (*puskat' k sebe*)'. Witte let Gesse speak about gay men, in an utterly off-handed remark that itself hinted at male sexuality: 'I know him from childhood, he has an excellent ability to speak and writes splendidly. . . . As to his vices, they are not a danger to me, because I will never allow him anywhere near my boys (*oni mne ne opasny, potomu chto ia ego vmest s moimi mal'chikami nikuda ne puskaiu*).'[41]

Whether through the intellectual empowerment of university science and mathematics, the civic autonomy of student life in Odessa, or the swirling cultural life of a young adult man, Witte by 1870, the year of his graduation from New Russia University, already could be said to have experienced much in the new world emerging from the so-called 'Great Reforms'. At the same time, he remained an Orthodox Christian, a service nobleman, and a loyal subject of the Russian emperor, subject to the traditions, mores, and assumptions of the imperial world into which he had been born. He himself, in a sense, remembered this transitional milieu when he recalled his 'firm intention to remain in the university' and take up an academic career in theoretical mathematics. Both his widowed mother and his uncle Fadeev, who journeyed to Odessa at this time, 'very much looked askance at my desire to be a professor', he testified. They argued that 'this occupation did not suit me because it was not a nobleman's business (*dvorianskoe delo*)', and he paused to explain how frequently such opinions were voiced in the society of those days, 'especially in those of its parts which clung to the former traditions'. Even his uncle, 'an entirely cultured and educated man, nevertheless in his soul remained that same "prere-form"—if this can be said—nobleman'. Paradoxically enough, Fadeev would persuade his nephew to abandon the university and take a job instead on the railroads.[42]

Odessa and St Petersburg: The Railway Man in an Age of Empire

In 1870, as war raged in western Europe between Prussia and France, Witte accompanied his uncle Fadeev to socialize at the Odessa apartments of the imperial governor-general, Count Kotsubey. Through Fadeev's prodding and influence, the recent university graduate, still intent on an academic career, had agreed to become a personal assistant on the governor-general's staff. The position required no actual work, but did provide the young nobleman a rank from which to begin a career advancing through the hierarchy of the civil service. Especially from his family's perspective, it also insured him against the foolhardy notion of continuing his studies and becoming a professor. Witte recalled evenings where members of Kotsu-bey's social company, most of them military officers, gathered around maps strewn with markers denoting the positions of German and French armies, and how, given 'human weakness', these Francophiles refused to believe that France was suffering total defeat. A young man of 21, Witte was entering public life at a critical juncture in Europe's history, a period when the wars of Italian, American, and German national unification had unsettled international relations throughout the European Atlantic world.

Five years previously, a victorious federal state had defeated a secessionist movement to become the sponsor and crucible of national unity in North America. Monarchical states had assumed this mission in Italy by 1860, and in Germany, where, around the core of the Prussian royal state and its North German Confederation, King Wilhelm I and his chancellor, Otto von Bismarck, constructed the diplomatic and military strategies that led to the proclamation of a German Empire in January 1871. In east central and eastern Europe, similar shifts in the geopolitical landscape were occurring as the three empires confronting each other in the east all acted variously to aggrandize their imperial power with the fuel of nationalist aspirations. This was especially the case in the Balkan peninsula, where Ottoman, Austro-Hungarian, and Russian empires maneuvered for dominance among the polyglot religious, ethnic, and political communities that populated the region. The ideas of nationalism that had dominated European intellectual life in the first half of the century were proving through war to be the catalyst that could nationalize the imperial state and empower empires.[43]

In this same year, Rostislav Fadeev had published *The Eastern Question (Vostochnyi vopros)*, which Witte acknowledged having read with respect. It was one important voice in a larger chorus of so-called panslavic sentiment, which was prominent in Russian imperial public opinion in these years, and accorded Russian state power a manifest destiny to exert its cultural and political hegemony over all ethnically 'Slavic' communities in the Balkans.[44] Fadeev greeted the inevitability of a general European war, sure to result from a great power struggle over sponsorship of the national awakenings occurring across the region. Foreseeing a chain reaction of events initiated by Russia's own strategic objectives in the Black Sea region, Fadeev predicted Austria would combat Russia's drive to occupy 'Constantinople', the Ottoman capital he ostentatiously called by its Christian Byzantine name, and thereby achieve unfettered access to the Mediterranean Sea. Inevitably as well, Fadeev maintained, this war would extend beyond the force of arms, and necessitate winning popular support from Slavic peoples in the Hapsburg domains. Efforts foreshadowing modern propaganda, again inevitably, would lead Austria to agitate for some offer of national representation in its Polish territories, a nascent nation state divided among three empires since the late eighteenth century. Fadeev's own view of the so-called Polish question reflected the lofty pretensions and harsh realities of Russian panslavism when it was directed against the ethnic communities it claimed to represent. Fadeev believed Poland incapable of ever becoming a nation state, but instead disingenuously envisioned it as either a German province or one of the autonomous Slavic homelands, stretching from Poland to the Balkans, in an idealized imperial protectorate under the international and military sovereignty of the Russian tsar. 'I know that many will call my conclusions fiction,' Fadeev, ever the dreamer, testified, but asserted that a millennium of Orthodox Christian history, as well as a contemporary era of national unification, lent credence to his arguments. Russia, in Fadeev's view, either could be a nation state or an empire . . . of nations. Nothing about the world he shared with his nephew—which now incorporated both the Caucasus and the truly metropolitan world of Odessa—would make that choice a difficult one. 'The spirit of the time together with a realistic analysis of our situation leads only to one of two decisions,' Fadeev wrote: 'Russia, as a local state (*mestnoe gosudarstvo*) of the Russian people, or Russia, as the focus (*sredotochie*) of a Slavic and orthodox world.'[45]

Whether at the time these views were Witte's as well cannot be ascertained. As we shall see, Witte's own panslavic sympathies in the 1870s were pronounced and he acknowledged Fadeev's intellectual influence at this critical juncture in his young life.[46] Otherwise, all that can be noted is the memory of evenings spent at Governor-General Kotsubey's salon in 1870. As he dictated, he reminisced and recalled the moment, and then, literally, his narrative attention swerved: 'At these assemblages appeared General in the Suite of His Majesty Count Vladimir Bobrinsky, who at the time was passing through Odessa and recently had been appointed Minister of Ways of Communication.'[47] Witte thus began to recall the details of how his own career in the service of the imperial state began on the railroad—a technology that with increasing intensity was transforming economy, society, and imagination itself in the nineteenth century. Through the prism of the imperial—the salon of the imperial governor-general, a time of imperial wars, imperial pretensions to sovereignty, Witte remembered encountering the railroad, an imperial technology, which would engage both his talents and his imagination.[48]

One evening during the summer of 1870, at Kotsubey's salon, Fadeev introduced his nephew to V. A. Bobrinsky, the Minister of Ways of Communication. As such, Bobrinsky was the final arbiter over what formally was known as the Administration of the Crown Odessa Railroad, a state-owned and operated railroad whose sale to the Russian Steamship and Commerce Company the minister then was negotiating as part of a general privatization of existing crown railroads and future rail construction.[49] Founded in 1856, this company dominated steamship routes on the Black Sea, had already begun to manufacture its own vessels in the Crimea, and would become an even larger corporate entity over the ensuing twenty years. The state charter through which it operated the railroad mandated new construction in two directions. Toward the east, a new railroad would link Odessa to the coal and iron ore of the Donets Basin of eastern Ukraine, for consumption and export. Toward the west, Odessa would be connected to Iassy, in Romania, and through that terminus to the agricultural markets of the lower Danube, and the strategic frontier with the Ottoman and Austro-Hungarian Empires to the north-west.[50]

Looking back on this critical turning point, Witte related how Bobrinsky convinced him to abandon dreams of a university life and 'to trade his professorial career for the career of a railwayman (*zhelezno-dorozhnyi deia-tel'*)'. Witte, at least as he recalled the story, wanted to move to St Petersburg and pass the examinations required to enter the Corps of Transportation Engineers, which since the late 1830s had produced military engineers expert in the construction and operation of railroads. Although a general of engineers himself, Bobrinsky 'loudly opposed' that approach, Witte remembered, as he explained the origins of his most prized identity. Bobrinsky desired 'a man just having finished university, with a broad education in general and in mathematics in particular, one not ruined yet by the corporate, narrow spirit of the specialist'. Because these engineers were trained within traditions of education and professional practice that were chiefly technical and administrative in character, Bobrinsky believed they did not comprehend the commercial potential of railroads. The minister thus offered Witte the opportunity to learn railroad management, and its economics, in practice, as a railwayman. For six months he learned the business, from ticketing and freight dispatch, through stationmaster and traffic controller, to management of outlying stations of the Odessa system. He claimed to have negotiated a salary of 200 rubles per month, a sum double or even triple the amounts normally earned at these jobs. That level of financial success, as well as the new ministerial uniform he wore to mark his advance in the service hierarchy, indeed the fact that it lacked the special insignia of the Corps of Engineers which he had coveted, were also memories marking the first major step of Witte's public career.[51]

The Odessa Railroad was privatized within the year. For the next fifteen years, Witte would work for privately owned and managed railroad companies. Yet, the state-corporate business world of the railroad industry that he joined intricately balanced the theoretical ideals of a laissez-faire, free market capitalism, and the practical realities of Russian business practices long shaped by a state officialdom that was accustomed to governing, and living from, the economy. When the first railroads were built in the 1840s in the reign of the arch-autocrat Nicholas I, crown ownership and management of railroads were the key characteristic influencing the organization of this nineteenth-century business venture. State bonds sold by the treasury on international markets financed railroad construction and operations with the investment capital thus acquired—a natural impulse in the autocratic design bequeathed his empire by Peter the Great. Russian military defeat in the Crimean War, however, nearly bankrupted the imperial treasury and strained underdeveloped domestic credit markets. With the ascension to the throne of the future tsar-emancipator Alexander II, who found the new railroad technology alluring for both strategic and commercial reasons, the problem of mobilizing financial resources on a scale necessary to construct a network of railroads spanning European Russia beckoned to the new sovereign. So too did practical solutions rooted in the laissez-faire, free-trade economic theories then dominating continental European statecraft. Alexander approved the first in what through the late 1870s would prove a series of corporate charters to syndicates of private investors, whose purchases of equity shares created the investment capital necessary to form joint-stock companies empowered to construct, operate, and profit from the railroad line thereby created. A major purchaser, and by corporate law the ultimate guarantor of company stock, was the imperial treasury. The state was thus involved at the conception of these market economies and the publicly owned business firms that inhabited them.[52]

   The terms of these concessions varied, as did the international composition of the private consortia of financiers, bankers, and commercial-industrial entrepreneurs who bid against each other to win them. All, however, shared common attributes. First, each concession was a legal charter (*ustav*) that obliged the two contracting parties. Chief among these, from the government's perspective, was the stipulation that the ownership group construct new railroad lines or extend existing ones at a guaranteed price. In exchange, the company operated, and if it was able, profited from the line. Second, each concession was precisely that, a long-term lease of ownership rights by the state to private investors. After eighty-five years, the state could exercise its right of eminent domain and expropriate private owners, but, as an escape clause, could so act after twenty—a process that Witte would initiate as a minister in the 1890s. Of greatest importance, each concession was financed through a complex set of commercial loan transactions and sale of stock shares in both domestic and foreign markets, all ultimately brokered and guaranteed by the credit worthiness of the Russian state. Maintaining this reputation in the later nineteenth century was no small feat for a treasury whose solvency rested on a paper currency itself the object of sufficient investor speculation to make currency markets, and the profits that could be taken from them, objects of study in the imperial Ministry of Finances during these years. Finally, the financial instability of the imperial state all but dictated that concessions be offered on terms advantageous enough to attract investors. As a rule, annual dividends from company stocks and bonds were guaranteed at 4–5 per cent. These were first paid from company profits but, when these private firms operated at a loss, as they frequently did, dividends flowed to private investors directly from the state treasury. That expenditure only further complicated the problems, and opportunities, of credit markets that were the objects of profiteering and speculation.[53]

One early twentieth-century historian represented the late 1860s and 1870s as years of 'concession fever'.[54] The promise of speculative profit drew investors to railroad stocks and bonds not only from abroad, but from within the empire as well. Chronic company construction cost overruns and operating deficits, however, were silent testimony to the nature of nineteenth-century business practice, and perhaps as well to the bidding process brokered by imperial officials. By 1880, government statistics suggested, only five of thirty-seven Russian railroad companies were profitable. The others, among which was the Odessa line, owed the treasury over 550 million credit rubles, a figure that had tripled in a decade as scarce treasury resources paid the annual dividends that company charters had guaranteed investors.[55] Such commercial debt constituted one part of a larger market in the stocks and bonds of Russian railroad companies, in 1880 estimated to be capitalized at 1.6 billion credit rubles. A major player in this sizeable commercial and capital market was the imperial treasury, which owned over 85 per cent of this paper.[56]

A system of concessions, where the state provided the legal framework and financial guarantees for the entrepreneurial capital necessary to accelerate the construction of a rail network in European Russia, was successful to a point, however. Compared to the United Kingdom, which in 1867 conveyed 273,000 passengers and 135 million tons of freight over 20,000 kilometers of track, the Russian network was still in its infancy. In 1867, its 'iron roads (*zheleznye dorogi*)' as they literally were called in Russian, extended over only some 5,000 kilometers. Over the ensuing decade, however, this system quadrupled in size to some 21,000 kilometers. The amount of freight shipped on it grew seven times to 36 million tons; 29,000 passengers, four times the number ten years earlier, traveled by rail in 1877. A system constituted from large and small corporate businesses, as well as direct state management, incorporated strategically important main lines linking St Petersburg with Warsaw, Kiev, and Moscow. Through the hub of the empire's second capital, a second network, constructed and operated by the Main Society of Russian Imperial Railroads, connected to other lines and incorporated not only a strategic, but a commercial rail network: the industrializing territories of Russian Poland (Warsaw), the export markets of eastern Prussia (Konigsberg), the commercial entrepot of the Baltic Sea (St Petersburg), the urban centers of Ukraine (Kiev and Kharkov), the chief ports of the Black Sea (Feodosia and Odessa), and the commercial artery of the upper Volga River valley (Nizhnii-Novgorod).[57]

One of these rail lines was the Odessa Railroad, now owned by The Russian Steamship and Commerce Company. Witte spent nine years there, from 1870 to 1878, in a succession of increasingly responsible commercial and managerial positions. His public roles within the civic world that blazed in Russia during the 1870s were invested with increasing amounts of status as well.[58] Yet, his tales of these years, which the memoirist recapitulated in dogged pursuit of each such public moment, were just as frequently revealing of the private self of this most image-conscious Victorian man. Thus, as he began to explain the origins of his career advancement, a topic Witte treasured, his narration turned first to a person, a man, his predecessor as Chief of Traffic, 'Fedor Moiseevich Shtern', who had died within the year of the text Witte was then dictating. Why Witte began his reminiscences of a distinguished railroad career with Shtern will never be known—but there are reasons to dwell for a moment on these details, for Fedor Moiseevich Shtern, any Russian reader of this text would know, was a Jew.[59]

Shtern was the low-born son of a watchmaker, a man with little education who had parlayed talent and practical experience into civic status. Refracting these memories through his own lifetime of civic activity, Witte emphasized Shtern's 'ability to conduct himself in society, which was a distinction of all Odessan young people', and their 'cultured and public' city, he added. Given the evident relationship between the social company an individual kept and the position (*dolzhnost'*) he held, Witte appreciated as well how 'Shtern similarly made his career, moving gradually from office to office', finally becoming the Chief of Traffic of the Odessa Railroad. In these recollections, however, there also echoed the voices of a European century that was discovering racial and ethnic categories to be scientifically grounded keys to understanding human identity. The assumptions held by one ethnic group about another echoed throughout Witte's memoirs. To be a Russian, or a Pole, Ukrainian, German, Georgian, Armenian, Chinese, Jew, or a raft of other ethnic signifiers meant in his eyes, and those of his contemporaries, to be and behave according to certain predictable patterns. Without diminishing its connections to the virulent ideological racisms that would darken the twentieth century, such language was deemed acceptable and natural, or, as a part of the surrounding cultural landscape, simply went unnoticed.[60]

Hence, thinking of Shtern, Witte mused over his 'one shortcoming', one he deemed 'typical of his race', what he called 'bold impudence (*na-khal'stvo*)'. The fact that he was 'the most jewish of jews, (*sovershenneishii evrei*), a Jew who never once concealed his nationality (*natsional'nost'*)' from anyone in Odessa intrigued Witte. He plainly admired such assertiveness in a man. A central part of that identity, at least as Witte unfolded it, was masculine beauty and sexuality, for Shtern was a man who 'had very gallant manners and in fact was incredibly handsome'. He used these traits to woo the wife of his superior, a woman of rank at the imperial court, and thus advance his career. Witte dwelled upon this meeting of beauty and ethnicity, and thought of Shtern again, 'one of the most handsome men I have met in my life, even though his was a type that was somewhat jewish (*tip neskol'ko evreiskii*)'. Shtern perhaps provides a glimpse of Witte himself in the 1870s—or of what Witte wished he had been. Shtern moved through the winter season of Odessa, and enjoyed 'the greatest success' among its aristocratic women, especially those within 'the Polish colony', Witte added, packing every detail into his autobiographical musings. In the end, however, the accent in this tale belonged to the careerist, whose personal language was always deeply shadowed by the racialist and ethnic edifices embedded in his heritage. Fedor Moiseevich Shtern was the man Witte replaced, in part, he remembered, because the new company director, N. M. Chikhachev, resented his 'arrogant manner of speech'—leaving forever unanswered whether Witte had uttered, or simply heard, what were, in essence, anti-Semitic slurs.[61]

Less speculatively, his memories of these first years attribute career success to both individual talent and patronage. Through Fadeev, he was a young protégé in a network grouped around his uncle's mentor and military superior, the former viceroy of the Caucasus, Prince A. I. Bariatinskii. Through this aristocratic counselor, Witte, to be sure from a very great distance, was connected to the heir to the throne, the future Alexander III.[62] Bariatinskii's formal letter of introduction to N. M. Chikhachev, which asked the director of the newly formed Russian Steamship and Commerce Company to 'advance' the young Witte, was a prized artifact of his personal archive. Patronage notwithstanding, his talent was undeniable, as was the connection between his growing prominence as a manager and the increasingly evident power of his intellect. The accomplished university mathematician began in these years to display an ability to synthesize sweeping practical solutions in a railroad system whose variables were time, motion, and space.[63] In 1874, only 25, Witte attended the 12th General Congress of Representatives of Russian Railroads, a consultative and regulatory body through which the Ministry of Transportation attempted to coordinate the operation of the rail network. He had frequented international congresses of railroad executives since 1876, and made his voice heard on topics that ranged from the commercial and corporate to the economic and geopolitical.[64] In early 1877 he was invited to join the Baranov Commission, a high-level government body in St Petersburg charged to standardize the operation of what had become a haphazardly integrated rail system of crown and privately operated lines. The Russian jurist A. F. Koni first met Witte that year and remarked the 'deep knowledge' Witte then had displayed and the general agreement with which 'other specialists' greeted his views.[65]

Personal identity, career paths, growing prominence in business and public life: all were central to the memoirist as he mused over these first years as a railwayman. As his narrative attention swerved yet again, however, and he took up 'the status of the railroad during the Eastern War of 1877', what became apparent was that Witte's experience of the Odessa Railroad centrally entailed the linkage he discovered there between the railway and the empire, the one a new technological instrument shaping the international politics, economy, and culture of the other. By the later 1870s, the Odessa Railroad had become a pivotal link in a growing imperial rail network. It connected to a terminus on the northern shores of the Black Sea, from which traffic could flow southwards, via steamship lines, toward the Caucasus, the Mediterranean Sea, and the Ottoman Empire, and westward, via international connections, to the lands of the lower Danube and the Balkan peninsula beyond. The Odessa Railroad, in short, was a conduit through which, beginning with security and commerce, the fundamental interests of the Russian imperial state flowed.

On the Odessa line, judging from the scrupulous fashion Witte recorded all things having to do with the symbols of monarchy, he became a participant for the first time in the imperial court and the rituals that maintained it. Imperial trains carried Alexander II from St Petersburg to Crimea via the Odessa port, or, in 1877, via Iassy, to war. Each time Witte, as appropriate to his office, met or accompanied the train—the memory of his role probably no less glowing for the reality of being one participant in a large cast surrounding the emperor.[66] The railroad linked him to imperialist rhetoric and adventure, as both stewed in Odessa during the 1870s, especially with the outbreak of war in 1876 between an all but independent Serbia and its formal suzerain, the Ottoman Empire. 'A general surge of Russian (*russkii*) patriotic self-consciousness in the sense of Slavic unity' filled the air, especially among the young, Witte wrote, 'because we were swept away by "the Slavic idea"—the idea of taking Constantinople and we enthusiastically worked to send volunteers there.' His entire upbringing shadowed by imperial conflict between Christian Russia and Muslim Turkey, Witte eagerly joined this struggle. He was the vice-chair of the Odessa Slavic Charitable Society, and, by his own testimony, used its premises, healthy bribes for customs officials, and the good offices of his company to dispatch Russians to a military adventure that, Witte failed to mention, ended in disaster.[67] Among the some 100 international diplomas and medals he was awarded over his lifetime, Witte preserved a Takovskii Cross, awarded him in 1877 by the Serbian Prince Milan Obrenovic IV for his support of Serbian military efforts against the Turks.[68] In 1876, a government investigation found that the Odessa Railroad employed two refugees, one a 'Jew-Serb' and the other 'a Turkish subject' named 'Kollar-Wagner', both of whom most likely had fled ethnic strife in a Bulgaria gripped by popular rebellion and Ottoman military occupation.[69] Both men, the record stipulated, had been given jobs through the offices of 'chief of traffic titular councilor Witte' and his associates in the local Slavonic society.[70]

Yet, only with the outbreak of the Russo-Turkish War in 1877 did Witte first experience the railroad as an instrument of imperial power. He recalled with great detail the role that the Odessa line and its chief operations officer played in the mobilization, concentration, and transportation of a Russian field army from the interior and across the Romanian frontier into the Balkans. Displaying the managerial skill, even audacity he had acquired since 1870—'a decisive and firm character' he called it—Witte went to war, not so much against the Ottoman enemy as the chaos ensuing on his railroad when it fell under the purview of army mobilization. Rather than 'strict correspondence with a plan, calculated to the hour and minute, running as surely as a chronometer', Witte entoned, he confronted a maze of conflicts and bottlenecks. The Russian artist Konstantin Savitsky famously captured this wild disorder and cacophony in his portrayal of dazed yet bold army reservists and their peasant families crowded together at a train platform, a steaming locomotive waiting to carry this jumble of men and their equipment to battle.[71] Troops outnumbered the locomotives and rolling stock needed to move them. Cavalry was forced to detrain and move by horse, the animals' places given to soldiers instead. Eventually Witte created out of this disarray the mathematician's orderly progression of men, material, and even returning empty boxcars filled with evacuated wounded soldiers, but along the way he learned as well the full value of the unorthodox solution. Witte mused about his introduction of the 'American system' of railroad operation, where men in shifts serviced constantly operating machines, or how, abandoning the use of the telegraph to move rail traffic safely from station to station, he instead dispatched trains, at a quicker tempo, at regular intervals of time.[72] In the bloody combat and military occupation that followed, imperial arms reached near to Istanbul before the Ottoman Porte sued for peace. Victorious and glorious, the Russian Empire subsequently found its military victory turned into the diplomatic defeat engineered by the German Chancellor Bismarck at the Congress of Berlin in 1878.[73] But Witte had been transformed. Almost twenty-five years later, upon becoming the acting Minister of Communications in 1892 amidst a famine unrelieved by a bottlenecked railroad system, one of his first formal requests, in terms that were synthetic, generalized, and analytical, was to review the army high command's plans for the railroads during a general mobilization.[74]

The railroad symbolized not only power, but modernity as well. In this regard, Witte's experience of the railroad reflected less the eager embrace, and more the unease and uncertainty that often characterized his relationship with the modern. Two categories of modern nineteenth-century public life—disaster and notoriety—swirled within his retelling of 'The

Tilligul'sk Catastrophe', a fiery train wreck in December 1875 on the Odessa Railroad upon which, because he was the lead actor in the public drama that unfolded, Witte lavished his attention. The wreck occurred when a troop train carrying new army draftees to Odessa, traveling along an embankment atop the Tiligulsk Ravine, derailed and burned in a 'howling gale' (*strashnaia miatel'*), costing over 100 lives. He remembered being dispatched to the scene, how 'the picture, of course, was extremely sorrowful. The accident had been horrific.' Telling the tale with a technician's eye, Witte explained how the telegraph had been used to move the train safely from one junction in the system to another, remembered the mile marker where the wreck had occurred, and detailed how a large drainage pipe had acted like a bellows and caused part of the train to be incinerated.

What burned more brightly in Witte's memory, however, was the public notoriety, much of it scorn and criticism, which the incident attracted. Suggesting the degree to which an increasingly sophisticated Russian educated public, and the complex civic discourses it was creating, used print media and its narratives to become participants and judges of public events, Witte lamented 'a public mood (*obshchestvennoe nastroenie*)' that had assigned blame and demanded retribution for the terrible accident. Writing in the Victorian frame that had led a stout defender of liberalism like John Stuart Mill to uphold the liberty of the individual against the homogeneity of the mass, Witte also retrieved an older monarchical politics rooted in his youth that disdained all radical populism. 'This was in 1875–1876', a time when, he explained, 'the press and public opinion had been seized by a spirit of particular hate for individuals, who, given their standing or their material assets, stand out [sic] from the ranks of middling people (*srednye liudi*)'. Witte scrupulously detailed the lengthy criminal investigation prosecutors conducted into the wreck launched by prosecutors. No evidence exists to parry his claim that government authorities scapegoated N. M. Chikhachev—an admiral, an adjutant of the imperial court (*fligel'-adiutant*), and director of the railroad—and himself, whom 'public opinion had deemed to be the heart and soul of the railroad's administration'. Willing to shoulder some responsibility 'because we both after all were supervisors (*nachal'niki*)', Witte followed procedure to blame first of all the 'horrific negligence' of the track crew foreman who had abandoned the work site, and, following the disaster, disappeared, some said insane. Odessa prosecutors eventually declined to indict Chikhachev and Witte, but the public outcry and 'psuedo-liberal (*lozhno-liberal'noe*) attitude' reigning in St Petersburg were such that the case was eventually transferred to an old, unreformed, and more reliable criminal chamber in Ukrainian Kamenets-Podolya, which sentenced both men to four months' imprisonment.[75]

In 1879, after each had garnered additional prominence for the parts they and their railroad played in the victorious Russo-Turkish War, Alexander II commuted the court's sentence and instead himself punished each 'in a fatherly way (po-otecheski)'. Chikhachev was confined for two weeks to the fashionable Hotel Europa in downtown St Petersburg, while Witte, by this time already transferred to railroad company headquarters in the capital, served his four-month sentence by spending nights sleeping under guard in a crown-owned apartment located on Haymarket Square. Because subsequently in his public and ministerial life Witte's reputation for the widespread and always strategic way in which he exercised influence over correspondents and government officials alike was also notorious, what was most noticeable in this tale was that he never once mentioned bribery.[76]

We have arrived at a key moment in the railwayman's career. When the war ended in 1878, he remembered with pride, the emperor extended his formal thanks for Witte's 'magnificent' work transporting the army. Clearly, his star was in the ascendant. Shortly after the end of hostilities, the Odessa Railroad was merged with two other lines to create the privately owned Southwest Railroads Company (SWRR), an extensive network that reached from the middle Volga River basin in the east, through an interior system linking Moscow, Kiev, and St Petersburg, to export termini at Brest-Litovsk on the German frontier and Odessa on the Black Sea. Minister of Finances Reitern favored an enterprise that aimed to cheapen and speed the transport of goods for export, and saw merger as an effective means of reducing costs, increasing profitability, and lessening the strain placed on a treasury guaranteeing the rail system's financial stability.[77] For some two years Witte worked as the business director (nachal'nik otdela eksploatatsii) in the St Petersburg headquarters of the new company, as a chief assistant to the SWRR's vice-president and managing director, I. A. Vyshnegradskii, the patron who later, when he became Minister of Finances, proved instrumental in recruiting Witte to work in his ministry.[78] From the company headquarters building at No. 27 Bolshoi Koniushennyi, one could spy, around the corner several blocks away, the ministry's creamy golden facade facing onto the Moika Canal. The railroad's office building itself was in the center of the imperial capital's own City, its banks and

insurance companies clustered in the nearby blocks around Nevskii Prospect and The Great Sea Street (*Bolshaia Morskaya*).[79]

During this interlude when he 'spent some two years' in the
imperial capital, he contributed his proto-technocratic expertise as a railway
manager to the Baranov Commission. Led by the Director of the Department of Economy in the Imperial State Council, Count E. T. Baranov, the
commission reflected a typical Russian bureaucratic practice of gathering
together ministerial officials and 'enlightened' local experts to resolve administrative dilemmas. Such commissions in the late nineteenth century
were the equivalent of parliamentary investigations in an age when autocratic Russia still lacked national representative institutions.[80] Seeking to
produce a general railroad charter that could regularize operations, administrative practices, and transit prices for an imperial rail network still constituted chiefly from disaggregated private companies, the Baranov
Commission convened a railroad 'congress' in St Petersburg in 1881,
attended by some eighty-five ministers, railroad company owners, academic
experts, and representatives of municipal councils, provincial zemstvo assemblies, and commercial associations. Witte was a noticeable contributor,
one of the participants later remembered, cogent in his defense of an orderly
and unified pricing system. He also spoke against regulation of workers'
hours and defended the right of the employer to dismiss employees without
cause. His ability to support an argument with data and practice drawn from
professional experience, in this case from his work as an assistant and then a
director of a railroad station, was a skill that would serve him increasingly
well in his public life and career.[81]

These two years in St Petersburg thus exposed him to the ministerial
bureaucracy, with its caste-like influence and privileges. Given what we
know of Witte's subsequent life, ministerial power, perhaps already beckoned. Most readers of his life tend to think in such terms about Witte,
always maneuvering toward power and intent on seizing every opportunity
to aggrandize it. Yet, judging from the way he remembered these years,
if he was learning such lessons in the years 1879–81, Witte encountered
them, not in the salons and offices where officialdom dwelled, but in an
equally powerful, private, and corporate culture created, as he styled it, by
'the railroad kings (*zheleznodorozhnye koroli*)', the wealthy business barons
who monopolized control of the Russian railroad industry at this time. In a
public address of 1910, where he never once uttered the word 'entrepreneur', Witte expressed his fascination for this 'peculiar wielder of power

(*vlastitel'*) in the state'. In fact mere subjects of the Crown, these individuals acted royally, their 'retainers and courtiers' markers of the 'dynasties' created from the 'enormous' capital funds accumulated through their privately owned banks, which purchased government-guaranteed railroad bonds and controlling interests in the railroad companies they created.[82] Again detailing his fascination for public celebrity, and personal influence, he especially mused over the social obscurity from which each had emerged. Here were Jews, some converting to Christianity. Here too were former serfs and Old Believers, who first became prosperous as liquor tax-farmers (*otkupshchiki*), civil service clerks, and engineers. Each of them had a different life story, but all had become prominent, he remarked, 'thanks to accidental circumstance, intellect, cunning and a certain amount of adaptability (*proidoshestvo*)', a colloquialism that conveyed an individual ability to change from one frame of reference to another.[83] A talent that Witte had first witnessed in the adults who framed his childhood, such adaptability to circumstance was, in a transitional era, an instrument critical to the nobleman, the courtier, the aspiring careerist, and the railroad king.

Chief among them was Ivan S. Bliokh (1836–1901), the owner and director of the Southwestern Railroad, and a figure who occupied high ground in the landscape of Witte's memories. Contemporaries knew him as a Jew born in Russian Poland, who first emerged on the public scene in the 1860s as an investor in railroad concessions, banks, insurance companies, and the Main Society of Imperial Russian Railroads. The latter, a joint venture between Russian and French capital founded in 1856, constructed, owned, and operated a major strategic and commercial rail network, which linked European Russia through St Petersburg to Warsaw, Moscow, Nizhnii-Novgorod, and the Crimea. Having accumulated his fortune, Bliokh turned to scholarship, and from the later 1870s authored a series of studies on the Russian railroad industry, and the imperial economy for which it increasingly was a foundation.[84] Musing in his memoirs, Witte dwelled on 'the quite interesting career' of a man who acquired 'enormous influence and enormous wealth, and who, thanks to his railroads and banks, wielded enormous authority (*avtoritet*)... even in the propertied upper class'.[85] Enticing indeed was the example of a man who had begun with nothing. The biographer only can speculate about a memory which suggests how encountering such a man might have influenced Witte's subsequent public career.

'Bliukh had been a subcontractor' for the building of some railroad station, Witte wrote with the bluntness he applied to all ethnic identities, 'in short a small-time little subcontractor-jew (*poddriadchik evreichik*), entirely uneducated but ... extraordinarily capable'. Eventually, 'when he had become rich enough and established himself, he was so intelligent' that he went abroad to Germany and there 'educated himself'. Returning to Russian Poland 'as a proper young man', Bliokh fell in love with a Catholic woman, 'a beauty (*krasavitsa*)', Witte exclaimed with the word he often used to categorize females, 'very beautiful, educated, intelligent, an entirely fashionable (*svetskaia*) woman'. Converting to Catholicism, Bliokh married her, 'bought a large home' in Warsaw, and amassed a fortune sufficient enough by 1878 to obtain controlling interest in the three railroad companies that merged to become the Southwestern Railroad.

It was then that a young Witte, still only some 30 years old, first encountered Bliokh, who periodically traveled to St Petersburg to confer with company officers. As if comparing himself yet again in the mirror that this powerful man had once provided him, Witte remembered Bliokh as 'a fellow by nature not stupid [sic], to the highest degree educated and talented, but with the shortcomings so strongly inherent in the majority of Jews (*evreev*), that capacity to put on airs (*zaznavat'sia*), and with a goodly amount of impudence (*nakhal'stvo*) to boot'. Any number of commentators noted similar patterns of behavior in the adult Witte, and he himself, in tones that suggested less anti-Semitism and more the same, previously observed skirting of ethnic boundaries and the patterning of behavior that occurred there, allowed that Bliokh tolerated but never 'sympathized' with him, 'because', he explained, 'from my youth I never bowed and scraped before anyone (*ni pered kem spiny ne gnul*) and always spoke the truth straight into the eyes of everyone, even though I was then a man entirely dependent on others (*zavisiashchii*) and lacking means'. Bliokh, Witte recalled, 'always complained about my brazenness (*rezkost'*), or, as he put it, arrogance (*nadmennost'*)' which, at base, differed little from the impudence he remembered his former superior to have displayed. Noteworthy as well was Bliokh's ready use of 'assistants' wherever he went, a work strategy that left him free to pursue 'politics and scholarly study', although even here he employed 'various writers and specialists for money' to write texts according to programmatic outlines he established. Scholars who have read in the rich archives of the imperial Ministry of Finances during Witte's tenure will surely recognize in this description a pattern of behavior he would display in his subsequent public and ministerial life.

At the core of this tale, however, Witte registered uncertainty, as he dwelled upon the subordinate behavior others displayed toward this powerful individual. Even Ivan Vyshnegradskii, who then was the chief executive officer of the Southwestern, displayed 'a servility (*nizkopoklonstvo*)' toward Bliokh that, at base, Witte found shocking in a man whom he also knew subsequently as a powerful minister. 'Even though then just a young man, I sooner would have gone begging (*poiti po miru*) than conduct myself that way toward Bliokh, and not because he was a Jew,' Witte hastened to add, 'but because, in essence, he stood for nothing (*on nichego soboi ne predstavlial*); in the end, all the power of these gentlemen was to be found in their pockets'.[86] Was this a moment when Witte also remembered a conflicted young man, barely 30 years of age in 1880, caught between, on the one hand, an old Russia that had ascribed him nobility and cultural value, and, on the other, a new Russia pointing toward the modernity that was establishing the dominion of individual talent, wealth, power—and meaninglessness?

His private life, at least as this most constructed aspect of his memories revealed, had altered as well. In St Petersburg, he married for the first time.[87] His wife, whose first name he never uttered in print, was a divorcee, N. A. Spiridinova, whom he first met in Odessa while she was still living with her husband. What Witte claimed to be her compromised reputation in Kiev, where supposedly her dissolute gambler husband had forced her to steal to support his gaming, influenced his decision to work in St Petersburg. Given the scandalous reputation still attached to her, he remembered, 'it would have been awkward for me to move to Kiev with Spiridinova as my wife'.[88] Of equal import for a man with eyes now squarely fixed on career advancement had been the invitation to participate in the Baranov Commission.[89] Spiridinova, the daughter of a provincial noble family from Chernigov province in eastern Ukraine, had been pursued by Witte even while she was still married: 'she was beautiful, you could say a beauty (*krasavitsa*)', he remembered. He paid the husband to divorce her. She lived with Witte for ten years, dying prematurely of heart disease in 1889. They had no natural children. He financially supported but never legally adopted a daughter from his wife's first marriage, Sonia Mering. Their relationship, at least judging from Witte's perspective, was strained and cold. Whether a marriage of convenience or love—some biographers note the paucity of attention he accords the marriage in his memoirs—they lived together as a couple. A close subordinate of Witte's, returning to Kiev in 1906 and sampling the stories that still circulated about him among former co-workers, reported that Witte and his wife 'lived "like two love-birds (*dusha k dushu*)", enflamed with love for each other, carefree and happy', that he 'worship(ed) his wife'.[90]

Conclusion: A New Russian

Toward the end of 1880, the couple moved to Kiev. Witte was ordered there by the Southwestern as business manager to stabilize its unsteady financial position. A year after his marriage, the couple apparently felt more secure in their public reputation.[91] In Kiev, he took up 'the reins of the administration on the ground', and reorganized it entirely, showing for the first time his penchant to control and centralize, 'in the sense of a greater centralization of power', he detailed.[92] The ancient citadel of Orthodox Christian Rus', as well as the chief city in what he generally called Little Russia, and twenty-first-century contemporaries know as Ukraine, Kiev in the early 1880s was a boom town. It had a rapidly expanding population of over 125,000 people, much of that growth following the arrival in 1869 of a railroad connection to Moscow, and thus St Petersburg. In 1870, the city's first main railway station was completed, as was its rail link to the port of Odessa. A historian of the city writes that the Southwestern Railroad dominated the Kiev economy, which had added seven new major banks, a new stock exchange and city hall, and the Southwest's own Main Railway Shops, Kiev's largest employer, over those twelve years.[93] Witte took up residence in the Lipki neighborhood, a high-rent district that he remembered as 'the aristocratic quarter', near to the old citadel, the neighboring St Vladimir University, and the main commercial boulevard of the city, the Kreshchatyk.

Within a year of his arrival, I. S. Bliokh, now well acquainted with the young executive he had met several years before, nominated Witte to be the managing director of the Southwestern, a position requiring the confirmation of the Ministry of Communications. Because his lack of railroad engineering credentials had so complicated the ascent of his career, audible indeed was the undertone of triumph in the memory of an achievement where bureaucratic regulation could no longer trump 'the authority (*avtoritet*) that I had garnered on the railroads . . .'. From that position, by his own testimony, he earned a salary larger than any amount he received in state service prior to 1905. He recalled the loyal professional subordinates that he began to gather around him in these years; they were talented, knowledgeable proto-technocrats and railroad administrators, whom he assessed seriously and sometimes caustically, even from the hindsight of so many years.[94] Perhaps somewhat wistfully, he remembered as well that then he had been his own man, free from St Petersburg interference, with 'the most enormous (*gromadneishie*) business affairs' all his to manage. He achieved a standard of living that assured him entry to the company of 'many families from high society, who lived in their own separate little world (*kruzhok*), one to which', he hastened to add with characteristic bluntness, he now 'belonged'.[95] Claims of belonging often concealed realities of exclusion, but the southern colonial railwayman was beginning to exhibit that same adaptability he so admired in the railroad kings. Thus, he attached himself to a patronage network reaching into the extended family of the Romanov royal house by frequenting the salon of the Grand Duchess Alexandra Petrovna, the estranged, elderly, and eccentric wife of the brother of Tsar Alexander II, the Grand Duke Nikolai Nikolaevich the Elder. There he met, and became a whist partner of his son, the Grand Duke Nikolai Nikolaevich the Younger, destined to become the commander-in-chief of the imperial army at the outbreak of World War I.[96]

Witte arrived in Kiev in the fall of 1880. These were times of great civic and political uncertainty. By 1879, government and society found themselves confronting what was becoming a phenomenon spreading across the industrializing world, an outburst of revolutionary terrorist violence directed against the state. Organized by a radical, populist, conspiratorial party called The People's Will, a failed plot to assassinate the sovereign, Alexander II, by detonating dynamite beneath the royal family's private dining quarters in the Winter Palace, had produced two responses from the government. One, a burst of liberal reformism led by a military hero of the recent Eastern War, M. T. Loris-Melikov, promised to undertake economic, social, and political policies that hinted at the possibilities of substantive constitutional reform within the imperial state. The other, heightened state security measures designed to crush such terror, in effect contradicted the image of a reformist state by unleashing administrative police power to run roughshod over enemies and loyalists alike. All the more shockingly then did an entire generation seem to register the shattering assassination of the

Tsar-Emancipator, Alexander II, on 1 March 1881.[97] As was true of so many memoirists of that era, Witte well recalled where he had been and what he had done upon hearing the news. Yet, in his case, his reaction to regicide went beyond the personal trauma experienced by a dutiful monarchist. Witte resolved to act. He involved himself in the conspiratorial, monarchist, anti-terrorist plot of the Holy Druzhina. He contemplated counter-terror.

As he framed it in his memoirs, this shadowy affair germinated as an idea as he rushed home with his wife from the theater the evening when he first heard rumors of a telegram reporting that the emperor had been killed.[98] In his memoirs—as well as in organized correspondence that almost deliberately hinted he had arrived first at the idea—he summarized the contents of a letter he wrote late on the evening he heard the news of Alexander's death. Writing to his uncle Fadeev, who briefly in the period 1878–81 was an influential counselor to both Alexander II and Alexander III, Witte proposed that the revolutionaries who had conspired successfully to kill the Tsar-Emancipator were a microscopically small but powerful force against which the 'might of the state' was powerless. Therefore, he reasoned, it was necessary to turn their own weapons against them. Confront revolutionary conspiracy with a secret society that would answer assassination with assassination, he raged, and 'just as predatorily and just as traitorously . . . murder them'. Several days later he received a letter back from Fadeev reporting that his nephew's words now lay on Alexander III's desk, and that he soon would receive a summons.[99]

With close and crisp attention, Witte recalled that soon afterwards he did receive a telegram from I. I. Vorontsov-Dashkov, a former military officer who knew Fadeev and his family from the time when all served in the Caucasus, a close confidant at the court of the new tsar, Alexander III. As the newly appointed chief of security at the royal suburban palace of Gatchina, where Alexander sheltered with his family in the aftermath of his father's bloody death, Vorontsov instructed Witte to come to St Petersburg. Arriving in the capital, Witte, in an interview with the palace commandant, replied under questioning that he indeed did stand by his letter, and then was passed along to P. A. Shuvalov. This aristocratic counselor of both Alexander II and his son swore Witte to a secret oath as a member of the society which, based on the idea in his letter, had already been organized under the name of Holy Druzhina.[100] Or so Witte told the story, leaving in dispute only the degree of his responsibility for the original idea. The *druzhina* was a Russian reference to the armed retinues that the princes of medieval Rus' gathered about them as servitors and warriors. In a fashion that hinted at the mysticist and Masonic environments that had coursed through the Fadeev household in Tiflis, Witte explained that 'this was a secret society, on the order of those that existed in the middle ages in Venice and obliged themselves to combat their enemies with both weapons and poison'. What ensued was an almost tragicomic tale, that nevertheless included travel to Paris and plotting to kill the People's Will refugee Gartman, implicated in another foiled plot to explode the royal train. Witte eventually withdrew from what, he maintained, became a 'laughable if not embarrassing institution'.[101]

That a man now well established in career and public life had engaged in it, however, was yet another facet of what this noble, mathematically inclined, university-educated, panslavist railwayman had experienced over the course of the two decades that historians traditionally have labeled the era of the great reforms. Affecting every area of Russian life, from the peasant village where serfdom had been abolished to the university lecture hall alight with the possibilities of radical empowerment, these years saw tectonic shifts in the economy, society, politics, and culture of the Russian Empire. From them emerged, to judge from one remembered life, the kaleidoscopic identity that a young man of the Victorian age had created over the years he had lived in Odessa, Petersburg, and Kiev. He had come to Odessa a colonial parvenu, but one with connections that a noble family long attuned to patronage, status, and hierarchy had provided. Set upon this foundation, and caught in the accelerating complexity of the European Age of Empire, Witte confronted choices as he began adult life—whether to be a professor of mathematics, a state servitor, a railwayman, or a panslavic enthusiast—that were all much richer and more varied than those his forebears had experienced even a generation earlier. Embracing and intermingling them all, his early adulthood belonged to the burgeoning Victorian era—its railroad technology, business careers, friendships, erotic attractions, and emotional love. He was an admirer of beauty and manners, talent and knowledge, synthesis and action, adaptability and reputation. The railway had brought him far indeed through the Russian Empire: from its frontier outpost in Georgia, through its chief southern port, to one of its citadels, the 'mother of Russian cities, Kiev'. Sergei Witte was a new Russian.

3

Kiev: Dreaming in the Victorian 1880s

To impart the proper economic growth to our fatherland, we must make possible the easier distribution of natural resources throughout the broad expanse of our Empire. . . . If such in fact should be the objective, then how to attain it in an area of more than 5 million square versts, that of European Russia, and how to attain the same thing in the future in an area of over 18 million square versts, that of European Russia and Siberia together with the central asian [sic] possessions.

The Principles of Railroad Tariffs for the Transporting of Freight
(Printsipy zheleznodorozhnykh tarifov po perevozke gruzov) [Kiev, 1883][1]

I became acquainted with this statesman, who created such an uproar by himself and around himself, at a time when, all about him, everything was still peaceful. . . . Witte immediately seemed likeable, with his natural manner, the genuine way he had about him. In a black frock coat, uninhibited and free in what he said and how he acted, he reminded me in his appearance of an English statesman. I also noticed this remarkable, intelligently engaged look with which he listened to comments his minister directed to him, and later, in conversations with him eye to eye, I saw before me this same attentive listener, so rare among our bureaucrats. . . . (His) chief misfortune consisted in this, that (after he became a minister) he could not remain an autodidact (*samorodok*), but wanted to adorn himself with the glitter of vanity.[2]

Prince V. P. Meshchersky, *Memoirs*

As for Madame Shabel'skaia . . . I remember her when she still was an altogether young girl, and I still served on the Odessa Railroad. She was the daughter of General Shabel'skii, but ran away from her relatives and I met her, in Odessa, being then a young man, in Iashchuka's restaurant, in the Northern Hotel, in a company of revelers (*kutiashchaia kompaniia*). Then, she was very enchanting (*zabavnaia*), because she was still a very young girl, who was receiving a relatively good education, and . . . in the sense she drank a terrible amount and was extremely free and easy (*kraine razviazna*). She devoted herself to the theater and was an actress, and later went abroad, as an actress, on the Vienna stage.

Memoirs/tales in stenographic record/of
Count Sergei Iul'evich Witte, 3 March 1911[3]

the body of the deceased Emperor Alexander III lay in state in the Peter and Paul Cathedral. . . . The entire time a mass of people came and bowed to the body of the Emperor. . . . Several days after the internment I paid my respects to the dowager Empress . . . (S)he received me in a very kind manner (*ochen' laskovo*) and said the following words.

'I think that the death of the Emperor must be terribly burdensome for you, because, indeed, he loved you very much.' My subsequent tales will deal with the reign of the Emperor Nicholas.

*Memoirs/Tales in stenographic record/of
Count Sergei Iul'evich Witte,* 18 May 1911[4]

H istorians of Russia have tended to view the decade of the 1880s darkly, refracted through the prism provided by the reign of Tsar Alexander III. Reflecting themes first posited by liberal and socialist historians before 1917, they long have been accustomed to think of the reign of Alexander III as the era of the counter reforms. Some historians see his reign as ending a liberal flowering first promised by the abolition of serfdom and other 'Great Reforms' initiated at mid-century under his father, the Tsar-Emancipator Alexander II.[5] Others accentuate what they see to have been a hotbed of reactionary monarchical politics, even a birthplace of the modern totalitarian police state, and certainly the grounds from which grew the radical and revolutionary politics of the early twentieth century.[6] Still others, noting the explosion of official nationalism or russification that swept the empire after he ascended the throne in 1881, see the reign as a fatal turning point away from a coherent imperial polity under a unitary monarchical crown toward the nationalist-inspired dismembering of the empire that would occur with war and revolution after 1914.[7] Finally, although his reign saw policies that accelerated Russian industrialization, initiated construction of the Trans-Siberian Railroad, cemented a strategic alliance with republican France, and elevated the Romanov dynasty to a position of unquestioned prominence in the extended family network that linked the royal houses of Europe, historians tend to disdain Alexander III, a modern Victorian gentleman whose ugly anti-Semitism and political obscurantism were characteristics of the Europe that shaped him.[8]

Witte's views of Alexander and his reign were different, even though, as he reminisced about these years in winter 1912, the opinions set out above all circulated in the public discourse of the day. He was well aware, he commented in a representative passage, of a prevalent public view of the tsar 'as a man who was reactionary, as a man who was cruel, as a man limited and dull.'[9] Alexander III's policies initially were 'reactionary', Witte retorted, but the tsar had grown and matured during a thirteen-year reign that had begun with the murder of his father and sovereign by radical terrorists. He 'became markedly more liberal' as he became assured that neither revolution at home nor international conflict abroad would threaten the domestic order of the empire or the political stability of the autocratic crown that ruled over it. Alexander, in this view, began moving toward what Witte ambiguously called 'the path of peaceful liberalism (*put' spokoinogo liberalizma*)', where 'the state existed not for itself alone, but for the welfare of the people (*ono zhivet ne egoisticheskoi zhizn'iu, a zhizn'iu dlia pol'zy naroda*).' 'Had Emperor Alexander III been fated to continue his reign yet again as many years as he already had ruled,' Witte insisted, 'his reign would have been one of the very greatest reigns of the Russian Empire. But (he) did not succeed in doing so, because God summoned him.'[10]

What Witte envisioned as he imagined this turn from reaction to moderate reform can only be surmised. Judging from what echoed decades later in his recollections of the tsar, his relationship with Alexander was that of a protégé to a mentor, who promoted career, whetted personal ambition, and instilled genuine loyalty, perhaps even filial love. That Witte thus sought to burnish Alexander's historical reputation can be explained as an obligation repaid. Making Alexander a moderate also allowed Witte to disassociate himself from political reaction. It hardly seems coincidence that Witte dated Alexander's pivot toward reform to the early 1890s, by which time the provincial railwayman had utilized the protection of his most powerful patron to achieve appointment to high office in the bureaucracy of the imperial state, and begin to dominate it as few had done before him. Finally, any commentary Witte offered after the fact about Alexander inevitably also entailed the even more complex relationship he maintained with his son, Nicholas II, and that second, much longer reign that led Russia into a twentieth century marked by military defeat, political turmoil, and eventually the son's rejection of his father's most influential counselor. It is impossible to read the aged memoirist in 1911–12 and escape the impression that he preferred to muse about a distant past that had existed before all of this.

Was there something more to the elder man's musings about a tsar whom so many of his contemporaries assailed? Might there have been resonating in these reminiscences what once had been, in the 1880s, compelling dreams? That Europeans dreamed in the last decades of the nineteenth century goes without saying. They explored dreams to understand personality, identity, disease, and human imagination itself. In an age when, historians agree, new forms of imperialism and colonialism extended European cultural, economic, and political hegemony around the globe, citizens and subjects not surprisingly also dreamt about empire. Accustomed as we are in our own, postcolonial era to analyze the nightmares empire imposed upon the colonized, we also are reminded that empire could, and did, create identities, cultures, and entire civilizations.[11] It expanded the truth of science or religious faith, generated personal fortune, underpinned national economic wealth, and secured communal well-being. Indeed, at the end of a century in which, historians often tell us, the nation was the focus of political thinking, empire dominated the imagination, whether in Disraeli's Britain, McKinley's America, Bismarck's Germany, de Lesseps's France, or Conrad's Poland. Not surprisingly, Sergei Witte, the scion of an archly imperial family, was dreaming, repeatedly by the 1880s, about empire.

Three recurring and interconnected dreams of empire shaped his thinking during this decade. All imagined a Russian imperial polity: enriched by industrial modernity; ruled by a Russian monarchical sovereign made legitimate by the social and economic well-being thus created for all imperial subjects; and rendered powerful by its vast natural resources and territorial expanses. First, as his experience in Kiev would reveal, Witte envisioned a Russian imperial polity that industrial modernity was enriching and strengthening. Key to that vision was his experience of the railroad, a transportation and communications technology that could overcome the impediments to economic growth that space and time historically had created within the vast expanses of the Russian Empire. Second, as his devotion to the memory of Alexander III suggested, and his lifetime repeatedly had demonstrated, Witte could envision the Russian monarchy as a legitimate political authority within the empire. The colonial boy raised amidst the rituals of monarchical rule perhaps not surprisingly became the adult monarchist, whose wellsprings of emotional loyalty to a ruler shaped—certainly many might say distorted—his understanding of the legitimacy of Russian autocratic rule in the empire. By the 1880s, however, Witte's professional experience was deeply influencing these personal dispositions, as the railroad allowed him to imagine levels of economic and social well-being of such scale that they could become the foundation of political allegiance and subjecthood (*poddanstvo*) for the disparate communities subject to the Russian imperial crown.

Finally, Witte did not simply imagine a vast Russian empire, rich in territory, natural resources, and future potential. As had several generations of his family before him, he traveled through it. Yet, unlike grandparents who spent grueling weeks conveyed in carriages across notoriously inadequate roads, the railwayman swept in steamboats and railroads across much vaster, continental distances, where expanse ceased to be an impediment and became instead an alluring harbinger of future power and modernity. Not only his memoirs, but also other public and private records, contain descriptions and schedules of travel. Correspondence with his second wife, Mathil'da Ivanovna Nurok-Witte, dating from the first years of the twentieth century, displayed a near fetish for railroad timetables, routes of travel, and speed of transit, both within Russia, and to and from Europe.[12] In June 1894, he had journeyed to the Russian Far North, at the behest of Tsar Alexander III, to inspect sites for a warm water naval port. His travelogue-like report subsequently detailed a geopolitical fascination for the strategic location of ports, the ethnographic diversity of populations, and the sheer expanse of the land and its resources.[13] Travel itineraries in the records of the Finance Ministry reveal a professional career in which the imperial official—much as Witte's grandfather had done on horseback—traveled through the territories he was charged to administer.[14]

The earliest such extant itinerary detailed a trip that Witte undertook to Central Asia, from late August to early October 1889, shortly after his appointment to the Ministry of Finances, when he accompanied his mentor and now superior, the minister Ivan Vyshnegradsky, to inspect lands abutting the recently constructed Transcaspian Railroad. Still at times traveling by carriage and horse, Witte moved much more rapidly by river steamer and rail from St Petersburg, down the Volga, across the Caucasus and the Caspian Sea to travel through what the formal itinerary called 'our central Asian possessions'. With scrupulous attention to distance and time traveled, this document conveyed the expanses that were opening before an entire generation. The traveler could, as Witte did in 1889, use the three trains and thirty hours required to cover the 1,000 kilometers from the capital Moscow to Nizhnii Novgorod on the upper Volga, embark upon a fifteen-hour steamship voyage across the Caspian Sea, or travel the nearly

2,000 kilometers of the Transcaspian express railroad, which via Samarkand, Tashkent, and Kokand, carried him to the central Asian termini of medieval Europe's Great Silk Road.[15]

Travelers, however, were not necessarily imperial dreamers, even if they experienced the expanses of time and space that international rail, steam, and telegraph were compressing. In Witte's case, however, we have access to two texts that he wrote during the 1880s, which, if readers too will use imagination, can be read as objective records of these dreams. During his tenure as an executive officer of the Southwestern Railroad, a network that speeded communication, commerce, and travel throughout and beyond Ukraine, Witte had become, as we have seen, an increasingly prominent public commentator on the operation of the expanding railway system of the empire, and made his voice heard on topics that ranged from the commercial and corporate to the economic and geopolitical. In a series of articles he first wrote in 1883 in a reputable technical journal, *Engineer [Inzhener]*, and then reissued a year later as a book, *The Principles of Railroad Tariffs for the Transporting of Freight*, Witte joined ongoing public debates about the role of railroads in fostering commerce, business, and economic development in the key agricultural and urban markets served by the Southwestern. A treatise which proclaimed itself to be a study of prices devoted notable attention to both the imperial economy and the international economic order of which, he believed, it was a constituent element.[16]

Some five years later, in 1887–88, as he moved from business to ministerial office in St Petersburg, he would write a second economic treatise, entitled *National Economy and Friedrich List (Natsional'naia Ekonomiia i Fridrikh List)*, an annotated and heavily excerpted summary of a prominent mid nineteenth-century text written by the German political economist Friedrich List. Historians typically have classified List as an economic nationalist, whose arguments for protectionist tariffs in Germany linked industrial modernity and political power together as the motors necessary to overcome the global power early industrialization had created for Great Britain. Certainly, through the lens afforded by Witte's reading of it, List's writing also examined the creation of the North German Tariff Union, the *Zollverein*, a free-trade zone that brought all independent north German states into the economic orbit of autocratic Prussia in the 1840s. He assessed the political, economic, and, without so naming it, cultural bonds of unity that created polity.[17] Together with what he wrote in *Principles*, Witte elucidated his vision of the late nineteenth-century imperial economy, the place of technology within it, and the imperial polity both could solidify. What he saw was a Eurasian empire that filled a geographical nation-space from northeastern Europe to the northern Pacific. What follows is Witte's understanding of that world, of 'the reality surrounding us', as he experienced it in both his public and much less frequently glimpsed private lives. Scholars might consider this a hermeneutic; others will find the constituent elements of Witte's imperial dreams.

'The Reality That Surrounds Us':[18] Imperial Economy and Polity

Witte was a synthetic thinker and a pragmatist. Having celebrated his thirtieth birthday in 1879, he was still far removed from the corridors of ministerial power and the grand conceptual vistas of economic and political change that marked his later career. His *Principles of Railroad Tariffs* was a technical study of railroad freight rates. Its methodology reflected his training in mathematics and a pattern of inductive thinking that proceeded from facts to generalized hypothesis. The text modeled what its author repeatedly labeled 'scientific data', drawn primarily from the records and managerial practice of the Southwestern, and proposed a schedule of shipping rates that would apply to all railroads operating in the empire (*preiskuranty*). At a time when price-cutting wars were wracking both the Russian railroad industry and the imperial treasury, *Principles* offered a hypothetical solution to declining company profits, growing industry-wide deficits, and increasing treasury subsidies to guarantee the dividends of imperial railroad bonds.[19] His proposed innovation required the purview of a supervising bureaucratic agency and a pragmatic innovator to oversee it. That individual was Witte, who in this tract effectively described the directorship of a Department of Railroad Affairs in the Ministry of Finances, the newly created job that Ivan Vyshnegradskii would offer his protégé in 1888.[20] A half-decade earlier, however, rather than careerist motives, much more apparent in this writing was a pronounced intellectual penchant for synthesis, reinforced by a pragmatism he already had displayed in his managerial work on the railroad. In an introduction to a second edition of the book written in 1883, Witte insisted that his text went far beyond the technical issue of pricing. He sought instead to examine 'the interplay of elements that are parts of the economic, political, and even intellectual life of the people'. This 'locus (*igra vlianiia*)', Witte opined in embracing both roles, was 'a worthy subject of study for the thinker (*myslitel'*) and the economist'.[21] The pragmatic man of action offered his vision of the imperial economy and the polity it was creating.

At the foundation of his understanding was the commercial network of roads, rivers, sea lanes, and railroads which circulated goods and people throughout the empire. Refuting critics who charged railroads were monopolies, for example, Witte displayed his detailed knowledge of competing road and water transportation networks 'along which in the course of centuries enormous commercial interchange has been taking place'. Even at present, Witte noted, 'the mass of the poor population in Russia travels not only by horse, but simply on foot, even for great distances, parallel to the railroads . . .', while the teamster (*podvodchik*), hauling goods on local highways and roads, practiced a craft as profitable today for whole sections of the population as it had been in the past.[22] Water transport, a critical and traditional pathway for Russian trade, posed an even greater challenge to railroads, he continued. Passenger traffic on steamship lines, for example on the Volga River, Black Sea, and Dnieper River, was growing rapidly, assisted by the development of rail lines that expanded access to these traditional commercial conduits. He also noted the even larger regional commercial networks to which these lines connected, commercial sea lanes which united disparate regions of the European 'peninsula' and bore its trade with the more distant markets of the eastern Mediterranean, the Pacific, and the Far East. He was aware that a 'mass of products . . . moves among countries of the European continent and even among points within the same country by sea', and knew as well, from his Odessa experience, that 'rail transport makes possible access to a seaport or the movement of freight from a seaport into a country's interior'. On the Southwestern, Witte noted, Ukrainian grain both transited overland toward Berlin and from the interior to Odessa, from which it was conveyed by sea to both the Mediterranean and Atlantic ports of western and central Europe. He knew well 'the low prices of towage on the interior rivers and canals' of the country, especially for raw materials like lumber, salt, fuel, and grain, as well as the development of commercial wholesale enterprises, which warehoused cheaply transported goods and supplied them to markets during the long winter months.[23]

Critical to the act of experiencing and imagining the political and economic space of empire was the technology of the railroad. It was new, even for the industrial age, or so at least Witte intimated. He wondered whether the railroad as an industry might one day preempt the primacy of agriculture, whose produce satisfied a basic human necessity, or manufacturing, which created material 'products' that railroads only served 'to move ... from one place to another'. He certainly recognized the technological power that the railroad created. Not even the formalistic language of his treatise could conceal the enchantment of a system whose 'only purpose ... (was) to eliminate the limitations of distance (*pregrad razstoianii*) and, in this manner, supply the opportunity for identical products to be competitive on many markets'. Sounding the entrepreneurial tone that often inflected this text, Witte allowed that the railroad was quickening market development in regions it traversed, encouraging with lower prices for long-distance freight shipments of grain and other commodities, both business volume and company profits. Railroads operating in this manner, he exclaimed, 'had increased the transport of goods to levels about which previously they had not dreamed'. Statistics from the Southwestern Railroad emphasized the point. Almost 70 per cent of the 2,100 million kilograms (130 million *puds*) of freight transported in 1881 had been shipped at low rates set to encourage long-distance commerce.[24] Business practices such as these gave some sense of the imperial economy that Witte was envisioning as the railroad moved him, figuratively and literally, through Russian imperial space.

Despite its ponderous title, *Principles of Railroad Freight Rates* exuded the optimism of the proto-technocrat. A still young railroad executive, Witte deemed himself to be the standard-bearer of a new commercial-industrial culture, confident he could comprehend the forces propelling Russia toward the modern. To call him a technocrat would be to implant in the 1880s a cultural typology that was only emerging in the late nineteenth century. That he already sensed the technocratic power that technology and scientifically based technical knowledge could bring the administrator, however, seems a plausible claim. Here was one source of the confidence that girded both his professional life and his views of Russia's future. Unquestioned was the capacity of that administrator to establish prices on an empire-wide basis and thereby control a rail system where 'thousands of commodities of varied type' were transported among 'thousands of stations' at prices that could fluctuate, sometimes daily. Keenly appreciated was the perception of the imperial economic space that railroads girded, as they in turn encouraged commercial exchange, 'systematize(d) business practice (*vedenie khoziastva*), and, by means of offering the selling price to a greater number of consumers, energize(d) demand (*sluzhat' k vozbuzhdeniiu energii sprosa*) and consequently enlarge(d) consumption'.[25] Ultimately envisioned was what many subjects of the Russian empire did not yet understand about railroads, but soon, especially after they were 'extended into all the border-lands . . . (would) stare them in the face'. Because the railroad could over-come distance, its technological impact on the imperial economy, he believed, could be immense. In the West, he wrote, such considerations were less important simply because these countries were small in territorial size. England only occupied 3 per cent of Europe's land mass, Germany 5.5 per cent, but 'in Russia the European part alone . . . represents 55 per cent of Europe's expanse. To impart the proper economic growth to our father-land', he continued, required what in effect was an imperial economic zone 'throughout the broad expanse of our Empire'. Local goods and regional markets needed to be superseded by spaces in which 'every producer has the broadest possible market (*raion rasprostraneniia*) for his products, because the interests of consumers are advanced considerably through such an expansion of supply'. He envisioned an imperial rail network intensifying commercial and economic exchange and energizing economic life 'in the future in an area of over 18 million square versts, that of European Russian and Siberia together with the central asian (sic) possessions'.[26]

Underlying this proto-technocratic vision of an imperial economy was a basic assumption. That economy was creating a modern polity, and Witte's writing explored this conjuncture of political economy at some length.[27] In the process he exhibited a familiarity with the intellectual discourses of his era and, more pointedly, added his voice to debates, which coursed through Russian public life in the 1880s and 1890s, about the desirability and con-sequences of such development for Russia's future. Much has been made of Witte's Slavophil sympathies, which inclined him to idealize the inherent communalism of the Great Russian peasant and suspect the urban proletari-an anomie and disorder of industrializing Europe. Certainly his views of that future were evolving and, as such, at times confused and conflicted, but they always presumed that capitalism was a civilizing, integrative force in the modern world.[28] Hence, Witte's unease with what he deemed the overly crude, materialist, and utilitarian calculus of classical laissez-faire theorists, who could reduce all human intercourse to economic relationships that rested on a struggle for existence between self-interested buyers and sellers. Somewhere within him resided religious sensibilities strong enough to deride the social Darwinism of those 'disillusioned pessimists' who could deem human beings made in 'the image and likeness of God' to be mere 'rational beasts (*razumnyi zver'*)' governed by 'brute egoism (*zhivotnyi egoizm*)'. He could explain that such unrestrained self-interest only dominated in those societies at 'lower levels of social existence', and insist that it was receding in a modern industrial civilization developing its unlimited potential to expand production, consumption, and demand.

Grown more complex and interrelated with 'the evolution of a spirit of organicity (*dukh organichnosti*), the establishment of . . . credit, the diversification of occupations, and generally the spread of enlightenment and knowledge that serves as the fundamental source of all capital', such societies were moving gradually from a situation in which market economics was governed by 'a law of struggle,' toward what Witte viewed as a more civilized stage of 'mutual dependency (*menovaia zavisimost'*)' and 'mutual advantage (*vzaimnost'udovletvoreniia zhelanii*)' created by modern capitalist economies. When entering into a transaction, he illustrated, both buyer and seller sought minimal financial loss: the former desired to purchase at the lowest price, and the latter sought the highest possible profit. '(E)ach of them can satisfy their desire only by satisfying the corresponding desire of the other,' he insisted. Commercial-industrial society thus rested on the mutual interest of exchange. Rather than a Darwinian universe dominated by the strong, Witte, entranced by the apparently inevitable progress of the age and knowing Rousseau's social contract, envisioned a magical 'ideal where it is natural that the well-being of each would depend upon the well-being of all others'. But '(h)ow', he asked, 'is one to achieve this ideal?'[29]

The question was rhetorical. Witte knew that the reality of the late nineteenth-century imperial polity differed from this idealized vision of political and economic modernity in two fundamental ways. First, it ignored the glaring socio-economic inequality of industrializing Europe. Second, it accepted the fundamental principle of laissez-faire economics and relegated to the marketplace the regulatory control of such conflict that in a continental society like imperial Russia's traditionally had belonged to the bureaucratic state. Since Adam Smith, he instructed, classical economists had argued for 'the total elimination of active state involvement in the national economy' because markets were themselves 'fully capable of achieving the best economic order'. Propagandized especially by English free traders, this precept 'had been axiomatic for statesmen in the first half of this century', and remained influential, especially in Russia. Yet, Witte cautioned, that principled stance was becoming an increasingly dubious proposition as industrial progress spawned public disorder, poverty, and class hostility. '(E)ntire classes of proletarian-workers living from day to day exclusively by their physical labor', he wrote in a passage that mixed slavophile and socialist undertones, were the inevitable result of 'the development of machine production', which had lowered wages, lengthened work days, and produced such 'dissatisfaction with the existing economic status quo' that not only 'local unrest' but a socialist 'internationalist movement' was exerting an ever more powerful influence upon European public life.[30]

Paralleling this explosion of protest was the emergence of 'an economic literature imbued with sympathy for the interests of labor'. In affording a glimpse at his reading habits, he admitted how this work 'was exerting an ever greater influence on public thinking (na umy).' Two 'new economic schools'—'realist' and 'socialist'—since mid century had addressed this most glaring contradiction of classical economics: the contrast between the actual 'economic inequality existing in today's social structure (*ekonomicheskoe neravenstvo sushchestvuiushchee pri nastoiashchem stroe obshchezhitiia*)' and 'the ideal of justice' that classical theory promised free markets would deliver. Moreover, both schools accorded the state a greatly expanded role in resolving this core dilemma of imperial economic and political life.[31] Both thus offered Witte, whose assumptions about the centrality of the Russian imperial state in contemporary life were axiomatic, propitious grounds to imagine a modern Russian imperial polity. Many of his contemporaries, and historians after them, of course, saw a very different reality—autocratic despotism, agrarian backwardness, and gross socio-economic inequality. Witte was not willfully suspending disbelief, but his more progressive and optimistic views were instructive.

What Witte called the realist school proved especially alluring to him. In fact, a group of German scholars known as academic socialists, the *Katheder-Socialisten* developed, in active counterpoint to classical laissez-faire theory, a methodology called 'historical economics'. It framed geography, and the human experience particular physical environments created, as the primary factors explaining how and why the universal laws of classical economics in practice operated differently depending upon the national-geographical context to which they were applied.[32] Emerging amidst the statist nationalism of Bismarck's new German Empire, academic socialists assumed that the nation was the civic polity, and the state an instrument guaranteeing, and perhaps even creating, its existence. In this view, however, both nation and state were grounded within and shaped by the peculiarities of geographical spaces and the welter of cultural, institutional, and ethnonational factors that a particular geographical environment was deemed to have created. Thus, what Witte called economic realism or 'rational opportunism (*razumnyi opportunizm*)' allowed him both to escape the intellectual universality of classical political economy, and to embrace instead the particularities of human societies that differed depending upon 'time, place, and the presence of other concrete circumstances'.[33]

Rather than Britain, Germany appealed as a template that had melded industrial modernity and an absolutist bureaucratic political tradition to create a powerful imperial polity. Quoting approvingly and at length from a Reichstag speech given in 1872 by a leading German historical economist, Gustav Schmoller, Witte emphasized for his readers the 'brilliant, unprecedented successes . . . in technology and production, in commerce and the development of communication', that had occurred in recent decades in Germany. The state had played a central role in developing this national brilliance and wealth, but so too did it regulate the consequences of free market capitalism: 'deep social ulcers, growing inequality of income and property, a tendency toward dishonesty in industrial affairs, insufficient solidarity among different classes of the commercial world, (and) the crudeness and uncontrollable character that grows as a result of all this in a certain section of the lower classes.'[34] In Germany, a centralized, bureaucratic, and autocratic state had been necessary to facilitate and guide the emergence of industrial modernity.

Such views undoubtedly comforted a Russian of Witte's background, imbued as he was in the statist traditions of the service nobility. Yet, Witte was too much the railwayman to embrace unquestioningly the routinized control of a bureaucratic state, which, as his own administrative and business experience certainly suggested, all too often only obstructed innovation, especially in economic life. Perhaps 'Prussian officialdom . . . had shown itself able to regulate the impact of the law of supply and demand in a way that gives better results than (does market) freedom in economic life,' Witte admitted rhetorically, but, for other countries—the Ottoman straw man was always available to stand in Russia's place—'for example, Turkey, which does not have such officials, it is understandable that all the wonderful desires expressed by Schmoller not only may remain in the realm of dreams, but (may result in) a Turkish officialdom, which, desiring to regulate free displays of economic life, can entirely obstruct its movement'.[35] It could hardly be forgotten, he wrote, 'that government is not an abstract entity, but consists of people who move from one position to another, have their own cravings and personal proclivities, or that, if the instruments to effect and implement (state designs) deep in the social organism are lacking or corrupted, the most beneficent desires of the supreme government, as we see at every turn, not only remain inconsequential but often produce results directly opposite those intended'.[36] Witte then could not have known how often in the years ahead he would have opportunity to ponder those ideas.

He was considering the consequences of unconstrained state power as he wrote in the 1880s, however. Displaying his familiarity with 'scientific socialism', and what he deemed to be its commitment to displace the laws of the market with 'state and legal compulsion', Witte uncharacteristically in this text wrote without references to any literature to explore 'the scheme of society recommended by this school'. Most likely drawing upon a familiarity with Russian radical populism and European republican radicalism, he detailed its envisioned 'federation of communes', 'collective ownership of the means of production', 'social organization of labor', distribution of goods according to 'the material labor of each producer', and displacement of commerce by 'a central bureau' overseeing domestic and foreign exchange. On the central issue of market-driven price, he turned to the German text of *Das Kapital* and Marx's labor theory of value, taking seriously its contention that the prices of goods could be calculated based on the amount of 'socially necessary work required for their creation'.[37] Engaging what he took as the root of socialist political economy, Witte disagreed fundamentally with ideas whose implementation, he believed, would necessitate an unimaginable expansion of state power. In his view, socialists were logically consistent in their thinking. Bent on the creation of a new collective social order, '(t)hey understand that this law (of supply and demand) is a consequence of the contemporary structure of society, which, presupposing significant freedom in its use, is based on private property, and thus (they) theoretically seize on the cause and not the consequence'. Their call to eliminate property altogether, however, would necessitate that the state proscribe human nature itself, Witte rejoined, an impossibility 'as long as the idea continued to exist in humanity that the division into "mine and thine", and consequently the formal laws which it creates, was a just one'.

If a state were to make the attempt, thus going far beyond any other effort to regulate the law of supply and demand, it would necessarily have to undertake 'the forceful elimination of the idea in society' and, in effect, allow 'its own self-destruction, if we understand,' Witte concluded as he indicated that for him the state was coterminous with a propertied society, 'the word state in its contemporary, realistic, and not socialistic context'.[38]

What role, then, could a state legitimately assume in the polity? Setting about to determine the answer, Witte examined historical examples of what he considered legitimate state intervention in economic life, among them most notably the Russian abolition of serfdom, but dwelled at length on the 'state socialism' of the German chancellor, Otto von Bismarck, whose career we know Witte had followed at least since the time of the Franco-Prussian War. In both Bismarck's dominating statesmanship and his willingness to use the state as an instrument in economic life, Witte found much that appealed. There was no mistaking the admiration, if not adulation that overcame him when he looked to the great practitioner of continental *Realpolitik*—whether a desire to imitate filled Witte's heart as well is a question that will never be entirely resolved, although his life is littered with subsequent examples of his affection for all things Bismarckian and Germanic. In the realpolitik of Bismarck certainly Witte found a masculine self-image that he treasured. 'Mankind', he exclaimed, 'believes much more in results than opinions. Prince Bismarck, who has done so much and achieved such success, stands beyond the criticism of this generation,' Witte insisted. What he viewed as Bismarck's greatest accomplishment was less the political unification of the Germanies. Instead, he was intrigued by the engagement of the German imperial state in all phases of German civic life, especially the social welfare legislation it implemented to combat the excesses of modern industrialism, and counter the appeal of a socialist ideology deeply rooted in German universities, popular press, and electoral politics. Witte called this welfare state a 'social monarchy (*monarkhiia sotsial'naia*)', a reference he took from German economists who maintained that Bismarck was striving to adapt a monarchical tradition of paternal care to modern life by returning the Crown to its ancient foundations and assuming responsibility for, 'in both theory and practice, the defense of the rights of the weak and the protection (*pokrovitel'stvo*) of the unfortunate'. Bismarckian policy rested on a simple assumption, Witte wrote: 'he recognizes the necessity of enhancing the state's intervention in the economic life of the country'. The practical example that Witte had sought, Bismarck was to be 'numbered among the representatives of the realist school'. As did they, Bismarck too configured national difference, a nearly ethereal category that allowed him, or so at least Witte surmised, to counter a laissez-faire market economics with a national economics that accounted for 'the presence in Germany of political, social and economic conditions' unique to it alone.[39]

Germany, for Witte, was an ideal, a geopolitical polity, both national and imperial in scope, reflected in history itself. Bismarck's statecraft guided a modern, nineteenth-century German Empire, but it had grown from a centuries-long experience in which national character emerged organically from geopolitical space. The 'economy and thrift' demanded to survive in the sandy soils of the north-eastern German Duchy of Brandenburg, the Prussian heartland of the German Empire, were 'qualities seemingly bequeathed to its posterity', Witte explained. 'Such historical, hereditary leavening of the character of the nation (*istoricheskaia preemstvennaia zakvaska kharaktera natsii*) is not an exceptional phenomenon,' he added, pointing to the 'ingenuity' Americans had inherited from their country's foundations or 'the spiritual unity' Russians had taken from Orthodox Christianity. Economy and thrift alone, however, would not have assured the 'grand historical future of the country'. Ever the monarchist, Witte romanticized royal history and proclaimed historical greatness to be the domain of 'destiny (*sud'ba*)', which sent Prussia Frederick the Great. He 'took economy and thrift to extremes' and used the state to build the economic and cultural foundations upon which 'the nation could develop, not perishing from hunger'. Advancing as a first principle of his statecraft 'the total subordination of the individual to the well-being of the state,' Frederick, Witte noted approvingly, 'converted the Prussian state into a political machine, which took the human being in hand from childhood, at first by means of the school, later by means of the army, and finally by means of the regulation of economic and social life through constant state intervention.' Nevertheless, he instructed, the machine 'had not been powerful enough' to prevent the evolution within society of that 'dangerous enemy of Germany—socialism. Hunger', he wrote, 'had proven more powerful than the machine intended to hold each citizen in its hands.' Thus, he concluded, historical circumstances shaped by national differences justified the abandonment in Germany of laissez-faire economic principles and their replacement by realist Bismarckian policies that aimed 'to increase the machine's strength by deepening the intervention of the state in the country's economic life'.[40]

Witte fully embraced these foundations of what routinely would come to be known as the welfare state.

That his thoughts consistently had returned to Russia as he explored German history is indisputable. He now took up the comparison explicitly. Laissez-faire theory, which had dominated government policy for the last half-century, 'significantly had developed the wealth of Russia' and generated 'enormous successes in production, technology, commerce, communications, and the like', he began. Yet, Russian public and government opinion was now shifting against this dominant trend, 'demanding that the principles of free-trade economics be brought into accord with the concrete conditions in which our fatherland finds itself'. That reference, some biographers have argued, hinted at Witte's alignment with conservative critics grouped around the arch-conservative Procurator of the Holy Synod, Konstantine Pobedonostsev, the nationalist conservative publisher Mikhail Katkov, and the aristocratic court confidant Prince Vladimir Meshchersky.[41] He certainly was aware of, and sympathetic to, a steady drumbeat of criticism of classical economics, but he also recognized that these same critics were prone to embrace alternative models with just as much enthusiasm and abstraction. Many found it fashionable to mimic Bismarck, he remarked, but 'they forget that the great chancellor of Germany would speak and act somewhat, perhaps entirely differently . . . were he the state pilot of Russia.' Having conjured up a Russian Bismarck, Witte assumed his identity, and surveyed the circumstances that the physical and historical environment of the Russian empire might dictate to such an individual. 'What underlay the policies of Prince Bismarck?' he queried.[42]

He turned again to the challenge posed to Germany, and Russia, by socialism, and linked its rise in Germany and its prevention in Russia to religious faith. Much as Max Weber in the early twentieth century linked capitalism and Protestantism, Witte in the 1880s linked German socialism to a religion that historically had inculcated the values of intellectual criticism, individualism, and a singular profession of faith by the individual believer. By the nineteenth century, the resulting secular culture naturally had produced radical socialism, he argued, with its 'artful criticisms of economic laws . . . the artificial creations of collective property and public labor . . . new forms of association . . . (and) the political propagandization of the words of the Gospels and Holy Fathers to attract new followers into political societies.' The Russian Bismarck instead would find 'orthodoxy, based on unconditional faith, orthodoxy—which is creating the Russian Empire'. Given the community of believers that existed together within the church and that community's connection to the divine, orthodoxy was 'our own socialism, based on our faith'. Because he believed Orthodox Christianity capable of achieving 'the inner perfection (*vnutrennoe usovershenstvovanie*) preached by the teaching of Christ', Witte saw his religion able to assure 'the moral renewal of the individual' and 'serve as the source of all progress'. Orthodox Christianity could reduce impoverishment because 'the teaching of Christ preaches to us love for the destitute and the higher ideal of social justice (*vyshee chuvstvo obshchestvennoi spravedlivosti*)'. It could 'inspire the upper classes to provide examples to the people of simplicity in life, diligence in labor, and fairness in one's affairs'. It could close the gap between rich and poor, because it alone, he insisted, 'can inspire the upper classes to work for the improvement of the majority ... (and) summon individuals who earn profit to use their surpluses not in the search for pleasure, not in the satisfaction of their desires, but for the benefit of humans like themselves'. It could instill in the common people 'a spirit of self-sacrifice, obedience and good conduct. It condemns drunkenness and profligacy, and reinforces a tendency toward obtaining property by hard work and thrift.'[43]

That the upper classes *might* act in this fashion, or the mass population *could* behave differently, of course, did suggest his underlying uncertainty about whether Orthodoxy could remain constituent in a culture displaying every one of the fault lines that Witte claimed religion still cemented. His critics might object, Witte noted rhetorically, that Orthodox faith was neither 'moderating the harsh manifestations of economic laws' nor obstructing the allure of socialism. Such criticism was inevitable, however, because much contemporary opinion in the West, inflected as it was by materialism or public indifference, dismissed the social utility of religious faith. They 'do not see anything other than brute egoism in economic relationships among people', and thus failed to understand that, while 'egoism played a quite important role' in economic life, it was moderated 'in cultured societies by ethical morality (*moral'*)'. Orthodoxy remained a vital integrative force in contemporary life, he maintained, because, unlike Roman Catholicism, it did 'not inhibit the civic development of society', and, unlike 'the Protestant quest for faith, which resembles a search for physical certainty ...', Orthodoxy 'rested upon the union of believers who are united in the Church, and not upon a lone faith outside the Church, as in Protestantism'. He acknowledged that, especially 'in classes cut off from the people'—such as his own, he implied strongly—the power of faith and the community of belief had become 'an abstract concept, almost incomprehensible in practical life'. A Russian Bismarck, he concluded, would 'concern himself first of all to regenerate a vital and active Church, which would imbue all popular life with the spirit of love and freedom, rather than compulsion, and open itself, in turn, to the influence of secular society'.[44]

If a Russian Bismarck would find configurations of religiosity different than those in the West, he would also encounter an entirely different physical environment in the empire as well. Here too Witte reflected an uncertainty about the influence of this factor upon policies of state. Unlike the purported poor soil and scarce arable of Germany, which had caused poverty and thus discontent, Russia possessed 'beautiful land', adequate enough to support the population 'for many, many generations'.[45] The problem was not a shortage of land, but its unequal regional distribution, so that in one area 'hundreds of thousands of hectares of fertile land went unworked', while in another, equally fertile locale, 'the population crowded together, materially deprived and sometimes starving'. Population density per square kilometer varied significantly across Europe, from 178 people/sq. km. in Belgium to 36/sg. km. in Turkey. In European Russia this figure was 14/sq.km, he noted, but those figures varied wildly elsewhere in the empire: 10.6 in the Caucasus; 1.06 in Central Asia; 0.27 in Siberia. When he asked how a 'Russian Bismarck' would use the state to address this problem, he envisioned a distribution of population 'to the degree possible equally among the enormous, fertile lands of the Russian Empire', facilitated by government policies that supplied new settlers with property, either unowned or 'made free' from lands owned by the state. The most effective precautionary means against the expansion of 'radical (*voinstvuiushchii*) socialism', he insisted, 'was the expansion of property. When property becomes the privilege of the minority, plundering it usually becomes the dream of the majority. The more democratic (*demokraticheskii*) the property structure of a country, the less will radical socialism expand there,' he concluded.[46]

Finally, Witte returned to Bismarck's imperial state and the bureaucracy that represented it—and nowhere else was his uncertainty about this comparison between Germany and Russia more pronounced. He reiterated a view that was becoming, for him, foundational: 'State authority (*vlast'*) is a force (*sila*) which usually contains in itself the highest ideals of justice, and thus, in many instances, the action of this force can produce quite beneficial consequences.' As with any force of nature, however, be it wind, water, or the warmth of the sun, the key issue became the quality of 'the transformer (*peredatochnyi mekhanizm*)' that converted force into action. The officialdom that represented and implemented the state's policies thus was his crucial concern. None was more idealized than the purportedly efficient, prudent, and disciplined bureaucracy of the German imperial state. However inaccurate in actuality such a characterization might have been, it was nevertheless widespread, and Witte shared the view of a German national character both efficient and rational. A historical result of the German quest for the philosophical 'spirit of criticism', and the relatively small extent of its physical territory, the German ideal provided Witte a template to assess its Russian equivalent. However beneficial its influence upon society and culture—and here too Witte expressed his doubts, Orthodox Christianity's 'spirit of faith, spirit of selflessness, spirit of self-development and humility' appeared to have had little effect on Russian officialdom. 'Those people who think that good will, regardless of historical conditions, is sufficient to create a state organization similar to the German one are badly mistaken,' he noted acidly. Worse, the German 'state machine (*gosudarstvennaia mashina*) . . . converted the force of (central) authority)' over an area of some half-million square kilometers and 43 million people, while Russian officialdom 'had to serve as a conductor of that same force over an area of 21,000,000 sq. km. and act upon 90 million residents'. Railroads might have condensed space and time across the empire's vast space, but the idea of Russian officialdom administering it served as a constraining brake upon a vision of a state capable of regulating, accelerating, and, perhaps most of all, transforming the economy and polity of the Russian Empire.[47]

When Witte published this text in 1883, and its speculative imagining of a Russian Bismarck wielding the instruments through which the state could shape political economy, he was an acknowledged expert and railroad professional, dreaming about state power. Four years later, in January 1887, the appointment as Minister of Finances of his patron and superior Ivan Vyshnegradskii was creating the opportunity that would lead him within a year to join the very officialdom whose capacities he had doubted. While he understood the precepts of classical political economy, beginning with the works of 'Adam Smith and his followers', Witte fixed his own views, he wrote in 1883, firmly in 'the realist school' and its 'principle' that the laws of the market 'were to be altered for each nationality (*natsional'-nost'*), according to its individual peculiarities'. He maintained that ideas already influential in Germany, where theorists spoke, not of classical, but 'national economy', had to become widespread in the Russian Empire as well. In 1887, as he considered moving to St Petersburg, Witte returned to the idea of a political economy shaped by national differences. He published a pamphlet entitled *National Economy and Friedrich List*, an annotated and wildly abridged version of the latter's *The National System of Political Economy*, which the German-born List (1796–1846) had published in 1841. List's critique of classical political economy, frequently labeled economic nationalism, accepted the classical school's emphasis on markets but argued that its key actor was not the hypothetical individual buying or selling, but the nation states that were the constituent elements of the international economic order to which all polities belonged. Inscribed with the epigram 'Et la patrie et l'humanite! (Both country and humanity!)', List's work insisted that an international economic order in which all individuals and nations shared equally in the prosperity of the modern world was an unrealized and still distant dream of classical economics, which only abetted British commercial hegemony and precluded other European polities from following the path of economic and political development blazed first by Great Britain.[48]

List, and Witte, or possibly a ghost-writer under his dictation, cut and pasted selected passages of List's text to assemble this annotated brochure, which repudiated the theoretical individual found at the root of classical political economy. 'The single individual,' they wrote, 'alienated from others like himself, is weak and powerless.' Power was the result of association and, they insisted, 'the highest association of individuals which at present can be realized, is that of the state, the nation'.[49] That Witte stumbled when he spoke of the state and nation was not surprising. Not only did the term possess pejorative political connotations for a late nineteenth-century monarchist who well knew the challenge posed by the popular sovereignty of the nation to the legitimacy of tsarist authority. The nation also lacked ready analogs in an imperial polity where numerous ethnic and religious communities increasingly embraced distinct national identities, and even opinion-making Russians themselves found it difficult to identify the bonds of common identity unifying a member of an Europeanized elite and the but recently emancipated bulk of its uncivilized, one might even say colonized, peasant population.[50] Ever disdainful of the overtly nationalist politics that increasingly marked Russian state policies of russification at, and after, the turn of the century, Witte, when he thought of the nation, perceived an economic and cultural association that, while it naturally privileged Russian Orthodox Christians like himself, encompassed all imperial Russian subjects.

'The nation,' he entoned, '. . . (this) organic whole, bound by common faith, territory, blood, language, literature and popular creativity, morals and customs, state principles and institutions, the instinct of self-preservation, a striving for progress and independence, and so on. These entities are not the product of human fantasy or caprice, but have evolved historically from nature and the laws of society. They constitute a necessary condition of human development.'[51] 'The wealth of nations', he explained somewhat later in a way that only underlined how difficult the task of definition actually was, 'depends upon a mass of the most varied causes, of both a material and spiritual character. It depends upon national strength, geographical conditions, political and civil institutions, laws, religions, moral codes and so on', Witte broke off, only to resume, 'Christianity, the destruction of slavery, monogamy, the royal succession, printed matter, the press, the post, the currency, the establishment of a police guaranteeing the safety of citizens, and so on and so on'. That he could not exactly define the reality he found surrounding him in 1887 does not belittle, it perhaps even enhances the panoramic vision and dream of an imperial polity that Witte harbored. Economic modernity remained its key. 'Manufacturing, commerce, and commercial seafaring have a future which surpasses the present to the same degree as the present supersedes the past. It is sufficient', he wrote, 'to have the courage to believe in a vast national future and begin the trek with this hope.' Above all he saw the need for the state, 'a national rationality' that 'would plant and cultivate now the tree which will give enormous fruits to future generations'.

Such rhetoric was accompanied by a policy agenda that over the next decade would organize much of the work of the Ministry of Finances. Loudly advocating protectionist tariffs to supply price supports for Russian manufacturing, and a flow of revenue to the imperial treasury from the levies collected at ports of entry, Witte averred that '(f)irst of all the fatherland must conquer its own markets for itself.'[52] Attention was paid to the accumulation of investment capital, the importance of luring foreigners to invest directly in protected national markets, and the stabilization of the ruble currency by accumulating gold reserves and moving toward the gold standard. Following List, Witte agreed that, to become fully modern, Russia must escape its status as a 'purely agricultural' nation, subject to the imperial hegemony of more developed nations, and become instead one

a new

aims

based on manufacturing, commerce, and agriculture. '... (A) purely agricultural nation cannot develop fully its internal and foreign commerce, its
means of communication and commercial fleet; it cannot achieve significant
successes in intellectual, social, and political development; it cannot obtain
political significance commensurate with the position supplied it by nature;
it is in no condition to influence the civilization and progress of backwards
peoples and establish colonies,' Witte wrote, outlining as he did his vision of
the nascent imperial polity.

Russia, he knew, possessed or was in the process of acquiring everything
required to construct such polity: territory, varied material sources of
wealth, a population adequate to such territory, the idea of the 'moral and
material development of a nation and its political might', without which,
especially when the population lacked 'a common language', 'literature,
science, and the arts' could not develop. It required free access to the seas,
and a national fleet to project 'global political significance, influence peoples
of backward culture and have the means for stable and independent international commerce'. His historical realism, and the vestiges of his own
religious faith, led him to understand that 'the economic significance of a
nation resulted not only from these factors; it also depended on the religion
of a people, its moral foundations, its state idea and all its individual
peculiarities'. His hard-headed Victorian practicality, however, already
had convinced him what 'history shows', that achievement of the highest
stage was not possible without 'state assistance'. Only when a nation reached
the highest stage of development, when its 'national manufacturing and fleet
had so established themselves that foreign competition was no longer
dangerous', could it engage in 'free trade'. 'The civilization, political education and power of nations, depend chiefly on their economical condition', List wrote, and Witte approvingly transcribed, 'and reciprocally; the
more advanced their economy, the more civilized and powerful will be
the nation, the more rapidly will its civilization and power increase, and
the more will its economical culture be developed'.[53]

Witte, this quintessentially Victorian imperial Russian, had set his sights
high indeed. That his views assumed the superiority of ethnic Russian
culture over the myriad ethnic communities constituting the empire war-
rants mention, of course. Any number of individuals sharing Witte's frame
of reference could object vehemently to his assumptions, which so contradicted their own, even as the Pole, the Ukrainian, the Armenian, the
Muslim, the Jew, and the scores of other ethno-national communities

subject to the Romanov Crown might strive to repeat Witte's own sentiments, albeit expressed instead in their own ethnic sensibilities. Equally true
would be the observation that these years of his life reveal a man engaged in
an at times quixotic search for a language that bespoke community in the
autocratic empire, whether this required the precepts of religious belief or
the presumptions of Russian monarchism. That Witte could still dream in
the 1880s of an imperial society that was organic, rather than a political
collection of disassociated ethnic communities and proto-nations testified to
the power of a modern nationalism that, over the next four decades, would
create just such a reality and destroy the empire. It also testified to the power
of his dreams. Indeed, Witte was now coming to envision that the imperial
economy, the foundation of an imperial polity that the Romanov Crown
provided the vast empire, was the pathway toward a future that rested on
industrial prosperity and Russian (*rossiiskii*) civilization.

Public and Private Lives

As he dictated his memoirs in 1911–12, Witte devoted only passing attention to these visions of the Russian Empire's economic and political future.
Reminiscing about the decade of the 1880s, he devoted much more attention to his public life in Kiev and the webs of acquaintances and professional
associates he spun, contemporaries remarked, with consummate skill. Again
and again he turned his attention to gossip, often malicious, about the
individuals within these networks, such information itself a source of
influence and standing. Here too were glimpses of a family and private life
that he closely guarded from public view, yet repeatedly revisited as he
remembered his past.[54] At the end of his life a powerful statesman and
influential counselor of two Romanov emperors, Witte tended to be seen
by both contemporaries, and after them scholars, as the bureaucratic careerist and influence peddler whose meteoric rise from obscurity to international repute illuminated what for many was his own, self-aggrandizing pursuit
of personal power.[55] They tended not to see the Victorian man, 40 years of
age in 1889, who still lived on in the old statesman's memories. Who was
Sergei Witte, this Victorian-era, European gentleman with grand dreams
for himself and the Russian Empire?

Contact with its high society, reputation in its business community,
growing access to both the ministerial government and the imperial court

in St Petersburg, even his entanglement in the shadowy, aristocratic and counter-terrorist Holy Druzhina following Alexander II's assassination in 1881, all testified to his involvement in public life in these years. Writing an obituary in 1915, A. A. Spasskii noted that a veritable 'cult of Witte worship (kul't obozhaniia Vitte)' still lingered in Kiev among those who had worked under him or benefited from his influence.[56] Prince Vladimir Meshchersky remembered not this public persona, but instead Witte the man. Writing in 1912, Meshchersky recalled first meeting Witte in 1888, shortly after he had arrived in St Petersburg from Kiev.[57] Then, Meshchersky wrote, 'nobody could have foreseen that raging storm (buria)' that Witte would become in the public life of the empire over the ensuing decades. Instead, 'I saw before me a man tall, of fine physique (khorosho slozhennyi), with a face that was intelligent, lively, and affable.' Embracing the ubiquitous stereotype of the Russian official, Meshchersky enthused that Witte lacked the clerk's characteristic 'self-abnegation (samonizhennost')' in the presence of the powerful and 'self-aggrandizement (samopoklonenie)' before the meek, and thus found him to be even more 'likeable, with his natural manner, the genuine way he had about him'. Perhaps the highest compliment that Meshchersky could pay Witte was that, 'in his black daycoat, uninhibited and free in what he said and how he acted, he reminded me in his appearance of an English statesman' rather than the staid officials that Russian literature and culture had lampooned for over a century. Later, Meshchersky believed, Witte was corrupted by power. In the 1880s, however, 'gradually becoming acquainted with what for me was a new type of man,' Meshchersky observed of his early acquaintance with Witte, 'I experienced great pleasure (udovolstvie).'[58]

How did this new type of man remember himself? What memories preoccupied Witte as he dictated to his stenographer, in the early winter of 1911, the story of his Kiev years? Judging from the order of his memories, a central facet of his public and private self remained his loyalty to monarchical rule. Although it occurred some three months after he moved to the city, the assassination of Alexander II was his first memory of Kiev. The blow of that event still echoed in his mind thirty years later. We have previously seen how he dwelled on the conspiratorial episode of the Holy Druzhina, whose cloak and dagger intrigue had led Witte briefly to trail a suspected terrorist to Paris, and how the aged memoirist proclaimed it all ultimately to have been 'stupid' and 'laughable'. Perhaps an older man did look back upon that time and find only youthful indiscretion. His lengthy and intense recollections, which marked the bloody regicide not only as a divider between two different monarchical reigns, but also two eras in his life, however, suggested how deeply rooted in his personality were the monarchist sentiments that framed his personality. Indeed, attached to the front of the memoir manuscript was a secret oath, written in Witte's own hand, that swore members of the secret organization to loyalty and pulsated still with the genuine rage of a man who, confronted by the upheaval of a tsar's violent death, had dedicated himself then 'in the name of the Father and the Son and the Holy Spirit (+)' to 'the protection of the Sovereign as well as the unmasking of the treason that has disgraced the name of Russia (*russkoe imia*) (+)'.[59]

Musing over regicide, and one set of events that had shaped his life, he paused, and swerved, from the public to the private moments of these years, moments that reflected much about the man he had become. In the first instance, he attended to his failed relationship with the daughter of his wife's first marriage, Sonia Mering. She won little affection from either Witte or her mother, Spiridinova, who passed 'the girl' to the care of her grandmother when she moved to St Petersburg and married Witte. Returning to Kiev in late 1880, the couple placed Sonia at a boarding school, the Institute for Noble Girls, where she spent all but a few days per year, her mother never displaying any 'special tenderness toward her'. Witte himself recalled her, coldly, as a child he almost never saw, certainly 'never nurtured any attachment with', and found to be, unlike her 'beautiful' mother, more akin to her natural father, altogether 'unattractive and . . . unsympathetic'. Sometime around her mother's sudden death in 1889, Sonia married 'a very capable young man', a young Finance Ministry official who was the son of the wealthy, prominent Kiev physician Mering. Equipped with the 'very adequate dowry' that Witte had supplied, Sonia and her 'wealthy' husband returned to Kiev. There, liberally 'exploiting my name', as Witte put it, the couple became embroiled in speculative banking schemes that nearly bankrupted the husband, and led Witte to sever relations with Sonia, an adopted daughter whom he viciously slandered. 'In general,' he concluded, 'she displayed the exact same personality as that of her father, a liar and petty intriguer.'[60] However crudely he sometimes indulged that interest, Witte, when he looked at any woman, typically saw her through her relationships with men. In a Victorian nineteenth century where upper- and middle-class female autonomy was still a sporadic, if not exotic, exception found most frequently in novels, on stage, or in the radical underground, a man of

Witte's social standing encountered women in the social networks spun by marriage, parenthood, social acquaintanceship, and sexual liaison.[61] His reminiscences repeatedly suggested how often such relationships with women informed both his public and private life.

Chronicling the succession of the imperial viceroys who ruled Ukraine as governors-general during his years in Kiev, Witte attended to the male patronage networks that these representatives of imperial power created. In so doing, he also displayed the status and personal influence that such male acquaintanceship created. Gazing just as closely at the women associated with these men, he also revealed their centrality in the networks through which power and influence in the city's society was constituted. Adjutant-General A. R. Drentel'n, a career military officer connected to the court of Alexander III, was a very 'cruel (*zhestok*)' but 'unconditionally honorable and proper man'. His firmness and fairness, Witte insisted in framing the typically benevolent tsarist administrator, won the respect of all Kiev's population, 'both the Russians and the ethnics (*inorodtsy*)'. His wife, 'Maria Aleksandrovna Drentel'n', and her children, seemed naturally a part of this story. Still an acquaintance of his family in 1912, the honorable 'old woman (*starushka*)', still possessing 'a sharp memory (*svezhaia pamiat'*)', also had a son, whose accolades of university graduate, guards officer, and, eventually, courtier he dutifully detailed. The young man achieved success, Witte acidly noted as he surfaced a memory of private life, in part because he 'did not have a wife and thus avoided the various petty intrigues' in which women inevitably involved their men.[62] He directed his attention as well to Drenteln's successor, 'Chertkov', a wealthy Petersburg aristocrat who, given his evident administrative inexperience, apparently owed his appointment to his status in St Petersburg high society. Judging both the length and the character of the reminiscence, Witte found the chief distinction of the man to be his wife. She was 'quite an enchanting lady (*zabavnaia dama*) and a real beauty (*polozhitel'naia krasavitsa*)', he remembered, noting that even 'to the present day she remained quite flirtatious (*ona ves'ma frantitsia*)'. Once an unhappily married woman, Chertkov saved her from her entrapment in a dutiful but mundane marriage. 'Olga Ivanovna Chertkova' was a divorcee—a married woman that encountered a man who wooed her, then 'fell in love with (her), divorced her from her husband, and married her'. Her story was a cultural set piece of contemporary society, a game or a combat that men of Witte's class played repeatedly, and that Leo Tolstoy narrated in his classically Victorian novel *Anna Karenina*. It was the story of Witte's own first marriage, and mimicked his own approaching courtship of his second wife, Mathil'da Ivanovna Lisanevich-Nurok. That 'Madame Chertkova' was also 'of Jewish origins' only added to the allure of 'this very proper (*poriadochnaia*) and quite well educated woman, one full of life (*zhiznera-dostnaia*)', who 'always enjoyed herself' and had 'many admirers (*poklonniki*)' among the young officers who attended her husband—'although all of them (in large part)', he added lasciviously, 'were platonic.'[63]

Such assessments of male and female personalities thus also opened the door to explore the sexual and the erotic. Although he certainly never used these terms, and such themes *were not* the main narrative line as he dictated his Kiev reminiscences, Witte still, often in ciphered language, touched upon both the sexual mores of the day and the public notoriety of individuals who flaunted or violated them. Because gossip was a primary means by which Victorians discussed their otherwise highly secluded private worlds, it remains a primary avenue for the historian to explore them.[64] Memories of his first royal patroness in Kiev, the Grand Duchess Alexandra Petrovna, for example, dwelled at length upon her failed marriage to the Grand Duke Nikolai Nikolaevich the Elder, the brother of Tsar Alexander II. The collapse of this Romanov family marriage, prompted by the husband's public affair with the ballerina Chislova and their illegitimate daughter, given the surname Nikolaeva, had been a salacious public scandal. Protesting how difficult it was 'to judge from the outside why a husband lives well with a wife and why often a marriage is unhappy', Witte eagerly rummaged about in their private lives. Although 'fault lay with both parties' for this marital disaster, the man was a man, the man acknowledged, and perhaps 'a bit too much loved to be the playboy and frolic (*zhuirovat' i veselit'sia*)'. The burden of guilt, however, resided with the woman. She was 'somewhat abnormal (*anormal'naia*)'. That characterization released a stream of consciousness about inherited degeneracy in her family, the Oldenburg line of the Romanov royal house, which caused not only her perceived deviance but that of her three brothers as well. One was a homosexual, another an alcoholic, and the third 'a drunkard (*kutila*), in debt up to his ears', whose scandalous behavior caused his exile to the Caucasus, where he seduced and married the divorcée he created. The grand duchess herself, aged and confined to a wheelchair, was rumored to have been enamored of the priest who attended her court. A man with 'an unattractive face but a very masculine body', who 'played the dandy (*frantit'*) as much as a cleric could', the priest exerted 'overwhelming' influence over her. 'She undoubtedly more than loved him,' he remarked. Witte, who by his own testimony scrambled to ingratiate himself with both the woman and the priest, concluded that, 'beyond a platonic relationship, there was nothing else between them'. Hers was, he concluded, 'some kind of psychopathic love (*psikhopaticheskaia liubov'*), a marker precisely of that psychiatric abnormality (*psikhicheskaia anormal'nost'*) which the grand duchess inherited' from her forbears.[65]

Erotic love—or male fantasy about it—was to be found in the oddest corners, in newspaper offices and university lecture halls, between older men and younger women. Witness the daily newspaper *The Kievan*, and its two successive editors, Vitalii Shulgin and Dmitrii Pikhno. Shulgin was a professor of general history at Kiev's St. Vladimir University and the author of a series of secondary-school history textbooks that Witte admired and had used as a student.[66] Remembered by Witte to have been a mediocre scholar but 'one of the most talented lecturers' among Kiev's professors, Shulgin in the 1860s had assumed the editorship of an official government publication, increased its circulation, and eventually purchased the paper outright. 'Very eloquent', this man was plainly as adept as was Witte at the use of both the printed and spoken word. He proved irresistible to young women, Witte observed with evident fascination, despite his being 'very ugly . . . hunchbacked and . . . quite old'. A young woman student, an 'institutka, . . . so fell in love with him' that she asked Shulgin to marry her, a request that the 'old man' obliged. Such 'infatuation', however, passed as soon as 'she became his wife and discovered the secrets of life (*tainy zhizni*)'.[67] After Shulgin's death in 1878, Pikhno assumed the editorship of *The Kievan*. Although he engaged Witte in heated debate over issues of railroad development in Ukraine, in these reminiscences he was merely the man who 'wooed' (*ukhazhivat'*) Shulgin's young and apparently estranged wife while his predecessor at the paper was still alive, possibly fathered Shulgin's son, married the woman after her husband's death, and after that woman in turn died, married Shulgin's daughter, the heiress of her father's estate.[68]

One of Witte's most talented subordinates during his ministerial years, Vladimir Kovalevskii remarked in his own memoirs that his superior always displayed an 'amazing capacity for work', never spending less than twelve hours each day immersed in the array of meetings, readings, and conversations that filled his waking hours. 'Family matters diverted him little,' Kovalevskii attested, although other evidence suggests this to be the view of a workplace colleague.[69] Perhaps the aged memoirist had more time in

1912 to devote to the family and private lives of himself and his acquaintances. Perhaps that alone explains this passion for recounting sexual indiscretion and abnormality. Yet, within the commentaries of this Russian man
about the women who touched his life, and especially his judgments about
them that penetrated beneath the formal roles of wife and mother that social
convention ascribed to them, Witte the dreamer appears again, albeit in the
much more private space where a man could fantasize about women as
sexual objects and amorous objectives.

Consider what Witte had to say about Kovalevskii, whom he first met in
1888 when he began working in the Ministry of Finances, and immediately
hired. Witte's respect for Kovalevskii, one of the most talented officials to
serve the imperial government at the end of the nineteenth century, was
enormous, and Witte promoted him repeatedly. At some length, moreover, he defended his subordinate against charges of political radicalism,
which had swirled about Kovalevskii ever since his youthful encounter
with the infamous radical Sergei Nechaev led in 1869 to more than a year's
confinement for political crimes in the Peter and Paul Fortress of
St Petersburg.[70] As Witte recalled in his memoirs, Kovalevskii's reputation
'as a politically disloyal man' could not override his talent. He 'was a very
lively man, extraordinarily talented and extraordinarily industrious'. Yet,
'Vladimir Ivanovich Kovalevskii had one weakness', which appeared only
late in his life, 'a passion for ladies (*uvlechenie damami*)', Witte wrote,
explaining how his prized subordinate, a married man older than 50 years
of age, 'became involved (*sputalsia*) with a certain Shabel'skaia . . .'. She was
'a lady of improper conduct, in both a physical and moral sense', he huffed
in the cramped language used to describe the sexual and erotic. She
'ensnared (*zavlech' v svoi seti*)' Kovalevskii, Witte insisted, using 'talk of
freedom generally and women's freedom especially' to entice him into an
extra-marital affair that not only destroyed his marriage but landed him in
civil court to defend himself against creditors who demanded payment on
promissory notes allegedly forged by Shabel'skaia. That relationship ended,
but Kovalevskii took up with yet another woman, 'also not of unimpeach-
able demeanor', who was twice married before she 'took Kovalevskii into
her arms, hooked him and now lives with him, together with children from
the first two husbands'. His disapproval of a woman whom he stereotyped
as 'one of those ladies who cannot live without affairs (*avantiur'*)' was as
loud as had been his scathing remarks about Madame Shabel'skaia.[71]

'As for Madame Shabel'skaia', continued Witte in what was yet another stream of consciousness where the lines between his recollections of Kovalevskii's past and the memories of his own youth they had summoned forth blurred, '... I remember her when she still was an altogether young girl, and I still served on the Odessa Railroad'. The noble daughter of an army general who sought to escape the straightjacket of provincial noble life by running away to the city, Shabel'skaia's story was prototypical for the 1860s, found in literature of the day, subsequently among scholars, and, judging from these reminiscences, among Victorian Russian men of the era as well. She 'ran away from her relatives and I met her, in Odessa, being then a young man, in Iashchuka's restaurant, in the Northern Hotel, in a company of revelers (*kutiashchaia kompaniia*),' he mused. 'Then she was very enchanting (*zabavnaia*), because she was still a very young girl with a relatively good education, and ... in the sense she drank a terrible amount and was extremely free and easy (*kraine razviazna*). She devoted herself to the theater and was an actress, and later went abroad, as an actress, on the Vienna stage.'[72] Here was the woman's world of a nascent bourgeois culture viewed through a man's eyes. Much like the narrative that Leo Tolstoy laid down in the novel *Anna Karenina* in 1877, it was a world where, behind the screen of proper marriage, resided tempestuous love affairs, frequent divorce, common-law marriage, and male sexual conquest. Wives, mothers, acquaintances, and lovers: women, in the eyes of the men who attached themselves to them, were accorded roles that assured the capacity of males to dominate in what was a patriarchal society, and to fantasize in what increasingly was a modern one.

Such glimpses of his private life and passions, however, should not override the fact that Witte's attention as he recalled his Kiev years never strayed far from what increasingly occupied both his public and private life: his professional work. Created, Witte opined, by the talent of 'a good mathematician' and the experience of a railwayman concerned for 'the practical side of the business', his prominence and success as chief executive officer (*upravliaiushchii*) of the Southwestern Railroad were cardinal aspects of his public identity.[73] V. I. Kovalevskii remembered the 'administrator of this vast railroad network, (who) made it a model of order, expanded it, developed enormous passenger and freight traffic on it—truth be told,' he added, 'often resorting to cagey (*khitroumnyi*) strategies' in doing so.[74] As did Kovalevskii, for he was one of them, Witte knew that his professional success had depended as much on the networks of 'talented co-workers'

he attracted into his service. Labeling his ability to identify talented individuals as a 'feel for people (*niukh k liudiam*)' that was, if not 'innate, very
developed', he emphasized the 'large pleaide of talented and capable workers' he gathered about him during his business career on the railroads, and
subsequently in the ministerial world of St Petersburg.[75]

All of them, given the parameters of professional life in the late nineteenth century empire, unsurprisingly, were men. Having selected talent,
Witte used it intensively and rewarded it loyally. Although the records for
the Southwestern are scattered, his management of the Ministry of Finance
is fully documented, and those papers reflect a liveliness and informality
within the working groups of an institution that sharply contrasted the more
regularized, hierarchical, and plodding discourse of other imperial ministries. 'To work with him was pleasurable and easy', Kovalevskii recalled of
Witte the manager. He easily grasped new ideas, 'as they say, on the fly (*na
letu*). He had great trust in his close associates, and allowed them extensive
independence and great initiative.'[76] Their success registered long afterwards in his memoirs. Some went on to become influential bankers and
financiers, others businessmen or imperial officials.[77] Others became 'prominent railwaymen'; that many of these were Poles and 'several were even
Jews,' Witte remarked, indicated that he hired talent over ethnicity even as
these ethnic communities increasingly experienced the discrimination that
official Russian nationalism visited upon them from the 1880s onward. Still
others were civil engineers, proto-technocrats upon whose specialized
knowledge of railroad technology he relied in operating the railroad.[78]
His professional work as a railroad administrator, he acknowledged, left
him 'entirely satisfied (*ves'ma dovolen*)'. It provided wealth and social status,
everything, he seemed to suggest, a man could want in his public life. He
enjoyed 'a very large salary', the professional autonomy afforded him by the
management of 'the most enormous business' of one of the largest railroad
networks in the empire, and a 'good family life (*schast'e*)'.[79] Work even
penetrated the private world of his prized aristocratic Lipki neighborhood
and the home located, Witte once pointedly remarked, 'across from the
residence of the imperial governor-general', but connected to his office by
the 'telegraph apparatus' attended around the clock by employees who
monitored the business of the railroad that poured from it 'day and
night'.[80] Work, however, was not the only path by which Witte made his
way through imperial civil society during these Kievan years.

Journalism, as we have seen, was another such pathway. His published treatise on railroad freight rates originally had been a public response to criticisms of the Southwestern Railroad launched by D. I. Pikhno's newspaper, *The Kievan*. Generally, Witte was eager to engage public debate over issues of railroad management and imperial financial policy. An occasional essayist in the periodical press, most notably in the slavophile Ivan Aksakov's Moscow-based weekly, *Rus'*, Witte in these years also revealed for the first time his willingness to fund newspapers and thereby sway public debates toward positions he favored.[81] Confronting the public criticism of a major city newspaper, Witte used the financial resources of his company to establish a competitor sympathetic to his views, *The Kievan Word* (*Kievskoe slovo*). He claimed that his position at the Southwestern was 'incompatible' with the editorship of a newspaper, but his actions showed more simply a desire to create the public impression of an independent press organ whose views were, not coincidentally, his own. He enticed an assistant editor of *The Kievan*, A. Ia. Antonovich, a professor of law at the university, to take on the responsibilities of publisher and editor of the newspaper, and left unexplained how editorial policy there was crafted, except to say that 'we constantly were polemicizing on all questions'.[82] To find correspondence referring to monies expended or individuals promoted in efforts to influence press opinion was not an unusual occurrence later in Witte's ministerial years.[83] It was standard practice.

Antonovich, like Pikhno, was a professor at Kiev's St Vladimir University. That he was drawn to the university, a repository and fount of scientific knowledge, as well as to the men who created and upheld it, was not just a natural consequence of his oft-stated nostalgia for an academic world he had abandoned upon graduating from it. Judging from his recollections, he sought out the university repeatedly during his public life. His reminiscences of Kiev mentioned an array of faculty, always displaying their academic titles, research specializations, and an accompanying comment about the intellectual quality of their work. All of them, by law and unquestioned social convention, were males, whose networks constituted yet another civic space that he frequented in these years. Nikolai Khristianovich Bunge, the university rector when Witte first arrived in Kiev in 1880, was 'one of the best professors of finance (*finansovoe pravo*) in Russia', whose writing on the circulation of currency he 'valued very highly'—and whose savaging, in which Witte participated when Bunge was Minister of Finances (1881–86), he conveniently had forgotten. Bunge's successor as rector, Professor Rennenkampf, was 'a professor of the philosophy of law and international law, and in the scholarly world a figure of some repute (*izvestnaia velichina*)'.[84] D. I. Pikhno publicly had defended his professorial dissertation on railroad development at the university and won appointment as a 'doctor of finance and university professor'.[85] 'Beyond the individuals I have mentioned, among Kiev's professors of that time were still other . . . renowned scholarly names,' Witte remarked, reflecting a final time on a milieu where professionalism, scientific knowledge, and talented work could create public renown.[86]

Propelled toward the university by his burgeoning interest in finance, economics, and systems of law, Witte also associated with professors of medicine and other physicians, who not only occupied a prominent position in later nineteenth-century Russian science, but seemed to salve a personal tendency toward physical illness and hypochondria. At various junctures in his adult life, Witte complained of ailments of the nose and throat, skin, stomach, and nerves. He frequently summered at various mineral water spas across the continent, and repeatedly consulted physicians about the variety of physical ailments that afflicted him.[87] Thus, the professor of surgery Karavaev was 'a luminary', whose 'authority (*avtoritetnost'*)' was recognized throughout Ukraine and abroad. Mering, a physician born and educated in Germany but first employed in Russia by a privately-owned sugar-processing factory near Kiev, was 'a very talented man' whose skills as a physician created for him such a public reputation that he eventually moved to the city, took university doctoral examinations in his specialty, and was appointed a professor of internal diseases at St Vladimir. Although the father-in-law of Sonia Mering, Witte had great respect for a university professor who built for himself 'an enormous medical practice', an 'excellent' university clinic, the 'mass of knowledge' it allowed him to accumulate, 'great notoriety as a physician', and, certainly not the least of Witte's concerns, 'a very substantial income'. Indeed, he luxuriated in this last attribute, explaining at some length that Mering constructed his wealth from real-estate transactions whose handsome profits resulted, Witte claimed, from Mering's access to Jewish property markets in the city. Because he extended free medical treatment to impoverished Jews in Kiev, even traveling to their 'poor Jewish hovels (*lachugi*)' to treat the ill, Mering developed 'an enormous popularity within the lower class of Jews', and benefited from an exchange in kind: health care for information about 'various deals' from which he benefited financially. Witte remembered this 'most honorable man' with unusually warm regard for 'the universal respect he enjoyed not only in Kiev but throughout the southwestern region'.[88]

A final civic arena that more and more preoccupied his attention was the world of business and finance. In Kiev, at least as he recalled that time, it swirled around Jews, Poles, aristocrats and self-made men, an ethnic and social polyglot that suggested both the intensity and complexity of his emergent civic experience. His administrative positions on the Southwestern, first as its chief business officer and then as its managing director, brought him into close contact with commercial, financial, and banking interests in the city. Dominant among them, and the most prominent 'among the Jews in Kiev, of whom then there lived quite a large number', was the Brodsky family. One located in Odessa and the other in Kiev, its two branches were headed respectively by the brothers Abram Moiseevich and Izrael Moiseevich Brodsky. Together they were major figures in Black Sea grain export from the port of Odessa, sugar beet cultivation and processing, and, by the turn of the century, commercial banking and finance in both Ukraine and St Petersburg.[89] Grain, sugar beets, and sugar were all key commodities in the regional economy, and they all moved with increasing intensity along its expanding railroad network. Witte had first encountered the Brodsky name when he worked in Odessa, then in Kiev held 'purely business conversations (*delovye besedy*)' with the family as an agent of the Southwestern, and maintained social and official contacts with them over the rest of his life. Their Jewish ethnicity greatly complicated his views of men whose wealth he respected and whose business he sought. The 'Kievan' Brodsky, as Witte labeled Izrael Moiseevich, 'on first encounter seemed a very honorable elder (*starik*), in appearance almost a biblical patriarch', not at all, Witte hastened to add, a man who appeared to be Jewish. Little evidence remains to imagine the demeanor that the railwayman might have assumed with the Jewish sugar magnate. Although presumably Witte's business dealings with the Jewish bourgeois in the Pale of Settlement was extensive, he only recalled, with healthy respect, an individual whose wealth made him 'one of the great capitalists of the entire southwestern region' and who 'produced the impression of a man incredibly intelligent but almost entirely uneducated'. Such a self-made man, of which the world of late imperial Russian capitalism offered a growing number of examples, was a type Witte personally favored. Yet, although also a man of talent and wealth, the 'Odessite Brodsky', Abram Moiseevich, could not, or chose not to, escape his Jewish ethnicity. 'This Brodsky was also very rich', Witte wrote, but 'he was . . . at first glance repulsive (*protiv-nyi*); his physiognomy, all his allure and even demeanor was entirely jewish (*evreiskie*)', a physical impression, he noted, that he found off-putting. That fact, however, apparently did not prevent Witte from doing business with him. It once again bore witness to an imperial Russian's conflicted relationship with a Jewish world that was a source of business and a target of Gentile rage, as his eyewitness memories of the violent pogroms of Jewish homes and shops that swept across Kiev in the aftermath of Alexander II's assassination testified.[90]

Business and finance also brought Witte into contact with members of the Polish landowning nobility, who descended on the city for the 'Kiev contracting', when the business of negotiating the sale, purchase, and transport of their estate agriculture was combined with the pleasures of the urban cultural season. Because grain was another essential commodity in the mix of the Southwestern Railroad's freight business, Witte was much in evidence during what he called 'my attendance' at this intermingling of deal-making and socializing. Chief, or most mentionable, among such acquaintances was Count Alfred Pototsky, the scion of one of the wealthiest and most influential aristocratic clans of post-partition Poland. An elderly Austrian statesman of Polish descent who in the early 1880s was the viceroy of Galicia, Pototsky would take up residence in his Kiev townhouse, give small private dinners that Witte 'occasionally attended', and meet with the railroad's director 'concerning various business matters, because he was a very substantial landowner'. Stereotypes of ethnicity, here intermingled with class, shaped Witte's appraisal of public men and colored his understanding of the civic space he inhabited. Pototsky, he recalled, was 'a type of Polish magnate'. His manner elegant, his French impeccable, his public demeanor haughty, Pototsky demeaned any 'common man (*prostoi chelovek*)', as essentially did all Polish magnates, as cattle', a view, he added, that applied 'especially to the Russian peasant, (whom) generally all Poles considered one step removed from oxen, if not worse'.[91]

Finally, here too mention was made of that 'renowned rich man (*izvest-nyi bogach*)', Alexander Polovtsev. One of the more influential behind-the-scenes players of the late imperial bureaucracy—and a scrupulous diarist who recorded its personalities and events for himself but not the posterity that has read it—Polovtsov was variously an ally and opponent during their time together in the central government of St Petersburg. The two first met each other in Kiev in 1880, but much of their acquaintance, Witte acknowledged, developed only after he had moved to the imperial capital in the following decade. Although acerbically critical of an individual with whom he more than once had crossed swords, Witte's tale of this 'amazing fellow (*udivitel'nyi chelovek*)' acknowledged not only the power of wealth literally to make men, but also captured the turbulence of a Victorian world where public and private identities were being fractured and remade at an increasingly frenetic pace. Here was Polovtsov, a man, quite like himself Witte must have reflected, 'born to a simple noble family, graduated from (the Imperial School of) Jurisprudence, before whom stood the life of a petty, poor government official (*chinovnik*), perhaps, in the end, he might through long service promote himself to some high administrative post'. This oft-satirized portrayal of an official life, however, was interrupted, really altogether altered, not only by wealth, but by women, beauty, male sexuality, and perhaps above all fateful circumstances. Literally into this picture stepped A. L. Shtiglitz, 'at that time one of the very richest bankers' in the empire, a man whom one historian termed the last of the 'court bankers' who financed the lives and policies of the Russian imperial court down through the early nineteenth century.[92] 'Shtiglitz had an adopted daughter and no heirs,' Witte remarked. 'So, this young official Polovtsov, absolutely impoverished, began systematically to woo this adopted daughter of Shtiglitz, and by the way, she was very beautiful. Of course,' he remarked, as if knowingly confirming acknowledged patterns of behavior, 'he wooed her not so much for her beauty as for his own benefit (*iz za razcheta*).' Eventually, 'he achieved what he was after and married her'. When Shtiglitz died in 1884 and left his extensive estate to his daughter, Polovtsov, by implication controlling his wife and her fortune, 'became a very wealthy man'. This wealth, combined with his own ability to establish networks of patronage and protection reaching into the Romanov court, created a powerful political personality who rose to the heights of power in the imperial government.[93] Yet, circumstances, especially in the modern world, could dictate both the rise and fall of fortune. During the course of his life, Witte mused as he dictated about a man who had died the previous year, Polovtsov managed to squander much of the wealth he had married. 'All the time he was engaged in various affairs; he sold, bought, speculated, and speculated to such an extent that he speculated right through almost the entire fortune of his wife.'

In the end, Polovtsev, whose personality Witte admitted 'always had attracted my attention', simply remained 'a riddle'. How, he wondered, could he be at one and the same time publicly 'a man intelligent, business-like (*tolkovyi*), a man undoubtedly with a certain statesman-like mind', but 'impossibly frivolous (*legkomyslennyi*) and stupid in his private affairs?' Typically supplying the answer to his own query, Witte explained that 'as a man, Polovtsev was very antipathetic (*antipatichnyi*), he was in the fullest sense of the word a parvenu'. An insult repeatedly leveled at Witte during his years negotiating the high society of the imperial capital, the term had a meaning in Witte's lexicon. Such an individual was fawning and submissive toward highly placed personages or others on whom he might depend, but haughty and even rude to those below. 'In general, he was not a good man . . . not even an orderly fellow (*poriadochnyi chelovek*). . . . He was not', Witte concluded, 'a man whom one would entirely trust (*vpolne doverit'sia*).' What better characterization than this might one find to describe the modern man that Witte was becoming, and that captured as well his own ambivalence about that process? Traditional noble official turned wealthy banker's son-in-law and financial speculator; insignificant, petty government clerk transformed into the male conqueror wooing woman and fortune; intelligent businessman and statesman become supercilious and senseless in his private affairs: Polovtsov, like Witte, was a thoroughly modern Victorian man, the attributes of personality and identity increasingly kaleidoscopic, and thus destabilizing, in their complexity. It was not—and isn't this what Witte meant?—a personality one could altogether trust.

Imagining Autocracy

There was a final masculine figure who appeared at intermittent junctures in these reminiscences of his Kiev years: Tsar Alexander III. In Witte's memories, he was both a powerful symbol of the legitimacy of Romanov imperial rule and an ideal type of man, one proper, truthful, honest, and strong, who instilled in Witte a sense of certainty, confidence, even belief, despite the kaleidoscopic future looming before him. Among all the individuals who influenced Witte's private and public identities, who helped to shape and connect Witte's understanding of himself as a man and an imperial subject, arguably none influenced him more than the sovereign whom he loyally served and whose memory he zealously protected. The Emperor Alexander Alexandrovich, as Witte invariably referred to him, promoted the railway executive to the Ministry of Finances in 1889.

patronized his subsequent meteoric rise to the heights of government power, and instilled in him deep feelings of personal fealty that still reverberated in his recollections of the man almost twenty years later. 'Emperor Alexander III was a great Emperor'—the keystone to Witte's understanding of a Russian imperial polity strengthened by the industrial modernity of his contemporary era. He was a paragon of Victorian manhood and a symbol of imperial sovereignty, who understood the responsibility of the monarchy to assure, at the least represent, order, prosperity, and well-being in the polyglot empire.[94]

Witte's adult political life was informed profoundly by the assassination of Alexander II in 1881, a watershed event that marked the coming of his own generation to power. The son ascending 'a throne stained red by the blood of his father' metaphorically colored the perspective of a generation, and Witte, even decades afterwards, framed the moment as one shared by all fathers and sons. Four years Alexander III's junior, Witte partially blamed the weak father for his own death. The 'great Emancipator Alexander II' in the later years of his reign had displayed a propensity 'to vacillate and even retreat' from his early liberalism, Witte agreed. Military victory in the Eastern War and diplomatic defeat at the Congress of Berlin also had played its part in creating public dissent among conservative and liberal monarchists alike. Witte, whose own understanding of this political moment evolved over the quarter-century separating the memoirist from it, believed that this perception of indecisive weakness allowed revolutionary radicalism to raise its head and instigate the disaster of regicide that had followed in March 1881. Yet, interlaced into this political explanation of the assassination was his personal revulsion before a father who had allowed rampant dishonesty to infect commerce, industry, and government service, and corrupted decadence to characterize his own private life. Alexander II's notorious relationship with the Princess Iurevskaya, the tsar's common-law wife with whom he fathered a second family while his estranged, ailing empress governed the royal family's hearth, had created a bifurcated family. The situation became even more scandalous when the empress died and Alexander, in violation of the etiquette of mourning, made Iurevskaya his so-called morganatic spouse. Marriage 'after sixty years of age,' Witte explained, when the tsar 'already had so many, entirely adult children and even grandchildren' could not but have affected the 'psychology' of a son whose own public image rested on his 'moral uprightness'.[95]

Witte's earliest recollections of Alexander III, however, were tied not to these heights of power, but instead to his public life as a railway executive, imperial subject, and Victorian man. His first encounters with the tsar were official. As an executive of the Southwestern Railroad, he conveyed the sovereign and his family through the western and south-western territories of the empire: hunting in Poland, attending strategic maneuvers in Ukraine, traveling to vacation resorts in Crimea.[96] As was always the case when he recalled encounters with any one of the three Russian emperors who reigned during his lifetime, so too these first opportunities to see Alexander III received the still rapt attention of the aged memoirist. The storyteller attended repeatedly to these displays of monarchical power and authority, which were, the historian Richard Wortman explains, 'scenarios of power' that the Romanov imperial court, through complex rituals and symbols, created to bolster its political legitimacy. 'I remember as if it were yesterday (*pomniu, kak teper'*)', Witte, who was himself both a spectator and an actor, said as he recalled his first opportunity to observe Alexander III, sometime shortly after the traumatic regicide that had brought him so violently to the throne. Waiting in the royal pavilion of the Kiev city train station amidst 'a large public accompanying the Sovereign, all in parade dress', Witte remembered, he witnessed a choreographed performance as first grand dukes, and then 'several minutes later the Emperor with the Empress and the children' entered the royal waiting room. Amidst this portraiture of familial propriety, the two young sons, a still boyish heir, the future Nicholas II, and his brother Georgii, 'misbehaved terribly . . . all the while darting about between the legs' of those in attendance, until suddenly one of their uncles, the Grand Duke Vladimir Aleksandrovich, grabbed the young heir by the ear, shook him, and shouted, 'I told you.—stop misbehaving!' Witte recalled commenting to another bystander that the time would come when that boy, grown to succeed his father on the throne, might remind his uncle of this event. Unfortunately, he mused in 1912, that moment had come much sooner than anyone had expected, bringing 'unexpectedly to the throne a young man who was entirely unprepared for the role of Emperor'.[97] That was by no means the last such lash that Witte directed during his memoir years at Nicholas II.

At times, as was the case at this point in his work, the memoir text that Witte dictated registered calendar markings. Witte, now in a regular rhythm of work, ended a day of dictation with this story of Alexander III, and returned to the task four days later. He took up the same thread of reminiscences.[98] A second memory of Alexander III allowed another opportunity to muse over this sovereign man. Sometime after he had succeeded Ivan Vyshnegradsky as chief executive officer of the Southwestern, Witte accompanied the tsar on the railroad in an entourage to observe military maneuvers near Bialystok, in eastern Poland. His story centered upon the unanticipated meeting of Alexander III with the future Kaiser Wilhelm II, at the time a young man dispatched by his grandfather, William I, to greet the Russian emperor near the borders of the two empires. A ceremony redolent with the trappings of nineteenth-century continental European diplomacy, Witte's role in the drama required him to commandeer an express locomotive to St Petersburg in order to fetch the Prussian officer's uniform required for Alexander to greet the young Wilhelm properly. Here again was the spectator, eager to share with his listeners his own proximity to royal persons, the detailed knowledge of personalities it had garnered him, and the lessons he had drawn from such public displays. Chief among them was what Witte remembered as the 'autocratic majesty (*samoderzhavnaia tsarstvennost'*)' of Alexander III.[99]

Physically 'a very imposing' figure, Alexander was less handsome and more 'large like a bear (*medvezhatyi*)', Witte recalled, less 'strong and muscular than husky and fat'. He was a man who, even if he were to have appeared anonymously 'in a crowd', would have drawn the attention of all to his 'physical figure', with 'his imposing presence, calm demeanor, and the firm but good-natured countenance found in his face'. Witte knew full well the accepted public wisdom that Alexander, who had grown up in the shadow of his older brother Nicholas before the latter's death in 1865 made the younger man heir to the throne, had not been prepared to become emperor. He acknowledged that 'Emperor Alexander III had been (a man) of entirely pedestrian intellect, even, if you will, less than average intellect, less than average capabilities, and less than average education'. He was 'in appearance an absolute lout (*vakhlak*), (who) resembled a big Russian peasant from the central provinces', but, much like the peasant whom his reign repeatedly idealized, Alexander impressed not with intellect but with 'enormous character, a lovely heart, a good nature, a sense of justice as well as firmness'. It had been an older Wilhelm, already the German emperor, who later supplied Witte, he claimed, the observation that 'he envied the majesty, the autocratic majesty, which manifested itself in the figure of Alexander III'. Witte remembered watching the two men at a formal banquet, to which he had not been invited because he was then still a man 'small in rank (*mal chinom*)', but, much as he had done as a boy in the Caucasus, here too he watched from the balcony of the banquet hall, his gaze turned on the imposing, majestic figure of the man who was his sovereign. Wilhelm, he continued, 'in all his mannerisms, in all his affectations, was a fop (*fert'*) . . . the most typical of Prussian guards officers, with his trimmed moustaches and all his *vyverty pri khodbe*, all his feigned elegance'. His polar opposite in manner and external appearance, Alexander 'was to the highest degree a simple (man)'.[100] However much time and memory had idealized him, Alexander was a man, and a sovereign, in whom Witte trusted.

The actual event that supplied the key to their relationship, however, was a train wreck: the derailment of the imperial train near Borka, in eastern Ukraine, on 17 October 1888. The last encounter with the tsar that Witte memorialized in these reminiscences of his Kievan years, the 'catastrophe' as he described it in 1912, had become a ritualized centerpiece of Alexander III's reign even before the tsar died in 1894. 'Borka' also constituted the actual prelude to Witte's own personal scenario of power, his appointment to the imperial bureaucracy in 1889. Witte produced a stream of detailed and heavily stylized memories about the incident, which rested in part on his own eyewitness account, and in part on the public images that the imperial court had created around Alexander III, who was said to have saved his wife and children by bearing on his back, 'thanks to his gigantic strength (*gigantskaia sila*)', the collapsing roof of the family's overturned dining car. Apocryphal tale or not, the event came to be celebrated as a miracle, a counterpoint to the disaster of regicide with which the reign had begun. Publications and memorials subsidized by the imperial treasury portrayed the suffering of the family, and the bravery and mercy they showed to all injured in the wreck.[101] One of Witte's first matters of business as a department director in the Ministry of Finances was to volunteer funds to pay his old company, the Southwestern, for the transportation of two church bells to the Monastery of Christ of the Nativity, struck by subscription 'in honor of the miraculous rescue on 17 October 1888 of Your Imperial Majesty and August Family from catastrophe'.[102]

A vague and circumstantial uncertainty characterizes the record at this critical juncture in Witte's public life. Some observers see him cagily maneuvering to utilize his professional standing and the patronage of Ivan Vyshnegradskii, who the previous year had become Minister of Finances, to secure the appointment he won in March 1889 as director of a new Department of Railroad Affairs within the ministry. Immediately after the

Borka crash occurred, he had been summoned from Kiev as an expert investigator on a commission created to determine its causes. The liberal jurist A. F. Koni, also a member, described in his own memoirs how a nearly distraught Witte feared that the disaster might be blamed on him and upset all his carefully crafted plans. In the months preceding the accident, railroad engineers, over Witte's signature, twice had issued formal warnings about the unsafe speeds at which the excessively heavy train traveled while on the Southwestern's network.[103] In his own memoirs, Witte at length explained these circumstances, and heaped blame on bureaucratic officials in the imperial court and the Ministry of Communications who had been responsible for the scheduling and maintenance of these trains—and ignored his technical advice.[104] He emphasized the violation of safety rules governing the weight and speed of this 'most enormous imperial train', which weighed more than the typical freight train and thus required two heavy locomotives to haul it, at speeds usually reserved only for lighter passenger trains, Witte instructed. Ever the technical expert, he detailed how that combination of weight and speed caused the parallel tracks to separate and derail the train. Ever the professional businessman and proto-technocrat, he objected that officials within the imperial court and the Communications Ministry wrote the schedule for the tsar's travel, with speed their paramount concern. He recalled that, as the responsible Southwestern official accompanying the train on one of these trips, he spent an entire night fretting 'in a fever (v likhoradke)' about a possible accident, even as all night long everyone else slept, including the Minister Pos'et and the chief railroad inspector, the engineer Sherval'. Handing off the train to another railroad line, he remembered, he returned to Kiev and immediately filed an official report with the Ministry of Communications that cited the dangerous safety violations, but admitted 'he had not had the courage to stop the train' because he feared creating a scandal. The report insisted, however, that future travel on the Southwestern required slower speed and increased time, and 'failing that, I wrote, I will not escort the imperial train'.[105] Soon he was informed that 'in view of his categorical declaration', the tsar's timetable would be rewritten and travel time on this network increased.

Shortly afterwards, the tale continued, Witte again accompanied the imperial train. He found himself nearly accosted, however, by the retinue of officials and courtiers traveling with the tsar. They 'all looked down their noses at me', even Count Vorontsov-Dashkov, 'who was so intimate with my close relatives and had known me since childhood' and acted as if they were not even acquainted. Finally, he recalled, the tsar's personal court adjutant and companion, General Cherevin, approached Witte to inform him that 'the emperor was dissatisfied with his travel' on the Southwestern, and, as the railwayman again attempted to explain the technical reasoning behind his protests, Alexander entered the car, overheard the conversation, turned to Witte and said, 'What are you saying! I travel on other lines and no one lessens my speed, but on your line it is forbidden to travel, simply because yours is a yid line (*vasha doroga zhidovskaia*).' That comment, Witte immediately added, referred to the fact that the owner of the line was 'the jew (I. S.) Bliokh'. Of course, Witte continued, he made no reply to the notoriously anti-semitic Emperor, but instead 'stayed silent'. When Minister of Communications Poset raised the same comments, only insinuating the anti-Semitic remark and charging instead that disorderly administration on the Southwestern explained why it had required slower speeds than 'anyone at any time had dared to demand', Witte exploded, even after a quarter-century. 'Realize, Your Most Esteemed Excellency, others can do as they like, but I do not want to bash in the head of the Sovereign, because that is how this will end, you will eventually break open the Sovereign's skull.' Alexander, Witte continued, overheard this comment, 'of course was very displeased with my impertinence', but said nothing, 'because he was a genteel, calm, and noble fellow'.[106] Two months later came Borka.

In Witte's telling, this episode served to cement a personal relationship with Alexander III, who came to regard this abrasive but knowledgeable railroad executive as a protégé to be promoted toward the heights of power. That bond, Witte remembered, had been central to his promotion to the St Petersburg bureaucracy. Greater government coordination of the imperial rail network and a Department of Railroad Affairs within the Finance Ministry to oversee its financial and commercial-industrial practices were both ideas he had supported for a decade. Vyshnegradskii had asked Witte to come to St Petersburg, he explained, and participate in a special conference, the first of countless such bodies he would come to dominate with his presence over the subsequent years. Chaired by State Comptroller Dmitrii Sol'skii, who over the years became one of the younger Witte's staunchest allies, it approved the project as he had outlined it. The conference finished, Vyshnegradskii thanked him and Witte returned to Kiev. No mention was made of his nomination to direct the new department, he continued, and even had Vyshnegradskii asked, he had no interest in sacrificing his place as director of a line of over 3,200 km, which rewarded him with an enormous

salary and allowed him to be 'utterly a free man, my own master', in order to
obtain 'an official place (*chinovnich'e mesto*)', even if attached to it was high
rank. A second communication from Vyshnegradskii, however, informed
him that he could not refuse, because the emperor wanted the director of
the SWRR, because he looked to advance Witte's career. The story that
attached to the episode, and such were one of the treasure troves that
imperial Russians of his class collected avidly, was that the sovereign had
characterized him as that 'brazen (*rezkii*)' fellow who had the impertinence
to say in his hearing that he would not obey a superior whose decisions
threatened the emperor's life. He had proven himself correct, Alexander
remarked. 'I see great things ahead for him'.

Having protested ever so loudly in his memoirs how he did not seek rank
or position, he did detail that, having loyally acceded to the tsar's request, he
maneuvered for salary, noting the 50,000 rubles he was currently making
and the 8-10,000 rubles a department director would earn. 'Were I alone,
but I have a young wife, and I do not want to move to Petersburg and later
find myself wanting, so that at least they should give me a salary on which
I could live comfortably (*bezbedno*),' Witte remembered himself lamenting.
Alexander added 8,000 rubles to the 8,000 ruble housing allowance
provided to men in this office, to be paid from the sovereign's own
'purse'. 'Thus I began my career against my own desire,' Witte exhaled.
Because 'the Sovereign insisted (*Gosudar' potreboval*)', he and his wife
moved to St Petersburg. She found the move displeasing, given that 'in
Petersburg we could not live as luxuriously (*shiroko*) as we had in Kiev', and
the climate suited neither of them. They settled on Bell Street (*ulitsa
Kolokol'naia*). He was promoted from titular councilor to actual state councilor, an unprecedented leap across four rungs on the Table of Ranks that
provided him access to a city of dreams.[107]

Conclusion: A Tale of the Counter-reforms

As he concluded dictating reminiscences of this crucial move from the
private world of railroads to the realm of ministerial power, Witte offered
a final soliloquy. 'The Emperor Alexander III', he remembered, was 'the
single man before whom I was never restrained in either my words or
actions, said whatever I thought, with the brazenness (*rezkost'*) and indeli-
cacies (*nedelikantnost'*) that were part of my character'. The tsar never gave

any hint 'in the turn of his body or in the expression on his face' that he ever objected. Witte acknowledged that a 'certain lack of discipline and bra-zenness of speech' was 'a weak part of my character', and admitted as well that this explained 'why in the end I never could, either as a man or as a statesman, win over the now benevolently reigning Emperor (*nyne blagopo-luchno tsarstvuiushchii Imperator*)'. That term, one of the countless Byzantine formulae demanded by the ritual of the Russian imperial court, was one that Witte typically deployed when he spoke of Nicholas II, who was entirely different from his father. 'He was an incredibly well-bred man, I never in my life saw a man as well-bred as he...he never allowed himself any brazenness (*rezkost'*), vulgarity (*uglavatost'*) in his speech or manners, and thus naturally he did not like my manner or speech', he remarked to himself, 'it jarred on him and this was one of the chief causes of that chilliness he came to display toward me.' 'I should admit', he concluded, 'that in this regard he was correct. My only justification was that I knew him from his early youth. When after a meeting I would be criticized: why did you speak so sharply, so impudently. I would answer that I always talked that way with his father and that it was very difficult for me to change.'[108] Witte dictated these lines in February 1911.

Later that spring, on 18 May, having reviewed much of his tenure as Alexander's Minister of Communications and Minister of Finances, Witte dictated remarks he entitled 'The Illness and Death of Alexander III'.[109] He remembered the unexpected sudden death and public funeral of his patron in autumn 1894 with an emotion that seemed derived from genuine grief. His daughter Vera recalled his 'teary eyes' and 'breaking voice' as he told her the news of the tsar's death.[110] Given all that followed the death of Alexander and the ascension of Nicholas, there was in these lines a profound sense of lost opportunities as well. Witte ended that day's work on an anecdotal, yet deeply personal note. He recalled how, at an audience with Alexander's widow several days after her husband had been buried, the Empress Marie Fedorovna had tried to comfort the solemn minister. She assured him that she knew how 'the death of the Emperor must be terribly burdensome for you, because, indeed, he loved you very much'. Witte then added one last sentence—'My subsequent tales will deal with the reign of the Emperor Nicholas '—and here halted his work.[111] He did not resume it again for another six months. Why the memoirist ceased work is unknown—although delaying his first formal confrontation with what for him was the long nightmare of Nicholas II's reign is a tempting explanation.

What can be emphasized with more certainty, however, was the importance for Witte of Alexander III's love, a word that conveyed in the first instance his deep personal loyalties to a tsar who promoted his career, policies, and power in the ministerial state. Authoritative if not authoritarian, incorruptible, morally upright, huge and powerful, Alexander, judging from Witte's memoirs, had bolstered his personal belief in the symbolic power of autocracy even before he assumed ministerial office. Yet, beneath these external characteristics of the tsarist persona, Witte discovered an emotional core—a sense of honor, honesty, and intuitive goodness—which evoked his allegiance, a fact that seemed to amaze him, careerist that in part he was. In observations that could only have come from his personal dealings with the tsar, Witte mused aloud that 'Emperor Alexander III possessed the most noble—most noble is not saying enough,' he interrupted himself, 'he really possessed a tsar's heart.' Such 'nobility', such an 'inviolably pure heart', Witte said, could only exist among Russian sovereigns, born as they were into 'conditions which do not force a man, concerned for his own situation or concerned for the situation of those near and dear to him, to betray his conscience or close his eyes to that which he would prefer not to see'. Witte sharply distinguished such 'mere mortals', assaulted as they were by 'egoistic, material interests which so often ruin a human heart', and Alexander III. Indicatively enough, he did so by taking issue with public critics who, employing a rational discourse, discounted the tsar as intellectually mediocre. 'It all depends', Witte countered, 'on what one understands by intelligence.' 'Perhaps', he allowed, 'Emperor Alexander III was short on an intelligence derived from reason (*um-razsudka*), but he had a huge, remarkable intuition (*um-serdtsa*), a kind of intelligence whose presence is incomparably more important than reason, especially often among people who must use their intelligence to foresee, presage, and fashion.'[112] Rulers acted in this way and Witte, given 'the remarkable nobility and purity of (his) heart, the purity of his morals and thinking', numbered 'Emperor Alexander III' among them:

> His words never differed from his actions. He might not speak his mind on matters about which he was uncertain, he might be silent, or wait you out, but if he said anything you could rely on his word as if it were a mountain of stone (*kak na kamennuiu goru*). As a result, Emperor Alexander III enjoyed, on the one hand, the general confidence and respect of all those around him and, on the other, which was even more important, the respect and confidence of the entire world.[113]

In these retrospective views of prerevolutionary autocracy, remarkable indeed, after the quarter-century that followed from this moment—through gilded age, triumphal power, a new century, depression, defeat, revolution, and personal crisis—were the still resilient depths of the confidence, respect, and emotional allegiance that Alexander III had engendered in Witte. Similarly noteworthy in 1911, after the disaster of defeat and the near implosion of the empire in 1905, were the poignant reminders of the imperial power and grandeur that the emperor Alexander III had represented before the entire world—a fundamental piece of Witte's own imperial dream. That dream, resting on the very tangible possibilities of a unified imperial economic market, was constituted as well from the alluring visions of imperial and autocratic power that were adrift in Russia at the end of the nineteenth century and that Witte, as we have seen, fundamentally shared. Indeed, under an autocrat like Alexander III and in an empire that stretched from Europe to the Pacific Ocean, Witte could dream of a unified imperial polity made powerful and wealthy by the underpinnings of a modern industrial economy. It was easy to dream when there were few nightmares—or little contrary evidence to disrupt them. This then too was a tale of the decade of the counterreforms.

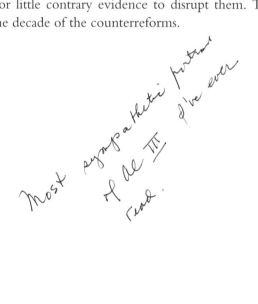

4

A City of Dreams: St Petersburg, the Empire of the Tsars, and Imperial Horizons in the Gilded Age (1889–1903)

After several days my father and I set out for the Ministry of Finances, on the Moika. As it turned out, we had to wait (at his formal receiving hour). Witte emerged before the assembled public and began to make the rounds of those attending him. He came up to us. He knew my father. He said that (minister of Justice) N. V. Muraviev had forewarned him about our request (for a service position in the Ministry). He took the formal request (*proshenie*) from me, handed it to a secretary, and directed me to the director of the department of railroad affairs V. V. Maksimov . . . The work was boring.

V. P. Lopukhin, 'Notes of a former department director
in the Ministry of Foreign Affairs, 1894–1917'[1]

. . . a certain well-known . . . (I forget his last name) an Englishman, if I'm not mistaken a Jew, who earned enormous personal wealth in african [sic] gold (this was before the Boer War; as much as I can recall his last name it was Ro(d-added over markout)es or something like that.)

*Memoirs/Tales in stenographic record/of
Count Sergei Iul'evich Witte*, 3 April 1911[2]

As the example of America has shown, the attraction (to domestic markets) of foreign capital, able to acclimate rapidly and generally not recognizing national distinctions, and accompanied by a protectionist policy, facilitates as nothing else can the growth of industry and, following that, the rapid creation of investment capital within the country itself, thereby encouraging widespread engagement of its laboring energy and bringing to life its natural riches. The Ministry of Finances has turned its attention first of all to the widespread attraction of capital to industry.

'Abstract of a program and a survey of the activity of the Ministry
of Finances in 1892 and subsequent years as presented
to the minister of finances in 1896', January 1896[3]

...the Asiatic East until recently was for the peoples of Europe an almost unexplored world...(B)uilding the Siberian Railway opens the gates of this formerly sealed world to Europe (and) places her face to face with the populous tribes of the Mongol race.

'Most Humble Report of the Minister of Finances
on Travel to the Far East', 1902[4]

After all one cannot forget that the tsarevich Nicholas became the Emperor Nicholas a year or a year and a half after his most august father, who loved him very much, himself said to me that his most august son was a boy and uninterested in state affairs or, at the least, was incapable of managing state affairs on his own.

*Memoirs/Tales in stenographic record/of Count
Sergei Iul'evich Witte*, 3 April 1911[5]

B y the time he resigned his office as Minister of Finances in August 1903 and became Chairman of the Committee of Ministers, the titular senior civil servitor in the Russian Empire, Actual Privy Councilor and State Secretary Sergei Iul'evich Witte, at age 54, was one of the most powerful men in the Russian Empire.[6] He had been a trusted adviser of one tsar, Alexander III, and a contentious but omnipresent counsel to his son, Nicholas II. He had built a Eurasian transcontinental railroad linking European Russia to the Far East. He had overseen the enrichment of the imperial treasury and placed its currency on the gold standard. He had expanded the tsarist state's stake in an imperial economy that had become an attractive commercial-industrial investment for foreign and domestic capitalists alike. He had become an international diplomatic figure through his adroit management of the empire's bond portfolio and banking affairs in Europe, China, North America, and Central Asia. He wielded power and influence in every corner of St Petersburg.

From the moment he had arrived in the imperial capital in 1889, he had begun to expand this power and influence: institutionally, culturally, and politically. Assuming direction of the Department of Railroad Affairs within the Ministry of Finances, he set about crafting an imperial rail network, still partly privately owned, but managed and regulated by a state that also aggressively expanded its direct ownership of an empire-wide system— managed, of course, from his office. Within two years, he won appointment

as the Minister of Ways of Communications, charged in particular to
mobilize famine relief in severely drought-afflicted provinces of the Volga
River valley. He oversaw railroad construction projects in the Caucasus, the
eastern coasts of the Black Sea, Central Asia and the Caspian Sea, Finland
and the Arctic north, and, as the decade wore on, across the vast expanses
of western and central Siberia toward Manchuria and the Pacific Far East.[7]
Asia long had shaped Witte's imperial imagination, just as it had several
generations of his contemporaries in the nineteenth century.[8] The trans-
Eurasian continental, the Great Siberian Way as the Russian government
called the Trans-Siberian Railroad, leveraged this imperial dream into
reality. The culmination of Witte's railroad career, the Trans-Siberian,
especially as he envisioned it, was designed to be a conduit for expanding
Russian commerce, political influence, and imperial hegemony in Asia and
the Pacific Far East. After a fateful decision in 1896 to lessen the distance
between Europe and the Pacific by constructing a rail line from Lake Baikal
across Chinese northern Manchuria to the Russian coastal city of Vladivostok, the Trans-Siberian was also embroiled in the international geopolitics
that resulted in Russia's disastrous military defeat by Japan in 1904–05.
Witte's controlling presence in the archived records of this project becomes
apparent after August 1892, when he replaced his ailing mentor and chief,
Ivan Vyshnegradskii, as Minister of Finances, and gained unrestricted access
to the treasury resources that his new office controlled.[9] He was 43.

These Petersburg years began what amounted to the story of the rest of
his life. He pursued his dreams: the socio-economic, cultural, and—by the
time war and revolution in 1904–05 began wracking the empire—the
political renovation of what he understood to be an imperial polity. One
part of telling Witte's story entails explaining his continuing insistence upon
what, throughout the rest of Europe by the end of the nineteenth century,
was an artificial demarche between the socio-economic needs of a society
and the political rights of a nation to address them. Ever a believer in
monarchy and, with increasing difficulty in the reign of Nicholas II, Russian
autocracy as well, Witte accepted the legitimacy of these institutions as fully as
he had in earlier decades of his life. They alone preserved the political power of
the servitor class from which he had come. They also assured the prerogatives
of the 'ruling house', as Witte would at times refer to the Romanov monarchy,
and its insistent familial identification with autocratic prerogatives unchallenged by national elections, parliamentary government, or constitutional
law. Only in 1905 would the Russian Empire be forced by military defeat

and revolutionary upheaval to assimilate these trappings of European democratic politics. They did not exist in 1900. Indeed, at the time of his coronation in 1896, Nicholas II, at the urging of his most conservative advisers, dismissed as 'senseless dreaming' the suggestion of moderate liberal opinion that the tsar consult with elected representatives of his people. A gilded age of economic and imperial expansion across and beyond the European continent, the 1890s was a decade in which the governing educated elites of imperial Russian society were left, relatively untouched by the necessities and demands of the country's majority populations, to imagine, and pursue, the wealth, power, and expanding horizons of the Russian Empire.[10]

Witte spent twelve years of these years (1892–1903) at the helm of the Ministry of Finances. At the core of his activity were four assumptions that had evolved from his thinking and experience since the 1860s. First, in his modern nineteenth century, Russian imperial power required an economy 1) based on industrial capitalism, an economic system that integrated industrial manufacturing, commerce, and agriculture to produce a seemingly limitless stream of investment capital, the motive force for its own expansion. Equally axiomatic was a second contention. Because natural limits existed to the amount of wealth that it could produce, an economy based chiefly 2) upon agriculture was backward. Amounts of land were fixed. The yield from agricultural labor often was consumed rather than marketed. Growing population placed more demand on fixed amounts of land and created impoverishment, unless new forms of technology and growing market demand sparked by industrial expansion could enrich agriculture as well. 3) Third, Witte also understood the increasingly international character of industrial capitalism. Labor, commodities, and capital all circulated with growing intensity, both inside individual nations and among the units of an increasingly interdependent international capitalist order, especially as the transportation and communication systems necessary to move people, goods, and capital across the globe became ever more technologically sophisticated. Finally, in an emerging global economy where other states—England, France, Germany, the USA—were more industrially advanced, modern, and powerful, polities like the Russian empire, whose economies remained reliant on agriculture and the export of raw materials, could not remain competitive and powerful if they allowed market forces to govern economic development. That was the lesson derived from an imperial age that saw European industrial powers using both their advanced militaries and cheap manufactured goods to dominate and colonize agrarian societies in Africa, Asia, and other non-European parts of the world. An Age of Empire required the state to govern the economy and assure its industrial modernity.[11]

Although articulated in late imperial Russian public discourse, firmly so within the Ministry of Finances even before Witte's arrival on the Moika, this equating of imperial power with industrial modernity was not an uncontested assumption in tsarist society. Its elites remained noble, aristocratic, and agrarian. Its majority population was peasant. Its dominant forms of economic activity were agriculture, commerce, and the production of raw materials. Contrasting views of the empire's future and thus of the proper role that the state should play in contemporary life collided across a spectrum of conservative, liberal, and radical public opinion. Was the state's chief appointment to maintain social order and popular welfare, as argued both traditionalists concerned to preserve overtly romanticized rural cultures and radical populists repulsed by the proletarianization and urbanization of Europe and America? Should the state, as many classical laissez-faire theorists and populist critics alike contended, restrict its interference in the national economy and allow industry to evolve organically, via a rural market economy that eventually would produce abundant labor, savings, investment capital, and consumer demand for the manufactured goods and technology of industry? Even were the argument accepted that an empire could not afford to wait for the market to work its magic, could the state treasury and its tax-paying population afford to work this magic itself? How, in a society whose population remained overwhelmingly rural, peasant, illiterate, and impoverished, could the state obtain the financial resources required to fund the development of industrial modernity?

Such questions, as well as the broader issues they raised about the character and development of the late imperial economy, are deeply ingrained in modern Russian history. They were the focus of debate during Witte's years in the Ministry of Finances, and remain so for economic historians today. Three consensus positions exist in this literature. The first is perhaps the most weathered and least convincing, although perhaps the most widespread in popular perception of Russian history. The state's drive to industrialize ultimately failed because, in order to augment an industrial infrastructure that supported the imperial state's military and imperial ambitions, the government exhausted the fiscal, financial, and physical capacities of a peasant population that was the primary source of investment capital and market demand. Government policy thus further exacerbated the impoverishment, immiseration, and backwardness it purportedly was intended to escape—and thus contributed to the revolutionary crisis the empire confronted in the early twentieth century.[12] A second, still well established view, first offered at the heights of the twentieth-century cold war by modernization theorists, recognized Witte as an avatar of state-sponsored industrial modernization. Foreshadowing the much grander soviet industrialization drive of the 1930s under Stalin, Witte's industrialization from above sought to escape Russian agrarian backwardness, not via a market economy, but via direct state investment in the coal, iron, steel, and chemical technological infrastructures of the first and second industrial revolutions. That investment, and the wages, savings, and capital it created rippled outward through the rest of the national economy, in particular its banking, commercial, and agricultural sectors, to become self-sustaining by the time of the First World War.[13] A third consensus, shared here, is that by the end of the long nineteenth century, between 1885 and 1914, the Russian Empire was witnessing a self-sustaining commercial and industrial expansion of its national economy. Emphasizing that Russia in this period displayed an 'Asian pattern of development', characterized by high capital investment, high government spending, and low rates of per capita consumption, Paul Gregory has characterized the late empire as 'an economy taking the first steps toward affluence'. This view holds, correctly, that the chief result and objective of nineteeth-century industrial capitalism were capital and its further investment. On both fronts, tsarist Russia was becoming a relatively successful member of the European community, even if the bulk of its population continued to exhibit some of the lowest standards of living on the continent.[14]

Rather than industrialization—a word rarely if ever found in the late nineteenth-century Russian lexicon—Witte's economic vision saw a 'commercial-industrial' (*torgovo-promyshlennaia*) economy that was a constituent element of an international capitalist order. In a global economy, every state sought to attract investment capital, employ labor, and produce commodities, including capital, the source of future wealth. The challenge, Witte knew, was to entice this capital, whether foreign or domestic, to the Russian Empire. An imperial currency backed by gold, the international denominator of value at the end of the nineteenth century, became his talisman. The *Imperial*, the gold coin established in 1896, was intended to signify to domestic and foreign investors alike the stability, prosperity, and future commercial-industrial expansion of the Russian Empire that Witte envisioned. As the old memoirist remembered it in December 1911, placing the imperial economy on the gold standard was 'one of the most fundamental reforms which it befell me to complete during all the time of my being in power (and) finally stabilized Russian credit and placed Russia financially in the rank of a great European power'.[15] In a memo that constituted formal bureaucratic rationale, he assumed that this measure ensured Russia's place, 'like other countries of Europe', in an international system of circulating gold species that ebbed and flowed from country to country depending upon the investment climates of individual national markets. Europeans would seek profitable investments in Russia, where interest and dividend income was higher than elsewhere on the continent, because 'bonds naturally seek the buyer who will pay most', the report laconically noted.[16]

The future, Witte believed, rested on economic wealth and imperial power. He sought to augment them both in the 1890s. From the Ministry of Finances, a pinnacle of bureaucratic power in the imperial capital, he consummately supervised the commercial-industrial economy of the empire, allocated the treasury resources that increasingly in the 1890s poured into it, and, through these instruments, influenced a multitude of issues that his ministry's sprawling operations funded or controlled. In St Petersburg, a city that both Fedor Dostoevskii and Andrei Bely knew to be a city of dreams, Witte set about realizing what he had spent at least the previous decade imagining: an imperial polity rooted in commercial-industrial prosperity throughout the Eurasian expanse of the Russian Empire.[17] That quest led him to involvement in the international geopolitics of the Asian Pacific and a fateful partnership with the son of Alexander III. Witte's dreams led not only to commercial prosperity and imperial power, but foreign entanglement, military adventurism, and war with the Empire of Japan. It was a paradox—and ultimately Sergei Witte's personal crisis of faith—that the effort to realize his dreams also created nightmares of military defeat, political turmoil, and personal abandonment that haunted him for the rest of his life.

Gospodin Minister: Witte as Imperial Official

Russian literature has never been kind to the *chinovnik*, the Russian official who haunted the labyrinth of offices, departments, and ministries that together were the imperial state. Looming over the type was Chichikov, Nikolay Gogol's vampish investigator, whose knowledge of byzantine regulations allowed him to scheme his way toward social standing by purchasing 'dead souls', deceased peasant serfs still registered on the tax rolls of thick-headed Russian country gentry and thus alive in the eyes of the state. Mikhail Saltykov-Shchedrin, the mid nineteenth century satirist, produced novels and short stories that made tsarist officialdom an impossible impediment to progress, even civilization. Anton Chekhov drew the type repeatedly in drama and especially prose. His short story 'Anna Round the Neck' played on the older male official, Modest Alekseevich, who married the 18-year-old daughter of a debt-ridden family and displayed her beauty like the St Anne's Cross he lusted to hang round his neck, one award in a peacock fan of medals, ribbons, gifts, and monetary rewards that all communicated standing and favor to refined imperial sensibilities. When she learned that youth and beauty could create freedom from the dull embrace of her insufferable husband, her escalating demands for his money and self-effacement made of her, Chekhov punned, an altogether different Anna that hung heavily round his neck. If Chekhov satirized, Leo Tolstoy revealed Alexei Karenin, obsessed with the case file (*delo*), the administrative or legal project whose movement through that maze of offices required technical knowledge and created power (*deloproizvodstvo*). He was an honest man, slow to anger and easily taken advantage of, but thoroughly vindictive. He spent most of his time at work. He made his marriage to the young, vivacious Anna Karenina lifeless, and drove her into the arms of a lover and onto the tracks of a railroad.

Certainly there was something of Chichikov in Witte, and the years that unfolded from his appointment in 1889 as an imperial official repeatedly tested his ability to distinguish wiliness and honesty. His climb toward power was meteoric. Most observers suspect Witte's ego if not megalomania, and underestimate his talent and intellect. A departmental director in the Ministry of Finances in 1889, by April 1892 he had become Minister of Ways of Communication, and by the end of that summer, when it became clear that the ailing Vyshnegradsky would not recover his health, Alexander III turned to Witte as acting Minister of Finances.[18] B. A. Romanov related how legend had it that Alexander III appointed Witte a minister because the tsar was stunned by his 'knowledgeability (*osvedomlennost'*)'—what Romanov portrayed as some combination of intellectual power, natural reservoirs of physical and emotional energy, and an ability to join the masquerade of the heavily ritualized political and public life of tsarist Russia. Witte knew how 'to have the look of a person who knew a secret he never would reveal entirely but only in snippets (*lish' odnim kraem*)', wrote Romanov of a man who as a boy on the far-off frontier of imperial Georgia had learned the masquerade in the salons and banquet halls of his grandparents.[19]

Those who worked with Witte praised his honesty, hard-working example, and the reliability of both his intellect and his patronage. A. S. Ermolov, a protégé whom Witte promoted to ministerial rank in 1893, wrote in a letter that Witte preserved in his private papers how he 'had learned to value (Witte) not only as a supervisor, but as a man who is direct, open, on whose word one can rely'.[20] Others would testify of corruption— or a willingness to do business. V. P. Lopukhin by 1896 was working under V. I. Kovalevskii to organize the great Nizhnii–Novgorod Trade Fair of that year. Lopukhin recounted how Kovalevskii, heading a project intended to display the commercial-industrial achievements of the empire and its Ministry of Finances, found himself suspected at every turn by the provincial governor, who reported to the rival Ministry of Internal Affairs and bore imperial appointment from the tsar. To overcome this impediment, Kovalevskii promised the governor 200,000 rubles to fete the emperor and his entourage when they visited the fair, and another 20,000 rubles as an imperial favor bestowed upon the governor at Witte's request as an award for bringing the trade fair to fruition. All this activity was legal.[21] In 1910, Kovalevskii, Witte's closest and most skilled collaborator, also wrote a letter, again preserved by Witte in his archive, that warmly recalled their work together. 'You were the central figure of this epoch . . . around you gathered bold activists, who rejoiced in the new, the better, the future.'[22] Kovalevskii described a generation of officials who, beginning careers in the Ministry of Finances, after the turn of the century in turn filled key positions in the commercial-industrial, banking, and managerial elites of the empire.[23]

Witte was anything but immune to the legendary penchant of the imperial official to display his status, privilege, and influence.[24] Alexander III awarded Witte his St Anne's, first-class, in 1894. Buried in his personal archive was a large box containing ninety-three different awards from foreign governments, and, reflecting his complex positioning in public life, numerous honorary memberships in academic, scientific, technical, charitable, and artistic societies.[25] A slow yet steady advance upward through the fourteen rungs of the civilian Table of Ranks marked his life, each one marked out by uniform, formal title of address, salary, medals,

housing and travel allowances, and ever more commodious crown apartments and vacation homes. He distributed the same as rewards to loyal and
hardworking subordinates. 'On awards to individuals for service in rank'
was a routine report in the ministry's archives. Salary increases, gifts and
cash bonuses at the new year holiday, child support cash payments, the
continuance of salary and housing for widows of ministry officials, a
230,000 ruble renovation of a former royal palace to house ministerial
departments, even a pilgrimage to Jerusalem, and repetitive requests for
medical leaves to recover ruined or strained male health: Witte rewarded
his subordinates.[26]

In return, they worked for him. V. P. Meshchersky observed that the
omnipresent V. I. Kovalevskii always seemed to be awash in the affairs of his
department, so much so that it seemed 'that nobody could ever find him,
and then five minutes of conversation with V. I. Kovalevskii equaled days of
hopeless searching. He was never hiding, but simply seemed to those
searching for him to have disappeared because in the course of a day he
managed to be in several commissions and conferences, or visiting various
individuals, and everywhere he was talking, everywhere he was building
castles in the air that were of undoubted benefit for those listening to him.'
Kovalevskii had what Meshcherskii called 'a capacity for improvisation at
work (delovaia improvizatsiia)'. Lost amidst a day's worth of commissions,
Kovalevskii, ascertaining his next appointment while traveling there in a
cab, would improvise his tenth speech of the day without even having read
a formal memorandum about the subject, so immersed was he in the stream
of correspondence, draft projects, statistics, and paperwork that flowed
through his department.[27]

The records of the Ministry of Finances were filled with work in
maddening detail, bursts of policy deliberations and petty detail haphazardly
intermingled. Witte at work read everything, digested concepts, searched
out the main ideas as can be seen in his underlining and marginalia. His staff
were key—he relied on them for information, expertise, and relentless
labor. 'Discuss this again (peregovorit')', 'Report about this (dolozhit')',
'Write a summary abstract (sostavit' spravku)' were imperatives scrawled in
increasingly illegible pencil in the margins of typed and hand-written draft
reports, correspondence, legislative projects, telegrams, and budget state-
ments. Life in a hierarchically ordered workplace created an endless processing of the files (deloproizvodstvo) that flowed across his desk. Some required
his decision, others he distributed to subordinates or passed upwards to

more powerful 'chiefs' (*nachal'niki*), who, once he became a minister, was the emperor himself. Still others he handed laterally to other officials in hierarchical organizations similar to his own, knowing that he required their support or approval to move his own idea forward. All of this occurred at a pace and level of intensity that made his work day extend from late morning until well past midnight, a social life of salons, dinners, theater, opera, and card playing never entirely divorced from the personal and institutional contacts and networks that he assiduously cultivated and influenced during the day.[28]

Much of the work, however, was routine. Witte often paced the office in debate with both himself and subordinates, or dictated commentaries to attentive subordinates struggling to stay abreast of the flow of his thoughts. His ministerial files contain very little preparatory paperwork from inside the ministry itself. Much more typical is a letter or document from an outside petitioner or correspondent, his remark on the document, at times a request to a subordinate of the proper department or desk for advice or further work, the consultation with that subordinate, and a draft by the appropriate official of his original comment into the formal—and stultifying—prose of the bureaucrat state. In very important cases he might edit and review, especially if the matter went to the sovereign in what was known as 'A Most Humble Report (*vsepoddaneishii doklad*)' transmitted from subordinates to supervisors throughout the ministry and treated in great detail when they contained anything Witte deemed to be in his interests. An early set of such reports compiled by Witte in 1889 while still a department director, although because he was still so junior in the ministry's ranks his were *report notes* (*dokladnye zapiski*), reflected the mixture of small detail and policy initiatives, as well as the range of Witte's tastes, to be found littered in the records of this ministry—church construction in Trans-Caucasia, monuments to Catherine II and Lermontov, a memorial to mark the wreck of the imperial train at Borka, expropriation of a privately owned railroad line, and new railroad tariff legislation. These first footprints also contained evidence of his continuing obsession with the press and his manipulation of its opinion through cash subsidies to journalists out of ministerial funds.[29]

By all accounts, he appeared in St Petersburg and took it by storm, becoming a fixture in its '*obshchestvo*', that 'society' of salons, townhouses, gentlemen's clubs, investment and banking houses, editorial offices, university departments and academic institutes, government offices and receiving halls, churches and charitable organizations, scholarly societies, and bedrooms which constituted it. More than simply a sociological construct, society was also a cultural receptacle for layer upon layer of what Alfred Rieber has called the 'sedimentary society', whose rich cultural heritage had accumulated in the educated and westernizing experience of the families and clans that had gravitated to the empire's capital ever since Peter the Great had made it the residence of the imperial court in the early eighteenth century.[30] As had been true in his boyhood, so too now did the salon stand at the forefront of his recollections. Witte began his reminiscences of his years in the Ministry of Finances with the salon of his patron, Ivan Vyshnegradsky, the critical acquaintanceship he struck up there with a beautiful, influential, and aristocratic woman, and the introduction she supplied to the adjutant-general and favored companion of Alexander III, P. A. Cherevin.[31] P. L. Bark, a young official of the ministry during the 1890s, recalled this social world as very much an extension of work. The most noticeable contrast between the German Reichsbank, where he was posted for seven months of training, and the Russian State Bank were the hours of work. In Berlin, he became accustomed to a full day and a busy social life in the evening. Upon returning to Russia, he discovered committee meetings late into the evening, and then a round of socializing that he would be forced to leave if he were to be at work in the morning. 'We Russians turned night into day like the Spaniards,' he recalled in his own memoirs, 'and usually came home in the early morning when we had been out to a function the evening before.'[32]

That social world and the connections it created were recapitulated, as we have seen, in crenellated detail by the old memoirist, each time his reminiscences came across an episode that connected his life to the apex of the Russian social and political order, the Imperial Court. As his stature grew in St Petersburg—and few ministers wielded more influence institutionally than the Minister of Finances, who held in his hands the purse strings of the state treasury—so too did his access to, and preoccupation with, the Romanov imperial court. To some, the court simply was 'behind the scenes (*za kulisami*)', its internecine politics an ongoing shadow war of intrigue among the most aristocratic, traditionalist, conservative, and, after the turn of the century, proto-fascist elements of imperial Russian society. At the center and apex of the court was the royal family, a line of the Romanov imperial house that reached back directly to Catherine the Great and culminated in Alexander III and his son Nicholas II, together with their influential wives, Marie and Alexandra, the latter a niece of Queen Victoria of England. Around this head of the ruling house was a pantheon of princely grand dukes and duchesses, whole lines of often distantly related cousins descended from a sibling of a sovereign. They exerted great influence upon imperial politics and the cultural life of high society, more often by the end of the old regime not on the basis of their talent, but by virtue of bloodlines that did not guarantee against mediocrity. The court also was a center of public ritual and performance—religious services, military pageantry, formal rituals of state, public appearances—that propagated the prestige, authority, and culture of tsarist monarchy. Echoing systems of status dating back to late medieval Muscovy resting on proximity to the person of the tsar, the imperial court also evoked a sociological hierarchy for an imperial world still envisioned by many as a pyramid culminating at the royal throne.[33]

For Witte, that proximity to tsar was an elixir, one that with time he came to crave. Typically, he met weekly with the sovereign to report on ministerial business, although often the venue of these meetings would change, depending on the residence of a royal family that created for itself some of the great palaces of eastern Europe and vacation spas of the Black Sea basin. In his reminiscences, Witte repeatedly referenced its movement—to visit relatives or heads of state in Europe, hunt in Poland, cruise in the Baltic Sea, recuperate in Crimea, or travel through the empire. An invitation to dine with the family was a sign of royal favor. These were infrequent, although more often when Alexander III reigned and rarely, as we shall have opportunity to see, after the younger Nicholas came to the throne. Witte remembered seemingly any conversation with a royal personage, perhaps because he already had repeated it in society to exhibit his own proximity and access to power, prestige, and influence.[34] In the end, however, Witte was an official, a *chinovnik*, whose social access to the imperial court was limited, in part by his outsider, noveau, *arriviste* reputation in St Petersburg high society, in part by his marriages to divorcées, and in part as well by the middling standing of his own family background. Witte received invitations to court functions and, given his high civil rank, enjoyed great formal respect and entitlement. However, neither he nor his wife or step-daughter was ever granted a formal ceremonial title as an attendant at court. That fact, judging at least from the evidence of his memoirs, vexed him.[35] Witte was an official. Karenin, although he walked the corridors of power, rarely approached the throne.

Perhaps more akin to the age of empire in the 1890s, other rhythms also informed his daily life. His penchant for travel and exploration, now fully empowered by a ministerial portfolio, led him to tour far northern Murmansk, to order ethnographic expeditions to the Arctic, and to travel at the first opportunity in 1902 to the Pacific coast on the newly completed transcontinental railroad.[36] Education and culture remained foci of his attention, from primary education in clerical schools through technological universities to an array of cultural sponsorships he supported. These ranged from the Academy of Sciences' centenary celebrations of Pushkin's birth to a scholarship for families of SWRR employees at Novorossiisk University for a student of his old faculty, physics–mathematics, to become a professor of theoretical mathematics.[37] In April 1899, he was appointed a corresponding member of the Physics-Mathematics Division of the Imperial Academy of Sciences.[38] His studies also included most notably his mastery of what in the imperial bureaucratic world was called 'the peasant question', modernizing Russia's ever shifting understanding of agrarian Russia and the colonizer's conviction that law, administration, and courts could influence and shape proprietary and public behavior at the frontier that separated his world of society (obshchestvo) from that of the peasant hut and village (izba and selo).[39] Witte was involved intimately with the fiscal and investment policies of the empire, as he seized opportunities for making Russia a market open to foreign capital investment, and thus better positioned for increased commercial exchange in near, central, and far eastern Asia.[40] By 1896 he thought of himself as a statesman with international reputation, as his work with Nicholas II in the international disarmament movement would attest, most notably at the Hague Peace Conference of that year.[41] The appointment in 1900 of his card-playing friend and noble ally Dmitrii Sipiagin to be the Minister of Internal Affairs marked his continuing political ascendancy.[42] The great Nizhnii-Novgorod Trade Fair of 1896, the construction of the Siberian Pavilion at the 1900 Paris World's Fair, the ritualized public celebration in 1902 of the centenary of the Ministry of Finance: all of these and an avalanche more constituted Witte's life as an imperial official.[43]

Leo Tolstoy, when he wrote Karenin as the imperial official, knew that marriage to Anna, and the turbulent world in which the institution of marriage found itself in the late Victorian era, was the subject of a novel. That Tolstoy knew men of Witte's class, and their apparent attraction to wooing married women and cuckolding their husbands, does not explain Witte's two marriages to women whose divorces he arranged. In summer 1892, Witte married again, his bride Matilda Ivanovna Khotinskaia-Lisanevich, a divorcée of Jewish heritage whom Witte courted and married within three years of the death of his first wife.[44] When the two met, he had been a widower, living alone. 'I almost accidentally in the theater noticed in the loge one lady, who made a great impression on me, but I did not then pursue finding out who this lady was,' he began a story he told at length. 'That summer I saw her again on the islands' north of St Petersburg, where the city's elites escaped to their dachas, he remembered, 'and then discovered that she was Madame Lisanevich, whose husband was a relative of Adjutant-General O. B. Rikhter, the tutor of Alexander III and head of his petitions commission.' One can only imagine Witte that summer . . . burdened by work, dinner parties and cards on evenings, circulating in salon society. 'I accidentally became acquainted with the Lisaneviches. Madame Lisanevich turned out to be that woman who had made such an impression on me in the theater,' he continued. How he would have then become part of their company, enough that the old man could ponder how 'occasionally afterwards' he would be in the couple's company and notice how the husband conducted himself in 'a most impossible way toward his wife and that their familial happiness (schast'e) was entirely destroyed', Witte left unexplained. At that point he decided to persuade Madame Lisanevich to leave her husband and marry him, which was 'very easy' given the husband's behavior toward her.[45]

When the divorce had been arranged, Witte continued in what seemed a highly stylized narrative, it occurred to him that he could not remain Minister of Communications after marrying a divorced woman. That status was then viewed as extraordinary and socially unacceptable, especially at the court of Alexander III and his wife, Marie Fedorovna, whose own familial happiness was a set piece of the court's official ideology during the reign. He intended to marry Lisanevich, and return to private business, and protocol dictated that he report this fact and decision to the sovereign. Through a fellow minister, Ivan Durnovo, Witte conveyed to Alexander that his decision to marry the divorced Lisanevich was irreversible, and that he found his personal situation untenable, given that only recently had he agreed to serve the sovereign as his minister. At his next audience with the emperor, Witte formally offered his resignation, which Alexander refused, aware of the details of the case and implicitly suggesting how valorous he found saving this woman in distress to be. That showed what 'an honorable fellow' he was, Witte remembered the emperor saying about him—hearsay of hearsay!—and 'how this action only deepened the emperor's confidence and respect.'[46]

Several days later he married her, in the church of the Institute of his ministry. Much as Karenin likely would have done, the next day Witte went back to work. An international railroad congress then taking place, for the first time in St Petersburg, drew him the day after his wedding to a dinner for the congress at the Winter Palace. The event was remembered, plainly, for the spectacle that was played out that evening as public attention in the banquet hall turned to Witte and Rikhter, because all knew, as Witte recalled the tale, that this courtier was a relative of the Lisanevich whom Witte had just embroiled in divorce proceedings. Witte claimed his relationship with Rikhter remained business-like and cordial, but then huffed that he never again spoke with or bowed to his wife. 'When I married, a horrific hub-bub of every sort of gossip immediately was raised in all the high society women's spheres. And this hub-bub and gossip flowed not so much at me, because I did not pay it the least attention, as to my wife....'[47]

She also was Jewish. A former university classmate and personal friend, G.E. Afanasiev, told this same story differently in a 1915 obituary of Witte. She was 'a jewess (*evreika*)', and Witte's fears of her origins, and not her status as a divorcée, were his real concern in going to the tsar. He was resolved, Afanasiev wrote, that he would resign, 'put a cross on top of my entire career and travel abroad to live'.[48] Mathil'da Ivanovna Witte, at the end of her own life in 1922 the Countess Witte, is the heroine of this story, the guardian of her husband's writings that are the basis of this book. Their love for each other is to this observer genuine and his devotion to her unwavering. So testified their daughter, whom Witte made his ward in 1896.[49] A grandson's correspondence in 1913–14 to his grandfather testified to the warm love that reached from Witte, through Mathil'da's daughter Vera, to Vera's son, Leva Naryshkin.[50] Correspondence hand-written by Sergei to Mathil'da at the turn of the century is warm, caring, passionate, and, at times reflective and despondent. He loved and sought comfort in her.[51]

The Witte System and the Empire of Gold

Moving to his offices 'on the Moika', the building of the Ministry of Finances with its sweeping vistas onto Palace Square and the Winter Palace, Witte, in autumn 1892, inquired of Alexander III regarding his 'most humble obligation to request of His Imperial Majesty an indication as to what salary His Majesty will be so good as to designate for the Acting

Minister of Finances'. Alexander merely wrote in the margin '18,000 r,' but added an additional 25,000 rubles to renovate and furnish the minister's private apartments. Generous but hardly startling, the compensation paled before the volume of work that he found on his desk that autumn. Vyshnegradskii, who had suffered a stroke the previous February and taken a leave of absence, had been assaulted by the fiscal crisis caused by the famine and cholera epidemic still afflicting the middle and lower reaches of the Volga River valley. This ecological and human disaster had complicated ongoing ministerial policy, which aimed to stabilize a ruble paper currency whose fluctuating value had made it an object of speculative investment on Russian and European markets. That objective dictated rigorous constraint of government spending, intensified efforts at tax collection, encouragement of grain export despite famine, the negotiation of commercial treaties with Russia's major trading partners, and the slow accumulation of treasury reserves to allow the eventual establishment of an imperial gold currency. In his last report to Alexander of February 1892, he detailed four different bond issues or loan guarantees currently being managed by the treasury. Vyshnegradskii also was using the new Department of Railroad Affairs to assert treasury control over unprofitable private railroad companies which relied on state guarantees to pay shareholders dividends and every year cost the treasury, he wrote in a letter to Witte, 'a weighty sum in the millions'.[52]

Witte's first entry in the record of the finance ministry echoed many of these same concerns. His handwritten commentary and instructions littered an internal survey on 'the status of the economy of Russia', written in September by F. G. Terner, the acting minister whom he was replacing.[53] Addressing the famine, Terner advocated various water and reforestation public works projects to decrease the aridity of the soil, which drew from Witte an acerbic veto: 'with such energetic decisions about the allocation of revenues,' he remarked, 'the treasury would be deprived of both them and of bountiful harvests.' He was far more interested in accelerating resettlement into Siberia from the overpopulated rural provinces of central European Russia, especially with construction of the Trans-Siberian under way. Witte devoted singular attention to a state budget deficit in 1892–93 approaching 93 million rubles for the year. Marginalia scribbled in large blue pencil across the page made even more pronounced his insistence that the state treasury's gold reserve of some 35–55 million rubles not be used to cover this shortfall, which would only lend credence to rumors of Russian state bankruptcy circulating on European credit markets. Accumulated painstakingly over the decade of the 1880s, state gold reserves, and the creditworthiness of both imperial treasury bonds and the Russian paper ruble which gold purportedly supported, were non-negotiable. Hewing to a strategy of indirect taxation that the imperial state had pursued throughout the century, Witte ordered the deficits covered by increased excise taxes on wine, beer, and alcohol. The following summer the ministry gained approval to begin field testing a state liquor monopoly and excise tax in four eastern provinces of European Russia, which by the end of the decade would be universal across the empire and a significant treasury fiscal resource.[54] He rejected the idea of an income tax as unrealizable in a country where so many peasant households lacked the base income that would make such a tax, he argued, simple and just. Left unmentioned was the general lack of state administrative resources necessary to create and administer it.[55]

A desperate search for tax revenues, especially when wrung from a rural population that had developed complex strategies to avoid paying them, was a weathered cultural pattern exhibited by the tsarist state and a succession of its finance ministers.[56] Witte was no exception, but the scale and scope of the expenditures he intended these revenues to support extended well beyond the accumulation of gold reserves. They encompassed a roster of budgetary expenditures, first among which were his plans to construct the Trans-Siberian Railroad, expand and improve the imperial railroad net-work, and begin its nationalization. Initially confirmed by imperial rescript in March 1891, the trans-Siberian project had languished since then over concerns about its costs. Within four months of Witte assuming control of the state's finances, he had produced a financing scheme, a set of hopelessly low estimates, to construct the line over a ten-year period. By early the following winter he had convened the interministerial committee, chaired by the young heir Nicholas, to mediate conflicts among the bureaucratic interests vying to control this grandiose state enterprise.[57] The archival records of the construction project were to be found within an office called the Siberian Desk of the Chancellory of the Minister of Finances. From there, the minister oversaw a project whose tentacles over the next ten years extended across Eurasia toward the Pacific: the 'colonization' of Siberia and the land surveying necessary to support it; the construction of rail factories; topographical, economic, hydrographic, and botanical research along the Arctic Sea coastline, Siberian river systems, and Lake Baikal; the exploration of mineral deposits, especially coal and gold, in Siberia; and various con-struction projects, from schools and churches to a commercial port in

Vladivostok and the development of a fishing industry in Pacific Ocean waters off Sakhalin Island.[58] He intensified an ongoing drive to expand the imperial rail network, which sparked perennial debates among the Communications, Finances, and War Ministries over the costs, commercial impact, and strategic significance of railroad construction, but nevertheless resulted in a significant expansion of the network during the years that Witte headed two of these three competitors.[59] At the same time, he began to exercise the treasury's contractual right to expropriate some 8,000 miles of privately owned rail lines, one of a series of measures he directed toward the consolidation of a crown railroad network. That work involved negotiating with European and Russian banks representing private shareholders and chartered corporations that in many cases continued to operate the line and pay a negotiated percentage of annual revenues to the treasury.[60]

Opening European credit and commercial markets to Russian treasury obligations and exported raw materials, a chief appointment of the Ministry of Finances, grew in importance, given the scale of expenditures that his ministry began to undertake. Negotiations to facilitate Russian commerce in the Danube River valley, construct a freight highway into northern Iran, or establish commercial trade treaties with Egypt and Serbia all were under way within his first year of work.[61] Of greater import to his own reputation was the successful conclusion of a new commercial treaty with Germany. Stalemated negotiations since 1891 had pitted increased Russian import tariffs on German manufactured goods against the higher tariffs Germany imposed in retaliation upon its imports of Russian grains, forest products, and cattle. Witte hardened the Russian negotiating position. In October 1892 he offered the carrot of an arranged marriage and the stick of a tariff war. The two empires would extend each other most-favored nation status by negotiating lowered tariffs for favored categories of exports and imports. Failure to agree on mutually beneficial terms, he threatened, would create an escalating round of tariff increases. Confronting German intransigence, Witte fired the first shot, and set off what in his memoirs he called 'a most vociferous, show-no-mercy (bezposhchadnaia) trade war'. Its intensity, and the uncertainty about challenging powerful Germany that it provoked, by the following summer had provoked murmurings at the imperial court— what he remembered as near social ostracism at public events—against the overly rash actions of a finance minister seemingly bent on provoking outright military conflict.[62] Eventual German concessions that fall, and a lowering of Russian rates in response, produced in January 1894 a new treaty that greatly heightened Witte's reputation, both at home and abroad. 'My debut on the world stage greatly surprised all in Europe,' the old memoirist recalled, thinking back on the rapid expansion of his power and prestige. This included, he recorded with evident pride, the retired German chancellor, Bismarck.[63]

The Department of Trade and Manufacturing, once Witte appointed V. I. Kovalevskii to be its director in fall 1892, became the ministry's clearing house for commercial–industrial affairs. It oversaw the negotiation of commercial treaties, sought to accelerate commercial shipbuilding and marine freight, looked to facilitate the long-distance shipment of grain to export termini, and unsurprisingly searched for new sources of commercial and industrial taxation.[64] It also developed commercial–technical education and law. It proposed an expansion of the factory inspectorate, a force of ministry officials operating in industrial regions charged to supervise an industrial workplace increasingly affected by working-class unrest and violence, and mediate the conflicting interests of ownership and labor. Legislation governing workers' insurance for industrial disability and accidental death, as well as children's and women's labor, was also developed. In June of that year, Alexander III approved the department's proposal for 'The All-Russian Industrial Exposition in Nizhnii-Novgorod' to be held in 1896 at the Nizhnii-Novgorod trade fair, a great annual gathering of commercial wholesalers and merchants at the confluence of the Oka and Volga Rivers. With public pomp and ritual, this event was intended to demonstrate 'the successes achieved in various branches of national industry and the invigoration of our commerce'. Situating the fair in Nizhnii was ideal, 'given its central position on the trade route to the East, as well as its excellent rail and river transportation connections and proximity to the Moscow industrial region.' The exposition's exhibits would accentuate the trade routes that historically had bound Nizhnii-Novgorod 'with Persia, Central Asia, and China', and feature as accurate a presentation as possible of 'the commerce conducted with these countries by Russia and the States competing with us'. Witte personally made the announcement in July and entered into formal dialogue with representatives of the Nizhni-Novgorod 'merchantry' (*kupechestvo*), the state corporation of this municipality's self-administration, about celebrating through the Fair and the Trans-Siberian Railroad the achievements of national industry.[65]

Marxist political commentators of the era privileged this moment to signal the rising of a new commercial–industrial class in the empire that was displacing the landed gentry and noble aristocracy that traditionally had held sway in tsarist society.[66] That explanation of historical transformation is much less convincing today, although Witte himself embraced its constituent parts, arguing in 1897 that failure to ennoble commercial and industrial wealth could weaken the social structures of a conservative, monarchical political order.[67] Both illustrated, however, an awareness of the profound underlying transformations of tsarist economy and society contemporaries believed were occurring in the late imperial era. Within the Ministry of Finances, the fullest accounting of these structural shifts, and the strategies the ministry was deploying to leverage them, was written in January 1896 for the ministry's General Chancellory. This seventy-page 'abstract of a program and survey' of all ministerial policy since Witte had assumed office in 1892 was a text that the minister reviewed and approved for publication. It is the fullest and most succinct explication of Witte's vision of the imperial Russian economy, as well as the frankest explication of the numerous obstacles that Russian law and culture placed in the path of its realization.[68]

The ministry proclaimed its program to be 'the expansion of the economic well-being of the population as the only pathway to improving the national economy and assuring its future growth'. In utilitarian language that valued capital, labor, and commodities, the report argued that personal and national wealth within the empire derived from accelerating the exploitation of Russia's rich but often underutilized, even 'dormant' natural and human resources. To accomplish that goal required increased capital investment in the imperial economy. Investment increased production of mineral and agricultural commodities, as well as manufactured goods. Expanding wealth throughout the economy in turn created greater market demand and consumption. This increased circulation of capital, goods, and labor was already creating 'more favorable conditions of action for all participants of the national economy', the report maintained. The economy, in short, was creating conditions for its own self-sustaining expansion—although nothing here suggested a contradiction between that goal and a continuing significant role for the state as economic arbiter and investor. Indeed, because this report surveyed not only every sector of the imperial economy, but also the commercial–industrial business cultures each created, what was also evident in the text was just how sweeping were the statist impulses now governing Witte's thinking. To achieve his vision of a modern imperial economy required the transformation of Russian commercial-industrial life. Not even that was beyond Witte's dreams in this gilded age.[69]

Given the extent to which capital investment informed the ministry's views, it should not be surprising that the report's first concern was the ruble currency and the gold standard. Frequently an object of speculative investment on European financial markets, the paper ruble's instability was one of the key 'factors retarding the proper course of the country's economic development.' Foreign capital markets, doubting Russia's reliability as a creditor (*kreditosposobnost'*), hosted a costly, speculative 'game' on the ruble's fluctuating value. Domestically, a volatile money system also created opportunities for speculative profit-taking that diverted capital from productive uses. Prices of commodities fluctuated unpredictably, 'healthy entrepreneurialism (*zdorovaia predpriimchivost'*)' sapped by 'outbursts of price speculation (*azhiatozhnye vspyshki*)' developed weakly, and, it was argued, Russia witnessed 'the slow accumulation of capital (*tikhii rost kapitalov*) in a country richly endowed by nature'. A series of 'energetic measures' undertaken since 1892 aimed to stabilize the market value of the paper ruble and move toward the establishment of a gold standard. A series of measures sought to aggrandize 'the powerful, ready weapon of a large gold reserve' that the ministry had accumulated in the last decade. The use of gold in private market transactions was forbidden. All transactions in foreign currency (*valiuta*) were to be conducted only through organs of the Finance Ministry—the treasury, the State Bank, or the customs service. Private banks found to be engaged in speculative currency transactions were subject to ministerial audit. Astute refinancing that lowered interest rates on state bond issues and over time reduced the total indebtedness of the treasury also raised the creditworthiness of the imperial state. Efforts to increase the attractiveness of Russian business opportunities on foreign capital markets also were under way. The State Bank guaranteed the foreign credit of any Russian business engaged in foreign trade. Treasury bonds that financed projects with 'strictly productive purposes', as with the railroad network, were touted. The opening of first English and then, following the trade war of 1894, German markets to Russian imperial bonds was a critical step. No measure was more important, however, than the impression made abroad by Russian imperial penetration in Asia. 'The bold intervention in eastern affairs', it was noted, was 'increasing our prestige in the East and in Europe.'

All of these measures, taken together, were designed to eliminate speculation on the value of the ruble, stabilize Russian credit, and allow the 'second stage' of currency reform, the introduction of 'the gold standard (*zolotaia edinitsa*)'—a measure finalized by imperial edict in August 1897.[70]

That edict guaranteed that owners of the paper ruble on demand could purchase gold rubles at a rate of 1 paper ruble to 0.66 gold rubles. That guarantee was backed by regulations that required the State Bank to limit the total amount of paper currency in circulation to 300 million rubles; beyond that sum, the ruble and gold were required to be traded at parity. A fifteen-ruble gold-coin Imperial symbolized this new structure. Although critics, in particular agrarian interests tied to the landowning nobility, bitterly protested the effective devaluation of the paper currency then in circulation, the ministry favored the Olympian view—and long-term foreign capital investment: '(t)he population gradually is being prepared for monetary exchange (*monetnoe obrashchenie*) and for open access to the country for foreign gold'.[71]

Monetary policy led logically to the banking system, and its crown, the State Bank. The State Bank was the central fulcrum of commercial–industrial life in Russia, and the ministry sought to expand its institutional presence throughout the empire. It issued currency, and thus regulated the amount in circulation. It supplied pools of investment credit to large and small enterprises. It regulated domestic interest rates and terms of loans in a manner designed to 'encourage commercial activity'. Most importantly, it served as the 'regulator (*regulator*) of the country's credit exchange'. The bank explicitly was forbidden from intervening in specific commercial transactions, but charged instead to use its control of currency, interest rates, and the state treasury, and impart 'tone' to the country's system of corporate and privately owned banks, mutual credit institutions, and savings and loan cooperatives.[72]

Capital and credit sought markets. Hence, a commercial policy that expanded demand for Russian commodities, industrial goods, and investment opportunities became a priority for the ministry. It continued to defend a system of protectionist tariffs that was a source of treasury revenues and shield for fledgling Russian industries, and thus advocated protectionism. Recognizing the interdependent character of the international economy, however, the ministry argued the need to balance the protection of national industry, and the encouragement of the international commercial relations essential for marketing its goods.'(O)nly consistent and constantly expanding trade between countries provides the proper framework for both commercial relations and domestic productivity, which in turn encourages new production,' the report proclaimed in introducing its strategy of negotiating a dual-tiered or 'differentiated' structure of customs duties with each of its major trading partners. A strategy that accounted for local terms of trade and affecting the commercial interplay of two trading partners, it was deemed to increase the likelihood of actually achieving effective protection of 'national industry'. Over the decade these treaties were negotiated with Egypt, Serbia, France, Germany, Austro-Hungary, Denmark, Portugal, Spain, Greece, Turkey, Japan, and the United States.[73] Russian tariffs, which were a form of indirect taxation levied on the purchasers of imported goods, nevertheless remained, in the words of the report, 'in other circumstances, almost prohibitive'. Historians calculate that these assessments on imports, much of it manufactured goods and technology, by 1903 constituted some 14 per cent of all treasury revenues.[74]

Russian commercial development was, to repeat, a balancing act. The ministry's recourse to protectionist policies cannot obscure its efforts, evident in these treaties, to advance international commerce and business. Commercial agents of the ministry were being appointed to staffs of Russian embassies to supply intelligence about, and encourage, a favorable environment for Russian business and investment in the countries where they were posted. Private banks were encouraged to open foreign branches. The formation of public associations within sectors of industry to encourage exports, the reform of the Russian stock exchange in St Petersburg, consistent government participation in the bacchanalia of international trade fairs taking place across Europe and North America as the new century approached, the creation of an international merchant marine, and the encouragement of steamship lines: all these measures being undertaken in Witte's ministry were justified in terms of an international economy where capital sought markets wherever they were to be discovered.[75]

'In terms of seeking out markets', commercial expansion in the near and far east especially bore Witte's imprint. 'The expansion of the natural sphere of Russian political and commercial influence in the countries of the east, which are in close proximity to us and are less cultured [sic],' the report proclaimed, 'is an immediate priority.' Central to that vision, as we have seen, was the Trans-Siberian Railroad. The 'great siberian way' would foster Russian interests in Asia by 'opening free access for the products of Russian industry to its huge markets . . . (and) . . . channeling the great traffic of cultured Europe through Russia to the far east'. Population from European Russia would be resettled 'into Siberia and the east', thereby assuring that, 'given the Russian people's penchant for colonization, our might (*mogu-chestvo*) is created and strengthened'. A Siberian expanse was envisioned,

linked east to west by rail, and north to south by river systems that
themselves might become more open to international shipping moving
seasonally along its Arctic coast, which possibility the ministry was exploring and surveying. It was sponsoring commercial expeditions as a first step
toward organizing ocean transit from the Pacific coast terminus of the
Trans-Siberian Railroad at Vladivostok to the ports of China and Japan.
Developing commerce with Central Asia and Persia also was a priority,
especially along the trans-Caspian railroad that bisected these imperial
possessions from the Caspian to Bukhara and Samarkand, tracing out a
southern boundary of the empire's authority and commercial influence in
that region.[76]

Turning to 'the close linkage between foreign and domestic commerce
and the extreme disarray of the latter', the report shifted focus. In an
arresting exposé of business practice, the ministry found that 'commercial-
industrial activity (*torgovo-promyshlennaia deiatel'nost'*)' often did not display
the 'autonomy, widespread initiative, and knowledge' that Witte's business
model of a 'modern international commerce' idealized, and thus dissipated
government efforts to expand Russian commercial wealth. Both business
and government were to blame, however. The report targeted *opeka*, a word
but dimly translated as patronage, because the Russian bore the connotation
of overweening parent policing minor child. Russian commercial–industrial
culture historically had confronted 'a mass of formalities placed before it by
laws and administration in an effort to protect against possible abuses'. The
effort required to deal with such 'detailed reglamentation' wasted energy
and bred habits of mind 'oriented to receiving favors, special privileges over
foreign or domestic competitors'. Understanding the symbiotic relationship
that had evolved over time, the ministry called for 'the inculcation of a new
spirit', which would, the ministry pledged, decrease regulation, reduce
'impediments and formalities', gradually wean commercial–industrial elites
from 'petitions and efforts at influence-peddling', and increase knowledgeable risk-taking. A series of measures aimed to effect cultural change. First
among them was the creation of a Central Board of Weights and Measures
to combat widespread falsification. Its first director was D. I. Mendeleev.
Here too were measures fostering vocational and polytechnic education,
commercial credit, commercial infrastructure construction, and resources
to support statistical study of commercial–industrial life.[77]

Central to both foreign and domestic commerce was the railroad, 'one of
the chief instruments of progress in our time'. It was bringing the Russian

Empire into closer proximity with both 'foreign lands (*zagranitsa*)' and her constituent territories. 'With the help of all types of railroad, the slogan of the present Ministry of Finances has become,' the report exclaimed, 'Make Russia Transitable (*sdelat' Rossiiu proezzhei*)'. Since 1888–89, the ministry had developed 'an entire plan of railroad construction'. It tied the Far North to central European Russia and the Baltic Sea, as well as opened 'a new transit route to Europe for the east and Siberia'. The Urals Mountains, with their rich mines, were tied to both central Russia and Siberia. The South, 'promising to become our rich industrial center', was the site of new construction, and both the Caucasus and Central Asia were tied to central Russia—and all of this was set within 'a detailed economic study of the country, an investigation of its regions, the elucidation of its industrial and agricultural needs, and consequently the creation of an entire system of main and secondary railroad lines, necessary for the growth of national wealth'. Second, railroads were de facto nationalized. Their economic import as earners of currency and generators of commerce made them 'a powerful economic factor . . . whose supervision, affecting the most varied state and public interests, the Government could not leave to private initiative'. Finally, the report emphasized the ministry's centralized control of freight and passenger rate structures, which had been Witte's initial accomplishment in 1889. Centralized control served the fiscal 'interests of the treasury', the report noted, but also gave 'priority to the country's economic interests, the development of its productive forces, and the proper pace of its commerce'.[78]

Together, a stable currency, expanding foreign and domestic commercial markets, and an empire-wide communications network were the framework within which 'the products of national labor' circulated and engendered wealth. The key question 'at the root of the economic welfare of the country, the source for the creation of its new wealth and further prosperity' was finding sufficient investment capital to create an ever expanding flow of these commodities, industrial goods, and services. The ministry's solution to this problem was direct and clear: open Russian industrial markets to foreign investors. They would build and operate enterprises inside the empire, especially within those branches of industry made even more attractive as investments, given the high protectionist tariffs already sheltering them—textiles, petroleum, metal-working, iron and steel. It was assumed as nearly axiomatic that Western investors would bring with them cutting-edge technology and business practices. A neat trick, protecting industry owned

by foreigners from competition by foreigners, but such was the stratagem its
wily chief designed to foster greater competition within an underdeveloped
Russian industrial culture.[79]

Excessive regulation and high protectionist tariffs had accustomed Russian business and capital 'to seek to invest only in the especially advantageous conditions of a monopoly', the report instructed. Under those
conditions, 'initiative loses its edge; under the influence of excessively
high and easily obtained profits, capital and after it labor do not seek new
outlets; the country's natural resources remain inert; productive technology
develops but weakly, (and) demand for specialized industrial knowledge is
constrained. . . . ' Why foreign owners would be any less likely to behave in
this manner was a question that went unacknowledged and unanswered—
although no more so than the degree to which the Ministry of Finances
itself facilitated the very forms of behavior it was condemning. Nevertheless, Russia looked to the United States after the civil war as an example of
the benefits foreign capital investment could bring to a national economy.
'As the example of America has shown, foreign capital, which acclimates
itself quickly and generally knows no national distinctions (*natsional'nost'*),
when combined with protectionism, incomparably encourages the growth
of industry and consequently the rapid creation of native capital (*sobstvennye
kapitaly*) within that country, which in turn provides huge outlets for her
labor power (*trudovaia energiia*) and allows the exploitation of her natural
resources.'[80] A long list of policies followed. The 'presentation of rights of
citizenship to gold', as the report framed the gold standard, was first among
them, but treasury-backed industrial credits and reform of corporate laws
governing joint-stock companies also were measures designed to attract
foreign and domestic capital investors. Designed to increase competition
and entrepreneurship, policies driven by the Department of Trade and
Manufacturing encouraged new enterprises, professional business
expertise, social welfare for industrial workers, and education in technology
and industrial labor skills. Reflecting a general drive to assess, measure, and
understand industrial development, the ministry compiled statistical and
census materials tracking indices of labor, commercial–industrial, or other
business activity. It encouraged, and tracked, regional, national, and international trade expositions and congresses.[81]

Agriculture did not go unmentioned. 'Industry (*promyshlennost'*)' encompassed all forms of economic production, including agriculture: from
extension of seasonal credits to peasant households, through refinancing of

mortgages on arable land and discounting of peasant debt, to encouraging
the restructuring of rural property distribution through the Peasant Land
Bank. The report acknowledged the hostility that its development strategies
had provoked within the ranks of a landowning nobility assaulted by the
long-term decline of noble agriculture since the 1861 abolition of serfdom
and two decades of low grain prices on international markets flooded with
North American and Australian supply. Having conducted extensive statistical evaluation of these phenomena, the ministry was well aware of the
difficulties they were producing, especially given the political protests they
provoked among Russian noble landowners throughout the 1880s and
1890s. The ministry's report, however, ignored those who were perishing—
Chekhov would famously paint the type with Madame Ranevskaya in *The
Cherry Orchard* in 1903.[82] Instead, it praised those who were making the
transition to more productive and market-driven agricultural enterprise, in
language that embraced status earned over status ascribed by birth: 'those
landowners who desire to emerge victorious from their present difficult
circumstances, in (whose) culture, knowledge, capacity for energetic struggle in new conditions of activity is their success, proof of their capabilities'.
Thoroughly intolerant of claims of aristocratic privilege, the ministry
declared that its agricultural policy entailed the support of profitable estate
landholding, agricultural and agronomic science, and general primary
education—'these are the pathways toward raising the level, and the combined energetic work of all participants in agriculture—the only means to its
real improvement.'[83]

Largely unmentioned in this report was the much more intractable issue
of peasant agriculture. At mid decade it had not yet become the political
problem it would be after the turn of the century, when Witte became an
advocate of legal, institutional, and economic reforms of Russian communal peasant agriculture.[84] It was not happenstance that led the ministry to
leave agriculture as the last sector of the imperial economy it surveyed in
this report. Written amidst a decade of economic growth and expansion,
the ministry, with Witte at its head, assumed that increasing the productive
capacities of the imperial economy eventually would render agriculture
more productive and modern as well. In this sense, his vision of a future
imperial polity *was* a reform of peasant agriculture and culture, a component element of that economy. Within the infrastructure supported by the
power and revenues of the state—entrepreneurial competition, domestic
and foreign capital investment, new entrepreneurial and business practices,

law that guaranteed both capital and labor their juridical rights—industry would expand enormously, given the 'autonomy, healthy initiative, and technical and commercial knowledge' that, the report assumed, marked out modern economic life. Driven to compete, '(domestic) industry . . . will begin to strive for improvements in technology and through mass production reach a stage where . . . it will then begin to concern itself with foreign markets, especially in the east'. Greater wealth generated greater demand and thus inevitable was 'a more extensive domestic market with higher prices for raw materials and grain, the chief products of our agricultural industry'. These raw materials would continue to be a valuable component of a more diversified imperial economy, but 'their export will not be, as now, a primary, but a secondary concern. Meanwhile, 'the report concluded, 'those who would purchase them abroad will have to meet our conditions, and not the reverse'.[85]

'But that is a matter for the future,' the report noted.[86] In the present, these legislative initiatives, programs, and strategic visions required revenues to fund them. It was a mark of the capitalist market mentality now fully ensconced in the Witte ministry that the first object of analysis emphasized in this regard was not taxation, but domestic capital accumulated through savings and insurance. Both served to strengthen 'in the people the habit of thrift (berezhlivost')' that led to 'the accumulation of popular wealth'. Savings banks in particular, with their strictly defined and government-controlled institutions paying interest rates set to market values, could serve generally as a source of 'petty credit', as did an insurance industry that reduced risk across pools of insured and thereby lowered the unit cost of its product for all participants. Much more central to the flow of revenue required to fund the imperial state was the crown monopoly on the sale of alcohol, now extended across the empire. Obligatory Victorian protestations about temperance and the 'evil of drunkenness' in the report found their way years later into Witte's reminiscences, where he was hopelessly hypocritical about a measure that substantially increased treasury revenues from the substantially increased alcohol consumption within imperial society.[87] Much more convincing were arguments that acknowledged the trade-off between deriving revenues from alcohol and using them to fund investments in primary education, technical and commercial education, parish schools, the first census of the imperial population, and investigations of peasant economic welfare.[88]

The longest, most complex, and ultimately indecipherable entry of the ministerial report, however, was 'taxation'.[89] Historians of the meandering, disjointed, and insistent search for tax revenues of the early eighteenth-century 'service state' created by Peter the Great would find it familiar. Despite some gestures toward reducing peasant redemption payments associated with the abolition of serfdom and easing repayment schedules for mortgaged rural property, the general direction of imperial policy was to increase old taxes and create new ones. By the end of the nineteenth century, the paradigm that justified a progressive income tax already existed, but its rebuttal was the report's dominant line. Acknowledging that theory preferred 'a more equitable distribution of the tax burden' when the government's reliance on indirect taxation upon consumption left the poorest elements of the population to shoulder proportionately the heaviest taxation, the ministry nevertheless opted for the maxim that 'any old, already established tax is better than a new one, even if the best in theory'. Especially following the decline of population, savings, and tax revenues that resulted from the famine and cholera epidemic of 1891–92, that truism also seemed the most direct pathway to increased revenues.[90]

Existing excise taxes on alcohol, beer, kerosene, and matches were increased. So too were direct taxes levied on the state corporate (*soslovie*) institutions of the merchantry, townsmen, and honorary citizens, as well as on privately owned, joint-stock companies, factories, and what was called urban immoveable property (land, structures, and personal residences). New taxes on capital (bank deposits, non-guaranteed dividends in railroad companies) were created. The tax-collecting capacities of the Ministry of Finances were strengthened in the Caucasus, Central Asia, Siberia, and, unsurprisingly given the similarity of imperial viewpoint, a tax on working-class wages was levied to cover deficits accumulated by the imperial court. The ministry's tax inspectorate, the provincial apparatus through which these revenues were collected, was expanded in provincial Russia proper and extended to the Urals region, Turgaisk, the Caucasus, and Siberia. The ministry—and its chief in particular—created conflict with provincial and county zemstvo assemblies by asserting a right to review the rural property assessments levied by these locally elected organs, in an evident effort to constrain this competition for scare tax revenues. Commercial tariffs on imports and exports, despite the ministry's legitimate effort to enhance 'the evolution of international commercial exchange, (and) the growth of Russia's participation on the world market', were also sources of income that served the 'interests of the fisc'. Tariffs on cotton were twice increased. An expanding textile export trade to Persia, China, the Caspian, and the Pacific Far East was made subject to an excise tax. Finland explicitly was included in an imperial customs zone designed to prevent untaxed goods being imported into the empire—and the Border Guards, a paramilitary organization whose Chief was also the Minister of Finances, were strengthened to police these borders. Almost as an afterthought, it was noted that the substantial landholdings of the Crown might at some future time serve as a revenue resource should the need arise. Little could Witte then have imagined that within the decade, amidst the revolution of 1905, such a moment would arrive.[91]

As a final note, the report concluded by returning to the issue that undergirded this entire discussion: state spending (*raskhodnye stati*). As Witte never ceased to stipulate, he honored 'those principles, which were indicated by our Sovereign, now eternally resting with God, Alexander III'. Alexander had been dead for more than a year, and Witte had become accustomed to reminding his son, Nicholas II, of his father's intentions. These principles, the report stipulated, were 'strictly scrupulous expenditure' of treasury funds, 'thorough discussion' of any budget proposal to elucidate its 'necessity and value', and the prohibition of extra-budgetary expenditures, which the autocratic sovereign possessed the right to include in annual budgets. Witte at that very time was enmeshed in the early stages of a struggle with the Grand Duke Alexander Mikhailovich, Nicholas II's cousin, over precisely that issue and funding a Pacific High Seas Fleet, an idea that he found economically wasteful and strategically indefensible.[92] The principles the report outlined assumed a talented, authoritative, and intentional decision-maker like Alexander III, and a minister able to support and realize them in action—such as the current Minister of Finances. In its last lines, his voice was audible. The ministry would undertake every effort to guard the creditworthiness of the Russian state, but it also intended to fund 'productive expenditures, which either cannot be delayed without damaging the moral or material prosperity of the country, or whose implementation now will pay dividends in the future for economic growth or the political might of Russia'.[93] Because, in the empire of gold, wealth was power, certainly this ministerial summary had left little doubt that the Russian Empire, under the firm guidance that only autocratic monarchy could afford a dreamer such as Sergei Witte, was becoming a modern and powerful imperial polity.

Three years later, in 1899, North America and Europe were witnessing the first signs of what, by the turn of the new century, had become a full-blown economic depression negatively affecting business growth, capital markets, and industrial productivity. Urging Nicholas II in the ponderously entitled 'Report of the Minister of Finance to His Majesty on the Necessity of Formulating and Thereafter Steadfastly Adhering to a Definite Program of a Commercial and Industrial Policy of the Empire', he argued that the sovereign do just that. Witte defended the agenda he had pursued across the decade: tariffs and commercial treaties to raise revenues and foster international commerce; foreign capital investment; the creation of a 'national industry', especially in metallurgy, textiles, and chemicals; development of agriculture; and the creation of stronger domestic markets 'based on two pillars, agriculture and industry, and the relations between them, profitable to both'. The key to the policy's success remained attracting international investment capital to the empire. 'Not even the most powerful government can create capital,' he declaimed. Capital sought a stable currency environment, he believed, and the guarantee of that stability was a gold coin, the *Imperial*' and the gold standard it symbolized. Witte chose the metaphors of late nineteenth-century imperialism to instruct that '(t)he relations of Russia with Western Europe are fully comparable to the relations of colonial countries with their metropolises'. He continued: 'The latter consider their colonies as advantageous markets in which they can freely sell the products of their labor and of their industry and from which they can draw with a powerful hand the raw materials necessary for them. . . . Russia was (in 1861), and to a considerable extent still is, such a hospitable colony for all industrially developed states, generously providing them with the cheap products of her soil and buying dearly the products of their labor.' The 'radical difference between Russia and a colony', Witte throughout his life never doubted, was her great power status. Monarchist that he was, he remained loyal to the Romanov crown, and spoke to Nicholas when he proclaimed '(s)he wants to be a metropolis herself'.[94] Writing at age 50, Witte also was speaking for himself about a vision that had been instilled in him from his boyhood. He had helped to instill it in the mind of the young man who had become his sovereign and master, Nicholas II, following the death of his beloved father, Alexander III. Witte, any photograph reveals, bore him striking physical resemblance.

hes died about 20 x already

Fathers and Sons on the Road to War

On 20 October 1894, Alexander III, at the still young age of 49, died at his Crimean estate in Livadia, the victim of kidney failure brought on, some said, by the wreck of the royal train at Borka, or complications from influenza, or alcohol. His eldest son, now Nicholas II, was only 26 the day that he lamented in his ever faithful diary: 'My God, my God, what a day! The Lord called to Himself our revered, dear, most heartedly beloved Papa. My head is spinning, I don't want to believe it. . . . This was the death of a saint! Lord, help us in these heavy days.'[95] Witte, dictating in May 1911, remembered the rapid decline of Alexander's health that summer and autumn, the 'very painful weeks' preceding 'the horrific news of his death', and the rituals surrounding his funeral and burial in the Cathedral of Sts Peter and Paul that dominated the public life of the capital. His grief was palpable even after seventeen years.[96] Although unmentioned in his memoirs, his ministry in the six weeks before the tsar's death propelled an unusually large number of legislative projects toward Alexander for his approval. Whether petty, such as the dismissal of a corrupt officer in the Border Guards, or significant, such as the twenty-four separate files to be submitted for review by the Imperial State Council which Alexander approved on the day before he died, this stream of projects, which abruptly halted when Alexander died, reflected both the scope of the ministry's writ, and the uncertainty surrounding the young and unpredictable Nicholas as Alexander lay dying.[97]

At the time, contemporaries were quick to draw the contrast between the stalwart father and young, inexperienced son. Vladimir Lamzdorf, an assistant Minister of Foreign Affairs whom Nicholas would promote to head that ministry in 1900, mused in his diary on 20 October that the country mourned the death of Alexander 'mainly because of the uncertainty being created by the anonymity of the heir to the throne, who almost until the last moment was kept in the nursery; the heir,' Lamzdorf continued, 'did not distinguish himself in any way, he was only known for certain weaknesses and excesses of youth, which did not inspire any kind of confidence (*doverie*) in him.'[98] However harsh that judgment, the aristocratic and bureaucratic worlds of the capital cities indulged similar sentiments. Witte recalled the Minister of Internal Affairs, I. N. Durnovo, fearing 'how much tragedy we will experience in his reign', and how the arch-conservative Konstantine

Pobedonostsev, the new tsar's former tutor, acknowledged as well his fears that 'emperor Nicholas, given his youth and inexperience,' would succumb to ill-intentioned advisers whom his father never would have tolerated.[99] Count S. D. Sheremetev, scion of one of the great aristocratic families of the empire and a boyhood playmate of Alexander, in his own memoirs recalled Alexander III extensively and emotionally. His unexpected illness and death caused 'the wheel of history' to turn away from the international peace and domestic reconstruction that had marked the reign of the father toward the 'far eastern entanglements' that would eventually result in military defeat and revolution during the reign of the son.[100] Only six years older than Nicholas, Vladimir Gurko, a civil official in 1894, recalled the varied gossip and speculation surrounding Nicholas, given his limited public exposure. 'But in one regard everyone agreed,' Gurko wrote, that 'tomorrow's guardian of the fate of Russia' altogether lacked experience and, not surprisingly, made that future 'just as unforeseeable as it seemed vague and troubling (*smutnoe*)'. The Naval Minister N. M. Chikhachev, Gurko wrote, allowed that 'the rudder of the ship of state has been taken from the firm hands of an experienced pilot and, in all likelihood, no other hands will take it up for an extended period of time. In what direction the ship of state will plot its course under such conditions—only God knows.'[101]

His most authoritative biographer, Dominic Lieven, agrees that Nicholas came to the throne at an age when he had not yet acquired enough experience to develop 'an independent conception of an autocrat's role', and remained, especially in the first years of his reign, 'fated not merely to attempt to emulate his father's role but also to know that he was doing so inadequately'. He lacked, Lieven writes, 'Alexander's experience, his authoritative manner and, very important given the symbolic nature of the Tsar's position, his majestic physical stature'.[102] Sergei Oldenburg, an émigré and monarchist historian who after the 1917 Revolution authored the first scholarly biography of Nicholas, acknowledged that 'Russia knew very little about its new emperor', shielded from him as it had been by 'the dominating personality of Alexander III'. Ministers especially, he wrote, found Nicholas to be 'undependable', too often diverging from policies that reflected institutional policies and precedents that they had established in the previous reign.[103] Certainly Witte complained loudly and often about such behavior in the winter of 1911–12, while he marched his way through reminiscences of his years as Minister of Finances. He lamented that Nicholas lacked his father's decisiveness, and thus, Witte mused, he had learned 'to seize the moment (*lovit' moment*)' with the tsar in order to dissuade Nicholas from arguments contradicting those of his peripatetic minister.[104] He was equally aware, however, that Nicholas, as autocrat, possessed unlimited power and ultimate responsibility for all affairs of state. When he supported Witte—the construction of the Trans-Siberian Railroad and the introduction of the gold standard were accomplished after the death of Alexander III—the minister acknowledged Nicholas's majesty. 'All of this I achieved and implemented going against the current,' Witte remembered about the gold standard. 'I had behind me the confidence of His Majesty and thanks to his firmness and support I managed to achieve this greatest reform . . . which undoubtedly will long adorn the reign of Nicholas II.'[105] But, at other times, Nicholas disagreed, heeded others, or prevaricated—and then Witte found Nicholas's indecisiveness galling, even maddening, especially as the tsar's unwillingness to heed Witte, his policies, and the realization of the dreams they contained, grew with time.

Fascinated by personality and psychology, Witte in his memoirs focused repeatedly on the young man whom fate had made his master, and thus on the relationship between them that so determined his own destiny. Nicholas, Witte mused in one recollection, 'from the very moment he came to the throne did not admire and even could not tolerate . . . a decisive personality, that is individuals firm in their opinions, their words and their actions'. Admittedly, such personalities in particular were inclined to forget that 'they were dealing with His Majesty . . . I (was) guilty of this myself,' he added. Less self-justification than objective analysis, he hinted at the tone of a human relationship between the two men that historians will never fully recover. ' . . . Prior to serving Nicholas II, we served Alexander III. The late Emperor never paid attention to turns of phrase (*vyrazhenie myslei*), to abrupt words, and, on the contrary, valued firm conviction in a man,' Witte mused, thinking undoubtedly of himself. '(T)he character of Alexander III was entirely different from the character of Nicholas II and any of His subjects, including we, should have kept this in view and attended to it.'[106] Explaining why Nicholas dismissed his father's confidant and Minister of Court I. I. Vorontsov-Dashkov in spring 1896, Witte recognized that the minister had been held responsible for the disaster of Khodynka Field at the coronation festivities in Moscow that May. Celebratory crowds congregating to receive souvenir gifts and food from royal pavilions became a surging, crushing mass of people that resulted in several thousand deaths and injuries. Always recapitulated subsequently in histories and memoirs of the reign as a foreboding harbinger of its disastrous ending, this public disaster cost the Minister of the Imperial Court his position. Witte, in his memories of the event, spent far more time exploring the 'psychology of relationships' between Nicholas and a minister who had 'known the young Emperor from the cradle' and been 'one of the closest confidants of his most august father'. That alone 'must have had some sort of depressing impact (*nekotoroe gnetushchee vliianie*)' on the tsar, he noted. Plainly he was thinking of himself ('this applies to me as well, I must admit') when he went on to describe how his father's ministers reinforced this emotional complex by their own inability to recognize fully 'that this young tsarevich, whom they had known as a youth or a lad, by the will of the Almighty had become the all-powerful Monarch of this great Empire', and spoke to him as if he were still the inexperienced son rather than 'the autocratic Sovereign of a great Empire'. This 'mentoring tone (*mentorskii ton*)', affected by older, established, and knowledgeable men tied to his father, Witte reflected, 'shocked the young Emperor and his most august spouse'.[107]

The son not only had become emperor in 1894, but also a betrothed and then married man. Four years younger than Nicholas, the 22-year old Alix of Hesse-Darmstadt was the maternal granddaughter of Queen Victoria of the United Kingdom, from whom she received her Victorian cultural sensibilities, her conservative beliefs in monarchical political order, and the gene that her hemophiliac son, the tsarevich Alexei Nikolaevich, inherited from her at his birth in 1904. Fetched to the Crimea by Nicholas in order to receive his father's blessing of the marriage, she arrived in Russia only days before Alexander's death. Her conversion to Russian Orthodoxy, her subsequent marriage at the beginning of the year-long public mourning declared to mark the late tsar's passing, and her abrupt immersion into an imperial court still dominated by the brothers and wife of her husband's deceased father all tended to reinforce in the Empress Alexandra Fedorovna a shyness and reticence that high society came to regard as inaccessibility and distance.[108] Popular writers and professional historians alike have devoted enormous attention to the royal couple Nicholas and Alexandra—as fated lovers, Victorian couple, doting parents, deeply religious or hopelessly mystical Orthodox religious believers, and exemplars of an imperial world that inevitably perished or perniciously was sacrificed amidst twentieth-century modernity. Oddly, few have regarded them as the emperor and empress of Russia who, within the cocoon of the marriage and family life that the two of them lovingly created and jealously guarded, together ruled the great empire.[109] Witte, ever vigilant to the world of the imperial court, here too proved an exception.

His relationship with the Empress Alexandra was, judging from the comments about her that he scattered across his reminiscences, distant and cold, reflecting what he certainly experienced from her. Seldom did he recall even meeting formally with her, as was the case with the Dowager Empress Marie Fedorovna, and when he did, the recollection was formalistic at best. In the files of the ministry, for example, was his handwritten request to Nicholas in 1898 for a copy of her photograph as a 'most precious Imperial gift', to which the tsar replied that 'Her Majesty agreed' he could retain one of them.[110] When his tale of Alexander's death, dictated in December 1911, touched the first time that he saw her in 1894, as 'our future Empress' stepped from the royal train bringing the body of Alexander III back to St Petersburg, his story contained the sort of vicious court gossip he indulged. First the young emperor exited the train, he recalled, followed by two women, one of whom was the Princess of Wales, the future Queen of England Alexandra, the sister of Nicholas's mother and, by her marriage to the future Edward VII, the aunt of Alix. Never having seen his future sovereign, Witte recounted, he assumed that this 'very beautiful lady, with an entirely youthful carriage, was the future Alexandra Fedorovna, the princess of Darmstadt', only to discover that he had been 'stunned' by the Englishwoman. Alix by comparison was 'less beautiful and less sympathetic ... but nevertheless the new Empress was beautiful and remains beautiful today, although there always was and remains something angry in the set of her mouth'.[111]

In his private notebooks, where he recorded his memoirs of the 1905 Revolution, he was much more candid, vicious, and perspicacious about the nature of autocratic rule under Nicholas. Writing in the summer and autumn of 1907, Witte viewed Alexandra, 'unfortunately for Russia the Empress', as a powerful but irrational woman susceptible to the mysticism and spiritualism rampant in Victorian society generally, and in the Romanov royal family in particular. Witte especially emphasized her conversion to Russian Orthodoxy, which imbued her with the fanaticism created by belief in an adopted religion. The empress 'with every fiber of her being' succumbed to what he called 'orthodox paganism ... that is submission to externalities without a consciousness of the spirit, preaching by force and not conviction', he wrote, slipping into the cadences he imagined her speaking. '(E)ither submit or you are my enemy and against you will be my "Autocratic and unrestricted" sword [sic]. I think in this way, thus it is so. I want it this way, thus it is just and justice is my right. Given such a psychology,' he concluded, 'surrounded by self-effacing lackeys and intriguers—it is easy to fall into all sorts of fantasies.' Always an admirer of those, like himself, who wielded power effectively, Witte found Alexandra to be a powerful personality in her own right, who, given her 'weak-willed husband', exerted 'firm and uninterrupted influence on Russia's sovereign Tsar. 'Add to this', he continued, allowing a glimpse of how Victorian men viewed the power of a woman, that not only was she the wife of the tsar but also 'she is beautiful, has a will, is an exemplary mother to her family'. That she too ruled, that 'in the end She took the Sovereign in hand', he did not doubt. Her fanaticism and indulgence of fantasy, however, made her 'a pernicious adviser for the Autocratic Master of the Russian Empire. In the end, she will bring much misfortune to herself, Him, and all Russia.'[112] How these tones might have made their way from Witte, counselor and erstwhile mentor, to the son of the father he had so loyally served, and to Alexandra, the empress who so zealously protected the prerogatives of her autocratic spouse and urged him repeatedly to be the man and father she knew him to be, is impossible to say. That they undoubtedly made themselves known to her, and were reciprocated in kind toward her husband's otherwise most influential adviser, was likely a significant factor undermining the relationship of tsar and minister.

What ultimately divided them, at least from Witte's perspective, was, paradoxically, their shared dream of a powerful Russian Empire reaching from Europe across Siberia to Asia and the Pacific Far East. Indeed, Witte had abetted that vision in the younger man by arranging his appointment in 1893 to chair the government committee overseeing construction of the Trans-Siberian Railroad, a position he retained once he became tsar.[113] Nicholas's dream had been kindled, however, in 1890–91, when Alexander III dispatched his 22-year-old heir to undertake what amounted to a circumnavigation of the Russian Empire, from Moscow, via Trieste and Suez, to India, Singapore, Bangkok, Hong Kong, and Japan. There, he was attacked and slightly wounded by a sword-wielding Japanese policeman. He drove a ceremonial spike of the transcontinental in the Russian Pacific citadel of Vladivostok, and then traveled back to European Russia across the vastness of Siberia. 'In my opinion,' Witte reminisced in 1911, 'this travel imprinted upon the future Emperor a certain tendency, which fatally found expression throughout his entire reign', not Witte's last reference to what for him was Nicholas's adventurist foreign policy in the Far East that eventually resulted in military confrontation, war, and defeat by Japan. In part, he argued, the attack upon the heir to the throne enflamed Russian nationalist opinion and fostered within Nicholas himself a sense that Japan was 'a hostile, insignificant and powerless nation, which could be destroyed with one flick of the hand (*shchelk*) of the Russian imperial giant'. In part, the entire tour ingrained upon the 'impressionable nature of the young Tsarevich' his standing as 'the Heir to the greatest throne in the world, the future Emperor of the greatest Empire in the world...', the 'majesty' of whose role was reinforced further by his return to Europe from Vladivostok by road and rail through the vastness of 'all Siberia'. As a result, Witte concluded, this experience occupied primacy of place in 'the world view of the young Tsarevich', so that he 'inclined his head, intellect, and emotions in the direction of the East and especially the Far East'. His travels of 1890–91, 'one could say, to a certain extent would predecide the character of his entire reign. It is for this reason that I say the tour was fateful.'[114]

Witte possessed his own vision of expanding Russian commercial, economic, and thus political influence in Asia. Its centerpiece was the transcontinental railroad, whose construction he was driving at an increasingly frenetic pace, and cost, by the time Nicholas came to the throne in 1894. His technical expertise unchallenged, Witte's larger problem in advancing the construction of the Trans-Siberian always had been overcoming the traditional cry of impoverishment from senior officials quick to argue that the extraordinary costs of such a grand project made its immediate realization impossible. Although as Minister of Finances he stifled such claims, the costs were enormous, and growing. At a November 1894 meeting of the Trans-Siberian Railroad Committee, the first that Nicholas chaired as tsar, the emperor reaffirmed his full intention to fulfill the wishes of his father to build the railroad, but emphasized the need to do so 'parsimoniously, but especially quickly and soundly'. The committee then approved 28 million rubles of expenditures for 1895; twelve months later, it added another 500 million rubles for construction in 1896.[115] That increase in funding reflected a decision, dated to mid 1895, to accelerate the construction of the transcontinental and reduce total construction costs by taking what for Witte was a step as fateful for him as had been Nicholas's tour of the Far East: the construction of the Chinese Eastern Railway (*Kitaisko-vostochnaia zheleznaia doroga*). From east of Lake Baikal, across northern Manchuria, Witte resolved to take a short-cut across China directly to Vladivostok on the Pacific.

As a construction project, the Trans-Siberian had been organized into parcels constructed east from the Ural Mountains and west from Vladivostok. As approved in 1892, construction plans had called for work in western and central Siberia from Cheliabinsk eastward across the Ob River toward Irkutsk near Lake Baikal, and northwestward from Vladivostok, where Nicholas as tsarevich had driven a ceremonial spike, along the Ussuri River where it joined the Amur near Khabarovsk. Those parts of the project that were most challenging from a topographical, engineering, and thus financial perspective were the tracts beyond Lake Baikal and especially along the Amur River, which roughly paralleled the empire's borders with China in a long looping arc northwards and eastwards.[116] In the 1892 version of the plan, the construction of 'these most difficult tracts' was to be delayed while the more affordable parts of the transcontinental line were completed. There is ample evidence that Witte no later than 1892 was already thinking about what the official record called 'a straightening' (*spriamlenie*) of the Trans-Siberian by charting a shorter and more direct route to Vladivostok across Manchuria. Shortening the line would decrease not only the overall cost of the project, but the amount of time required to bring the railroad into operation and begin producing the economic and commercial benefits that Witte's imperial dreams repeatedly had emphasized. Nicholas II approved Witte's proposal to begin surveying this route in mid 1895.[117]

International geopolitics, however, figured strongly in this decision. War between China and Japan over hegemony on the Korean peninsula, which had raged from August 1894 to April 1895, ended in a Japanese victory that revealed to the world a modernizing Meiji Japan and a shifting balance of power in the Far East. By the Treaty of Shimonoseki, defeated China agreed to pay an indemnity to Japan, and ceded its claims to sovereignty over Korea, as well as Taiwan and the Liaodong Peninsula. The peninsula, strategically jutting out into the northern reaches of the Yellow Sea, contained at its southern tip a large, deep, ice-free natural harbor that an English naval captain, William Arthur, put on European maps in 1856, China began fortifying in the 1880s, and Japan seized in 1894. The Chinese called it Lushan, Europeans Port Arthur. In April and May 1895, Russia, France, and Germany, concerned that there should be another competitor in a region where their own imperial ambitions already focused, together threatened to halt Japanese seizure of Chinese territory with the implied threat of military action in what diplomatic historians call the Triple Intervention.[118] In his memoirs, Witte claimed a central role in organizing this initiative, first by convincing Nicholas that the territorial integrity of China was in Russia's best interests and then by brokering on French capital markets the financing necessary for a Chinese government loan required to pay Japan the indemnity established by their peace treaty. 'As a consequence', he recalled in December 1912, 'at my initiative' the Ministry of Finances founded in November 1895 the Russian-Chinese Bank.

It was organized under the same state-private sector corporatist structures familiar from the Russian railroad industry. Its charter allowed the bank to engage in loan operations, insurance, commerce, and industry on Chinese markets, and 'participation in concessions for the construction of railroads and telegraph lines'.[119] Together with the Russian-Korean Bank and the Discount and Loan Bank of Persia, also established over the years 1894–97, the Russian-Chinese Bank aimed to bolster Russian imperial commercial and financial dealings in Asia.[120] P. L. Bark, a future minister of finances during the First World War whom Witte mentored and promoted as a junior banking official in the ministry, noted in his own memoirs that mainly the state treasury and the State Bank held these ostensibly private banks' shares. The banks were intended, Bark wrote in the tones of the imperialist age, not only to develop Russia's economic and financial interests: Witte wanted them to exercise 'political influence' in these countries as well.[121] In November 1895, Witte obtained approval from the emperor to send a memorandum of understanding through the Ministry of Foreign Affairs to Beijing outlining the terms of a concession allowing the construction of the Chinese Eastern from Chita through Harbin to Vladivostok.[122]

The key decisions that formalized the railroad concession Witte dated to the coronation of Nicholas II in May 1896, and the back-corridor diplomatic negotiations he conducted with the Chinese diplomatic plenipotentiary, Li Hongzhang. Witte took full credit for the idea and its realization. Chinese gratitude for Russian diplomatic intervention and financial support following its defeat at the hands of Japan, combined with the status of transsiberian construction, led him to a moment of discovery. 'Quite naturally, I had the idea of taking the railroad directly to Vladivostok, cutting through Mongolia and the northern part of Manchuria.' Insistently, and in cadences that reflected the catastrophic consequences that emanated from this decision, Witte reiterated that the railroad as he envisioned it had 'only economic significance; (military) significance defensively but not offensively; in particular it was not to have served as an instrument for any new seizures of territory'.[123]

He reflected as well on the diplomatic ritual of the negotiations with the Chinese ambassador, which occurred informally, first in St Petersburg and, once the imperial court moved there for the coronation ceremonies, in Moscow as well. His tastes and considerable abilities for ritual diplomatic performance and hard-headed policy making were fully displayed in his retelling of the event. The protocols of dress uniforms and formal greetings intermingled with calculated negotiation aimed to win Russian advantage. His ability to share confidences with Nicholas and win the Chinese ambassador a private audience with the tsar bolstered a critical moment in the negotiations. Rumor swirled then, and subsequently, that at the base of these negotiations were bribes to Chinese diplomats, but Witte restricted his public memories to what he claimed was the three-fold proposition he offered to justify building the Trans-Siberian across China. Russia, he argued in terms that made the military implications of his thinking quite explicit, could support the territorial integrity of China militarily only with 'a railroad transiting by the most direct route to Vladivostok . . . through Mongolia and the northern part of Manchuria'. Economically, in an old refrain, a railroad would increase 'the productivity (*proizvoditel'nost'*)' of both Russian territories and those Chinese territories through which it passed. Finally, in an argument that he had been repeating insistently ever since it proved to be so patently false when Japan went to war against Russia in 1904, Witte argued that Japan would not perceive this railroad to be a threat 'because this line essentially would unite Japan with all Western Europe'. Japan, given its embrace of European culture and especially its technology, would view this project 'favorably'.[124]

What eventually resulted from these negotiations was a concession granted the Russian-Chinese Bank to charter a Chinese Eastern Railway Society (CER), a privately owned company whose chief stockholder was the Russian state treasury and its Ministry of Finances. The terms of the concession, which utilized privately owned banks and corporations subject to Russian government control, granted the CER rights to construct and then manage the railroad for eighty years, while providing the Chinese state the right to expropriate the line beginning in 1933. Mitigating against that eventuality were a series of provisions stipulating how costly that act would be. The chairman of the CER's board of directors was to be a Chinese subject, but salaried by the company—and thus essentially the Russian state.

The railroad was to be built to Russian specifications and by Russian engineers, have its right of way in essence be imperial Russian territory policed by Border Guards of the Ministry of Finances, and benefit from significantly lower Chinese import and export tariffs levied on all goods in transit on the CER. Waiving its rights to levy taxes on the railroad, any of its construction materials, revenues, or rate structures, the Chinese government in return, once the railroad began to operate, would receive from the CER, and the Russian state treasury, a payment of five million gold rubles— for deposit in the Russian-Chinese Bank, where it would draw dividend income from the investment! A quintessential project for an imperial age, the railroad extended from Chita, east of Lake Baikal, through Manchuria to Vladivostok. Its length of almost 2,000 kilometers, 1,425 of which were within China, was significantly shorter than the originally planned route along the Amur River, and less expensive.[125] It also was a road to war.

Remembering these first years, when plainly the new tsar most closely hewed to the policies that the minister had set down for his father, Witte recalled a Nicholas with a 'spirit of good will (*blagozhelatel'nost'*) (that) shone from within him almost as if in rays of light', so wholeheartedly and sincerely did he desire 'for all of Russia, for all nationalities comprising Russia, for all its subjects good fortune and peaceful existence'.[126] Yet, as the old memoirist recognized in another place, as the decade proceeded, Witte's views of 'both economic and foreign policy questions... encountered great competition in the opinions of other ministers, and often His Majesty deigned to disagree with me and act against my opinions and my counsel'. That reaction, in part, was the result of the personal relationship between the son and his father's counselor. Yet, it also resulted from the personalized politics at the heart of tsarist government, where each ministry was a fiefdom of its minister, the power of the institution determined by the influence and skill of the man who directed it. Lacking a prime minister or a cabinet, the tsarist state was united only to the extent that each minister reported directly to the tsar, whose unconstrained autocratic power manifested itself in the sovereign's right to resolve any matter of state, no matter what its size or significance. Powerful ministers accumulated power by extending their policies and personal influence across this collection of parallel organizations. Ministers sought each other out as powerful allies and patrons—or deliberately undermined dangerous competitors. Because each depended upon the good will of the sovereign for his standing and status, too much power in the hands of any one minister potentially threatened the rest, and seemed inevitably to attract their coalescence and opposition—what Witte in one moment labeled 'a feeling of bureaucratic jealousy'.[127] To oppose, much less defeat the powerful minister was a dangerous game, because it required the competitor to denigrate the influ-ential councilor and possibly risk the good favor of his royal patron. From 1894 until Nicholas dismissed him in 1903, Witte argued a vision of the empire's place in Asia with which Nicholas increasingly disagreed, in part because the son eventually could not tolerate the adviser of his father, but also because he found an alternative set of policies more in accord with his own sympathies and counselors to advocate for them.

Witte knew this. 'It is likely that I was often mistaken,' Witte dictated on New Year's Day 1912, 'but, nevertheless, today I am deeply convinced that had His Imperial Majesty deigned to heed my opinions in questions of both domestic and foreign policy, there perhaps would have been mistakes made, even significant mistakes made, but, nevertheless, we would have avoided all those catastrophes which began starting in 1903, when I was forced to leave the post of minister of finances.'[128] There was a disingenuous note in these protestations to posterity. A chief preoccupation of the high politics of the imperial court in the years preceding the First World War was the question of responsibility for what Witte had rightly labeled the 'cata-strophes' of a Far Eastern imperial gambit that resulted by 1905 in military defeat by Japan and revolutionary upheaval at home. Witte strove mightily in his memoirs to assure that any blame for these 'catastrophes' fell not on him but others. In his reminiscences, he also reflected repeatedly on the geopolitical gamble he had undertaken in driving the Trans-Siberian toward the East, although surely the future that lay before him when Nicholas succeeded his father in 1894 must have been far less predictable than the inexorable pathway, which in retrospect informed his recollections of the past.

A measured reading of his memoirs and the official record of the Ministry of Finances in these years suggests the following story. In June 1896, Nicholas II's cousin and confidant, the Grand Duke Alexander Mikhailovich, pre-sented the tsar an argument justifying the construction of a Pacific High Seas squadron. Witte, now responsible for enormous sums of extraordinary expenditures, polemicized against the advisability of such additional spending on a Pacific fleet. Because the costly Trans-Siberian Railroad was intended to mobilize and transport the empire's primary weapon, its land army, to the Far East, Witte could declaim in the official journal that the army could 'assure the interests of Russia in the East of Asia and assert there her dignity (*dostoinstvo*)'. He was well aware by this date as well that Russia risked conflict with Japan, 'an island state' whose naval forces could defend the coasts of Japan or move on the high seas as interests of state dictated, whereas any fleet Russia constructed would be maneuvering within the closed 'Sea of Japan off the shores of Eastern Siberia, access to which from the high seas was guarded by the Japanese island of Tsushima'.[129] Nicholas II ignored that argument, and ordered Witte in early 1898 to appropriate up to 600 million rubles of extraordinary expenditures for this naval construction.[130]

Fate also intervenes in the story. The German emperor, Wilhelm II, Nicholas's cousin, chose this moment to write another chapter in the story of European imperialism in China. German naval and army units seized the Chinese port of Tsingtao in Jiaozhou Bay, purportedly to punish Chinese nationals murdering German missionaries, in fall 1897. In November, as Witte recounted the episode in his memoirs, he was invited to a special conference chaired by the tsar, through the auspices of Minister of Foreign Affairs Count N. V. Muraviev, which also was attended by the War Minister, Vannovski and the acting Naval Minister, Tyrtov. There, a memorandum authored by Muraviev argued that Russia in response should seize a port. At the tip of the Liaodong Peninsula was the warm-water anchorage at Port Arthur, or northwards on the same coast Da-lia-van, which remained alluringly ice-free throughout the year and, as he recalled the argument, 'because it would be desirable to have a port on the Pacific Ocean in the Far East... for strategic purposes.' Witte remembered his heated opposition, so adamantly did he feel that Russia's pledge to ensure the territorial integrity of China was being violated and that Japan would perceive this to be military aggression. He also argued that this strategic decision necessitated the construction of a southern branch line from the Chinese Eastern Railroad at Harbin through Mukden to Port Arthur. These Manchurian territories were 'thickly settled by Chinese' and the city of Mukden was the 'homeland of the Chinese imperial house'. All of this taken together, Witte warned, would 'lead us into such complications, which will end in the most regrettable results'.

Nicholas overruled him. 'Apparently somewhat upset,' as Witte recalled the audience with Nicholas where he was informed of the policy shift, 'the Sovereign Emperor said: "Did you know, Sergei Iul'evich, I have decided to seize Port Arthur and Da-lian-van and already have dispatched our flotilla with military units there?"' Witte snorted about Nicholas, 'the young emperor, lusting after glory, successes, and victories ...'. It was here that Witte began using the term 'the child's play (*rebiachestvo, rebiacheskaia igra*)' to describe Nicholas's control of policy and the clear break he had made with his father's counselor. Witte offered his resignation over this decision, Nicholas refused Witte's offer, asked him to acknowledge that policy could be different and that his duty was to execute the decision. Echoing the cadences of a world in which proper upbringing and polite behavior still governed the relations of men and women, Witte added as a last justification: 'and He personally asked me to do this'. Although chastened and his advice publicly rejected, Witte remained at his post and implemented the new policy. By March 1898, his personal ambassador in Beijing, Pokalitov, had telegraphed the Chinese government's tentative agreement for Russia to lease for twenty-five years the harbor and fortifications of Port Arthur, as well as the surrounding region of the southern Liadong peninsula. By May, a treaty agreement between the Chinese Eastern Railroad and the Chinese state had arranged the construction of the Southern Manchurian branch line to Port Arthur.[131]

Publicly, his star continued to shine, however. As part of the traditional round of royal favors distributed to loyal officials on New Year's Day, in 1899 Witte was promoted to the second highest civil service rank in the empire, Real Privy Councillor.[132] That same year, in May, he assisted Nicholas II in organizing the Hague Peace Conference, which brought together representatives of the great powers to discuss a disarmament that might lower the tempo of the arms race in which all of them were heatedly involved.[133] In October, his colleague and personal friend, the nobleman Dmitriii Sipiagin, was appointed by Nicholas to become Minister of Internal Affairs. Planning was fully under way for the opening of the Paris World Exposition in April 1900, where Russia intended to proclaim 'the non-stop route from Europe to Asia' in its Siberian Pavilion. Plans were being made for photographic exhibits of the Arctic Ocean coastline, Trans-Baikal and Manchuria, the printing of 100,000 free brochures about the Trans-Siberian Railroad, and large maps of 'Asiatic Russia and the possessions attached to it', ethnographic Russian colonization of Siberia, mineral deposits, and a large 'relief map of the entire expanse'.[134]

By the time the Paris exposition opened in the first spring of the new century, however, the international situation in the Far East was beginning to shift. Popular rebellion in China, what Europeans called the Boxer

Rebellion, was altering the international calculus. Anti-colonial and nationalist in character, it was Witte's first experience of agrarian revolt, which would explode around him again, but in Russia, in 1905–06. The ministry's records indicate that Witte in winter-spring 1900 brought reports of unrest in Manchuria, along the route of the Chinese Eastern Railway, to Nicholas's attention. The railroad was both a target and a proximate cause of the unrest.[135] By May, and throughout June, he was deluged with news of popular unrest, the siege of European diplomatic missions in Beijing, and military intervention to suppress it—all of it causing him to lose face before the sovereign to whom he reported this stream of ill tidings.[136] It also brought Russian army units into Manchuria to protect the rail route to Port Arthur, itself still under construction. More loudly in his memoirs than the archival record supports, Witte did seek to restrain military involvement, in the first instance because the intervention of the military meant the effective end of his own civilian administration of the region, and because he feared that the Japanese would view this as an aggressive shift in Russia's posture. That would mean growing military confrontation with Japan.[137] The emperor approved the first plan to transport the army from its European garrisons to the Far East eleven months later, in July 1901.[138]

Witte remained engaged in Far Eastern policy, particularly when it affected the empire's commercial and industrial interests. He petitioned Nicholas II, for example, to allow as shareholders in the East Asian Industrial Company, already chartered by the Vladivostok merchant Briner, individuals whose rank and office in state service made such activity impermissible without the sovereign's sanction. The shareholders included his former Minister of Court—and Witte's mentor, count I. I. Vorontsov-Dashkov, Nicholas's bastard cousin Prince Felix Usupov, counts Sumarov-Elston and V. A. Gendrikov, army colonel Serebriakov, and navy captain A. M. Abaza. His ministry continued to seek financial and commercial advantage in the region, chartering a Manchurian Mining Company in 1902 and beginning initial planning for the expansion of Dal'ny as a commercial port to the north of Port Arthur.[139] In the fall of 1901, the Chinese Eastern Railway was completed, and in August 1902 the first train from St Petersburg to Port Arthur, with the Japanese crown prince making the trip, arrived on the Pacific coast.[140] Witte followed shortly thereafter, traveling the entire route in September 1902. There had been, he recalled in his memoirs, some discussion of his continuing onwards from Vladivostok to visit Japan, but that plan had been scotched by a suggestion from the court that the emperor would look askance at such a display of Witte's prominence.[141] Instead, he inspected the Trans-Siberian project, including its branches into Manchuria, and took account, in the words of David McDonald, that 'the Witte kingdom' he had constructed over the previous decade in railroads, territory, institutional structures and personnel—as well as the revenues and expenditures under his control—now was crumbling under the full-throated assault of what he personally catalogued in his own archive as the *Bezobrazovshchina*, the days of Bezobrazov.[142]

That Witte labeled a period of such historic import to the late Russian Empire in such personal terms was indicative of both the man and the times in which a high official of that empire found himself in the first years of the twentieth century. By then, the civic world that had shaped Witte's own life was acquiring the trappings of modern politics. Political ideologies—socialism, populism, liberalism, and nationalism—offered distinct alternatives to dynastic monarchism, and were creating leaders, party organizations, constituencies, and agendas to realize their visions of the future. Such a politics, by its very presence, challenged the monopoly of power and authority claimed by the autocratic sovereign and his bureaucracy. Formally illegal, periodically policed and prosecuted, nascent and evolving, a civic politics was emerging in the empire. Its signs were unmistakable. Public dismay and volunteerism during the Great Famine of 1891–92. The refusal of the newly crowned Nicholas II to consider moderate reforms. The St Petersburg textile strikes of spring 1896. University student disorders in autumn 1899. An industrial depression after 1900. Peasant disturbances and labor unrest in eastern Ukraine during 1902–03. The re-emergence of political terrorism with the assassinations of Minister of Education Bogolepov in 1901 and Minister of Internal Affairs Sipiagin in 1902. That Witte at the time recognized and even partially understood the forces of opposition to unlimited autocracy and bureaucracy building within imperial society is undeniable.[143] That one of the empire's most accomplished statesman later in life instead focused his memories upon the opposition building against him within the closeted world of officialdom and imperial court is silent testimony to its isolation from the underlying disaffection that fed and radicalized public opposition to autocracy.

The 'Times of Bezobrazov', which really was the tale of Witte's final fall from grace and ministerial power, began in April 1902, when Witte's friend and ally Dmitrii Sipiagin was assassinated, and Nicholas appointed in his place Witte's arch-nemesis and rival, Viacheslav von Plehve. As Minister of Internal Affairs, the other primary domestic ministry in the imperial state, Plehve asserted his ministry's competing authority in almost every venue of Russian public life. Witte hated Pleve, suspiciously regarding him as the agent-provocateur of the diminution of his power, which he perceived to be slipping away as Nicholas ever more publicly tilted toward a coterie of allies that included the tsar's cousin, Grand Duke Alexander Mikhailovich; the court adjutant-general A. A. Bezobrazov; the navy admiral A. A. Abaza, and the military commanders Alekseev and Kuropatkin. Their ability to counter every weapon in Witte's arsenal—his intellect, institutional base, influence, and networks—eventually led to the decision, on 30 July 1903, to appoint Vice-Admiral E. I. Alekseev Viceroy of the Far East, and set in motion a final round of exchanges between Witte and Nicholas. The younger Nicholas II grew weary of the older Witte's tutelage, constant hectoring, and disagreement with his choice of policies and advisers.[144]

In June 1903, Witte's political position at the Russian imperial court, and with his now nearly hostile sovereign, the Emperor Nicholas II, was crumbling. A. F. Koni, a noted jurist and long-time acquaintance, remembered encountering Witte that month, exercising on horseback as he had done throughout his lifetime, at a summer health resort in Sestroetsk on the Finnish Gulf. Riding in bursts, first at a gallop and then a slow walk, Witte was hardly recognizable, Koni remembered. Where 'in this stooping, rumpled, distracted and worried face' was the 'self-assured and energetic figure of the minister of finances', Koni wondered. Witte greeted him warmly and engaged him in conversation, but it was apparent, said Koni, that he was speaking 'mechanical phrases' and seemed not even to heed Koni's answers, simply content to meet someone, given all the enemies surrounding him, 'who would not cause him any unpleasantness'.[145] Nicholas dismissed him two months later, in August 1903, by promoting him to be the chair of the largely ceremonial Committee of Ministers.

The chorus urging Nicholas II toward an aggressive posture in Manchuria and Korea, and thus the roots of war with Japan and the inexorable descent into military stalemate and revolution, was hardly less loud with Witte gone. Finance nevertheless dictated peace, and that always moderating influence was for Witte a bottom line. He recorded, in his own hand, on the cover of a copy of his official report to Nicholas of his travels to the Far East, his own chronicle of subsequent events, written sometime after the fact. 'S. Iu. Witte completed travel to the Far East in July–September

1902 and presented this report sixteen months prior to the war. A. N. Kuropatkin,' it continued, turning attention to the former governor-general of Turkestan who had become War Minister and then Commander-in-Chief of imperial forces in the Far East, 'traveled (there) in May–June 1903–8 months before the war. S. Iu. Witte left the post of Minister of Finances because of disagreement with the actions of the Viceroy Alekseev, State-Secretary Bezobrazov, and the committee on the Far East administered by Vice Admiral of the Suite A. A. Abaza in August 1903, a whole half-year before the war,' citing as well the state committee that represented the Finance Ministry's institutional divorce from Far East policy. The note concluded: 'S. Iu. Witte this entire time maintained that we were not prepared for war—and were conducting a policy, which inevitably was leading to war. In May 1903, some 7–8 months before the war ... Alekseev was made viceroy of the Far East and from that time Count Lamzdorf (the Foreign Affairs minister) was in practice ... isolated from the conduct of policy in the Far East. It was handed over to the viceroy, and in Petersburg to Abaza and Bezobrazov. Count Lamzdorf resigned, but his resignation was not accepted and he played the role of a powerless dressing curtain (*shirma*).' As a summarizing final note, Witte added his argument and what those surrounding Nicholas II said in reply: 'Conducting a policy leading inevitably to war for which we were seriously unprepared. The Japanese wouldn't dare, and were they to dare, then we fight.'[146]

By the time that a Japanese fleet used torpedoes to incapacitate Russia's imperial squadron, anchored in the roadstead of Port Arthur, in January 1904, Witte long since had vacated the Ministry of Finances, victim to the syndrome that perhaps had befallen his idol Bismarck's encounter with a brash, young Kaiser Wilhelm II. The story of Nicholas's disenchantment with his father's most trusted adviser was a familiar tale, often told by fathers and sons. Reflecting on his resignation from the ministry in August 1903, in what Witte termed 'an appointment to the pointless position of Chairman of the Committee of Ministers', he summarized a final time that this change of fortune 'was to be explained almost exclusively by my disagreement with policies in the Far East that led us to the Japanese war'. Yet, he also knew that his colleague Vladimir Lamzdorf, the Minister of Foreign Affairs who, with Witte, had opposed the Far Eastern policies that Nicholas now pursued, had been allowed to remain at his post. Witte thus mused how his own personality, even his own hubris, had led him to this moment when the man whom he once had regarded as his young protégé rejected him and drove him from power. Although as he told this tale he put the words anonymously in the mouth of 'one of the players of that time, who was close to the court', Witte was telling his own tale of imperial Russia.

'Imagine the father of a family, who has a son and a daughter,' he began, 'and imagine that this father is doing something that, in the opinion of his children, is deadly for the father.' That the father's sin was a passionate desire to divorce his wife and marry instead a 'young girl' was an interesting aside, but his point was to contrast the responses of the son and the daughter to their father's wishes. Plainly envisioning himself, Witte saw the son haranguing his father, telling him 'curtly' not to do harm to himself and lose all 'prestige', refusing to be silent even when his father plainly was losing his patience, until finally, exploding, he told him, '"Get the hell out! (*Ukhodi von!*)"—and drove his son from his home.' The 'quiet and modest daughter', instead, conveyed entirely the same message to her father, 'but in a different tone: "Dear papa, I advise you not to do this! You know, how I love you! You will do harm to yourself, and because I so love you and fear this harm, I beseech you, please, do not do this."' The father, Witte concluded, lovingly caressed his daughter's cheek, and went with her for an evening at the theater. The daughter was Lamzdorf; he was the son, who in the end willingly left his father's house. Recalling that he asked Lamzdorf at the time why he had not resigned, Lamzdorf, Witte explained, 'told me: it is one of two options. (E)ither our Sovereign is Autocratic or not Autocratic.' Because Lamzdorf considered him to be unlimited in his powers, the duty of an official counselor was to give his best advice and, once the tsar decided, 'unconditionally submit and strive to fulfill his decision'.

Witte, across a lifetime, certainly had shared this view. By the early twentieth century, as he found himself awakening from grand dreams of imperial prosperity and power, however, these thoughts of fathers and sons were increasingly preoccupying his attention. Because his vision of empire always had centered on a strong, powerful, and decisive personality to be Emperor and Autocrat of All the Russias, Witte could dream only so long as such a personality sat on the throne. Hence his own loyalties to the memories of his tsar-father, Alexander III. With the son as father, however, his certainty of the present and future became ever more murky. Witte admitted to himself that he ought to have agreed with Lamzdorf, and submitted to the will of his sovereign. But reality was beginning to dictate otherwise. 'It is impossible to repudiate the logic of this argument,' he concluded, adding 'although for such a form of behavior, one must have an extremely elastic "I", which, unfortunately, is not one of my attributes.'[147]

5

From Exile: Memories of Revolutionary Russia, 1903–1912

The 14th–15th May (1905) saw the disastrous Tsushima battle and our entire flotilla was entombed in Japanese waters! This was the last blow of that disastrous conspiracy, which brought us to the Japanese war. After this defeat everyone came to the realization that it was necessary to end the war with a peace and this tendency so strongly began to manifest itself that it reached, in the end, to the throne.[1]

Memoirs/Tales in stenographic record/of Count
Sergei Iul'evich Witte, February 1912

... and I, since the time of my arrival from America, was ill throughout my premiership and only an extreme nervous tension (*kraine nervnoe napriazhenie*) kept me going.

Notes of Count Witte, September 1909, Biarritz[2]

One could say without any exaggeration that all Russia had been swept up in the troubles and that the general slogan was a cry from the soul: 'To live like this any longer is impossible,' in other words—the existing regime had to come to an end.

Notes of Count Witte, September 1907, Biarritz[3]

In general the October days showed me clearly that under the influence of cowardice no one human characteristic increases in significance more than stupidity.

Notes of Count Witte, September 1909, Biarritz[4]

I took up the administration of the empire at a time of wholesale confusion, if not madness.... In a word, by (17 October)...a complete revolutionary nightmare in the country.

Notes of Count Witte, August 1912, Biarritz[5]

The Sovereign appeared in the hall, where members of the State Duma and the State Council were in attendance, in the formal order of a great public procession, with all the high officers of the Court and the entire royal suite. In the hall of the palace all the official world (*chinovnyi mir*) as well as high society were in attendance. This public procession...possessed, of course, historic significance, given that it was the first and only such appearance of the Sovereign Emperor before representatives of the people, before both the upper and lower Houses . . . I stayed in St. Petersburg until the opening of the State Duma and State Council, attended the new State Council for several weeks, and then went abroad.

Memoirs / Tales in stenographic record / of Count Sergei Iul'evich Witte, February 1912[6]

Sergei Witte awoke from his dreams of empire in 1903, to a world he apprehended, but could not, in the end, ever entirely comprehend. His was, after all, a world that had begun with his grandparents, still of an age that remembered the glories of the Catherinian empire. Resigning the Ministry of Finances in summer 1903, he became chairman of the Committee of Ministers, a largely ceremonial post without power, from which Witte watched events transpire that led the empire to war, military defeat, and revolution. Two years later, he traveled to Portsmouth, Maine, in the United States, as the tsar's plenipotentiary ambassador to peace talks with Japan, and rose to an international prominence enjoyed by no other Russian statesman of his generation. Granted the title of Count by a grateful sovereign, Witte returned to Russia in September 1905 and encountered the consequences of military defeat: revolutionary turmoil, chaotic and swirling across all classes of the population and regions of the empire. He experienced the depth and scale of what historians have called the 1905 Revolution, the first Russian revolution, or simply '1905'.[7] He called it, variously, anarchy, 'our damned revolution', disorder, or, simply, 'the troubles (*smuta*)'. By mid October, he had become the most visible advocate for an equally revolutionary solution to the turmoil. Despite its multiple causes, Witte argued to an ever suspicious Nicholas, the social and political unrest engulfing the empire was fed by a single, unifying cause: a broadly based public repudiation of unconstrained autocracy and bureaucratic rule, the regime that had led to this impasse. Compromise with the inevitable spirit of the age, and give the people the constitution they are demanding, Witte insisted, and public order, slowly but just as inevitably, would follow, providing the empire the breathing space it needed to undertake the fundamental social and political reforms that now stood on the order of the day.

Two historic moments ensued that engraved Witte's name in the history of modern Russia. One was the Manifesto of 17 October 1905. In it, the sovereign promised laws guaranteeing freedoms of speech, press, conscience, and assembly; an imperial legislature, the State Duma; and elections that extended a ballot to most adult males in the empire. The other was Witte's appointment to be Chairman of the Council of Ministers, a ministerial cabinet responsible to the Crown for its actions and policies; reminiscent of Bismarck's power, the chairman of the council modeled German rather than British parliamentary politics. Meant to unify the disparate activities of the ministerial state and corral the willfulness that Nicholas II had displayed prior to the war with Japan, Witte's de facto premiership was short-lived. For six months, he struggled to restore public order and broker a reformed constitutional order, which retained the Crown, the ministerial state, and the unitary empire, but allowed popular sovereignty, parliamentary representation, and normal civic politics. The possibilities of such a compromise, particularly within the *ancien regime* culture that dominated the imperial court, aristocratic high society and officialdom of St Petersburg, grew increasingly unlikely as autumn became winter and then early spring. His health and reputation under assault, and the confidence of Nicholas II yet again shattered by their ever stormy relationship, Witte resigned his office in April 1906, on the eve of the convocation of the First Duma. Nicholas elevated him to an appointed position in the reformed Imperial State Council, the upper house of Russia's new legislative order. Witte left Russia to travel abroad.

By mid July 1906, Witte's promises of reform and order seemed, if anything, to have deepened political radicalism and social disorder in the empire. Russia's national elections that spring had yielded a parliament. Witte had imagined the First Duma to be a constitutional pillar of a monarchical Russian Empire, which in many ways it was. It was a body dominated numerically by peasants demanding land reform, and politically by liberal, populist, and socialist politicians competing among themselves to represent, and resolve, popular social grievances, with policies more radical than imperial officials were willing to tolerate, much less imagine. When it was prorogued after less than four months of existence, as the new Fundamental Laws Witte had authored allowed, its liberal tribunes, leaders of the Constitutional Democrats, went to Vyborg in Finland and issued a manifesto to the population, calling upon it to refuse to pay taxes or submit to the military draft. The effort had little effect; as the law provided, new elections were set for the following winter. The young and dynamic Minister of Internal Affairs, the former provincial governor of Saratov province, Peter Arkadeevich Stolypin, replaced I. L. Goremykin, who had replaced Witte that April, as chairman of the Council of Ministers.

In Europe, Witte viewed all these events from afar. He spent the summer and fall traveling in Germany, France, and Belgium. His daughter Vera lived in Brussels with her husband, Kirill Naryshkin, an official of the Russian Embassy there, and Witte's young grandson, Lev. Judging from his dictated memoirs, Witte was adrift in these months, each cataloged dinner, encounter, or family gathering bearing silent witness to how far away he stood from affairs of state. He spent a month in Frankfurt with his wife, where he underwent surgery.[8] He reported in his memoirs mysterious plotting that targeted him for assassination in Europe and at home in Russia.[9] What fixated his attention in these months, however, were rumors emanating from St Petersburg that the royal couple, rather than showering him with the praise he thought he deserved for the October Manifesto, instead were scapegoating his reputation and blaming Witte for the chaos of the war with Japan, the revolution at home it had precipitated, and the manifesto he purportedly had torn from the hands of an unwilling tsar.

In mid July, while he was in Aix in France, Witte received a letter from Baron Fredericks, the Minister of the Court, in which the courtier noted a conversation with the tsar. Nicholas had mentioned that, given the unsettled 'present political situation', Witte's return to Russia at this time 'would be quite undesirable', Witte exploded, taking this as confirmation of his disfavor. He penned a reply that this news 'had quite surprised him' because he could not imagine how anyone could believe he would do 'harm to my Sovereign and fatherland, which I always have served with total and self-sacrificing loyalty', but, if he were mistaken, he threatened, he should hold neither rank nor office in the imperial state. Apparently thinking better of this tactic, Witte merely communicated to Fredericks that he had no plans to return to Russia at present. After six weeks, with no reply forthcoming from St Petersburg, he dispatched another letter in early September, sent through Fredericks to the emperor, in which he wrote that the silence from St Petersburg suggested the sovereign favored his resignation. In that case, 'self-respect' demanded that he retire altogether from state service—and, he recalled later in his memoirs, take up one of numerous offers to work in private business. Preferring in the letter the cadences of the imperial court, he added that resignation would not alter his loyalties to the Crown and 'to those principles instilled in me with mother's milk, which His Imperial Majesty, as the Russian Monarch, personifies'. Loyal to the institution, but slighting the man, the contents of this letter finally produced a response from Fredericks on 10 September that all had been a misunderstanding, that Nicholas continued to look kindly upon Witte, and that he desired him to continue in state service.[10] Witte's feathers were smoothed by this reply, although given his past experience with Nicholas he could not have been reassured as he returned to St Petersburg in the early autumn that either his narrative of 1905 or his reputation was intact.

This correspondence with Fredericks contained a first attempt to frame just such a narrative. In his letter of 2 September, Witte attempted to shift the blame for the demise of the first Duma to the ministry of I. L. Goremykin, who had replaced him following his resignation in April. Another long-serving bureaucratic rival who had led the Ministry of Internal Affairs during the 1890s, Goremykin, Witte correctly argued, had adopted a deliberately conservative and monarchical tone in his dealings with the new Duma. That attitude had agitated nothing but 'contemptuous enmity' within the assembly, and thus assured continuing dissent and protest rather than the cooperation and productive work that he had envisioned cooperation with the Duma producing among the moderate and liberal elements of society that supported the October compromise. Worse, Goremykin had trampled upon the Duma's prerogatives to introduce and debate agrarian land reform legislation, which included provisions for the forcible sale of private landholdings and their distribution to 'land hungry' peasants, the one question 'upon which it was most dangerous of all to prorogue the popular assembly'. 'What is terrible', he wrote, 'is that the Government provided utterly obvious grounds to convince the peasantry that the Government of the Sovereign Emperor, if it is not against them is in any case not for them.' His former cabinet was being unfairly maligned in both the Russian and foreign press, he complained. He especially focused upon 'the honorable and decisive' Stolypin, who as the chairman of the Council of Ministers had 'climbed into the saddle' where Witte once sat. Stolypin was benefiting, Witte sniped, from what really were his accomplishments: the October Manifesto; a program of government reform legislation to occupy the new Duma's attention; and the six million ruble state loan he had brokered in Europe to stabilize imperial finances nearly bankrupted by war and revolution.[11] Stolypin, whose own political star was now in the ascendancy, was displacing Witte from his accustomed place at the center of imperial politics—as later he would with historians as well. Somehow, the older man could never tolerate that challenge. Perhaps, the younger, dynamic, and politically savvy Stolypin had learned to speak with his contemporary, the Emperor Nicholas II, in ways that Witte the tutor had never mastered. Certainly Stolypin began to utilize the institutions and reformist legislation of the Witte era to craft a new, more authoritarian, and more nationalistic politics than any Witte had contemplated.[12]

Yet, as he returned to St Petersburg in the fall of 1906, it was far less the future and much more the present and the past that drew his attention. Plainly, his policies as Minister of Finances propelled the empire toward Russian involvement in the Pacific Far East. He could be blamed for the disastrous war with Japan. As sponsor of an October Manifesto that excised the premise 'unrestricted' from the autocrat's political authority, he could have been construed to have betrayed the sovereign—and in conservative, monarchical, and proto-fascist, Black-Hundreds circles of opinion, he was viewed in that way. Those perceptions, Witte continued to believe, dominated at court and influenced especially the Empress Alexandra Fedorovna. She had constructed her own interpretation of events, he wrote in early 1908, whereby Witte had extorted the October Manifesto from the hands of her unwilling husband. He lurked, as the right-wing press charged daily, as traitor, mason, and 'purchased tool of the yids [sic]', and secretly planned to be president of a Russian republic.[13]

In early 1907, such suspicions and rumored calumny led him to write again for Nicholas, this time a memorandum that narrated his version of the negotiations and immediate events that had led Nicholas to agree to issue the Manifesto of 17 October 1905. When he received it—and another two weeks of silence passed before a reply—the tsar, Witte was told, agreed with its contents, but insisted that his opinion only be conveyed orally.[14] This refusal to go on the record further enraged the old statesman. 'How do you like such a thing from the lips of an Autocratic Emperor?' Witte disdainfully scrawled into his notebook in November 1907. 'And to think that this is the son of that most noble and most fair crowned head, Alexander III.'[15] That acerbic comparison between the son who had forced him from power, Nicholas II, and the father who had promoted him to its apex, Alexander III, was the concluding two sentences in 250 notebook pages of laboriously scrawled recollections that he had written during the previous six months (June–November 1907), all of which he had spent again in Germany, southern France, and Belgium. What he entitled 'Part I. Forward. The

Notes of Count Witte (memoirs—composed on the quick-not having at hand any documentary materials)' examined the events that had led from his dismissal as Minister of Finances in 1903 through the outbreak of war with Japan to his return from America to St Petersburg in September 1905. They also were the first installment of his memoirs.[16]

This writing intermingled chronological narrative with reflections on the personalities who bore significance in tsarist Russia's high society during those years, the informal networks and personalized relationships that bound these individuals together and gave them significance, and thus especially the sub-cultural milieus which enveloped and influenced their behaviors and motivations. As Witte began to write his memoirs during that summer and fall of 1907, he did so by centering on events that remained for him, as they did for so many other imperial Russians of his class, immediate, emotional, even burning memories of *smuta*, upheaval, and end times. Through the seams of recollection ran memories of not simply revolutionary upheaval following military defeat, and constitutional reforms torn from an unwilling autocratic officialdom. Adept at fashioning identity and trenchant observer of milieus that shaped personality, Witte sensed how fundamentally the world that he knew, and the values that anchored it, were being drained of their capacity to instill hope and belief, inspire allegiance, and maintain their aura of legitimacy. What Witte remembered about 1905 was not, in this sense, political or institutional at all. Rather, he recalled the evisceration of the emotional bonds that had tied him to the world of the autocracy. He remembered his own loss of faith. That personal experience reinforced his sensibility that the Russian Empire was passing from a nineteenth-century world, in which experience could be classified and explained, into another, where it could not.

From Summer 1903 to October 1905:
War, America, and Revolution

Witte suffered his first fall from power in August 1903, when he was dismissed from the Ministry of Finances. Later recalling this 'unexpected decision', he remembered 'an apparently somewhat inhibited, confused' Nicholas offering him the office of chairman of the Committee of Ministers, a position that, the tsar hastened to add, was 'the highest post that exists in the Empire'. Witte derided this appointment privately, but remembered telling Nicholas simply that he imagined himself 'in a more active post' than the committee. The committee, which had existed throughout the nineteenth century, was used at the discretion of the sovereign to process routine files of state that, for whatever reason, could not bear more transparent scrutiny. Witte attempted to steer as much of this material as he could away from himself, and was bored by the rest of it. Nicholas asked him to lead the renegotiation of the trade treaty with Germany, which brought him to the attention of Kaiser Wilhelm II in late 1904.[17] He had to request of Nicholas, a slight Witte had considered to be deliberate, that he be allowed to retain his oversight of a project constructing a memorial to Alexander III being built on Znamensky Square before the portal of the Nicholas Railway Terminal, the western terminus of the Trans-Siberian Railway.[18] He also continued with a huge undertaking he had gathered through the Ministry of Finances and Tsar Nicholas, the Special Conference on the Needs of Agriculture. This commission solicited testimony in the counties and provinces of European Russia from committees of local nobility, landowners, peasants, ethnic minorities, and others about the technological, economic, and legal policies conducive to increasing the productivity and wealth of Russian agriculture. He continued to sit, now in his capacity as a former minister of finances, on the Finance Committee, an interministerial body that consulted on the Russian state's bond portfolio and the status of its finances. Still, while he remained a fixture of Petersburg society, he knew himself to be shunned by the tsar and the court, whose social occasions he only infrequently noted attending.[19]

He dueled with Viacheslav von Pleve—and there is no other way of envisioning their conflict over the arch-strategy of dealing with every consequential matter of domestic and foreign affairs, until a bomb-throwing anarchist-terrorist ended the confrontation when he assassinated the Minister of Internal Affairs in July 1904. In part a personalized version of a longstanding institutional conflict between the two key domestic ministries, finances and internal affairs, the clash between Witte and Pleve testified to the rapidity with which the issues confronting Russian imperial governance were multiplying. They struggled over policy toward the peasantry, especially the utility of the peasant land commune, which Witte was beginning to regard as a source of economic and social instability, while Pleve saw a segregated peasant estate (soslovie), administration, and laws as a guarantee that a conservative peasant monarchism would remain a foundation of tsarist rule. They struggled over how to treat an expanding and increasingly volatile labor movement, which Witte regarded as a normal, if potentially dangerous, phenomenon of industrial life that the state, through law and administration, could mediate, regulate, and, if necessary, suppress—much as was the case in Germany. Pleve used the power of the police to organize worker's unions, the so-called Zubatov movement (*Zubatovshchina*), which eventually was complicit in the events of the infamous St Petersburg Bloody Sunday of 9 January 1905. Witte, who never fully embraced emancipation as an immediate possibility for Jews in the empire but always quietly advocated for amelioration of their legal position, scorned Pleve's adminis-tration of the 'Jewish question', with its shameful neglect or rumored deliberate provocation of the Kishinev pogrom of April 1903. Pleve, Witte insisted, viewed any accommodation with nascent national politics as steps toward restriction of 'unrestricted' autocracy. He understood the development and complexity of contemporary imperial society, but, as Witte recalled in 1912, 'he was only an intelligent, cultured and amoral policeman', unable to treat 'public unrest' with anything other than force or cunning. Worse, by encouraging these sensibilities in Nicholas II, he only further abetted in the sovereign a growing irritation at any thing that smacked of the Russian intelligentsia and the ideologies it spawned.[20]

The intelligentsia was a true cultural construct, a tradition as much as it was a social group, an identity that demanded privilege serve the good of the people, culture be preserved and transmitted as Russia's greatest treasure, and freedom, no matter the cost, be the birthright of every individual.[21] Established from the end of the eighteenth century, Witte first encountered the phenomenon at university in the 1860s, and by the turn of the century, intelligentsia as a category bearing meaning in Russian public discourse had encountered the kaleidoscopic sociological intersection of science, profes-sion, and civic life. Wealthier, more educated, and more modern, imperial subjects in ever greater numbers gravitated toward more active involvement in public life and civic affairs, in an autocratic empire where politics was reserved to the monarch and his bureaucracy. Political dissidence and opposition to autocratic rule were not a historical inevitability, but its rumblings were ever more audible in the traditional sites of imperial public life—its universities, thick journals, state corporate organizations, elected municipal councils (*duma*), the elected rural zemstvo assemblies stretching across 34 provinces and over 300 counties of European Russia, the offices and salons of the capitals and provincial cities, even among officials and landowners, many of them the descendants of the same tradition of service to tsar and fatherland as had been Witte. So too were these rumblings heard in new sites of public and political life: voluntary civic associations, professional and business organizations, the stage and song, the working classes in its factories and neighborhoods, cities and the urban street, national minorities who were majorities in imperial borderlands, the press and public opinion, and the countryside, especially the village. Nascent political parties—with leadership cadres, potential constituencies, and political agendas—were emerging, identifiable when the historian in retrospect traces the great political ideologies of the age of empire. Liberalism, republicanism, socialism, populism, nationalism, and proto-fascism all offered political alternatives to unrestricted autocratic power and the bureaucratic regime that officials had constructed and lovingly tended in service to monarchical rule.[22]

In his Notes, Witte wrote scathingly of both *intelligenty* and officials—as always disregarding the fact that he fancied himself to be in part the former and certainly well knew himself to be the latter. In terms that captured the paternalistic ethos of the imperial official, he reduced a social and cultural phenomenon to a class of talented and well-intentioned individuals, adept at the strategy that 'the end justifies the means'. Certainly capable of displaying remarkable unity 'behind their goal of overturning the existing regime', they nevertheless were self-serving 'politicos (*politikany*)' whose own wavering, ill-defined convictions allowed many of them to be "public activists" one day and, 'after the joy of revolution (*prelest' revoliutsii*)' had passed, 'rightists' the next.[23] Witte similarly disdained Petersburg officials, representatives of the state who, he once noted sarcastically, 'in the current fashion (are called) bureaucrats'. Indicatively enough, while discussing V. K. Pleve, Witte wove a broader recollection of the Petersburg officialdom, which both he and his great adversary, each in their own way, had mastered so consummately. His was a picture of corruption, stagnation, and especially, willful isolation from popular concerns, 'a mass of people whose main occupation was to abuse one another with lies and slander, thereby seeking for themselves momentary advantage'.[24] Many contemporary observers, and subsequently some historians, always have placed Witte, especially during years when his hand did not control affairs of state directly, into this category.[25] [T]he cross that Witte bore was a vision of an empire, were power exercised wisely and prudently] Russia, however, was entering a time when neither prudence nor wisdom was a ready attribute of statesmanship.

Although at some remove from its apex, Witte used his extensive networks, insatiable thirst for information, and synthetic intellect to continue to play a role in the high politics of St Petersburg. He largely stood by and watched as, from summer 1903 onwards, the empire moved from military occupation of parts of Manchuria following the Boxer Rebellion of 1900–1901 toward war with the Empire of Japan at Port Arthur in January 1904. News from the front in the first year of the war was grim. Following the Japanese attack on Port Arthur in January, the Pacific Squadron's flagship, the armored cruiser Petropavlovsk, was sunk in March, together with its commander, Vice Admiral S. O. Makarov, an Arctic explorer and Russia's most qualified naval strategist. The Russian navy in the Far East, Witte remembered, subsequently was 'doomed to complete inactivity'. Without Russian naval forces to intervene, the Japanese army landed in Korea and by April had seized control of the entire peninsula. From there followed Japanese victories on the Liao-tung Peninsula that pushed Russian army units back to Port Arthur to endure a siege that would last until the following December—'the beginning of the death of Port Arthur', Witte remarked.

In part, this deteriorating military situation had been predetermined by Russian strategy, when confronted by the sudden and unanticipated outbreak of war. A. N. Kuropatkin, the Minister of War, was appointed to command the Russian army in the Far East when the war began. Kuropatkin promised a strategy that anticipated a Japanese siege against a seemingly impregnable fortress at Port Arthur, a series of defensive battles as the army retreated northwards toward Mukden, and a concentration of Russian forces there with those coming from European Russia on the Trans-Siberian Railroad. Then, he planned a counterattack that would drive the Japanese into the sea and force them to sue for peace. Nevertheless, by August all attempts to break the siege at Port Arthur had failed, and a major land battle between the Russian and Japanese armies at Liaoyang, an important junction town on the Chinese Eastern Railroad trunk line supplying Port Arthur, had resulted in a major Russian defeat and forced a wholesale withdrawal to Mukden. In October 1904, the decision was taken to dispatch the Russian Baltic Fleet, under the command of Vice Admiral Z. P. Rozhestvenskii, and renamed the Second Pacific Ocean Squadron, to relieve Port Arthur and turn the tide in the Pacific. Although not a participant in the discussions leading to it, Witte from the hindsight of his notebooks, thought the expedition likely to be a failure that would deprive Russia of naval forces in European waters.[26]

Witte, whose memoirs reflect very little patriotic enthusiasm for the war from the outset, seethed as he recollected incompetent commanders, military defeat on land and sea, and stark casualty lists that hinted at the destructiveness of modern industrial war. Behind it all, he knew, were the blows to imperial political authority that defeat created and the ever wider fissures in the structure of domestic order that inevitably resulted. Writing in September 1907, Witte recalled how the war was agitating the most varied responses from 'all strata of the population', that 'the psychology' of the population began to shift, that 'all were being driven to their wit's end, that in the end one could say: Russia went insane'. Why? 'In truth,' he mused, '(w)ho created the Russian Empire, turning it from a Muscovite half-asiatic tsardom to the most influential, most dominating, great European power? The force of the bayonet, the army,' was his reply. The world, he continued, did not bow down before Russian culture, religion, wealth, or standard of living. 'It bowed down before our strength,' he mused, and when enemies foreign and domestic 'saw that we are not at all as strong as they thought, that this Russia is "a colossus with feet of clay" . . . (they) begin to ignore us'.[27] The biographer here can only recall a young boy in the now distant Caucasus, where empire, army, and uncontestable power were also unquestioned assumptions of the imperial service class from which his family had come. That Witte sensed a population ceasing to heed 'us' hinted at the crisis that the autocratic regime that he served was beginning to experience by 1904–05. Historians of this era at times have too generously used the word 'crisis' to describe the upheaval the Russian Empire experienced after 1904, but Witte's characterization of the crisis that had seized his class, ensconced at the heights of imperial power, *na verkhu*, by the winter and spring of 1905, was a genuine artifact of the period. There, 'at the top', it seemed, at the apex of a hierarchically organized world where the medieval origins of old regime polities still lingered, allied but often clashing civilian, military, diplomatic, imperial court, and aristocratic sub-elites intermingled in their salons, offices, palaces, landed estates, and townhouses. They stared, increasingly aghast, at the rising waters lapping against their citadel that storms of political and social turmoil were creating within the empire.[28]

What followed was increasing government indecisiveness and paralysis. When he first reached this chronological moment in his notebooks, writing in Catleret, France, in August 1907, Witte synthesized a 'general law', which surely only reflected his own experience of the year. 'A people demands economic and social reforms,' he entoned. When a government systematically refuses to act on these demands, the people concludes 'that its desires cannot be satisfied by the given regime'. Consequently, the socio-economic recedes in importance before an emergent set of 'political demands as the means to attain economic and social reforms'. Should a government not 'wisely regulate this tendency, and even more should it begin to create insanity (the Japanese war),' Witte added just to clarify, 'revolution bursts into the open.' Failure to act decisively 'opens the door to anarchy'.[29] The summary captured a political chronicle that historians typically begin writing, as did Witte, with the Imperial Edict to the Ruling Senate of 12 December 1904.

Prince P. D. Sviatopolk-Mirskii had replaced the assassinated Pleve in July as Minister of Internal Affairs. Known for his liberal monarchism and reformist sympathies, Mirskii was an aristocratic army general favored at court, who had served in the Russo-Turkish War. He had been a provincial governor and an assistant Minister of Internal Affairs before Pleve, and since that time had been the governor-general of the Baltic provinces, where his reputation as a reform-minded administrator looking toward an accommodation between government and 'society' had been solidified. He urged Nicholas II to distance himself from the repudiated domestic policy of his murdered predecessor, with its suspicion of all public independence and frequent recourse to extra-legal actions. Instead, Mirskii insisted that the sovereign embrace a program of liberal bureaucratic reform, which would expand local self-administration, institutionalize the rule of law by strengthening the courts, easing censorship, and establishing individual rights for national minorities and religious sectarians, as well as undertake a review of all legislation affecting the position of the empire's peasantry.

Witte fully supported, and well before 1904 had advocated all of these policies, but by all accounts he maneuvered to obstruct the premise of Mirskii's plan. With the absence of parliamentary institutions fast becoming a rallying cry of public political opposition, Mirskii had argued, no state reform would be deemed significant unless it included the participation of popularly elected representatives in legislative affairs—although the actual proposal to include some elected delegates from the zemstvo and municipal assemblies as consultants in the Imperial State Council was a halting concession. Recognizing the danger of half-measures, and seeking to channel these discussions away from Mirskii to the Committee of Ministers where he could exert influence and control, Witte opposed that compromise. In several consultations with the tsar in early December, he made plain, as he had since 1898 in a memorandum entitled 'Autocracy and the Zemstvo', that self-administration and autocratic rule were incompatible, the former inevitably leading toward a constitutional order. Of course, precisely such arguments encouraged Nicholas, whose long awaited male heir, the hemophiliac Alexei Nikolaevich, had been born that July, eventually to excise any mention of elected representation from the edict. He only reinforced the very image of indecisiveness that Witte had bemoaned.[30]

Almost immediately, events exploded beyond any capacity to control them. Witte lived through the Bloody Sunday of 9 January 1905. The episode, a display of murderous military force against the lower-class civilian population of the imperial capital, became almost immediately an iconographic event in Russian political culture. Directed against peaceful Sunday-morning processions of workers, who marched toward the Winter Palace from the outlying industrial districts surrounding the central government district, bearing crosses, portraits of the tsar, and a petition to the tsar-father for the redress of their economic and political demands, the attendant disaster resulted in hundreds of civilian casualties and an explosion of industrial strikes across the empire, many with an overtly political hue. Bloody Sunday produced in Witte what was apparent among other official memoirists writing about this era—a mad dash to escape any responsibility for the carnage. Nevertheless, he recognized the boundary that had been crossed. 'This was the first blood, shed in quite an abundant quantity,' he dictated in 1912, 'which set us off toward a broad current of events, the so-called russian revolution of 1905.'[31]

In early February, the tsar's uncle, the obscurantist Grand Duke Sergei Aleksandrovich, who a month previously had resigned his position as governor-general of Moscow rather than serve with Mirskii, was blown apart by a terrorist's bomb near the gates of the Kremlin. Married to the sister of the Empress Alexandra, the grand duke had provided entrée to the imperial court for his protégé, a major general of the Household Cavalry Guards, Dmitrii Trepov, who had served as Moscow chief of police since 1896 and following Bloody Sunday was appointed to a new position as governor-general of St Petersburg, charged to bring order to the capital city. The arch-nemesis of Witte's tale of 1905, 'the central figure of our entire, insane revolution', Trepov increasingly won the ear and affection of

Nicholas and Alexandra. In Witte's eyes, Trepov undermined Mirskii after Bloody Sunday, and advocated that Nicholas replace him as Minister of Internal Affairs with A. G. Bulygin, who had served with Trepov in Moscow.[32] By mid February, Bulygin was advocating proposals that eventually appeared as yet another imperial manifesto, this the Bulygin Rescript, in which the sovereign commanded his newly appointed Minister of Internal Affairs to go beyond the policies of the man he had replaced, Mirskii, and begin the committee work necessary to create a State Duma. The most notable artifact left the contemporary Russian Federation by the Russian Empire, the State Duma would be accorded all the institutional parameters of a national parliament but one, the peculiarity of 'an advisory voice', in which, like the power of the State Council on which it was premised, the Crown retained the right to disagree with the majority and act accordingly.[33]

At the center of these months were the spectacular, and disastrous, military defeats of spring–summer 1905. After a siege lionized in the Russian-language press as a twentieth-century Sevastopol, Port Arthur had surrendered on 22 December 1904, which Witte later marked on a personal calendar as the date 'My efforts to end the war' began. In February, the great land battle of the war took place near the Manchurian city of Mukden, which raged for over two weeks and resulted in the defeat and retreat of the Russian army, with domestic political repercussions that further undermined government prestige. 'I remember not one other such enormous defeat on land endured by the Russian army like that which we endured at Mukden,' he later recalled.[34] In May 1905, the empire's crown jewel, the Baltic Fleet, having sailed for nearly seven months halfway around the world to engage the Japanese imperial fleet in its home waters, was destroyed in the Tsushima Straits. 'The 14th–15th May (1905) saw the disastrous Tsushima battle,' Witte later recalled. 'After this defeat everyone came to the realization that it was necessary to end the war with a peace and this tendency so strongly began to manifest itself that it reached, in the end, to the throne.'[35]

Theodore Roosevelt now becomes a figure in Witte's tale; the American president's intervention to bring about peace between the combatants initiated a train of events leading Witte to America. 'For the moment I have been unable to do anything in getting Russia and Japan together,' Roosevelt wrote on 13 May 1904. 'I like the Russian people, but I abhor the Russian system of government, and I cannot trust the word of those at the head,' he continued. As to Japan, its military victories in the first months of the war, while showing what 'a valuable factor in the civilization of the future' the Japanese would be, had inclined them to exaggerate their own strength. There was nothing to be done but let the two sides 'work out their own fates'.[36] Writing a year later on 1 June 1905, Roosevelt revealed that he had been attempting futilely since the winter to convene peace negotiations, and blamed chiefly 'the folly of the Russians, who refused to face facts and insisted, first that the Japs [sic] would never take Mukden, and then that Rojestvensky [sic] could beat (the Japanese admiral) Togo'. Now, Roosevelt added, in terms with which Witte agreed, 'Russia has nothing to offer and no threat to make.'[37] Shocked by the scale of the military defeat Russia had suffered at Tsushima, Roosevelt, by the first days of June, was investigating with both the Japanese and Russian ambassadors in Washington the terms required to bring the combatants to the bargaining table. 'The Japanese evidently want peace, but only if they can pretty nearly get it on their own terms. The Russians hitherto seem helplessly and soddenly unable to decide what they want or how they are to get anything if they want it,' Roosevelt again complained. He conveyed formally to the Russian ambassador Cassini 'to say to the Czar that I believed the war absolutely hopeless for Russia; that I earnestly desired that she and Japan should come together and see if they could not agree upon terms of peace'. That letter, which contained a formal communiqué of this offer to the emperor, also contained the confidential remark by the president to Massachusetts Senator Henry Cabot Lodge that 'I do not believe that there is much chance of this bringing about peace, for I suppose the Czar, who seems in a thoroughly Chinese mood, will refuse to do anything.' Accustomed, like Witte, to the categories of ethnicity and race and his instincts thoroughly aroused by the semi-Asiatic caste he cast upon Russia, Roosevelt warmed to the task. He assailed Russians as 'hopeless creatures with whom to deal. They are utterly insincere and treacherous; they have no conception of truth, no willingness to face facts in the face, no regard for others of any sort or kind, no knowledge of their own strength or weakness; and they are helplessly unable to meet emergencies.'[38]

These approaches to Russia through the Foreign Ministry led Nicholas II to a search for an ambassador to conduct the talks. After being rebuffed by two other candidates—the Russian ambassador to France N. I. Nelidov, and the ambassador to Italy, N. V. Muraviev—Nicholas finally swallowed his pride and through the foreign minister V. N. Lamzdorf approached Witte, whose anti-war position had been apparent throughout the year. 'Then

Count Lamzdorf began to appeal to my patriotism,' Witte recalled, so that he would not refuse the tsar's request. He agreed to accept the post, providing that 'the sovereign personally ask or command me'—a moment Witte must have relished. On the following day, 29 June, he met with Nicholas, 'who very graciously asked (the sovereign in personal communications never commanded)' Witte to be his plenipotentiary at a peace conference to be held in Portsmouth, Maine, at the Portsmouth Naval Yards, that August. At the same time, Nicholas made it very clear that he intended, if necessary, to continue the war if the Japanese were to insist on either Russian payment of an indemnity or any territorial concession.[39]

Roosevelt, who would win the Nobel Peace Prize for this work, in early July, on the eve of convening the two sides, wrote that 'Russia cannot expect peace unless she makes substantial concessions, for the Japanese triumph is absolute and Russia's position critical in the extreme. I earnestly hope the Czar will see that he must at all hazards and at all cost make peace with Japan now and turn his attention to internal affairs.' As prescient an observer of geopolitical landscape as was Witte, Roosevelt warned explicitly that domestic affairs in Russia were such that 'I believe that the disaster to Russia will be so great that she will cease to count among the great powers for a generation to come—unless indeed, as foreshadowed in your last letter, there is a revolution which makes her count as the French did after their revolution.'[40] Witte, who appreciated the domestic crisis the war had precipitated in the empire, also knew, as he recorded at some length in his notebooks, the precarious state of imperial credit, and thus the gold standard he had struggled to create. Given a decision in early 1904 not to seek loans to finance the war but to await Russian military victory and better terms on international markets, the costs of the war had been covered by more than doubling the amount of paper currency in circulation, which the law allowed.[41] He admitted, at least in retrospect, 'a feeling of patriotic depression and shame' upon arriving in Paris to embark for the United States. 'It was morally hard to be the representative of a nation, caught in such misfortune, hard to be the representative of the great military power Russia, so horribly and stupidly defeated', he remembered himself thinking at the time. He left for America convinced, however, that 'the Japanese had defeated not Russia, not the Russian army, but our governmental structures (nashi poriadki)'. That 'conviction'—a distinction drawn between autocracy and Russia—allowed him to 'hold his head up proudly' as he departed Cherbourg on 13/26 July, and, he added, gave him strength throughout the difficult peace negotiations to come.[42] Like Roosevelt, Witte also knew the strategic, financial, and personal political challenges the plenipotentiary of the Russian Empire confronted in America.

As he traveled for six days across the Atlantic on a German ocean liner, he remembered, he took advantage of the interlude that now presented itself 'to concentrate' and prepare a 'campaign plan' for the 'epic diplomatic battle' to come. It was a mark of Witte's personality and his experience in both public and official life that his plans dwelt exclusively on public demeanor, on how he would fashion himself to represent Russia to the eyes of American public opinion. He would not seem the supplicant, desperate for peace, but rather a plenipotentiary of a sovereign who had 'agreed to negotiations only in view of the general desire of almost all countries' for peace. He would 'carry himself as was proper . . . for the representative of a great empire, which had experienced a mild inconvenience'. He would play to the press, given its 'enormous role in America, and be 'especially forthcoming and accessible to all its representatives'. Finally, he recalled, 'given the significant influence of Jews in New York especially and the American press in general', he would not be hostile toward them, a form of behavior, he added, that 'corresponded to my views of the Jewish question' in any case. Strictly following this program, however, required him to be 'on view every minute, like an actor on a great stage, full of people'.[43] It was a strategy that a lifetime of fashioning identities had prepared Witte well to execute.

He thrived in America. As he had planned, he played to public opinion, especially the correspondents who flocked to the peace conference. Major newspapers in both Boston and New York, whose editorial lines had been loudly pro-Japanese, shifted toward an approving, even sympathetic treatment of the Russian position during that summer.[44] Much more striking, however, were memories of his personal interaction with the public and the celebrity it created—behavior, he recalled, that was strenuous given how unaccustomed to it he was. The press followed him everywhere. Curious passersby constantly photographed him through a window of his hotel suite as he worked at his desk. Especially 'ladies', he noted, approached him to spend a moment in conversation, and obtain his calling card as a souvenir. Collectors mailed to request copies of his signature, and pedestrians thrust pieces of paper at him to obtain an autograph. When he traveled by train between New York and Boston, he made a point of approaching the engineer, 'to the surprise of the public', extending his hand to thank him.

He visited both Harvard and Columbia, and at the latter, following conclusion of the peace, was granted an honorary doctor of laws degree.[45] The day after he arrived in New York City, he rented an automobile and with one official of the Russian mission traveled to tour Manhattan's Lower East Side, an area of dense Jewish immigrant settlement, much of its population speaking some Russian.[46]

If a celebrity, he was also a visitor, simply struck by the new world—or at ease with its lessened social constraints. In all he spent just over a month in the United States, most of it in Portsmouth. While in New England, he toured Portsmouth and its environs; before and after the conference, he traveled along the eastern seaboard. In Newport, Rhode Island, he was struck by the summer homes of the small up against those of the 'American rich', whose every summer dacha seemed 'a palace'. American men, riding horseback early on a morning, were dressed in flowery shirts tucked, 'in the foreign style' inside their light summer pants, going without top hats despite the sun. Women, 'amazons' Witte called them, also could be seen riding without hats and in equally light summer clothing. In Boston, he toured parts of the city and visited Harvard, where he lunched with faculty. He found the food in America generally 'very bad', and even worse if it were cold dishes. In hotels and restaurants during the summer, university students, dressed in the uniform of a waiter, properly served and cleared the dining tables, thereby earning the means to continue their educations. After their work, they changed clothes, often donning insignia of their universities, in order to pay court to young women, stroll in the parks, and play. Then they returned to work for the evening dinner. Russian university students, no matter how impoverished many of them were, would have been shocked at the idea of serving at table like a livery, he remarked. Equally surprising were the young women who would stroll 'with a young man, tête-à-tête', in the darkness of an evening, together in a park or boating in a lagoon for hours, and it occurred to no one to consider this (behavior) in any way blameworthy. The coastline of Maine and New Hampshire, despite the fact that it was the same ocean that washed the shores near Biarritz where he summered, was 'somehow more grandiose', as was 'the open ocean with stormy waves'. He sailed up the Hudson from New York to tour West Point, and visited Washington, where he saw 'the White House of the President, the Senate, the House of Representatives, and the libraries (of Congress)', but included as well a stop at the home of George Washington. The custom of ships large and small lowering their flags as they sailed past Mt Vernon to salute the founder of the United States was 'splendid'. In New York, he saw the 'tallest buildings' and went up to a 37th floor, 'of course, by elevator'. Witte remembered how, at the time, with winds blowing he could sense the room swaying. He visited the stock exchange on Wall Street, where trading was suspended for ten minutes in his honor.[47]

Witte had come to America, however, to make peace. Having landed in New York on July 20 [Russian Old Style] /August 1, he arrived in Portsmouth a week later, leading a Russian delegation that also included the Russian ambassador to the United States, Baron R. R. Rosen, and a staff of diplomatic officials, secretaries, and military attaches. He joined with the Japanese delegation, led by the Japanese Foreign Minister, Jutaro Komura, and Japan's ambassador to the United States, Kogoro Takahira, in a round of ceremonies and receptions prior to the opening of formal negotiations the following day.[48] The sessions took place in the arsenal of the Portsmouth Navy Yard in premises especially prepared for the negotiations. The two delegations faced each other across a long table, with Witte and Komura, who principally conducted the discussions, at the center of each side. Reflecting the results of military victory and defeat on the battlefield over the previous eighteen months, the initial Japanese negotiating position, which listed twelve demands, starkly highlighted the costs of the adventurist foreign policy upon which Russia had been embarked since the mid 1890s. Russia would recognize Korea as a Japanese sphere of influence, evacuate its military and civil officials from Manchuria, and be allowed to retain the Chinese Eastern Railway connecting the Trans-Siberian railroad to Vladivostok, providing it operated only for commercial purposes. She would transfer the concession of the Liaotung Peninsula to Japan, which included the fortress of Port Arthur, the port of Dalny, and the southern trunk line of the Chinese Eastern Railway connecting them to Harbin. All Sakhalin Island, which Japanese forces had occupied after Tsushima, would become Japanese sovereign territory. Russia would pay compensation to Japan to cover all its costs for fighting the war, in essence thereby acknowledging both its defeat and its guilt in having provoked the war. The few remnants of the two Pacific squadrons that had reached neutral Chinese ports were to be handed over to Japan as prizes of war. Russia would limit its naval strength in the Pacific, and grant Japan fishing rights along its Pacific coasts.[49]

Russia agreed to negotiate many of these demands: Japanese hegemony in Korea, the abandonment of all Russian claims to the Liaotung Peninsula, fishing rights in the Pacific, even the de facto demilitarization of Manchuria. Yet, given the tsar's insistence that he would tolerate neither concession of territory nor payment of indemnity, Japanese demands that Russia compensate its war costs, limit its naval power, and hand over Sakhalin Island brought the peace conference by 4/17 August to a stalemate that threatened the collapse of the talks. Witte's position that day was contained in a written summary recorded by G. A. Planson, the Russian delegation's secretary. Witte made it plain to the Japanese that Russia's desire for peace would not be purchased at any price. She was prepared to continue the war, Witte insisted, and would find the necessary financial resources to do so much more readily than those required to pay the costs of 'a humiliating treaty'. Indeed, the previous day V. N. Kokovtsov, now Minister of Finances, had telegraphed, 'at the behest of His Majesty', to ask that Witte assist negotiating new loans in America and France, particularly as it seemed that the peace conference might fail and the war continue.[50] Japan, Witte warned his counterparts, was basing its calculations on circumstances as they currently existed on the battlefield, as if Russia had been defeated. That was not the case, he reiterated. There was 'no place for concessions' on questions that affected 'the dignity of Russia'.[51]

Over the next eleven days, Witte stood at the center of an intense negotiation that involved the two delegations at Portsmouth, a flurry of transoceanic telegrams to and from St Petersburg and Tokyo, and the repeated interventions of Theodore Roosevelt, who pressured Japan, but especially Russia, toward the concessions necessary to make peace possible. Although brinksmanship is a word belonging to the diplomatic vocabulary of another era, it does describe the game that Witte played during these days. He was, after all, fully aware of the growing domestic instability that the war was causing at home—and telegrams received from St Petersburg that tracked news of industrial strikes, public demonstrations, and general disorder were a consistent reminder of its threat.[52] Despite his insistence that the empire would find the resources to fight on, he, far more than most, knew how precarious imperial finances had become. He knew that the general staff planned to continue mobilizing reserves and dispatching these troops to the Far East in order to reverse the balance of forces there within another year, but had little faith in the commanders' plotting strategy or the possibilities of victory without naval power to match Japan's. That geopolitical fact especially made him willing to compromise, if necessary, over Sakhalin, which Russia lacked the military means to recover.[53] Ultimately, there was Nicholas, whose vacillation and distrust Witte assumed, but whose stubbornness—'our immovability (*nepodvizhnost'*)' he called it in a telegram of 12 August[54]—was such that he would continue the war, no matter what the threats doing so might pose the empire and even his dynasty.

On 5/18 August, the Japanese delegation did attempt to break the impasse at the talks. Dropping its demands that Russia provide financial compensation for Japan's war costs and limit its now largely non-existent naval power in the Pacific, the Japanese proposed instead that Russia cede the southern half of Sakhalin Island and 'redeem' the northern half to Russian administration with a payment to Japan of 1.2 million yen.[55] Witte wired this new position to St Petersburg, and in a separate telegram to Kokovtsov wrote that the question of the peace treaty now hung in the balance.[56] Discussions at home among the ministers of foreign affairs, finances, war, and navy concluded that any financial compensation was out of the question, but left open the possibility of a territorial compromise dividing Sakhalin. 'The attitude of the sovereign', as Kokovtsov reported to Witte on 8 August, remained 'unyielding'. The following evening, a telegram from Lamzdorf instructed Witte that the 'Sovereign Emperor... commands that You break off further negotiations if the Japanese delegates do not abandon these extreme pretensions.' The Russian delegation was to thank the Americans for their hospitality and leave Portsmouth, promising they would return to the peace table when conditions for negotiation improved.

Earlier that same day, however, President Roosevelt had sent Witte a letter addressed to Nicholas, in which the president reiterated arguments that he had made in a previous communication to the tsar three days earlier. He urged that the Japanese proposal provided the path to a 'just and honorable' peace, advantageous both to Japan but especially Russia, whose eastern Siberian and Pacific coast possessions, as yet untouched, were threatened if war continued. Witte telegraphed Roosevelt's communiqué to the tsar, but advised the American president in a reply that he believed the tsar uncompromising.[57] The next day, on 10/23 August, Witte took advantage of the need to await the tsar's response and went to the negotiations, not to break off talks, but to find 'any combination' that would bring a peace treaty without Russia paying Japan financial compensation. Now the

Japanese proved immovable. Witte ended the session with acknowledged disagreement and scheduled a final meeting for 13/26 August. Depending on the answer to Roosevelt from St Petersburg, Witte planned either to close the conference or, if the tsar made concessions, continue the negotiations.[58]

That same day, in St Petersburg, Nicholas shifted his position. He received the American ambassador, George von Lengerke Meyer, ordered by Roosevelt to convey orally to the Russian sovereign what he had dispatched earlier through Witte. Foreign Minister Lamzdorf relayed to Portsmouth the contents of this conversation. Insisting most compromise at the conference had come about at the behest of Russia, not Japan, Nicholas emphasized again that any payment of financial indemnity to Japan was incompatible 'with the dignity of Russia', and thus entirely unacceptable. On Sakhalin, although desiring to reject the compromise, Nicholas, in the name of peace and in recognition of the efforts of 'Mr. Roosevelt', agreed to cede the southern half of the island to Japan providing Russia kept the northern half without any compensation. This was 'the extreme limit' of Russian willingness to compromise; were the talks to break down, 'the public opinion of the entire world' would blame Japan.[59] Roosevelt responded on the evening of 11/24 August with yet another missive to the emperor sent through Witte, in which he attempted to persuade the Russians that the proposed payment to redeem the northern half of Sakhalin, as well as what now had become funds provided Japan for the costs of caring for Russian prisoners-of-war, was being misconstrued as an indemnity. Despite Roosevelt's now dire warnings of 'horrible calamities' should the war continue, Witte responded to the president directly that he fully understood the Japanese terms, but the money being demanded in the new proposal was a concealed indemnity. Were that demand to be dropped— an outcome he found unlikely—prospects for success at the conference would improve. On 12/25 August, responding to yet another effort by Roosevelt, the tsar drew the final line: a division of Sakhalin without any financial compensation, although the emperor now would allow 'a generous but reasonable compensation of Japan for its expenses caring for Russian prisoners-of-war'. Lamzdorf's telegram concluded: 'The Sovereign has spoken his last word and will not retreat from it for anything. Our Most August Monarch leaves it to President Roosevelt and the entire world to judge how noble is the desire of the Japanese to obtain money at any cost, even by continuing the war.' Witte was instructed to convey this position at the session of the conference scheduled for the next day.[60]

The two delegations met on August 13/26, at which time Witte announced that Russia would agree to divide Sakhalin but not pay any compensation for it to Japan. He was prepared, he announced, to close the conference at its next session—a fact that had been deliberately publicized by the delegation's preparation to pay their hotel bills and leave the city. The Japanese 'plainly were upset, feared a break-up' of the conference, Witte was said to have reported to his secretarial staff. Twice he agreed to postpone this next meeting while the Japanese delegation awaited a final decision from Tokyo, all the while insisting that there was no other Russian concession forthcoming, and no point in making further proposals. Following yet another intervention by Roosevelt, in which he still pressed Nicholas to cede half of Sakhalin and pay Japan to keep the northern half, Lamzdorf wired Portsmouth Nicholas's final instructions, which arrived late in the night of August 15–16 before that day's scheduled session, when the Japanese would present their answer. Nicholas ordered Lamzdorf: 'Send Witte MY instruction to conclude negotiations tomorrow no matter what. I prefer to continue the war than to await merciful concessions by Japan.'[61] Writing later in his notebooks, Witte mused that he would never want anyone to go through the strain that he experienced in these last days at Portsmouth as the question of war or peace was being resolved. The night before the final session he did not sleep, beset by what seemed to approach psychosis, 'the most terrible frame of mind', as if his soul was 'divided in two', one part of him knowing that the next day might bring great good fortune and peace were he to reach an agreement, but the other equally certain that to sign the treaty would bring down on his head all blame for compromising Russia's position and precluding her inevitable future military victory. 'I spent the entire night in some kind of exhaustion, in a nightmare,' he remembered, 'in sobbing and prayer.'[62]

At 9:30 the next morning, the principal negotiators met privately without secretaries for forty-five minutes. Witte walked into the room where the Russian delegation awaited news of the outcome, one of them remembered. 'Well, gentleman, peace. They agreed to everything,' he announced. Sakhalin would be divided. There was to be no indemnity and no compensation paid the Japanese. In Portsmouth, there were scenes of jubilation as news that peace had been achieved spread through the city. Men threw their hats into the air, women wept, correspondents ran for the telegraph to

report the news to all corners of the world. 'When State Secretary Witte and
Baron Rosen drove up (to the delegation's hotel) in an automobile, they
were met with jubilant shouts and ovations, going on for several minutes;
they silently bowed to the crowd and shook extended hands,' G. A. Planson
remembered. Witte also remembered the celebration, especially the international thanksgiving service held that evening, where 'around the church
and the entire street leading to it stood masses of people, so that only with
great difficulty did we make our way through it'. A service that included
Russian Orthodox, Catholic, and Protestant clergy left him with memories
of a 'wondrous picture', as hymns and prayers of thanksgiving echoed in a
church where 'many of those praying were crying'. 'I never prayed so hard
in my life', Witte recalled, perhaps actually believing then that this display of
Christian unity, 'the unity of all sons of Christ under the mantle of the great
commandment, "thou shalt not kill" inspired them all. Uplifting and
emotional as well were the strains of the choir singing the Russian national
anthem, 'God, Save the Tsar' as he left the church.[63]

Most likely, Witte thought that he had. A letter from one of Russia's
wealthiest aristocrats, Count S. D. Sheremetev, to Witte's wife, which was
preserved in his papers, hailed 'this victory—this great historic event, which
Russia will never forget'.[64] When the plenipotentiaries signed the Treaty of
Portsmouth on 24 August/5 September, it inclined much more favorably to
Russian interests than had the original draft Japan had demanded a month
earlier. Widespread public dissatisfaction in Japan, even public disorders
when the news of the treaty was announced there, most directly testified to
the victory Russia won at the negotiating table, despite the many defeats she
had suffered on the battlefield. Witte left Portsmouth on 25 August and after
a brief visit to Washington and a farewell dinner with President Roosevelt at
his summer home at Oyster Bay, departed the United States on 30 August.
In the eyes of many, including his own, Witte was the hero of Portsmouth.
'As it seems to me, and the entire civilized world holds this opinion,' he
dictated to his memoirs in 1912, 'I did all that could be done with words,
diplomatic maneuver, and the pen to achieve the kind of results that none
expected.' Nevertheless, he continued, 'representing the defeated party,
I was unable to accomplish that which only the victor on the field of
battle . . . could attain'.[65] Witte recognized that the losses of territory and
prestige suffered by Russia in the Far East and now codified by the Treaty of
Portsmouth were blows to Russian imperial power, but he had been willing
to gamble these against an immediate end to the war—or unwilling to

gamble that its continuation might yield eventual victory and an end to the growing domestic disorder now seething at home. Ever vacillating, his sovereign, Nicholas II, was less certain. On 17 August he received 'the telegram of Witte with news that the negotiations for peace had been brought to a conclusion', he reported to his diary. 'I went around after this for the entire day stupefied (*s golovoi v durmane*)!' Whether relief at the successful conclusion of peace prompted this reaction or chagrin at a premature end to the war was to a degree clarified a week later in a second diary entry, written after the tsar had participated at a public religious service of thanksgiving held at the Winter Palace. He observed that the event left him at best dissatisfied. '(O)ne would acknowledge', the sovereign delicately remarked, 'a joyous mood was not discernible!'[66]

Witte arrived in France on 6 September. He stopped in Paris to consult with the French premier, Maurice Rouvier, and Emile Loubet, president of the French Republic, about France's ongoing conflict with Germany over Morocco, as well as the now even more pressing and complex financial arrangements that undergirded the Franco-Russian alliance. He then proceeded to Berlin, where he stayed overnight, twice going out to the balcony of his hotel suite to acknowledge the public attention being accorded him by attentive crowds. Invited to visit Kaiser Wilhelm II at his summer estate of Rominten, near the Russian border, Witte stayed there for a day and a night of recreation, dining, and intimate conversation. He then departed by express-train for St Petersburg, where he arrived on 14 September. As official protocol dictated, he immediately notified the sovereign of his arrival in Russia, and was invited to attend the royal family on its yacht in the Gulf of Finland. 'I presented myself to His Majesty,' Witte remembered. 'His Majesty, as well as Her Majesty, treated me with great kindness.' Nicholas bestowed on Witte the title of Count for his accomplishments in America. Witte later remembered the whispered conversation, when he 'kissed the hand of the Sovereign Emperor and asked him: "Your Majesty, allow me now to ask you openly: will you now cease to doubt my loyalty to You and the fact that I am not a revolutionary [sic], as many constantly desire to make me seem?" The tsar replied, Witte dutifully and maniacally reported, by saying, 'I entirely trust you and pay no attention to all these calumnies.'[67] That promise became almost immediately a matter of concern for the hero of Portsmouth, Count Sergei Witte. It would haunt the nightmare that was 1905.

The Nightmare of 1905

Upon returning from America in mid September, Witte immediately plunged back into the rounds of meetings, appointments, social gatherings, whispered rumors, and personal maneuvering that habitually consumed the world of imperial officialdom. Two questions of crucial importance to its future preoccupied the attention of its offices and salons. One was the State Duma, the national parliament with consultative powers that had been promised in the Bulygin Rescript the previous February. The statute defining its competence and powers, as well as a structure of indirect elections weighted to ensure the representation of wealth, landed property, and purportedly conservative and monarchical peasants had been announced in early August. Although then in America, Witte had tracked these discussions, and once back in St Petersburg was appointed to the Solskii Conference, the conclave of senior officials developing the statute law and administrative rulings necessary to accommodate these institutional alterations of the autocratic state. Chaired by Dmitri Solskii, Witte's elder friend and ally, this meeting, when he joined it in September, was debating how to police the public assemblies that were discussing state, public, and economic issues with impunity, and the advisability of closing altogether university campuses sheltering such speech.[68] Perhaps more pressing for these connoisseurs of hierarchical power was a second issue, known under the awkward heading of 'the unification of the activities of the ministries', which the Solskii Conference formally began discussing in the first two weeks of October. That euphemism conveyed the conundrum that a prime minister leading a cabinet of like-minded officials infringed the personal prerogatives of the autocratic monarch to rule supreme—and threatened powerful ministers whose political views perhaps did not accord with the dominant view of the day. Discussed but never created by reform-minded officials since the ministries were founded a century previously, united government had never seemed more urgent to reform-minded officials than it did that fall, in the aftermath of the adventurist foreign policy that had led Nicholas II and the empire to the disaster of the war. No other official sensed that urgency, or seemed a more likely candidate for such a post, than Witte, who had auditioned the role as Minister of Finances, suffered the capriciousness of Nicholas II since 1903, and now, returned from America, was convinced that unified or cabinet government under a first minister was a prerequisite of any attempt to confront the crisis now facing the empire.[69]

As all of this transpired along the corridors of power, outside raged a storm. That Witte, returning from a summer month in the United States, found himself stunned by both its scale and intensity was unquestionable. Writing in his notebooks in November 1907, when these memories remained stark and emotional, he remembered arriving home in mid September and finding 'Russia in total upheaval, with the revolution breaking out of the underground into the open'. In a stream of words that patterned the swirl of events they described, Witte recalled a government that 'had lost the initiative (*sila deistviia*)' as officials ceased to act or contradicted each other, ensuring that 'the authority of the existing regime and its supreme standard bearer entirely was trampled.' *Smuta*—this most Russian of words that conveyed chaos, anarchy, sedition, and rebellion—'grew not by the day but by the hour, a revolution (*revoliutsiia*) that leapt out onto the streets ever more ominously, it was enticing all classes of the population'. The entire upper class was 'dissatisfied and embittered'. University and even high-school youth rejected all authority 'but that of those preaching the most radical revolutionary and anti-state theories'. Much of the professoriate spoke out authoritatively, not only to their students but to many adults, 'against the government and the current regime', and proclaimed, ' "enough, everything has to be overturned" '. 'Liberal oppositionists in rural zemstvo assemblies and municipal town councils, increasingly unified in what had come to be known as the 'liberation movement', were concluding 'salvation only in a constitution'. 'The commercial–industrial class, rich people', he recalled, still practically uncomprehending, lent moral and financial support to such opposition. 'Workers' entirely had fallen under the influence of 'revolutionaries of all sorts'. 'All non-Russian aliens (*inorodtsy*), in the Russian empire ... some 35% of the entire population', saw a weakening of authority and concluded that the time had arrived to realize 'their dreams and desires'—Poles for autonomy, Jews for equal rights, and all for 'the elimination of those restrictions in which they were living their lives'. Peasants forcefully were beginning to seize property and act against unjust law. 'Petty officials', who daily witnessed in their chancelleries the corruption and patronage that had grown 'in the reign of Nicholas II to gigantic proportions, stood against the regime they served'. The army was 'agitated by all the disgraceful failures of the war', and, once peace was declared, even more by the desire of many newly mobilized reserves to return home. 'One could say without any exaggeration', Witte concluded, 'that all Russia had been swept up in the troubles and that the general slogan was a cry from the soul: "To live like this any longer is impossible", in other words—the existing regime had to come to an end.'[70]

These days, he recalled more than eight years later in August 1912, in one of the last commentaries written in his notebooks, were 'a complete revolutionary nightmare (*polnyi revoliutsionnyi koshmar*)'. It does bear noting that Witte, who complained of a variety of medical maladies including ailments of the nasal cavity and 'breathing organs', stomach pain, skin irritation, and the voguish psychiatric diagnosis of neurasthenia, had been suffering during and after his return from America from what most likely were sinus infections. To treat his symptoms doctors had prescribed strict dietary restrictions and 'applications of cocaine paste', which, perhaps explaining the mixed moods of malaise, excitement, and depression associated with neurasthenia, produced addiction, or, as he put it, extreme nervous tension that 'completely destroyed my nerves'.[71] Against the background of this cacophony, Witte and Nicholas II began yet another minuet in their long and complex relationship.

Following a formal request for an audience on 6 October, Witte traveled to Peterhof to meet with Nicholas on 9 October, and returned the following day, a Sunday, to repeat his arguments in the presence of a silent Empress Alexandra Fedorovna. He presented his views of the impasse he believed now threatened the existence of the Romanov dynasty, as well as the strategies by which he, if entrusted with the full power to do so, could extricate it and the empire from the crisis both now confronted.[72] He outlined what came to be known as his 'program': a ministerial state unified under the leadership of a prime minister who enjoyed the confidence of the sovereign; social and economic reforms to stabilize the imperial polity; and a constitutional settlement delineating the fundamental civil liberties of all imperial subjects and the powers of an elected parliament. The unrest now evident throughout society, he argued bluntly, originated in an essential imbalance between the political ideals and the political reality of contemporary Russian public life. 'Russia had outgrown the form of its existing governmental structure,' Witte told a sovereign whose unlimited autocratic authority both men—and certainly Alexandra as well—deemed to be the tsar's birthright. 'She was striving for a state system of laws (*pravovoi stroi*) established on the foundation of civil freedom.' Contemplating the abandonment of neither monarchy nor ministerial government, Witte nevertheless fully recognized the compromises that were necessary to reestablish the fractured political legitimacy of the monarch and his government.

Immediate guarantees by the government of 'freedoms of press, conscience, assembly, association, and person', and then their sanctioning through 'the normal legislative work' of the State Duma was his first priority. Freedoms granted rather than rights demanded, they nevertheless extended across the empire to encompass 'the equality of all subjects (of the crown) before the law', regardless of faith or nationality. Freedom was not unlimited, however, and he fully supported all limitations upon it that were required to assure the lives of government officials and the 'tranquility and safety' of the state. Second, his program assumed the existence of a bi-cameral national legislature, a lower-house State Duma and an upper-house State Council, with the power to make law, not just advise about it. Although their powers remained unspecified, legislative assemblies and the participation of elected representatives of the people in the making and sanctioning of imperial law, which had become the essential demand of the political opposition to autocracy by fall 1905, was a given. In words that balanced the demands of public opinion over the desires of autocratic prerogative, Witte explained the necessity of 'the establishment of such institutions and legislative norms, which would correspond to the emerging political ideas of the majority of Russian society and guarantee the inalienability of the beneficence of civic freedom that has been granted'. Third, with peasant legal and land reform in mind, he insisted that the government prepare to set before the new legislative institutions economic and social reforms directed at 'the welfare of the broad popular masses', but structured so as to protect the property and civil rights of private landowners.

Having established an agenda of parliamentary powers, civil rights, and broadly based reform, Witte insisted upon the creation of a unified ministerial government under his leadership. In tones pointedly directed at Nicholas, he argued that it was 'inadequate for the authorities to speak out only with the slogan of civil freedom' because reestablishing order in the empire required 'labor, unwavering firmness and coherence'. Hence, a 'Ministry' had to be constituted from individuals sharing similar political convictions and imbued with a single idea motivating all agents of government authority, from the highest to the lowest. 'The concern of the government ought to be the practical inculcation in our life of the chief stimuli of civic freedom,' Witte proclaimed. Following this path, compromise with the moderate majority of Russian society and the social order such cooperation would create were possible. 'I want to believe in the political tact of Russian society,' he concluded in his written remarks. 'It cannot be the case that Russian society wants anarchy, which threatens, in addition to the horrors of this conflict, the decomposition of the state.'[73]

The program that Witte advanced at these Saturday and Sunday Peterhof meetings did reflect the compromised nature of tsarist reform efforts in general. Civic freedom was a granted gift, not a constitutional or natural right. A unified and reform-minded ministerial cabinet enjoyed the confidence of the sovereign, not that of the elected majority of the parliament. A prime minister's program or a sovereign's intentions, not a written constitution, guaranteed the rule of law. The rule of law and the demand for order were compatible, not inherently contradictory. Nevertheless, at no other juncture in imperial history had the choice of civic freedom, parliamentary power, government reform, and the rule of law ever been so clearly advanced. The starkness of the choice with which Witte confronted Nicholas and Alexandra should not be underestimated. It was reflected in oral comments he made at both meetings, in which he acknowledged that two paths beckoned. One was contained in his program, which, although neither his written nor his oral remarks explicitly so stated, entailed two unpalatable limitations upon the personal will of the autocratic sovereign: the one imposed by a unified cabinet and the other by an elected legislature. There was as well, however, the path of dictatorship, which required investing unlimited powers in a single individual—he recommended a military officer—who would 'with unshakeable energy by force suppress the troubles in all their manifestations'. Nicholas accepted Witte's recommendations and gave no indication of the path that he intended to pursue.[74]

The issue hung in the balance for the next week, but was complicated even further by the intensifying disorder gripping the country. The old railwayman, writing about these days in 1912, recalled in some detail how industrial strikes that began on 8 October on rail lines emanating from the hub of Moscow had spread within a week and nearly paralyzed the entire imperial rail and telegraph network. Almost all significant industrial enterprises in the country had ceased work, including those of St Petersburg, where by 15 October 'business life . . . had halted entirely'. Even Nicholas, whose diary rarely marked events of public political life, noted on 12 October that railroad strikes initiated in Moscow had reached St Petersburg, necessitating that government steamers twice daily ferry between the capital and his residence at Peterhof to replace the usual train from the capital to Tsarskoe Selo.[75] The next day, on 13 October, Nicholas acceded to part of Witte's argument by entrusting him with the task of unifying the activities of the ministers in preparation for the convocation of the Duma, but pointedly neglected any mention of his program or the underlying alterations of autocratic political culture that it entailed. Indeed, he significantly reinterpreted it by charging the government instead with 'the goal to restore order everywhere', without which 'the cooperative, creative work of the government with the soon to be freely elected representatives of my people' was impossible.[76]

That reply brought Witte back to Peterhof on Friday, 14 October, where, as Nicholas reported to his diary, they spent nearly the entire afternoon 'discussing the program of future measures'. Witte by all accounts reiterated that, in effect, his leadership of a unified government had a price. With a decade-long experience of Nicholas's indecisiveness behind him, he was desperate to institutionalize the tsar's confidence, and assure himself the political power it conveyed. Embracing a strategy drawn from hallowed bureaucratic routine, Witte proposed the publication of a 'most humble report' from the first minister, approved by the sovereign, and containing the ministerial program and the constitutional changes it sought to promulgate. His secretaries already had reworked the earlier draft of his proposals into such a text. Willing to play this high stakes game, Nicholas, who had mentioned at their meeting the previous Sunday that he preferred announcing any reform measures in the form of an imperial manifesto that issued from his hand, now returned with greater insistence to this idea.[77]

With a final decision still in abeyance, but both form and content now at issue, Nicholas hesitated for three more days, during which time he consulted with favored courtiers, other officials, and members of his extended family about the course of action to pursue. Three moments were critical. The first was more a psychological moment: the tsar's powerful and influential wife, the Empress Alexandra. As Witte surmised from rumor and second-hand sources, which were the gold standard of high politics at the imperial court, Nicholas was being urged to issue a manifesto by those at court who argued 'that I wanted to be the president of an All-Russian republic, and thus wanted measures that would calm Russia to issue from me and not from the Sovereign'. Whether Nicholas believed such arguments any more than did Witte as he recalled them some two years after the fact is unlikely. Witte did suggest the authorship of that rumor, however, when, having produced it, he proceeded immediately to remember an anecdote told him by Prince N. D. Obolenskii. Witte's confidant as well as the tsar's chief secretary, Obolenskii dwelt upon the influence of Alexandra, whose animus for Witte was only matched by his often voiced disrespect of her. During these decisive days, Witte related, Obolenskii went to Alexandra; he was one of the few courtiers who had befriended the reserved and English-speaking woman when she had first arrived in Russia. Their relationship had been warm and cordial ever since. Obolenskii begged her on his knees not to allow Witte's appointment as chairman of the Council of Ministers. He argued that the sovereign did not trust Witte and the minister, now approaching 60 years of age, would never change his character and be 'an obedient instrument in anyone's hands'. Inevitably, Obolenskii warned, Nicholas would begin to heed others, 'and I will not stand for this', Witte wrote as he entered the tale, 'will begin to be obstinate, even in those instances when, trusting in each other, we would move toward compromise'. Then, he continued, 'in short order I will resign, and agitate toward myself dirty, vengeful, and ill-intentioned feelings on the part of the sovereign'. The empress, Witte wrote in concluding the tale, listened silently and then dismissed Obolenskii. After this, his relationship with her ended, and despite his official duties he rarely enjoyed the private company of the royal family as long had been the custom. Whether she too believed Witte aimed to become president of a Russian republic, and thus stood behind her husband's insistence that his royal manifesto and imperial will be the source of rights and reformed governing structures is a question Witte left to others to decide.[78]

The second critical moment also involved personality. The next day, on 15 October, Witte again traveled by steamer to Peterhof, this time bringing both a draft manifesto and his most humble report, in order to attend yet another extended meeting. The tsar's uncle, the Grand Duke Nikolai Nikolaevich, was present; Witte had first met him over a card table on summer evenings in Kiev twenty years previously. Now commanding general of the Imperial Guards and the St Petersburg Military District, the grand duke was a likely candidate to play the role of military dictator should the sovereign so choose. Making it plain that he thought suppression of disorder unlikely to succeed, he questioned Witte closely and then supported him, although more from cowardice and self-interest than conviction, Witte himself believed. According to some, Nikolai Nikolaevich famously threatened before his own intimates to shoot himself in the head in the presence of his nephew should Nicholas refuse the path of reform. That path now was encapsulated in Witte's draft manifesto, in which the sovereign charged his government to establish civil liberties, broaden where possible the Duma electoral franchise, and establish that no measure could become law without the approval of the State Duma. That last clause acknowledged that the idea of a consultative Duma, once deemed a fundamental concession when it was made the previous February, had become meaningless when moderate and leftist public critics of the regime routinely discussed their preferences for constitutional monarchy and republican forms of government. The tsar's diary that day merely marked a gathering that lasted past 4 p.m., and then a stroll in the gathering October dusk with his wife.[79]

Finally, the third significant moment was the night of 16–17 October, when Witte discovered that Nicholas now not only had firmly resolved to publish a manifesto, but was considering substantive alterations of the text Witte had drafted. In particular, he seemed ready to exclude any reference to the legislative powers of the State Duma or a stipulation that he was charging his government to implement reforms, even perhaps the publication of Witte's program altogether. Perhaps worse, the tsar seemed to be entertaining the idea of appointing I. L. Goremykin, a former Minister of Internal Affairs and Witte antagonist, to the post of premier. Witte later remembered the meeting that took place in his home with Baron Frederiks in the early morning hours of 17 October, when the minister of the imperial court confirmed that all these rumors were indeed possibilities. Witte's response was categorical—and the emotional turmoil of the moment still resonated two years later when he wrote these remarks. 'All this evasion, these unworthy games, secret meetings had made me entirely unstable, especially with my fatigue and ill health after Portsmouth,' he remembered. 'I resolved that this situation had to be ended, that is, to do everything so that they would leave me in peace.' That phrase, which he repeated five times in three notebook pages, reflected the categorical nature of Witte's stance that night, as well as his belief that he had nothing to lose. Readers who see Witte conniving in an ever insistent, near megalomaniacal search for power misunderstand the man and the times in which he found himself. His participation as chairman of the Council of Ministers, as the first minister would be called, required the tsar to approve his 'most humble report', he told Fredericks, and, if the sovereign continued to insist upon the manifesto, issue it and his most humble report in the version that reflected Witte's governing strategy. Having heard him out, Frederiks left Witte's home after 2 a.m. Left alone, Witte 'began to pray and ask the Almighty that he spare me from this interlaced body of cowardice, blindness, craftiness, and stupidity. I hoped that after everything I said to Frederiks, they will leave me in peace.'[80]

Monday, 17 October 1905, was the seventeenth anniversary of what was deemed the miraculous escape of Alexander III and his family from the derailment of the imperial train at Borka in 1888—'The anniversary of the wreck!' Nicholas noted in his diary. If Witte really had meant to be left in peace, his harsh demands, the conditions he imposed upon Nicholas in return for agreeing to lead a unified ministerial cabinet and guide the empire through the stormy upheaval it was experiencing did not produce their desired results. He was notified the next morning that he was to return to Peterhof, where Nicholas that evening at 6 pm signed both Witte's program and the Imperial Manifesto of 17 October 1905. 'After such a day,' the emperor told his diary, 'heads are heavy and thoughts are confused. God, help us, save and calm Russia.'[81] The exasperated yet exhausted and resigned man who recorded that entry did, in a few words, capture his own view of what had transpired on this day. In the words of his biographer, Andrew Verner, Nicholas 'had finally consented to a "constitution" against his own better judgment and with immense pain.... Having swallowed this bitter constitutional pill, the tsar expected order to return virtually overnight.'[82] Having secured a program of constitutional change and civil liberties premised on the capacity of law to create order, Witte understood that the political acts of October were part of a larger evolutionary history, whose results would not be apparent in any near term. His reasoning was more complex, and much more demanding of contemporary imperial politics, than was that of his sovereign.

Witte analyzed the historical import of the October Manifesto in a brief set of notebook entries that he penned in August 1908, two years after he resigned the office he had worked so assiduously to create. Weighing on his mind was the illness of his wife Mathilda Ivanovna, together with 'an apathy' that made 'any kind of systematic work' impossible, he began, explaining why he had not written in his notebooks for some eight months. He was confronting the key moment of his public life, and arguably that of the empire that he had served. He was categorical about its historical significance. 'Actually, the Manifesto of 17 October', he began, 'cuts

[margin note: How did he convert so quickly + easily?]

away yesterday from today, the past from the future.' Much could be said about the way in which the surgery had been conducted, whether it was done too quickly or in a sufficiently antiseptic manner, 'but the operation, in my conviction, sooner or later was necessary.' Positivist that he was, Witte believed that 'the inevitable march of history (and) human progress' had dictated and justified the constitutional changes undertaken in October. Russian monarchist that he remained, he also recognized that circumstances had weighed heavily in Russia's case, given the individual, Nicholas II, whom history or providence had empowered to rule the empire. If history dictated the October Manifesto, she had chosen to act because the institution of autocratic monarchy, in which he continued to believe, had rendered itself illegitimate through the weaknesses of the man who filled the office and the corrupting influence of the imperial court culture that surrounded him.[83]

Historians of the era often use the collective noun 'camarilla' to describe this world, which was powerful but opaque, conservative if not reactionary, powerful and impervious to law or public opinion.[84] Witte described the 'high court retinue (*vyshii dvortsovyi cheliad*)' as 'ravens' feeding off the living *[margin note: Court]* organism that was Russia, 'into which they sunk their beaks as if it were carrion, and this had become habitual', he continued, because a weak man like Nicholas had allowed it. 'When thunderous phrases, honor and nobility exist only for show, for tsarist processions and receptions, but within the soul resides only petty craftiness, stupid (childlike, he inserted–fw) cunning, timid dishonesty . . . then of course nothing else but ruin can be expected', and then Witte scratched out 'but if to such an individual God entrusts . . . the entire, great, most pure Russian people, then great bloody misfortune is inevitable from the unlimited Autocratic rule of such a Person'.[85] To read Witte musing, at times raging in this commentary is to see the monarchist, who had dreamed that unlimited autocracy could anchor a modern imperial polity, recall his own loss of faith in that institution.

He recalled arguing to Nicholas in the last days before the manifesto that 'people are created so that they strive for freedom, for self-administration'. Some—he did not need to say in the worlds of officialdom, court, and aristocracy from which he came—still debated whether this contemporary fact of modern life 'was good for humanity generally or a given nation in particular', but such talk was 'quite useless' for statesmen. 'If you do not give reasonable freedoms in time, they will carve out paths on their own,' he recalled telling the emperor—and there is no reason to think that Witte reserved this counsel only for the emperor in 1905. 'Russia', he continued to write, 'is a country in which all reforms aiming to establish rational freedom and citizenship have been tardy, and every contemporary malady (*vse boleznenye iavleniia*) follows from this fundamental cause.' Yet, not just delay or backwardness but the disaster of war and defeat 'shook the very foundation of that regime—its powerful strength and especially the prestige of that strength, a consciousness of that strength (*silu i osoblivo prestizh sily, soznanie sily*)' in all sectors of the population. What resulted was an upheaval of such scale and scope that the disenchantment of autocracy throughout imperial society was palpable, as was its growing allegiance to the idea of freedom—defined, even Witte knew, in wildly diverse ways. 'Now,' he had instructed Nicholas, 'there was no exit without significant reforms capable of attracting to the side of the authorities a majority of the public forces' of the country.[86]

In Witte's eyes, that rapprochement required a new constitutional settlement, which could reconstitute public support for the imperial Crown. Even more, however, it required a strong monarchical personality to wear it—or, lacking that, his resolute hand to guide Nicholas toward the future. Given their past, Witte knew full well the risk he took. 'I told the sovereign', he continued, 'that worst of all will be if he undertakes a decision counter to his conviction or instinct, for this decision will not be firm.' He claimed to have spun for Nicholas a tale, indicatively enough, given the repeated ship travel he had endured traveling to and from both America and Peterhof, using the metaphor of steamships on stormy seas. Witte compared the tsar to a passenger advised to choose between two vessels steering entirely different courses. Witte was convinced that 'my steamer and my course' were less dangerous and more advisable for the 'future of Russia', but once the emperor set sail with him, 'this is what will happen, Your Majesty'. He continued. 'When we depart the shore, we will begin to be tossed about, and then there will be mechanical breakdowns every day: something goes wrong in the engine, some cargo is carried off, a traveling companion is washed overboard'. The passenger begins to hear from every side that he should have traveled on a different ship, and, unable to ascertain the truth of any one claim, believes them all, 'and then,' he concluded, 'begin the doubts, the pulling and tugging, the intrigues, and all of this for me undoubtedly, but chiefly for the business of state (*delo*), will end very badly.' This narrative plot even entailed dynastic considerations. What would happen to the House of Romanov were Nicholas to die and his infant son Alexei come to the throne under a regency? The continuation of monarchical rule, in which Witte still believed, thus dictated that unrestrict- ed autocracy and bureaucracy be abandoned and replaced over time with a new order—'a regime of administration (*rezhim upravleniia*) resting on the broad platform of Russian public consciousness, despite all the inadequacies inherent in the consciousness of the mob, especially one so semi-cultured'. Such was the convoluted syntax he used to describe the nascent new era of civic life, competing ideologies, and public politics emerging in imperial Russia by 1905. Such too was testimony to how inchoate were the outlines of the world in which Witte now found himself. 'I said,' he concluded, 'better to make use of a harbor no matter how inadequate, but ride out the storm in the harbor, than on a raging ocean in a half-rotten ship.'[87]

Here was Witte's conundrum. Brashly and impatiently, he had urged an autocrat, whose honesty and resoluteness he doubted, to abandon his birthright and share his uncontested power and authority, not simply with a prime minister suspected of radical sympathies, but with an imperial society that, like a raging sea, threatened the existence of the dynasty. That Witte had persuaded the tsar to endorse his program and seek com- promise with the emergent public forces of imperial society bespoke the power of his intellect and the depths of his belief in an imperial polity he had spent the last thirty years experiencing, envisioning, and constructing. Predictable vision and the inchoate, transforming landscape of contempo- rary life, however, were increasingly disassociated, and, having promised that his charted course would guide both monarchical crown and empire to a future safe haven, Witte claimed to understand it. 'Society' was capable and willing, he believed, to acknowledge the leadership of a ministerial government carrying the banner of moderate constitutional reform. Perhaps more, he believed 'society' would acknowledge him, because he came from its same cultural circles and public elites. Ever in his own estimation an outsider, a southerner in northern climes, never quite refined enough to be accepted by the aristocracy, high officialdom, or court of the imperial capital, he never entirely had viewed himself to be a part of the old order, no matter how fully he enjoyed its privileges, power, and status. He had prided himself on his university degree and public career, luxuriated in railroad technology and commercial affairs, grasped the power of the mass press and public opinion, and glimpsed the habits and currents of mass democracy in America. In his own mind, he remained a public man (*obshchestvennyi deiatel'*), whose value to the Crown he served ultimately was found in what he claimed was his understanding of that complex, increasingly modern world. The opposition that had exploded within it was rooted in positivistic laws of history combined with an overwhelming, delegitimizing revulsion for the man who wore the crown, the aristocratic court that surrounded him, and the self-interested officialdom that monopolized power in his name. It was not directed at him—high-ranking official and entitled count—because he shared these sentiments and somehow stood apart from the status quo 'society' would no longer tolerate.

These sentiments were also found in his notebooks of August 1908, where he returned to the events of the late fall and winter of 1905.[88] Still scrawling furiously, he related here the impact of the October Manifesto, and recorded events that soviet-era historians once routinely described as a '*krizis verkhov*', literally a crisis of old regime political elites.[89] Those analysts had viewed this time as a moment of political paralysis before a mounting revolutionary challenge, but certainly Witte, staking the future of the imperial crown on a proactive platform of constitutional transformation, was anything but paralyzed. He did describe a crisis, however, a personal, nightmarish crisis of anxiety, uncertainty, isolation, even abandonment within the shifting social and cultural contexts of the day. All Petersburg, he remembered thinking back to October, knew that behind the scenes some sort of struggle had pitted 'count Witte, which [sic] was a synonym for liberal reforms' against 'the last fit of obscurantism, which this time, all revolutionaries impatiently expected, would bring down the dynasty'. Their hopes were not far-fetched, he argued, given a Tsar who provoked in society only 'feelings of disgust . . . or apathy', grand dukes who were 'compromised or without authority', and a ministerial government, which, 'not possessing either an army or money, not possessing the capacity to deal with the general dissatisfaction and uprisings, once and for all had lost its head'. Then, on the evening of the 17th, in both the capital and the provinces, issued forth the manifesto. He imagined it having a talismanic effect. 'All instinctively sensed that suddenly a great break (*perelom*) had happened', which separated 'Russia of the XX century from Russia before the XX century.' Beyond that instinctual sensibility, however, little else was resolved. As he put it, the separation was only one 'of the flesh but not of the spirit, for a spirit only can be extinguished, it cannot be divided in two'.[90]

A burst of recollection surveyed the altering patterns of authority, allegiance, and loyalty coalescing in society during these months, more often than not explained and referenced within the framework of his own lifetime. 'The manifesto', he wrote, 'stunned everyone.' 'All who were truly enlightened, not embittered, and had not lost their belief in the political honesty of the elites' understood that society had been given everything for which it had striven ever since the early nineteenth-century Decembrists. Those aristocratic officers and their even more renowned, self-sacrificing womenfolk had symbolized a hallowed tradition of liberal noble reform in families of a loyal, enlightened service nobility like the one from which Witte had issued. That tradition of constitutional monarchy, he was discovering, was a minority phenomenon within the ranks of noble aristocrats, officials, officers, and landholders who stood heir to it. Others, 'embittered, psychologically unbalanced, and altogether losing faith in autocracy', repudiated not only the bureaucratic regime through which he ruled, but 'above all the autocrat, who through his personal qualities had caused Russia so much harm'. That description, however amorphously, encompassed large segments of Russian liberal and moderate socialist public opinion, as well as his own understanding of ideologies that flirted with democratic republicanism and full-blown popular sovereignty. Still others, 'hundreds if not thousands' he noted, also denigrated the autocrat for the harm he had brought to Russia, but they attacked from the right. Enraged that 'frightened, he had surrendered', these were determined that Nicholas II be made to return again to the unconstrained power that shielded their 'swamp of lies and pettiness', where they could profit, feed, and gain power. Hence did Witte understand the potent mixture of urban mob violence, anti-Semitism, monarchism, and political mobilization that became 'black hundreds' proto-fascism. Its own political discourse heaped calumny on 'Count Half-Sakhalin (*polusakhalinskii*)' and lurked throughout Witte's writings as scapegoat and obsession, but the emergence of such a movement was a watershed in imperial politics. Finally, '(m)any, if not all, non-Russians (*inorodtsy*)', their endurance tested by russifying restrictions imposed upon them since the last years of Alexander II's reign and then with greater intensity under Alexander III and without restraint in the reign of his son, rejoiced at Russia's misfortune, and awaited their own 'emancipation from the "russian-mongol yoke"'. Thus did he treat the challenge nationalism now posed to imperial polity and citizenship.[91]

He devoted the largest passage in these recollections to Russia's youth, and the 'complete revolutionary bewilderment' that by 1905 had washed over seemingly every category of young people, from university to high school, from young men to young women. With a disbelief bordering on

incomprehension, he tried to explain how youth, 'a mirror . . . of the spiritual condition of society', had reached the point where they thought the
October Manifesto nothing more than 'a maneuver', and roamed the
streets, some singing 'God Save the Tsar' and far more of them the lyrics
of the 'Russian Marseillaise'. To understand them, he reached back deeply
into the nineteenth century to 'the atmosphere' of his own past, and
seemingly the spirit it had instilled in him, when youth, naturally prone to
exaggeration, were nevertheless confronted by the contradictions between
the political conditions prevailing in Russia and 'the cultured and progressive ideas' they repeatedly encountered. 'It is enough to recall,' he wrote of
the 1860s and 1870s, 'Pushkin was thrown into the dustbin and Nekrasov
was placed on the poet's pedestal, not chiefly for his poetry but for the
political pretensions contained in his poems.' From this plebian radicalism it
was but a short step to 'the enormous role' played during and after 17
October by 'socialist ideas of varied types and forms'. Without any clear
effort or evidence of understanding, heaped together were the thoughts of
Tolstoy, the teachings of Marx, and an extremist 'anarchistic socialism' that
used theory to conceal 'plunder' under the guise of the expropriation of
private property. Ideas that had dominated European intellectual life for a
half-century, he recognized, had found fertile ground in a Russia where
'respect for rights generally' and 'rights of private property' in particular
had developed but weakly within governing elites and semi-cultured masses
of the population alike. That powerful populist, social-democratic, communist, and anarchist ideologies were developing in the early twentieth-
century empire goes without saying. Witte reduced them to the threat they
posed to provoking explosions of unrest in the depths of the imperial world.
'When revolutionaries began to promise workers their factories and peasants
the landlord's lands, and to prove to them that, in essence, it all belonged to
them and wrongly had been taken from them,' he now raged as he
approached the end of this writing, 'workers were drawn into wild strikes
and peasants to acts of arson . . . the revolutionary explosions' of the months
that followed the October Manifesto.[92]

In September 1905, the hero of Portsmouth had returned from the
United States to the golden autumn of St Petersburg. The approval of
the American public still ringing in his ears, he reinserted himself into
the hierarchy and order of continental European, imperial Russia. The
contrast that Witte experienced between it and America must have been
striking. Received by a grateful emperor and empress on their yacht, invited

to dine with the royal family, and honored with the title of count, Witte stood again, vindicated if not yet empowered, at the apex of the imperial world. Yet, swirling outside the hermetically sealed universe of royal privilege and bureaucratic power was the looming consequences of Russia's military defeat, the domestic disorder and widespread political opposition to the autocracy of Nicholas II that by that time was sweeping seemingly every imperial Russian into its vortex. Despite his knowledge that hard-won royal approval could be lost much more quickly than it was gained, he ignored these misgivings as the statesman turned his consummate intellectual and political skills to address the crisis at hand. Those who then viewed Witte as an archetype of the Russian bureaucrat—and many subsequently would embrace this readily familiar view of the administrator—explained his involvement in the debates and byzantine infighting leading to the October Manifesto as a reflection of his unquenchable thirst for power. Either he suffered megalomania or, more accurately, understood that power, the currency of Russian imperial politics, allowed projects and policies to be realized and thus individual standing enhanced.

Yet, Witte was both a state man (*gosudarstvennyi deiatel'*), and certainly in his own estimation, a public man (*obshchestvennyi deiatel'*) as well. As an official, he had taken an oath to serve the sovereign; duty, honor, and a tradition that stretched back to his childhood compelled him to address the crisis as much as any overweening administrative imperative. As a public man, as a subject of the empire and a denizen of its habitats, he brought to the corridors of state power the belief and conviction that the imperial polity he had envisioned, experienced, and striven to enrich could survive the crisis if the sovereign could be convinced, or compelled, to allow a constitutional settlement that shared power among the Crown, its ministerial government, and elected parliamentary institutions. 'Society' would rally to reform, he told an ever-suspicious sovereign. To effect change and repair the damage inflicted by adventurism, arbitrary government, and military defeat would require time and resolute behavior, but, were the sovereign to trust him to navigate the ship of state, he in turn would guide it to the other shore and save the dynastic crown. Instead, the hero of Portsmouth, now chairman of His Imperial Majesty's Council of Ministers, was finding himself isolated and abandoned, his faith in the tsar shaken, and his perception of the imperial world that was emerging from 1905 confused and estranged.

Conclusion: 'My Six-Month Ministry'[93]

Witte formally assumed the position of chairman of the Council of Ministers on 19 October. Shortly thereafter, chiefly for reasons of security, he moved from his townhouse residence on Stone Island Prospect, near the Peter and Paul Fortress, to a crown apartment connected by interior corridors to the Winter Palace, across the Neva River on the Palace Embankment. From here, he would preside over the united ministry in which Nicholas II had invested his confidence and trust. Six months later, on 14 April, both confidence and trust irretrievably destroyed, he offered Nicholas his letter of resignation, which the emperor accepted the following day.[94] That was two weeks before the formal ceremonial opening of the First State Duma on 27 April. As he later remembered, that event 'possessed, of course, historic significance, given that it was the first and only such appearance of the Sovereign Emperor before representatives of the people, before both the upper and lower Houses', as he called the reformed State Council and State Duma.[95]

The latter had been elected in several rounds of elections during late March and early April. By that time, it had become apparent that the greatest gamble undertaken by the central government in 1905–6 had gone awry. An electoral law structured to allow a broadly based franchise that would lend a preponderant voice to a purportedly conservative and monarchist peasantry indeed had produced a near majority of peasant deputies. It also brought to St Petersburg their singular preoccupation: legislation that would exercise the state's right of eminent domain over rural private property and effect a fundamental redistribution of property holding in rural locales. That idea, which first surfaced widely in public and government circles that winter, was seen to be a necessary response to the scale and violence of rural disorders that had exploded after October in villages grown weary of war and defeated government authority, and enticed into action by their definitions of the word 'freedom' emanating from urban Russia in 1905.[96] The 'land question' or the 'peasant question', as the problem of the allocation of land, property, and wealth in rural Russia came to be known, also drove the single largest party in the assembly, the liberal Constitutional Democrats, even further toward populist, radical, and even republican political sympathies.[97] Finally, the dénouement of April had given the tsar the opportunity to reevaluate Witte's promised reconstitution of law and order, a final wedge between Nicholas and his first minister that ended their working relationship.

In his letter of resignation, Witte noted that, having realized early on how his position with the sovereign 'had been undermined', he previously had raised the question of resigning, but remained at his post in order to oversee the negotiations for an international loan to the imperial treasury, which were concluded in early April.[98] The 'Russian State (*Rossisskoe Gosudarstvo*) 5 ½% Bond', which a combination of principally French, but also English, Austrian, Dutch, and Russian banking interests brokered, was issued in the unprecedented sum of 2.25 billion French francs. It stabilized the empire's shaken finances and saved the gold standard that war spending had almost destroyed.[99] Having successfully fulfilled that promise, he considered it his 'moral right' to renew his request. His health and nerves had been 'shattered' by all to which he had been subjected over the previous six months, Witte complained, and, in a rare admission before a sovereign accustomed to his outbursts, doubted his ability to maintain the cool-headed composure required of a first minister defending the government's program in the Duma. He proclaimed himself unable to work any longer with the Minister of Internal Affairs, P. N. Durnovo, much less appear with him in the Duma where he would be forced to defend actions that the key domestic police ministry had undertaken 'without my knowledge or against my opinion'. Although Nicholas had repeatedly demanded and Witte in the main sponsored it, he disingenuously blamed Durnovo for the violent suppression of urban, rural, and national unrest undertaken that winter and spring in imperial borderlands and central European provinces. Witte blamed these policies for further enflaming opinion and creating the leftist tilt of the First Duma's deputies. At root, however, he was outraged by the fact that Durnovo increasingly allied with Witte's antagonist, the Palace Commandant D. F. Trepov, and, reporting directly to the tsar, governed his ministerial fief independently of the chairman.[100] Nothing conveyed Nicholas's refusal to adhere to the new governing order or the lost confidence of the sovereign more coldly than this reliance on the informal networks of power and influence Witte had sought to constrain.

He mentioned as well the explosion of protest from landowners, aristocratic courtiers, and officials that had broken out, beginning in late January, over his own flirtation with proposals to allow the forced sale of rural private property. Implying that the tsar was favoring these interests over those of the peasantry, he said he could not appear in the Duma defending policies in which he did not believe.[101] The core of his complaint, however, involved the wholesale criticism from every direction to which he had been subjected, and the inability, or worse refusal, of the emperor to support him. 'Revolutionaries slander(ed)' him for using repression against outright revolution. 'Liberals' attacked him 'because I defended, by the obligation of my oath and conscience, the prerogatives of imperial authority'. 'Conservatives' incorrectly blamed him for changes in state life that had been initiated in late 1904—he did not add under the sponsorship of the tsar himself. He was isolated, 'the subject of virulent attacks from all sides'. Yet, most 'harmful' were 'extreme conservatives', nobles, high officials, and courtiers with 'access to the tsar' and capable of sowing doubts at court about his actions and intentions. He was not only isolated, he was, without the tsar, alone.[102]

In a letter the following day accepting the resignation, Nicholas drove home the point. Writing that 'only God knows' how conditions would develop once the Duma convened, Nicholas revealed one of his rare insights into the man with whom he had worked over his entire public life when he insisted that 'I do not look on the near future as bleakly as you look upon it.' He also heaped blame on Witte. His strategy of liberal compromise with the Duma and society, in the sovereign's view, had intensified disorder. 'It seems to me', Nicholas wrote, 'that the Duma ended up so extremist not because of the repressive measures of the government, but thanks to the breadth of the (electoral) law, the inertness of the conservative masses of the population, and the wholesale withdrawal of all government authorities from the electoral campaign, which never occurs in other states.'[103] In the public announcement of Witte's resignation on 22 April, the emperor followed well-established tradition in releasing Witte from his responsibilities, as he had requested, for reasons of health. He awarded him the Order of Saint Alexander Nevsky, 'with diamonds'. Finally, even Nicholas acknowledged the significance of Witte's accomplishments in this brief six months: the creation of new representative institutions, the ongoing campaign to restore law and order, and the successful stabilization of the state's finances.[104]

Those accomplishments were astonishing, particularly when judged against the historical standards of the Russian imperial state. At few other junctures in its history had the state used its power and bureaucratic apparatus as sweepingly to restructure its governing institutions as did the Witte cabinet in 1905–06. The reign of Peter the Great or the mid-nineteenth-century legislation of the great reforms come to mind; they both were points of reference for Witte as well. To be sure, much of what was accomplished had been discussed in the chancelleries and ministries of the St Petersburg government previously. Precedents had been established and preparatory work undertaken, but Witte had moved the bureaucratic machine into action, with consequences still discernible today.[105] First among these accomplishments was the convocation of a Russian State Duma with parliamentary authority. Its powers were circumscribed, and its subsequent political history between 1906 and 1917 reflected the imbalance between the executive and legislative powers of imperial government and Duma that Witte had implanted from the outset. Nevertheless, its existence, together with the administrative mechanisms necessary to accommodate the trappings of modern political life, both unthinkable and deemed illegitimate only a decade earlier, were due principally to his sponsorship. Elections, moreover, took place across the empire: Poland, the Baltics, the Caucasus, Siberia, central Asia, and the Pacific Far East. The same could be said of the 'upper house', the reformed State Council, the assembly of appointed, and typically retired high officials, to which was added limited elected representation from universities, commercial-industrial organizations, and other corporate bodies of the realm. As the archives of the tsarist state suggest, the Council of Ministers from 1905 became a new focal point for the 'production of files (*deloproizvodstvo*)' that was the lifeblood of this bureaucratic organization. On the eve of the convocation of the First Duma, the Witte ministry had readied legislative proposals addressing an accumulated backlog of domestic priorities in a remarkably short period of time. This program especially addressed the concerns of the majority population: peasant communal landholding, village administration, rural judicial instances, liability for official malfeasance, worker health and disability insurance, factory housing, child and female labor law, length of the working day, hiring practices and wages, and industrial arbitration boards.[106] Given the predilections of the sovereign and the careerist sensibilities of the officials who filled its seats, the ministerial cabinet never entirely unified the imperial bureaucracy as its creator envisioned, but it did initiate new patterns of bureaucratic politics for government and public alike.[107]

Historians of imperial Russia always have been quick to note the burning immediacy attached to law *and* order in the early twentieth century. So too had Witte, who promised Nicholas that law would bring order to public life. Within a month of the October Manifesto's publication, personal safety, property, public tranquility, and even the security of the state, were broadly perceived as threatened. The six months of his ministry were chaotic testimony to the scale and scope of the disorders that threatened the dynasty, as well as the personal burden Witte must have shouldered to repress it. A chronicle suffices. This one was part of a typed document found in Witte's personal papers, which contained his hand-written marginalia on pages listing significant events from 1896 through 1912. Martial law in late October in Poland. The existence for six weeks of the St Petersburg Soviet of Worker's Deputies, until its arrest in early December. Police and military suppression of widespread rural disorders from November through the winter and early spring. Military suppression of armed revolutionary conflict during the Moscow uprising of 9–12 December. Special military units, so-called punitive expeditions, dispatched into the Baltic provinces, the middle-Volga region, and along the Trans-Siberian Railroad to restore order. Bans of all industrial and professional strikes against enterprises bearing public or state significance. Prohibitions of government officials participating in political parties. Criminal liability for libeling government officials or institutions.[108]

All the while 'more than a million' of the army remained in Manchuria, as Witte later recalled in September 1909, 'materially and morally enfeebled'. He left in those notebooks as well the arresting image of the army beginning to return to Europe in the weeks following the declaration of peace in late October 1905. Based on reports he received describing troops traveling on the Chinese Eastern Railroad, he remembered, he had the same 'impression that one has on our Russian trains, when sometimes at night the recreating public returns home from its dachas and almost come to blows to grab a seat on the train'. The sensibility that the state lacked the punitive force that ultimately guaranteed its stability further complicated the task of governing with which Witte wrestled in these months.[109] 'Nobody wants to understand,' Witte told A. F. Koni during conversation in January 1907, 'that, insisting on the manifesto of 17 October, I—a convinced adherent of autocracy as the best form of administration for Russia—went against my sympathies in the name of saving the motherland from anarchy and the dynasty from death. I threw a "lifesaving ring" into a raging sea for representatives of the latter, which they had to grab onto'.[110] The manifesto, then and subsequently often framed as an act of political liberalism, was intended ultimately to promote order. Witte's ability to restore it, whether with reform or with violence, was another service he performed for tsar and fatherland.

Law and order intersected especially at one critical juncture. In March and early April the ministry drafted, and prior to the Duma's convocation published, the Fundamental Laws of the Empire. As the official memorandum of these discussions made clear, the Fundamental Laws were intended to delineate, prior to the convocation of a Duma that might itself attempt to make that determination, the balance of power between it and the ministerial state—and the extent to which the old political order would yield to the new. One answer was never in doubt. Even to allow the Duma to discuss these constitutional issues was out of the question, given that inevitably, instead of 'business-like creative work' on legislative issues, 'the first elected representatives of the people would be drawn into dangerous and fruitless debate about the limits of their rights and the nature of their relationship to the Supreme Authority'. Not only did such prospects raise concerns for continuing disorder at a time when Witte desperately sought to calm political conflict and social disorder. They also crossed a line that in the end Witte himself never could imagine crossing. The Crown, and the imperial authority it represented, belonged to the ministerial state, supported to be sure by society and perhaps even the people, but it did not, and could not, in the imperial world from which Witte had emerged, belong to representatives of a sovereign people.

The sovereign retained the 'power of Supreme Administration'. In order to mark out 'a broader arena for the autonomous operations of the Government', the sovereign issued edicts, designed to protect state and public safety, bearing the force of law. The sovereign minted money, promulgated martial law, pardoned individual crime, acted as 'Supreme Leader' of the army and navy, and controlled foreign policy. In a draft chapter 'On Imperial Authority', his fellow ministers overruled Witte's proposal to allow the sovereign to issue 'commands (poveleniia)' that interpreted laws as they were implemented. All readily supported as fundamental the emperor's right, not only to appoint and dismiss his ministers and officials, but to determine and increase their salaries and pensions. A second chapter on 'the basic rights and obligations of imperial Russian subjects (rossiiskie poddanyye)' excluded the most basic right, that of habeus corpus, from the fundamental laws, because it already existed in various criminal law statutes. The cabinet rejected an article prohibiting the perlustration of private mail, citing the 'great damage to state safety' that might arise 'at present' were the state to be

deprived of this traditional weapon in its arsenal. A chapter on the powers of
the new State Duma and State Council listed not rights, but limitations: on
altering the budget of the imperial court or the royal family; on curtailing
payments on state treasury bond obligations; or on prohibiting additional,
extra-budgetary expenditures during wartime.[111]

Taken together, these provisions, each crafted in the same detailed legal
prose that filled the files which Witte himself had read, written, and
managed consummately for almost a quarter-century, defended the power
and prerogatives of the sovereign, and the ministerial officialdom that
always had acted in his name. V. I. Kovalevskii, Witte's former colleague
and trusted collaborator during the late 1890s, was more well-positioned
than most to recognize this fact. Since his resignation in 1902, Kovalevskii,
who remained a close friend, had gravitated first to corporate business and
then, by 1905, to the Kadet party. In mid-April, at the invitation of
D. F. Trepov, he joined other prominent Kadet liberals, including Pavel
Miliukov and I. V. Gessen, to write a critique of the fundamental laws
project, which Trepov passed to the tsar. The project, this essay stated,
'produces the most sorrowful impression', given its patent attempt 'to
protect the existing irresponsibility and arbitrariness of the ministers. The
defense of their own interests and their unwillingness to have done with the
irresponsible position (from which they administered the country), which
for so long our supreme officialdom utilized and which led Russia to its
present horrific situation—that was the driving force during the composition of these projects,' the authors protested. Worse, such legislation
eviscerated the October Manifesto. 'Almost everywhere exits for the
administration in almost every instance have been left open.' Kovalevskii
handed this text to Witte only in 1907, at which time he remarked on its
detail but did not confront the substance of its criticism.[112] Ironically,
similar sentiments to those expressed by Kovalevskii came from an individual of entirely different social standing and political conviction, but,
like Kovalevskii, a colleague, even a friend, of long standing. Prince
V. P. Meshcherskii, whose hostility to Witte's policies and alleged betrayal
of autocracy was unrestrained, wrote Witte on 21 February 1906 to com-
plain about a rumored cut-off of clandestine credits in support of his arch-
conservative publishing activities that he suspected Witte was orchestrating,
given the unrelenting attacks Meshcherskii directed against him. If Witte
had grown hostile to him over the years, the now aged Meshcherskii jibed,
'then I ask: where is Your liberalism, whose chief condition is respect for the

freedom of each opinion?' 'Yes,' Meshcherskii continued, he did criticize Witte, 'but not You personally, but that new Witte, whom with sadness I see advocating in his policies above all for a bureaucracy that is killing Russia (*gubiashchaia Rossii biurokratiia*).'[113]

Both Kovalevskii, from the left, and Meshcherskii, from the right, looked at Witte and saw him to be an official, whom for very different reasons they both spurned. Once colleagues and close friends, all three had moved in the same social circles, shared many of the same cultural assumptions, indeed assumed themselves to be public men, subjects or nascent citizens in an imperial polity that at the turn of the century had shown every indication of an increasingly wealthy, stable, and powerful future. As the age of Victorian empire had merged into the twentieth century, however, that polity had evolved in ways about which none of them then had dreamed, Witte perhaps most of all. Visions of international finance and economic commonweal had yielded to realities of foreign policy adventurism, military defeat, and domestic turmoil. The allure of technology and commercial-industrial wealth had yielded new classes and cultures that challenged, rather than strengthened, governing political and cultural regimes. Dreams of autocratic monarchy and imperial subjecthood had dissolved into a nightmare of competing ideologies that rendered the present uncertain and the future unpredictable. When he resigned in 1906, his health shattered, he was disoriented, spurned, and alone. Ironically, he had become the man whom Leo Tolstoy so strikingly portrayed in his novel of railroads, love, and psychological anxiety, Alexei Karenin.

Paul Miliukov, leader of the Kadet Party in the First Duma and a noted imperial historian, in 1911 wrote the 'Witte' entry for the Encyclopedic Dictionary. Miliukov, who like many believed Witte harbored a desire to return to power, characterized him in the five years following his resignation as a man fluctuating between two extremes. On the one hand, 'Witte ever more categorically spoke in favor of "a constitution,"' he noted, 'given that under the current circumstances this regime better guarantees the state against unanticipated catastrophes'. The reference captured how Witte's public critiques of his successor P. A. Stolypin's more authoritarian and nationalistic policies after 1907 drove him to ignore the cautious niceties he had employed with Nicholas in 1905, and simply call the October Manifesto a constitutional settlement—and, by implication, highlight that Nicholas II had reneged on its promise. On the other hand, Miliukov continued, 'making these concessions to practice . . . (Witte) continued to believe "in theory" in the enormous advantages of an autocratic regime'. Whether reflecting 'old habits of mind' or 'tactics' he deemed appropriate to the political moment Miliukov could not say, but he did believe that by so acting Witte assured his isolation in contemporary civic life. 'Not one public organization trusted Witte, although several were not against using his services,' he averred. Miliukov, who long since had lost faith in the reformist capacities of the tsarist bureaucracy, found it improbable that Witte believed he would ever return to power. Surely, 'as a man who looked at things realistically and was gifted with an exceptional intellect', Witte did not imagine that another historical conjuncture like the one that had brought a man of his talent and intellect to the heights of the tsarist state would repeat itself. Yet, it was not so much the 'caprice of history' that rendered this scenario unlikely, as it was 'his isolation among contemporary political currents, an isolation created by the idiosyncrasy of his psychology, his views and convictions, as well as the result of this psychology and these views—his entire political past'.[114]

A June 1908 interview with the American correspondent Herman Bernstein struck a similar note. Bernstein, who had met Witte in the United States in 1905 during the peace negotiations, visited him in his St Petersburg home. His study was furnished with 'dark-red, massive furniture', and its walls decorated with paintings and engravings of European rulers and statesman, a 'fine print of President Roosevelt', and appropriately displayed poses of Nicholas II; 'a large painting of Alexander III is on the left side, and the wall in front of his desk is almost entirely covered with portraits of the Count's ancestors. His huge desk was heaped with books.' Witte had 'aged considerably' and at first sight gave 'the impression of a very old man'. Yet, as he talked, 'his eyes brighten up . . . and only at times, when he spoke of death, was a note of hopelessness faintly heard'. Bernstein put the question directly. 'In America you are regarded by many as the man who gave the Constitution to Russia. Would you tell me something about this?' In tones that can only be imagined, the aged man replied, 'That is quite true, I am responsible for it.' 'Judgments about this act,' he noted, were 'a matter for the future historian', but, already engaged by 1908 in a memoir project that was intended to be history, Witte set about explaining what he believed he had accomplished.

Proclaiming himself opposed to 'Parliaments and constitutions' and intolerant of 'all these disputes, these discussions, these arguments', Witte, gesturing toward the portraits of his ancestors before him, said, 'Look at

these . . . I have been brought up in environments to which constitutional-
ism and parliamentarism were entirely foreign. I served under the most
autocratic of recent Russian Emperors, Alexander III.' No friend to either,
Witte nevertheless had advocated both, 'as a physician would urge a patient
to undergo an operation'. '"Without it,"' he continued, '"the Russian
Government was on the point of"'—and the Count lowered his hand to
the floor—"do you understand? On the point of crumbling away. There are
many people who cannot forgive me," ' he concluded, for what he believed
to be '"these achievements of mine."' [115] The Portsmouth peace treaty and
the October Manifesto were his greatest services to the empire that he
faithfully served—greater than any Karenin ever could have imagined,
much less achieved. Yet, in 1908, he was left in his study, uncertain of the
modern world in which he found himself, alone with his memories.

Conclusion: From the Alexander Nevsky Lavra, 1915

I have just returned from Mendelsohn (Robert). He's arranged it—and I signed a letter according to which in case of my death everything immediately goes over to your name.

Letter of S. Iu. Witte to M. I. Witte, Wednesday, no place, no date[1]

I was born a monarchist and hope to die as one, but when Nicholas II with all his pathetic inadequacies is no more, monarchy in Russia might be shaken to its very foundations. May God grant that I do not see this.

Notes of Count Witte, Biarritz, August 1912[2]

Thirteen years of concerted work together (in the ministry of finances), more than that thirteen years of struggle on all fronts in the name of what we considered our dark, poor and suffering motherland needed has created the strongest personal friendship that continues to the present . . . You were the central figure of this epoch, the one who personified purposeful state power and talent, the focus of all that was vital, toward You gravitated all the hopes, around You gathered men of action who were bold, who rejoiced in the new, the better, the future.

V. I. Kovalevskii to S. Iu. Witte, 31 May 1910[3]

In the course of my first lessons in religion I was taught that man should be kind to his fellow man, I was taught the principles of peace and love . . . I had learned these things as a child, but I have been spoiled by life. When I grew up I saw that human beings, instead of taking seriously these fundamental truths, deceived and harmed one another in their efforts to achieve what they call success. I was spoiled by life when I realized that none of the noble ideals, none of the truths which constitute the essence of true religion was applied in life.

Herman Bernstein, *With Master Minds. Interviews.* 1913[4]

I walked up and down the room for some time in silence, pondering the different aspects of the matter and giving utterance to my half-formed thoughts as they emerged into the realm of consciousness. They centered naturally and necessarily around my old pet idea. . . . And that started me.

E. J. Dillon, quoting Sergei Witte, *The Eclipse of Russia*, 1918[5]

The view from the Alexander Nevsky Lavra looks up the broad expanse of avenue that leads toward the Admiralty Spire at the center of imperial St Petersburg, the capital that the first All-Russian Emperor, Peter the Great, erected on the shores of the Gulf of Finland. Following Nevsky Prospect from there back to the monastery, whose baroque architecture tied Peter's new European culture to Russia's Orthodox and medieval past, the visitor finds its cemetery, where St Petersburg's city elite honored itself. There, tucked in a small, enclosed courtyard expanse, is to be found a large, granite grey tombstone, the length of his large frame, surrounded by a black wrought-iron fence, bearing the inscription 'S. Iu. Vitte'. It marks the site where the old statesman was laid to rest on 2 March 1915, seven months after the outbreak of what was becoming the Great War. What can be said about Witte's life story from the perspective of its own end time, only some two years removed from the destruction of the empire that had shaped it? That his death preceded this larger end time was Witte's good fortune, a gift that fate, which often had treated him cruelly, bestowed on him in the end. Yet, while this book has sought to give voice to his tales of the empire that existed before the crisis, inevitably lurking in any reading of his life is a second, singular, and persistent question. What light can that lifetime shed on the great issue of late imperial history: the end of the empire in 1917?

These last glimpses of Witte's life reveal three fault lines upon which the earthquake of 1917 would occur. Two are old, familiar set pieces, hallmarks first suggested a half-century ago by Leopold Haimson, and thus here dressed quite differently by the rich scholarship produced since that time. One was political, seen in the increasing isolation of the Crown—the Romanov House, the aristocratic clans tied to it through the imperial court, and the civil and military officialdom that upheld them—from the imperial society it governed. A second was socio-cultural, found in the gulfs that divided the *verkhi i nizy* of the imperial world—literally those above from those below, the higher-up from the low-born, the lord from the peasant, the owner from the worker, the officer from the soldier, the educated from the semi-literate, the professional from the client, and the boss from the subordinate.[6] A third fault line was embedded in the imperial world, however. Witte's life began in 1849 as the product of an imperial polity that Romanov emperors, with their aristocratic and service elites, had created in the eighteenth and early nineteenth centuries. Witte's faith in the empire had been instilled over a childhood spent on the Caucasus frontier, stoked in Ukraine, shaped from university in Odessa to railroad manager during the Russo-Turkish War and managerial technocrat in a booming 1880s Kiev, and finally undergirded by the unlimited ministerial power and extraordinary vision he had wielded from the Ministry of Finances. There, his economic policies—and dreaming is an appropriate marker of an orientation characteristic of imperial Russian culture in the long nineteenth century—aimed to strengthen and secure an imperial polity rooted in commercial–industrial wealth throughout the Eurasian expanse of the Russian Empire. His assumption had been that wealth would trump nationalism, imperial subjecthood the sirens of national independence and ethnic communalism. By 1915, war was tearing apart the international financial order upon which these assumptions were based, and, with its demise, extinguishing the powerful, modern, industrial empire that Witte had struggled throughout his life to create.

All we know of Witte after March 1915 is fleeting. The settlement of his last will and testament that May revealed a comfortable inheritance of state and corporate bonds, cash, and property in St Petersburg and Crimea left to his wife, Mathil'da Ivanovna Witte and his adopted daughter, Vera Naryshkina. His investment portfolio was an important last glance at his affairs, something to which the Victorian-age gentleman had attended throughout his life. Witte owned a substantial position in what had been one of his greatest imperial adventures, interest-bearing bonds of the Russo-Chinese Bank. They had been issued in 1897 as a semi-private Russian loan to the Chinese Empire, part of the forward strategy that, with Witte's eager assistance to drive the Russian transcontinental across Manchuria to the sea, had led Russia to its ruinous war with Japan. Swedish bankers in Stockholm held and managed this paper. The interconnectedness of the European world economy was reflected in a second position, bonds worth a half-million imperial marks, also held in Stockholm, issued by the Vladikavkaz Railroad Company, a state-corporate railroad that followed a path his grandparents and parents once transited by carriage and horseback, from New Russia across the Caucasus Mountains to the Caspian Sea. When first justified in June 1889 by Director of the Department of Railroad Affairs S. Witte, this railroad promised the 'hegemony of Russia (*gospodstvo Rossii*)' over the entire region of the Caspian basin.[7] Finally, he owned 175,000 rubles of mortgage guarantees (*zakladnye listy*) issued by the State Noble Land Bank and held in Petrograd in the Russian Bank for Foreign Trade—however ironically, given how infighting and power conflicts with the aristocratic clans and gentry landowners of Great Russia had afflicted his political career.[8] Witte had invested in the Russian Empire and the international financial order of which, through his efforts, Russia had become a constituent member. Those investments, and the world they assumed, collapsed in 1917. Orlando Figes finds the Countess Witte in Petrograd in 1918, reduced to peddling an old existence away in order to survive amidst a new one.[9] I. V. Gessen recorded visiting her in Copenhagen in 1922. Her modest hotel and straightened circumstances with daughter and two grandchildren did not prevent her from maintaining in exile the tattered social network remaining from the Petersburg salon she had overseen at the couple's 'White House', on Kamennoostrovsky Prospect. Clutching to herself the green-bound notebooks of her husband's memoirs, she assured Gessen that in 1905 the American Jewish financier Isaac Schiff had discussed with Witte a book advance of US$ 1 million for his memoirs. That market too had collapsed with the Russian Revolution.[10]

Of Witte's life before his death in 1915, of course, we know much more, because he related his life in the tales that have comprised the subject of this book. This storyteller, who we know dictated his policy positions to secretaries, his memoirs to a stenographer, and his ideas and positions to Nicholas II in a fashion that eventually cost him political exile in 1906, polished and enjoyed a series of personae. He came of age in the imperial borderlands, born to a family of noble military and civil servitors in Russian Tiflis. He was a graduate of the university, where he studied mathematics in the nihilist 1860s at Odessa's. New Russia University. His was the world of the Victorian gentleman, whose women were divas, divorcées, and Jewesses, and whose men included radicals and grand dukes, editors and physicians, charlatans and idealists, married men and gays. Here too was the railroad manager, entrepreneur, and proto-technocrat, ensconced in the emerging modern industrial world that technology, commerce, and international capital were expanding in the later nineteenth century. He was a man of talent, whose professional knowledge and expertise created both autonomy and power in a burgeoning civil society. Official, minister, financier, statesman, and diplomat, Witte saw his star ascendant across the end of the long nineteenth century, and fated by war and revolution to fall from the sky. Thus, finally, here too was the author of the Witte memoirs, Sergei Witte's stories of his lifetime. These he finished writing in the summer of 1912.[11]

After his fall from power in 1906, a chastened Witte lurked in the background of the political and cultural life of imperial St Petersburg. P. L. Bark, a Witte protégé who became Minister of Finances in 1914, recalled in his own memoir how, appointed to a portfolio that controlled the treasury, he 'acquired overnight a great number of friends who wisely had been awaiting that event to show me their feelings . . . One of the most prominent of my new friends', Bark recalled, 'was Count Witte.' Shortly after the outbreak of war in 1914, Bark proposed to I. L. Goremykin, now also grown old but a loyalist summoned again to chair the Council of Ministers, that Witte head a government committee to develop libraries, sports, cinemas, and other forms of popular entertainment in the wake of the tsar's patriotic prohibition of alcohol consumption. Witte 'had lost none of his previous energy and disliked the idleness enforced upon him' as a member of the State Council, Bark remembered, but Goremykin warned the new minister away from the suggestion, given the hostility of Nicholas II, who still harbored 'the painful impression' of the October Manifesto and the First State Duma.[12] That those promises of civil freedom and rule of law had become painful memories for the tsar, and certainly as well for that most Victorian woman, his wife the Empress Alexandra, stood as silent testimony to the chasm of understanding that separated them from what Witte had envisioned as the beginning of a new political era for the Russian Empire in October 1905. The most farsighted statesman of the late empire was expelled from a court and an officialdom that preferred not to engage the emergent political realities of the early twentieth century. Neither Crown nor court had grown irrelevant to imperial society in the intervening years, however. On the contrary, they remained powerful, still at its apex, wielding the financial, bureaucratic, and military instruments of modern government. They were, however, increasingly isolated, unpredictable, and unreliable, in an autocratic system where personal trust and confidence long had been the currency of authority and legitimacy. The isolation of the imperial crown and its most loyal elites was one fault line of the old order.

Witte did perceive, but could never entirely comprehend the second fault line running through the old regime's social and cultural order. Few Russian statesmen had labored as assiduously as he had to create infrastructures of economic prosperity and industrial modernity in the empire. That drive to modernize, however, had come at high costs: early twentieth-century Russian industrial capitalism rested on high rates of capital investment,

economic expansion, and some of the lowest per capita standards of living in
the world.[13] Fully immersed in the public and civic worlds of the late nineteenth century, Witte's views of imperial society were far from the least
enlightened among the high officials who had watched the empire's majority
populations explode onto the stage of modern Russian politics at the beginning
of the twentieth century. A man of his class, he tended to share, in the end, its
view of a grey, unknown and unknowing mass population—much of it
peasant, ethnic, laboring, and constructed into some stereotype of class, gender, or religion. Fundamentally, however, he understood, having experienced
it in the nightmare of 1905, the threatening, explosive power this population
potentially contained.

In June 1911, Herman Bernstein found Witte thinking about war, and
the mounting costs of preparing for it, which burdened all the great powers.
Musing 'whether armed peace is not really worse than war, with all its
bloodshed and its horrors and its enormous costs', Witte reprised the role of
peacemaking statesman he had played so consummately in the United States
in 1905. Immersed in a memoir project that again and again drew his
obsessive attention to the linkage of war and revolution, Witte worried
aloud about an international environment where 'the best of our people are
ruined, the best efforts, the greatest minds, the strongest intellects are now
wasted contriving and perfecting new life-destroying instruments. . . . We
are perfecting ourselves in the art of murder,' he exclaimed. Arguing that
the financial costs imposed by armed peace were 'the heaviest burden
humanity is carrying on its back', Witte warned that such burdens upon
the population were creating grounds for socialism and anarchism. He
added what he most likely never thought to be prophecy: 'The burden of
standing armies, the heavy taxes thus imposed upon the people in one form
or another, make their life intolerable, and the result must shape itself in
movements of discontent, protest, and revolution.'[14]

The outbreak of World War I found Witte in southern France, in Biarritz
where he often summered and wrote. He hastened home through the
Mediterranean and Black Sea to Odessa, traveling with P. L. Bark, whom
the declaration of war also had caught abroad. That Witte palpably felt the
suicidal step which the old European order had taken as it went to war is a
sense drawn from Bark's own memoirs, to be sure written through the
prism that war and revolution lowered onto the memoir genre of a generation of expatriates and exiles. Still, Bark remembered Witte prepared to
conclude a separate peace with Germany and Austro-Hungary, immediately

to withdraw from 'the catastrophe which had befallen Europe'. All but arguing that Germany went to war as an act of self-defense when faced with Russian general mobilization, Witte displayed both a political and cultural affinity for Germany, as well as hostility to a Great Britain that had rivaled almost every one of his own imperial dreams. Russia had nothing to gain in a war for world supremacy between England and Germany, one that Great Britain, Witte was noted to have said ironically, was prepared to fight 'until the last drop of Russian blood had been shed'. He was disbelieving when Bark informed him that secret treaty provisions bound the three entente powers to a victorious and unified prosecution of the war. 'Count Witte concluded,' Bark wrote, 'by saying that if statesmen did not heed his warning and did not take immediate steps to stop the slaughter, at least on our front, the sequel to the struggle, which would be nefarious for all the belligerents, would bring disaster and ruin to Russia. The Governments of Europe had begun the war—the people themselves would bring it to a close.'[15]

Witte formally filled only one official function in these years of enforced retirement from the imperial bureaucracy. He was a member of, and when war was declared in 1914 chaired, the Committee of Finances. This over-sight body attached to the Ministry of Finances reviewed the investment portfolio and international financial dealings of the imperial state, a task to which Witte himself had attended with enormous success in the 1890s. The Witte years had seen a self-sustaining commercial and industrial expansion of the imperial economy. Its motive power, in Witte's always neo-mercantilist mind, had been the international circulation of capital, which the empire by all means had sought to attract to its economy and thus intensify capital accumulation, investment, labor productivity, and commercial-industrial ex-pansion within, and beyond, its borders. An abundant international supply of investment capital was a hallmark of the age of empire and imperialism; equally abundant were opportunities for international investment in stocks, bonds, and paper currencies. Witte's own portfolio had illustrated how personal wealth could be built through a system of international credit that financed technolo-gy, communication, commodities, and property—and Russia's great industrial boom was financed in this same credit environment. For Witte, the symbol of Russia's standing and equality in this international capitalist order had been the gold standard—just as the gold *Imperial'* symbolized to imperial subjects the benefits of subjecthood in the Russian Empire. Created in 1896, the new currency was backed by the credit and painstakingly assembled gold reserves of the Russian Empire, always convertible to gold at a fixed and guaranteed rate. Gold guaranteed the certainty of current accounts, the stability of investments, the prospects of future prosperity, and even the construction of a cultural civilization which Witte, like most of his class, always assumed Russian hegemony brought to imperial borderlands and peasant Russia alike.

One of Witte's last appearances in the archives of the central government was a meeting of the Finance Committee in March 1913, which reviewed a ministerial overview of the empire's financial positions on international money markets. There was little to suggest that the world stood on the brink of cataclysm, although the report noted 'an alarmed frame of mind' on world markets. Investors were avoiding long-term contracts, and interest rates on world markets were rising as governments became concerned to protect their gold reserves as a hedge against currency inflation. That international situation, the report continued, impacted Russia, although on its domestic markets there was no shortage of available investment capital. The economy generally was strong, despite a less than satisfactory harvest that year. Many branches of the imperial economy showed 'markers of expanding wealth', especially industrial production, banking, and domestic deposits. All of this development, however, had been built on cheap, and readily available credit, and that environment was altering. The State Bank had increased the treasury's discount rate, in an attempt to attract foreign currency and gold, and calm Russian credit markets, where fears of inflation fueled speculative buying and selling of stocks and bonds. Moreover, the markets were glutted with interest-bearing paper from banks, railroads, municipalities, and the state treasury, lowering the profitability of all holdings, and constraining the likelihood that the credit markets would remain profitable. 'The possibility of the uninhibited realization of new loans is necessary for the economic growth of the country,' the report stated. Chairing the Finance Committee, certainly Witte felt these financial tremors, in particular the possibility that inflation might drive investors away from Russia. They might sell Russian investments, demand their conversion at the official exchange rate, drain Russian gold and foreign currency reserves further, and weaken the economic stability with which gold provided the empire.[16]

By December 1914, after three months of warfare, that stability was disintegrating. P. L. Bark noted that Witte in December 1914 was 'very distressed' by the international financial situation generally, and complained to Bark in particular that the position of Russian investments on French credit markets had reached a 'critical' point. In France, a general credit moratorium had been declared in order to address the increasing incidence of French banks which, fearing the inability of the Russian treasury to repay them, had refused to pay dividends or principal on Russian bonds without French government guarantees to cover their possible losses. The French government, in turn, placed the responsibility for this debt where it belonged, on the Russian state treasury, by opening a credit of 500 million francs at the Banque de France as guarantee of Russian bonds on French markets, and obliging Russia to repay the debt in gold within one year of the war's end. The proceedings of this meeting, which Witte chaired, note that the chairman wondered whether the imposed contractual condition of paying in gold rubles was a means of guaranteeing the market value of the French franc—leaving readers to wonder after the biographer whether Witte was also contemplating Russian gold serving as the anchor of another state's ambitions.[17]

Two months later Witte was dead. He died, after a brief and never fully explained illness, on 28 February. On 2 March he was buried, and on 4 March 1915, the Finance Committee, now chaired by Witte's old nemesis I. L. Goremykin, met to honor his memory. Goremykin's eulogy was mostly official, cold and business-like accolades for Witte's 'leadership', his 'outstanding capabilities, great knowledge, and a similarly great storehouse of state experience'. Goremykin could not but allow, appropriately, given that both men had spent their long public lives in its service, that 'grateful memories of the works and contributions of the deceased will ever remain for those who hold dear the prosperity and flourishing of the Russian Empire'. At that same meeting, however, the membership of the committee was acknowledging that the currency structures which had underpinned this prosperity and flourishing were collapsing. In July 1914, the State Bank had been empowered to print 1.5 billion paper rubles, short-term treasury obligations not covered by gold, a significant increase in the currency supply and a slippage away from gold; by February 1915, 90 per cent of that issue had been spent. The Committee heard that another 1 billion ruble credit was on the horizon, and expressed concerns for 'the extremely unfavorable impression' this might make on foreign markets, as well as the possible collapse of the ruble's buying power abroad. Bark, speaking for the ministerial record, probably accurately captured the view of the international financial order that his mentor Sergei Witte possessed in the last months of his life. On the one hand, Bark noted, the day of reckoning was drawing near when Russia, given military expenditures approaching 15 million rubles each day, in effect would go off the gold standard. On the other, in a fashion that underscored how he continued to think within the framework of a past that assumed the continued existence of his present and future, Bark insisted that, following victory, Russia's exports would renew, her gold reserves again increase, and her currency thus again regain its international value. His ministry repeated the arguments of 1896, promising 'the reestablishment of proper currency circulation based on the free exchange of gold and the most rapid liquidation of treasury debt to the State Bank'.[18] Two more years of warfare remained.

These last glimpses of Witte highlight a third fault line running through the Russian Empire to add to the political and socio-cultural ones emphasized above. While purchased and its foundations constructed in the eighteenth century, the empire's position as European great power, modern polity, and imperial hegemon all were products of the long nineteenth century, and especially of the specific international economics of the later nineteenth century. A series of Russian Finance Ministers—Bunge, Vyshnegradskii, and Witte—had worked assiduously, not to build national, autarkic economic power, but to incorporate Russia as a constituent member of the international economy that was enriching contemporary life in the nineteenth century. They sought to export raw materials, accumulate industrial capital, attract foreign investment, construct public infrastructure, and accelerate by these and other means the movement of capital, labor, and goods throughout the empire. In Witte's hands, indeed, this policy drive had assumed ideological dimensions, a definition of imperial polity that linked the unitary imperial crown with economic power for the state, and economic wealth, or its promise, for all its subjects. Much of this development, of course, was financed from wealth grown by agriculture, extracted from mineral and petroleum deposits, produced as profit from processing these materials in Russian industry, and freely given by international investors large and small who had been willing to place their capital in Russia's future. The disintegration of this international order, and the undermining of the future that it had promised, were also products of a world which, certainly in the case of Sergei Witte, had prompted sweeping dreams of imperial expanse and power.

Finally, the insistence by these policy makers that the old world would be put back together at the end of the war, that the conditions which existed in 1896 might be reconstituted when victory was achieved, brings us back to the political isolation of the autocracy and its bureaucratic elites. Economic thinking in Europe was altering radically during the war years, as all combatants wrestled with the increasingly self-evident demands of whole-sale national mobilization to prosecute industrial war.[19] The pages of the Ministry of Finance's official journal, *Vestnik finansov, promyshlennosti i torgovli*, were filled in these years with theoretical treatises on planned economies, market and price controls, cartelization of industry, requisition-ing and rationing as planned alternatives to markets, and the legitimate heightened role of a modern state capitalist economy.[20] Yet, the formal response of the Ministry of Finances to the collapse of the imperial currency was ritualized assurances that that which had existed in the past would persist into the future. Plainly, such would not be the case.

This pattern of thinking—oriented to precedent, tradition, to what had been—brings us a final time to Witte, writing in Biarritz, in August 1912, in what were the concluding notebook pages of the massive memoir project he had undertaken beginning in 1907. As had been the case when he began, so too at the end: Witte was still reviewing, redefining, and finally simply musing over the revolutionary crisis that had befallen the Russian Empire, 1904–06. Much of this writing continued to be, as it had been initially, self-justifying, with Witte praising his accomplishments, blaming failures on those around him, dispensing vitriol toward the weak-willed man who was his sovereign emperor and the statesman, Peter Stolypin, who alone, Witte knew, eclipsed his reputation. But there was here too, as there always had been in his memoirs, concrete and insightful analysis. Then, as he had when he first began writing his memoirs in these same notebooks some six years previously in 1907, Witte dwelled on what he called both 'revolution (*revoliutsiia*)' and 'the troubles (*smuta*)', the events of 1904–06, the height of his public career and a crisis of faith for this man of empire. In what was a palpable pause in the memoir text, made for some unknown reason, Witte returned yet again to his premiership in late 1905. He remembered 'the disintegration of public and state life' and the 'general dissatisfaction with the existing situation that unified all classes of the population', mused how 'the dreams of the various classes' expressed themselves as wildly diverse visions of the political order that stretched from constitutional monarchy to democratic republic, and knew as well how what he called various 'state constructions (*gosudarstvoustroitel'stvo*)'—and most likely meant ideologies—appealed to 'a working class (that) dreamt about overfilling its stomach' and 'the majority of Russia the peasantry', who sought an expansion of their landholdings and the 'destruction of arbitrary rule (*proizvol*)'. 'In every case,' he remembered, 'everyone desired change. Everything was reduced to an attack on Autocratic authority.' Witte remembered the critical role the October Manifesto had played in dividing the camp of the Crown's opponents, and creating a politics of stalemate that persisted to the present, where neither opponents nor supporters of autocratic power possessed the will or the vision to escape it. In these lines as well lurked the social anarchy that had haunted him since 1905. 'Manifestations of joy' following 17 October were met by gangs of black hundreds, hooligans, whose occasional support by local officials became more frequent, and then spilled over into 'pogroms directed primarily if not exclusively against jews'. 'Anarchist attacks on government authorities, disorders in institutions of higher education and even in many secondary schools, the general accompaniment of varied excesses and disorders in the armed forces, peasant and workers' disorders accompanied by the destruction of property, the wounded and the dead and the stoppage of orderly work (*zabastovki*)', Witte wrote in near stream of consciousness, recalling the events of autumn 1905, and 'the revolutionary nightmare (*revoliutsionnyi koshmar*)' they constituted.[21] Whether that view was a final memory of the past or a prescient view of the future—for a final time the biographer leaves the reader to decide.

In his 1918 book *The Eclipse of Russia*, the British journalist E. J. Dillon, whose acquaintance with Witte over some two decades before his death supplied him an insider's perspective to sell to Western journalism and Witte a mouthpiece to the West for his version of events, described how he had long argued to Witte that the downfall of tsarism—feudal, obscurantist, and cursed—was inevitable. Witte, Dillon recalled, 'never wholly abandoned hope' that the Russian Empire might be transformed into a more modern economy and polity without collapsing. 'I often told Witte that his hopes and aspirations were doomed to disappointment, and his natural sagacity made him aware of the fact,' Dillon wrote. 'He used to say that if Alexander III had lived, or if his son Michael had succeeded him or were yet to come to the throne, much might be changed for the better and Russia's international position strengthened.' Dillon claimed that in such conversations he would insist to Witte that 'it was much too late', that 'the tsardom's sands were running out'. And then, Dillon added, the ageing man, suffering enforced retirement and, the outside observer would add, the embittering disillusionment of his dreams, 'sometimes agreed with me during those fits of dejection which often came over him of late years.'[22]

A. F. Koni, who had known Witte since the 1880s, served alongside him in the reconstituted State Council, where, as an appointed senior official, he had been sent after his resignation in April 1906. Koni left an arresting, life-like portrayal of Witte in these years when, largely denied the power and authority that had shaped his life, he wrote the memoirs that have been the subject of this book. 'He spoke worse than he wrote, going on at some length with frequent repetitions, not always consistent and seeking some way or another to touch on his work' as a minister and a statesman. His intonation and accent those of a southerner, he loved to employ cunning aphorisms, but listeners often heard in his remarks 'a withering irony that not infrequently erupted into indignation'. At times that irony made its presence felt in an inflection of his voice upwards, speaking almost triumphantly and in a rapid fashion that was humorous. He never tired of emphasizing 'his high regard for the memory of "the greatest of monarchs and that knight of the Russian soul, Alexander III"', but, at any mention of his son, noticeably lowered his voice and rapidly muttered 'the reigning and most honorable monarch'. In the end, however, Koni also remembered the dreamer. It was especially difficult for him in his last years of retirement, Koni noted. During pauses of State Council sessions, he paced in the vestibule of the assembly hall, his long strides echoing loudly off the floor, 'with quite a somber expression on his face, reluctantly answering the questions of the rare interlocutor and hurrying to escape from him'. It was apparent that in this turbulent personality, deprived of any possibility to express itself either in word or in deed, resided a 'perpetual rumbling of the soul (*roptanie vechnoi dushi*).... This was a type of Gulliver, tied hand and foot in the kingdom of the Lilliputians.'[23]

Notes

EPIGRAPH

1. V. I. Lenin, 'Chto delat'?' *Polnoe sobranie sochinenii*, vol. 5 (Moscow, 1960), 172.

INTRODUCTION: THE STORYTELLER AND HIS STORY

1. Herman Bernstein, *With Master Minds: Interviews* (New York: Universal Series Publishing, 1913), 27.
2. Bakhmeteff Archive Witte Collection, Special Collections, Columbia University [hereafter BAR Witte]: Boxes 2–4 Vospominaniia [razskazy v stenograficheskoi zapisi] Grafa Sergeia Iul'evicha Vitte (1911–1912), Parts I–XVII [hereafter SZ]; Boxes 7–8, Zapisi Grafa Vitte, 1907–1912 (various places) [hereafter ZGV]. The author acknowledges the cooperation of Butler Library, Columbia University, Special Collections, Bakhmeteff Archive, Ellen Scaruffi, Curator, for their assistance in obtaining a copy of these texts, authorized for research purposes. These have been transcribed at St Petersburg Institute of History, Russian Academy of Sciences, B. V. Anan'ich and R. Sh. Ganelin (eds.) and B. V. Anan'ich, F. Vchislo et. al. (editorial collegium), *Iz arkhiva S. Iu. Vitte. Vospominaniia.* 3 vols. (St Petersburg: Dmitrii Bulanin, 2003). All citations from SZ are to the original manuscripts.
3. *Goodnight! A Novel by Abraham Tertz* (Andrei Sinyavsky). Translated and with an Introduction by Richard Lourie (New York and London: Penguin Books, 1989, 1991), 17–18.
4. ZGV [Biarritz, August 1907], 74a–75/127. These have been transcribed as St Petersburg Institute of History, Russian Academy of Sciences, B. V. Anan'ich and R. Sh. Ganelin (eds) and B. V. Anan'ich, F. Vchislo et. al. (editorial collegium), *Iz arkhiva S. Iu. Vitte. Vospominaniia. Vol. 2. Rukopisnye zametki* (St Petersburg: Dmitrii Bulanin, 2003). Page citations are to both the manuscript and printed texts.
5. V. Naryshkina-Vitte, *Zapiski devochki* (Izdanie avtora, 1922), 56, 118–28 and *passim*.
6. Russkii Gosudarstvennyi Istoricheskii Arkhiv [hereafter RGIA], fond 560 (General Chancellery of the Minister of Finances), vsepoddanneishie dokladnye zapiski ministra finansov, 1888–1903 [hereafter VD ministra].
7. V. V. Cheparukhin, *Knizhnoe sobranie S. Iu. Vitte* (St Petersburg: St Petersburg State Technological University, 1995).

8. S.Iu. Vitte, *Natsional'naia Ekonomika i Fridrikh List* (Kiev: Kievskoe slovo, 1889); *Po povodu natsionalizma. Natsional'naia Ekonomika i Fridrikh List*, 2-e izdanie (St Petersburg, Brokgauz i Efron, 1912); Sergei Vitte, *Printsipy zhelez-nodorozhnykh tarifov po perevozke gruzov* (St Petersburg: Brokgauz i Efron, 1910); Graf S. Iu. Vitte, 'Prichiny ubytochnosti russkikh zheleznykh dorog. Doklad, prochitannykh 7 aprelia v institute inzhenerov putei soobshchenii', *Vestnik Finansov, Promyshlennosti i Torgovli*, No. 16, 18 April 1910.

9. Especially RGIA fond 560 (General Chancellery of the Minister of Finances), op. 22 (Notes and Reports of the minister of finances and other individuals on various questions concerning the economy, domestic and foreign affairs of Russia, 1809–1917); op. 26 (Second Division, First Desk, correspondence of the minister); op. 27 (II Department, Siberian Desk on the construction of the Siberian railroad); op. 28 (Third Division, reports of Russian diplomatic re-presentatives and other materials on the situation in China and the construction of the Chinese Eastern Railway); op. 29 (On the situation of countries in the Far East and the policies of Russia and other states in these countries); op. 38 (Most Humble Reports of the minister of finances and reports of the ministry and its departments); op. 43 (Most Humble Reports of the minister of finances and his remarks on the projects of other departments, 1812–1917); f. 229 (Chancellery of the Minister of Ways of Communication); f. 268 (Department of Railroad Affairs, MF); f. 40 (Department of Commerce and Manufacture, MF); f. 573; op. 34 (Reports of the Minister on affairs of the Department of Direct Taxes, MF).

10. B.V. Anan'ich and R. Sh. Ganelin, 'I. A. Vyshnegradskii i Vitte—korrespon-denty 'Moskovskikh vedomostei', *Problemy obshchestvennoi mysli i ekonomiches-koi politiki Rossii XIX–XX vek* (Leningrad: USSR Academy of Sciences, 1972); BAR Witte, Box 1 [Sergei Sharapov to Witte, 1889, 1899, 1902]; and RGIA f. 564, op. 1 (Reports of editors to the minister of finances; correspondence . . . with correspondents located in Russia and abroad, 1884, 1889–1917) and op. 2 (Telegrams of foreign correspondents about events abroad, 1884–1917) and f. 560 and 1622 *passim*.

11. Theodore Von Laue, *Sergei Witte and the Industrialization of Russia* (New York: Studies of the Russian Institute and Columbia University Press, 1963); B. V. Anan'ich and R. Sh. Ganelin, *Sergei Iul'evich Vitte i ego vremia* (St Petersburg: Dmitrii Bulanin, 1999); Sidney Harcave, *Count Sergei Witte and the Twilight of Imperial Russia: A Biography* (Armonk, NY: M. E. Sharpe, 2004); A. Korelin and S. Stepanov, *S.Iu. Vitte—Finansist, Politik, Diplomat* (Moscow: Terra-Knizhnyi klub, 1998); Francis W. Wcislo, *Reforming Rural Russia: State, Local Society, and National Politics, 1855–1914* (Princeton: Studies of the Harri-man Institute and Princeton University Press, 1990); David M. McDonald, *United Government and Foreign Policy in Russia, 1900–1914* (Cambridge, Mass.: Harvard University Press, 1992); E. V. Tarle, *Graf S.Iu. Witte: Opyt' kharakter-istiki vneshnei politiki* (Leningrad: Knizhnye novinki, 1927); A. V. Ignat'ev,

S.Iu. Vitte—Diplomat (Moscow: Mezhdunarodnye otnosheniia, 1989); Steven Marks, *Road to Power: The Trans-Siberian Railroad and the Colonization of Asian Russia, 1850–1917* (Ithaca, NY: Cornell University Press, 1991); David Schimmelpenninck van der Oye, *Toward the Rising Sun: Russian Ideologies of Empire and the Path to War with Japan* (DeKalb, Ill.: Northern Illinois University Press, 2001); also D. N. Shilov, *Gosudarstvennye deiateli rossiiskoi imperii. 1802–1917: Biobibliograficheskii spravochnik* (St Petersburg: Dmitrii Bulanin, 2001), 127–30.

12. RGIA, Annotirovannyi reestr opisei, Chast' 1-aia, f. 560 [1973]. The General Chancellery was reorganized 3 June 1894.

13. Bakhmeteff Archive, Columbia University, BAR Witte, Boxes 1–11 and RGIA f. 1622 [lichnyi fond S. Iu. Vitte].

14. These texts are: ZGV, BAR Witte, Box 7, pp. 1–383 ob. [1 June 1907–5 October 1912]; SZ, BAR Witte, Boxes 2–4, pp. 1–2438 (1911–12). Witte's notations indicated that he considered a third portion of the memoir project to be Vozniknovenie Russko-iaponskoi Voiny. Obzor predshestvovavshikh voin sobytii sostavlennyi pod lichnym rukovodstvom i na osnovanii dokumentov lichnogo arkhiva Grafa S. Iu. Vitte (St Petersburg, 1907), 3 vols. in BAR Witte, Box 5.

15. The major editions of the memoirs are Avrahm Yarmolinsky (trans.), *The Memoirs of Count Witte* (New York; London, 1921); Graf S. Iu.Vitte, *Vospominaniia*, 3 vols. (I. V. Gessen [ed.]) (Berlin, 1922–23); Graf S. Iu. Vitte, *Vospominaniia Tsarstvovaniia Nikolaia II*, 2 vols (Moscow-Petrograd: Gosudarstvennoe izdatel'stvo, 1923); S. Iu. Witte, *Vospominaniia* (A. L. Sidorov [ed.] with B. V. Anan'ich and R. Sh. Ganelin) (Moscow, 1960); Sidney Harcave (ed. and trans.), *The Memoirs of Count Witte* (New York: M. E. Sharpe, 1990); B. V. Anan'ich and R. Sh. Ganelin (eds.) and B. V. Anan'ich, F. Vchislo et. al. (editorial collegium), *Iz arkhiva S. Iu. Vitte. Vospominaniia*. 3 vols. (Rossiiskaia akademiia nauk. Sankt-Peterburgskii institut istorii. Kolumbiiskii universitet v N"iu-Iorke. Bakhmetevskii arkhiv russkoi i vostochnoevropeiskoi istorii i kul'tury) (St Petersburg: Dmitrii Bulanin, 2003).

16. Abraham Ascher, *The Revolution of 1905 [electronic resource]: A Short History* (Stanford, California: Stanford University Press, 2004).

17. ZGV, np. The handwritten title page of the Zapisi reads: 'Part I. Introduction. Pages 1–125 (double-sided). Notes of Count Witte (memoirs, assembled in haste, not having at hand any materials. June–November 1907 (abroad)). [signed] Graf Witte, Brussels, 5 Nov. 1907'.

18. F. W. Wcislo, 'Witte, Memory, and the 1905 Revolution: A Reinterpretation of the Witte Memoirs', *Revolutionary Russia*, vol. 8, no. 2 [December 1995]: 166–78.

19. F. W. Wcislo, 'Sergei Witte and His Times: A Historiographical Note', *Kritika: Explorations in Russian and Eurasian History*. New Series, Volume 5, Number 4 (Fall 2004): 749–58.

20. B. A. Romanov, 'Retsenziia. Graf S.Iu. Vitte. Vospominaniia Tsarstvovaniia Nikolaia II [M–P, 1923]', in *Kniga i revoliutsiia: Ezhemesiachnyi kritiko-bibliograficheskii zhurnal* 1923 [No.2 (26)]: 54–56; also *Ocherki diplomaticheskoi istorii russko-iaponskoi voiny 1895–1907* (Leningrad: Akademiia nauk SSSR. Institut istorii. Leningradskoe otdelenie, 1947).

21. Victoria E. Bonnell, Richard Biernacki, and Lynn Hunt, *Beyond the Cultural Turn: New Directions in the Study of Society and Culture* (Berkeley: University of California Press, 1999); Benedict Anderson, *Imagined Communities: Reflections on the Origins and Spread of Nationalism*. Rev. ed. (New York: Verso, 1995); and Laura Engelstein and Stephanie Sandler (eds.), *Self and Story in Russian History* (Ithaca: Cornell University Press, 2000).

22. Vospominaniia Andreia Mikhailovicha Fadeeva (Nadezhda Andreevna Fadeeva, ed.), *Russkii arkhiv* 1891, no. 3: 289–329; 385–424; 465–94; 1891, no. 5: 14–60, 105–64, 229–57, 424–522 [hereafter VAMF RA].

23. Iu. L. Lotman, *Besedy o russkoi kul'ture: Byt i traditsii russkogo dvorianstva (XVIII–nachalo XIX veka)* (St Petersburg: Iskusstvo-SPB, 1994), 5–17. See also Helena Goscilo and Beth Holmgren (eds.), *Russia Women Culture* (Bloomington: Indiana University Press, 1996).

24. N. A. F(adeev)-a, 'Vospominaniia o Rostislave Fadeeve', in *Sobranie sochinenii R. A. Fadeeva*, vol. 1 (StP: V. V. Komarov, 1889).

25. C. D. Tomei, *Russian Women Writers*, vol. 1 (New York: Garland, 1999) and M. K. Nef, *Lichnye memyary E. P. Blavatskoi* (Moscow: Rossiiskoe Teosovskoe Obshchestvo, 1993).

26. Laura Engelstein, 'Combined Underdevelopment: Discipline and Law in Imperial and Soviet Russia,' *The American Historical Review*, Vol. 98, No. 2 (Apr., 1993), 338–53; David L. Hoffmann and Yanni Kotsonis, *Russian Modernity: Politics, Knowledge, Practices* (New York: St Martin's Press, 2000); B. N. Mironov, *Sotsial'naia istoriia Rossii perioda imperii: XVIII-nachalo XX v. Genezis lichnosti, demokraticheskoi sem'i, grazhdanskogo obshchestva i pravovogo gosudarstva*, 2 vols. (St Petersburg: D. Bulanin, 1999); Jane Burbank, 'Revisioning Imperial Russia', *Slavic Review*, Vol. 52, No. 3 (Autumn, 1993), 555–67; Peter Holquist, '"Information is the Alpha and Omega of Our Work": Bolshevik Surveillance in Its Pan-European Context', *The Journal of Modern History*, Vol. 69, No. 3 (Sep., 1997), 415–50.

27. Marshall Berman, *All That Is Solid Melts Into Air; The Experience of Modernity* (New York: Simon and Schuster, 1982); Katherine Crawford, *Perilous Performances: Gender and Regency in Early Modern France* (Harvard, 2004); Mikhail Bakhtin, *Rabelais and His World*. Translated by Helene Izwolsky (Tvorchestvo Fransua Rable, 1965).

28. Eric Hobsbawm, *The Age of Empire, 1875–1914* (New York: Pantheon Books, 1987), introduction. See also Peter Gay, *Schnitzler's Century: The Making of Middle-Class Culture, 1815–1914* (New York: W.W. Norton, 2002).

Fred + Jane?

29. For example, Linda Colley, *Captives: Britain, Empire and the World, 1600–1850* (London: Jonathan Cape, 2002); Niall Ferguson, *Empire: How Britain Made the Modern World* (London: Allen Lane, 2003); Partha Chatterjee, *Nationalist Thought and the Colonial World* (Minneapolis: University of Minnesota Press, 1986); David Cannadine, *Ornamentalism: How the British Saw Their Empire* (London: Allen Lane, 2001); Anne McClintock, *Imperial Leather: Race, Gender, and Sexuality in the Colonial Contest* (New York: Routledge, 1995).

Cite most modern work.

30. Alfred Rieber, 'Russian Imperialism: Popular, Emblematic, Ambiguous', in *Russian Review*, vol. 53, July 1994: 331–35; Laura Engelstein, 'New Thinking about the Old Empire: Post-Soviet Reflections', *Russian Review*, Vol. 60, No. 4 (Oct., 2001), 487–96; Ronald G. Suny, 'Constructing Primordialism: Old Histories for New Nations', *The Journal of Modern History*, Vol. 73, No. 4 (Dec., 2001), 862–96; Jane Burbank, Mark von Hagen, and Anatolyi Remnev (eds.), *Russian Empire: Space, People, Power, 1700–1930* (Bloomington: Indiana University Press, 2007); Nicholas B. Breyfogle, *Heretics and Colonizers: Forging Russia's Empire in the South Caucasus* (Ithaca, NY: Cornell University Press, 2005); Willard Sunderland, *Taming the Wild Field: Colonization and Empire on the Russian Steppe* (Ithaca: Cornell University Press, 2004); Michael Khodarkovsky, *Russia's Steppe Frontier. The Making of a Colonial Empire, 1500–1800* (Bloomington: Indiana University Press, 2002); Robert D. Crews, *For Prophet and Tsar. Islam and Empire in Russia and Central Asia* (Cambridge, Mass.: Harvard University Press, 2006); Robert P. Geraci, *Window on the East: National and Imperial Identities in Late Tsarist Russia* (Ithaca: Cornell University Press, 2001); Geoffrey Hosking. *Russia. People and Empire, 1552–1917* (Cambridge, MA: Harvard University Press, 1997).

31. Anderson, *Imagined Communities*, 19–21 and especially ch. 6.

32. Richard S. Wortman, *Scenarios of Power: Myth and Ceremony in Russian Monarchy* (Princeton, NJ: Princeton University Press, 1995), vol. 1, pp. 7–8.

33. Dominic Lieven, *Empire: The Russian Empire and Its Rivals* (London John Murray, 2000); also John LeDonne, *The Russian Empire and the World, 1700–1917. The Geopolitics of Expansion and Containment* (New York: Oxford University Press, 1997).

34. Alfred J. Rieber, 'The Sedimentary Society', in E. W. Clowes et.al., *Between Tsar and People: Educated Society and the Quest for Public identity in Late Imperial Russia* (Princeton: Princeton University Press, 1991), 348–49, 355–61.

35. Natalie Zemon Davis, *The Return of Martin Guerre* (Cambridge, Mass.: Harvard University Press, 1983) and Laurel Thatcher Ulrich, *A Midwife's Tale: The Life of Martha Ballard, Based on Her Diary, 1785–1812* (New York: Vintage Books, 1990). See also Inga Clendinnen, *Ambivalent Conquests: Maya and Spaniard in Yucatan, 1517–1570* (Cambridge [Cambridgeshire]; New York: Cambridge University Press, 1987).

36. Clifford Geertz, *The Interpretations of Culture* (New Haven: Yale University Press, 1968], Chapter 1; also *Local Knowledge: Further Essays in Interpretive Anthropology* (Basic Books, 1983).

37. Sinyavsky, 17–18.

38. Yosef Hayim Yerushalmi. *Zakhor: Jewish History and Jewish Memory* (New Jersey: Schocken, 1982); see also Simon Schama, *Dead Certainties: Unwarranted Speculations* (New York: Knopf, 1991).

39. Willard Sunderland, *Taming the Wild Field: Colonization and Empire on the Russian Steppe* (Ithaca: Cornell University Press, 2004).

40. James C. Scott, *Seeing Like a State: How Certain Schemes to Improve the Human Condition Have Failed* (New Haven: Yale University Press, 1998).

41. Paul R. Gregory, *Before Command: An Economic History of Russia from Emancipation to the First Five-Year Plan* (Princeton, NJ: Princeton University Press, 1994). Also Alexander Gerschenkron, *Continuity in History and Other Essays* Cambridge, MA: The Belknap Press of Harvard University Press, 1968); Arcadius Kahan, 'The Russian Economy, 1860–1913', in *Russian Economic History: The Nineteenth Century* (Chicago and London: University of Chicago Press, 1982).

42. Joseph Brodsky, 'Less Than One', in *Less Than One: Selected Essays* (New York: Farrar, Straus & Giroux, 1986).

CHAPTER I: BOYHOOD AND FAMILY ON
AN IMPERIAL FRONTIER, 1849–1865

1. SZ I: 1 ['O predkakh'].

2. VAMF RA 1891 (5), 112 ['Sovet upravleniia zakavkazskogo kraia'].

3. Nef, *Lichnye memuary*, 7 [E. P. Pisareva, *Theosophist*, Jan. 1913, 503].

4. VAMF, RA 1891 (5), 478–9 ['Trevozhnoe polozhenie Tiflisa'].

5. Iu. M. Lotman, *Besedy o russkoi kul'ture: Byt i traditsii russkogo dvorianstva (XVIII–nachalo XIX veka)* (StP: Isskusstvo-SPb, 1994), 9.

6. Aleksandr Nikitenko, Helen Saltz Jacobson (tr.), with foreword by Peter Kolchin, *Up from Serfdom: My Childhood and Youth in Russia, 1804–1824* (New Haven, Conn.: Yale University Press, 2001); Vera Broido, *Daughter of Revolution: A Russian Girlhood Remembered* (London: Constable, 1998); Catriona Kelly, *Children's World: Growing Up in Russia, 1890–1991* (New Haven [Conn.]; London: Yale University Press, 2007); Barbara Clements, Rebecca Friedman, and Dan Healey, *Russian Masculinities in History and Culture* (Palgrave, 2002).

7. Lotman, *Besedy*, 5–16. Mary W. Cavender, *Nests of the Gentry: Family, Estate, and Local Loyalties in Provincial Russia* (Newark: University of Delaware Press, 2007); John Randolph, *The House in the Garden: The Bakunin Family and the Romance of Russian Idealism* (Ithaca, NY: Cornell University Press, 2007); Michelle Lamarche Marrese, *A Woman's Kingdom: Noblewomen and the Control*

of Property in Russia, 1700–1861 (Ithaca, London: Cornell University Press, 2002]; Valerie A. Kivelson, *Autocracy in the Provinces: The Muscovite Gentry and Political Culture in the Seventeenth Century* (Stanford, Calif.: Stanford University Press, 1996); Gary Marker and Rachel May (eds. and trs.), *Days of a Russian Noblewoman: The Memories of Anna Labzina, 1758–1821* (DeKalb, Ill.: Northern Illinois University Press, 2001); Marc Raeff, *Origins of the Russian Intelligentsia: The Eighteenth-Century Nobility* (San Diego, New York: Harcourt Brace Jovanovich, 1966); and P. A. Zaionchkovskii, *Pravitel'stvennii apparat samoderzhavnoi Rossii v XIX veke* (Moskva: Mysl', 1978).

8. Nicholas B. Breyfogle, *Heretics and Colonizers: Forging Russia's Empire in the South Caucasus*; Austin Jersild, *Orientalism and Empire: North Caucasus Mountain Peoples and the Georgian Frontier, 1845–1917* (Montreal; Ithaca: McGill-Queen's University Press, 2002); Susan Layton, *Russian Literature and Empire: Conquest of the Caucasus from Pushkin to Tolstoy* (Cambridge: Cambridge UP 1994); R.A Fadeev, *Shest'desiat' let kavkazskoi voiny* in *Sobranie Sochinenii R. A. Fadeeva*, vol. 1 (St Petersburg, 1889); Daniel Brower and Edward Lazzerini (eds.), *Russia's Orient. Imperial Borderlands and Peoples, 1700–1917* (Michigan-Indiana Series in Russian and East European Studies Indiana 1997); Charles King, *The Ghost of Freedom; A History of the Caucuses* (Oxford, 2008).

9. VAMF RA 1891 (5) [Pereezd v Tiflis], 56–60.

10. VAMF RA 1891 (5): 127–31, 229–232, 244–45, 256–57, 434–36, 461–63, 466, 476–85; SZ I: 69–72 [Vospominaniia iz detstva]; N. A. Otarova, *Tbilisi, Stolitsa gruzinskoi SSR* (Moscow, 1951) and *Illiustririvannyi putevoditel' po Voenno-gruzinskoi doroge i gor. Tiflisu* (Tiflis, Zakavtopromtorg, 1924), 97–108.

11. V. M. Kabuzan, *Izmeneniia v razmeshchenii naseleniia Rossii v XVIII – pervoi polovine XIX v.* (Moscow: Nauka, 1971) and Terrence Emmons, *The Russian Landed Gentry and the Peasant Emancipation of 1861* (London: Cambridge University Press, 1968), 4.

12. SZ I: 1 [O predkakh] and BE 5: 497–98.

13. VAMF RA 1891 (3): 290–5 ['Otets'].

14. VAMF, RA 1891 (3): 474–75 [Kalmyki] and (5) *passim*.

15. SZ I: 28 [O sestrakh Ol'ge i Sofii].

16. VAMF RA 1891 (5): 427–32 [1849].

17. VAMF RA 1891 (5): 521 [1866–67].

18. SZ: II: 117 ['Podgotovka k postupleniiu v Universitet'].

19. M. K. Nef, *Lichnye memyary* 110 [P. S. Nikolaev, Vospominaniia o kniaze A. T. Bariatinskom]; VAMF RA 1891 (5): 120.

20. VAMF RA 1891 (5): 514 [Vospominaniia A. M. Fadeeva. 1864] and *passim*.

21. W. Bruce Lincoln, *In the Vanguard of Reform: Russia's Enlightened Bureaucrats, 1825–1861* (DeKalb: Northern Illinois University Press, 1982); M. E. Saltykov-Shchedrin (tr. I. P. Foote), *The History of A Town* (Oxford: W. A. Meeuws, 1980) and (tr. Samuel D. Cioran) *The Golovlyov Family* (Ann Arbor, Mich.: Ardis, 1977); Nikolai Gogol, *Dead Souls* (New York: Modern Library, 1997).

22. SZ I: 2.

23. SZ I: 27–8 [O brate Boris, O sestrakh Ol'ge i Sofii]; SZ II: 102–105 [O pervonachal'nom vospitanii i obrazovanii].

24. Anan'ich and Ganelin, 9–10; BAR M. M. Kovalevskii, Moia zhizn', notebook XXVII, p. 71.

25. RGIA f. 1622, op. 1, ed. khr. 1020 [originally Odessa Obl. Gos. Arkhiv f. 625, op. 1, arkh No.1 'Spravka o dvorianstve Vitte, dannaia v Pskove'], ll. 1–5; Anan'ich and Ganelin, 9; SZ I: 2 [O predkakh].

26. VAMF RA 1891 (5): 19 [Gubernatorstvo v Saratove].

27. VAMF, RA 1891 (5): 40–1 [Khoziastvennye Fermy].

28. VAMF RA 1891 (5): 112 [Nemetskie poseleniia v Gruzii] and 490–93 [Vospominaniia A. M. Fadeeva.1857].

29. SZ II: 102–110 [O pervonachal'nom vospitanii i obrazovanii], *passim*.

30. SZ I: 76–83 ['O gornoi promyshlennosti na Kavkaze i uchasti v nei ottsa'] and RGIA, f. 1622, op. 1, d. 1020, l. 16 [letter to R. A. Fadeev, 13 Aug. 1870, detailing imperial grant of an annual pension of R 1250 to 'your sister Madame Witte']; D. N. Shilov, *Gosudarstvennye deiateli rossiiskoi imperii, 1802–1917. Bibliograficheskii spravochnik*, 122; and N. A. F(adeevo)i, Vospominaniia o Rostislave Fadeeve, 44–5.

31. RGIA, f. 1622, op. 1, d. 1020, l. 16 [letter to R. A. Fadeev, 13 Aug. 1870, detailing imperial grant of an annual pension of R 1250 to 'your sister Madame Witte'].

32. RGIA f. 560, op. 22, d. 181, ll. 47 (E. Gudima), 131–134 (A. Shatrova) and d. 189, ll. 66–9 (N.Lukhmanova).

33. SZ I: 24 and 17–26 [O brate Aleksandre].

34. Susan Layton, *Russian Literature and Empire: The Conquest of the Caucasus from Pushkin to Tolstoy*, op. cit.; Leo Tolstoy, *Hadji Murat* (1912); Mikhail Lermontov, *A Hero of Our Time* (1839, 1841); Aleksandr Pushkin, *The Prisoner of the Caucases* (1820–21).

35. VAMF RA 1891 (5): 55 [Provoda iz Saratova].

36. SZ I: 17–18.

37. SZ I: 19–21; Lotman, op. cit., 'Duel',164–80.

38. SZ I: 21–24.

39. SZ I: 85–98 and R. A. Fadeev, *Shest'desiat' let*, 41–85 [ch. III, 'Pokorenie Kavkaza'].

40. SZ I: 25–26.

41. N. A. F(adeev)-a, 'Vospominaniia', op. cit., 44.

42. SZ I: 69–72 [Vospominania iz detstva].

43. SZ I: 30–44 [O Rostislave Andreeviche Fadeeve]; *Russkii Biograficheskii Slovar'* 21, 6–10; R. A. Fadeev, *Sobranie sochinenii R. A. Fadeeva*, 3 vols. (St Petersburg: V. V. Komarova, 1889–1890]. These include *Vostochnyi vopros, Chem nam byt, Vooruzhenye sily Rossii, 60 let kavkazskoi voiny, Pis'ma s Kavkaza, Zapiski o kavkazskikh delakh*.

44. N. A. F(adeeva) 'Vospominaniia' 48.
45. N. A. F(adeeva) 'Vospominaniia' 4–9.
46. N. A. F(adeeva) 'Vospominaniia' 9–12.
47. N. A. F(adeeva) 'Vospominaniia' 16.
48. Fadeev, *Shest'desiat' let kavkzskoi voiny*, esp. 85–95; also *Pis'ma s Kavkaza and Zapiski o kavkasskikh delakh* in *Sobranie sochinenii*, op. cit., vol. 1.
49. Geoffrey Hosking, *Russia. People and Empire, 1552–1917* (London: Harper Collins, 1997), 18–23; Gordin, Ia. A. and B. P. Milovidov, eds. *Osada Kavkaza: Vospominaniia uchastnikov kavkazskoi voiny XIX veka.* (St Petersburg: Izdatel'stvo zhurnala Zvezda, 2000); Thomas Sanders, Ernest Tucker and Gary Hamburg (eds.), *Russian-Muslim Confrontation in the Caucasus: Alternative Visions of the Conflict between Imam Shamil and the Russians, 1830–1859* (London, New York: Routledge Curzon, 2004]; Moshe Gammer, *Muslim Resistance to the Tsar: Shamil and the Conquest of Chechnia and Daghestan* (London, Portland, Or.: F. Cass, 1994).
50. Fadeeva, 'Vospominaniia' 35 and Fadeev, *Shest'desiat' let*, ch. 2, op. cit.
51. SZ I: 43.
52. SZ I: 30–33; also 43–44; Fadeeva, 'Vospominaniia' 17–39.
53. SZ I: 33–45, *passim*.
54. Iu. F. Samarin, 'Predislovie', *Sobranie sochinenii A. S. Khomiakova* (Moscow, 1867: reprinted in A. S. Khomiakov, *Tserkov Odna*. Izdateltel'stvo Prep. Iova Pochaevskago. Montréal, 1975) and SZ I: 37.
55. SZ I: 34–36.
56. SZ I: 1, 45.
57. SZ I: 1–31 [O Blavatskoi; O Zhelikovskikh; O sestrakh Ol'ge i Sofii; O babushke E. P. Fadeeve, urozh. Kn. Dolgorukoi]; 69–72 [Vospominaniia iz detstva].
58. See Toby W. Clyman and Judith Vowles (eds.), *Russia Through Women's Eyes: Autobiographies from Tsarist Russia* (Yale, 1996), and Helena Goscilo and Beth Holmgren, *Russia: Women. Culture* (Indiana, 1996); also Lotman, *Besedy*, 'Zhenskoe obrazovanie v XVIII – nachale XIX veka': 75–89.
59. Philippa Levine (ed.), *Gender and Empire* (Oxford; New York: Oxford University Press, 2004); Anne McClintock, *Imperial Leather: Race, Gender, and Sexuality in the Colonial Conquest* (New York: Routledge, 1995); Nupur Chaudhuri and Margaret Strobel (eds.), *Western Women and Imperialism. Complicity and Resistance* (Bloomington: Indiana University Press, 1992).
60. SZ I: 1–2 and II: 102–111 [O pervonachal'nom vospitanii i obrazovanii] and *passim*; VAMF 1891 (5): 112 and *passim*.
61. Fadeev, VAMF RA 1891 (3): 394 (Ekaterinoslav) and (5): 32–34 (Saratov), 112 (Astrakhan), 126–27 (Baku), 244–5 (Tiflis).
62. SZ I: 15–16 [O Zhelikhovskikh] and II: 155 [Predpolozhenie sdelat'sia professorom]; Nef, *Lichnye memuary*, 24–28 [Letters of H. P. Blavatsky to A. P. Sinnett].

63. SZ I: 69–71 [Vospominaniia iz detstva] and VAMF RA 1891 (5): 479 [Trevozhnoe polozhenie Tiflisa, 1854].

64. BAR Kovalevskii, 71; also Herman Bernstein, *With Master Minds*, 27.

65. SZ I: 16–17 ['O semeistve otsa'].

66. Vera Naryshkina-Vitte, *Zapiski devochki*, 94–95; SZ I: 27 ['O sestrakh Ol'gi i Sofii'].

67. Veronica Shapalova, 'Elena Gan' in C. D. Tomei, *Russian Women Writers*, vol. 1 (Garland, 1999): 71–8 and Nef, *Lichnye memuary*, 9–10 [V. P. Zhelikhovskaia, 'Detskie vospominaniia, sobrannye dlia moikh detei.']. Also, as in Tomei, 86: *Sochineniia*. '*Zinaida R-va*', 4 vols. (StP, 1843), and *Polnoe sobranie sochinenii* 6 vols (StP 1905) (2nd ed. 1909).

68. Shapovalov, 'From The Reminiscence of Zheleznovodsk', in Tomei, 85–86.

69. BE 9, 242.

70. Nef, *Lichnye memuary*, 16–21 [V. P. Zhelikhovskaia, 'Detskie vospominaniia, sobrannye dlia moikh detei.'].

71. Nef, *Lichnye memuary*, 110 [A. P. Sinnett, *Incidents in the Life of Madame Blavatsky* (London, 1886)] and 110–112 [P. S. Nikolaev, 'Vospominaniia o kniaze A.(I.) Bariatinskom'].

72. Nef, *Lichnye memuary*, 7, 19 [E. F. Pisareva, unpublished mss.].

73. BE 3, 287–8; Maria Carlson, 'Elena Blavatskaia' in Tomei, *Russian Women's Writers I*: 241–6; Bernice Glazer Rosenthal (ed.), *The Occult in Russian and Soviet Culture* (Ithaca: Cornell, 1997), esp. Maria Carlson, 'Fashionable Occultism: Spiritualism, Theosophy, Freemasonry, Hermeticism in Fin-de-Siecle Russia,' 135–52. See also 'The Blavatsky Net Foundation' at www.blavatsky.net, dedicated to the propagation of Theosophy, the spiritualist movement Blavatskaia founded.

74. SZ I: 2–14 ['O Blavatskoi'].

75. SZ I: 2–6 ['O Blavatskoi'] and Nef, *Lichnye memuary* [khronologicheskaia tablitsa], 302.

76. Nef, *Lichnye memuary*, 24 and 28–30 [Letters of H. P. Blavatsky] and 109 [Zhelikhovskaia].

77. Nef, *Lichnye memuary*, 110–11 [A. P. Sinnett, *Incidents in the Life of Madame Blavatsky*, London, 1886, 1913].

78. SZ I: 14.

79. RBS 21, 4–5. These included Sir R. I. Murchison, president of the London Geographical Society. See Sir Roderick Impey Murchison, *The Geology of Russia in Europe and the Ural Mountains By Roderick Impey Murchison, Edouard de Verneuil, Count Alexander von Keyserling* (2 vols) [London: J. Murray, 1845).

80. SZ I: 28 ('O babushke E. P. Fadeevoi, urozhd. kn. Dolgorukoi').

81. SZ I: 28–9 ['O drevnem kreste kniazia Mikhaila Chernigovskogo']; BE 13, 242.

82. BE 8, 621.

83. BE 8, 620–1; Prebel'skii et.al., *Dom Romanovykh. Biograficheskie svedeniia o chlenakh tsarstvovavshego doma, ikh predkakh i rodstvennikakh* (StP 1992).

84. Marc Raeff, *The Well-Ordered Police State: Social and Institutional Change through Law in the Germanies and Russia, 1600–1800* (New Haven: Yale University Press, 1983); A. Kamenskii, *Historica Rossica. Rossiiskaia imperiia v XVIII veke: traditsii i modernizatsiia* (Moscow: Novoe literaturnoe obozrenie, 1999).

85. Sunderland, *Taming the Wild Field*, op. cit.

86. Fadeev, VAMF 5 RA 1891 (5): 500–502 [E. P. Fadeeva].

87. Ibid.

88. David Saunders, *Russia in the Age of Reaction and Reform 1801–1881* (London; New York: Longman, 1992); A. E. Presniakov and Judith C. Zacek (ed. and tr.). *Emperor Nicholas I of Russia. The Apogee of Autocracy, 1825–1855* (Gulf Breeze, Fla.: Academic International Press, 1974); Alexander M. Martin, *Romantics, Reformers, Reactionaries. Russian Conservative Thought and Politics in the Reign of Alexander I* (DeKalb, Ill.: Northern Illinois University Press, 1997); W. Bruce Lincoln, *Nicholas I* (Bloomington: Indiana University Press, 1978); Isabel De Madariaga, *Catherine the Great. A Short History* (New Haven: Yale University Press, 1990); V. O. Kliuchevsky (Marshall S. Shatz ed. and tr.), *A Course in Russian History: The Time of Catherine the Great* (Armonk, NY: M. E. Sharpe, 1997).

89. VAMF RA 1891 (3): 302–3 [Bandre-du-Plessy and Zhizn' pod Kievom].

90. VAMF RA 1891 (3): 309–11 (Moskva 1814).

91. VAMF RA 1891 (3): 311–317; S. T. Aksakov, *The Family Chronicle* (1856) and *Childhood Years of Grandson Bagrov* (1858).

92. VAMF RA 1891 (3): 312–15 [Kn. P. V. Dolgorukii].

93. VAMF RA (3): 307–309.

94. Ibid., 307–8.

95. Ibid., 308–9.

96. Ibid., 309.

97. Nef, *Lichnye memuary*, 16 [Colonel N. S. Olcott, *Old Diary Leaves*, vol. 1–2 (London, 1892)].

CHAPTER 2: COMING OF AGE IN NEW RUSSIA, 1865–1881

1. SZ II: 112–13.

2. V. V. Kirkhner, 'K biografii S.Iu. Vitte', *Volny*, April 1915 [no. 4]: 118.

3. BAR Witte, Box 1, Corr: A–G, Letter, Prince A. I. Bariatinskii to N. M. Chikhachev, Director, Russian Steamship, Commerce, and Odessa Railroad Company, 28 January 1871.

4. R. A. Fadeev, *Russkoe obshchestvo v nastoiashchem i budushchem (Chem nam byt?)*, Russian Society in the Present and the Future (What Will We Be?), *Sobranie sochinenii R. A. Fadeeva* (StP: V. V. Komarov, 1889), vol. 1, ch. 1, 4–5.

5. BE 14: 327–9; Isaac Babel, Nathalie Babel (ed.) and Peter Constantine (tr.), *The Complete Works of Isaac Babel* (New York, London: W.W. Norton, 2002); Patricia Herlihy, *Odessa: A History, 1794–1914* (Cambridge: HUP; Harvard Ukrainian Research Institute, 1986), 1–3; Willard Sunderland, *Taming the Wild Field*, chs 1–3; Charles King, *The Black Sea: A History* (Oxford University Press, 2004); N. A. Kislinskii and A.N. Kulomzin, *Nasha zheleznodorozhnaia politika po dokumentam arkhiva Komiteta ministrov* (St Petersburg: Komitet ministrov, 1902) [hereafter Kislinskii], vol. 1: 121–145.

6. SZ II: 112–17 ['O podgotovke k postupleniiu v Universitet'].

7. SZ II: 102–9 ['O pervonachal'nom vospitanii i obrazovanii'].

8. BAR M. M. Kovalevskii, Moia zhizn', 19–31.

9. SZ II: 112, op. cit.

10. SZ II: 114–17, op. cit.

11. Lynn Hunt, unpublished remarks, Byrne History Seminar, Vanderbilt University, April 2000; Dietrich Geyer and Bruce Little (tr.), *Russian Imperialism: The Interaction of Domestic and Foreign Policy 1860–1914* (Leamington Spa: Berg, 1987); Louise McReynolds, *The News under Russia's Old Regime: The Development of a Mass-Circulation Press* (Princeton, NJ: Princeton University Press, 1991) and *Russia at Play: Leisure Activities at the End of the Tsarist Era* (Ithaca: Cornell University Press, 2003); Ben Eklof, John Bushnell, and Larissa Zakharova (eds.), *Russia's Great Reforms, 1855–1881* (Bloomington: Indiana University Press, 1994); Alexander Polunov, Thomas C. Owen and Larissa G. Zakharova (eds.), Marshall S. Shatz (tr), *Russia in the Nineteenth Century: Autocracy, Reform, and Social Change, 1814–1914* (Armonk, NY: M. E. Sharpe, 2005); Claudia Verhoeven, *The Odd Man Karakozov: Imperial Russia, Modernity, and the Birth of Terrorism* (Ithaca: Cornell University Press, 2009); David Christian, *Imperial and Soviet Russia: Power, Privilege, and the Challenge of Modernity* (Houndmills, Basingstoke, Hampshire: Macmillan, 1997); Cathy A. Frierson, *Peasant Icons: Representations of Rural People in Late Nineteenth Century Russia* (New York: Oxford University Press, 1993); W. Bruce Lincoln, *The Great Reforms: Autocracy, Bureaucracy, and the Politics of Change in Imperial Russia* (DeKalb, Ill: Northern Illinois University Press, 1990); Goscilo and Holmgren, *Russia: Culture. Women*, op. cit.

12. OR, RNL f. 833 [V.A. Tser], No. 479, 'Zapiska o studencheskikh volneniiakh v Peterburgskom universitete' [nd] Signed Witte, Protasov-Bakhmet'ev, Ermolov, Muraviev, and Khil'kov. The document is not dated, but context strongly suggests disturbances of autumn 1899, pp. 1–4.

13. Susan K. Morrissey, *Heralds of Revolution; Russian Students and the Mythologies of Radicalism* (New York: Oxford University Press, 1998); Barbara Alpern Engel, *Mothers and Daughters: Women of the Intelligentsia in Nineteenth Century Russia* (New York: Cambridge University Press, 1983); Barbara Alpern Engel and Clifford Rosenthal (eds. and trs.), *Five Sisters: Women Against the Tsar* (New York: Knopf; distributed by Random House, 1975); Abbott Gleason, *Young*

Russia: The Genesis of Russian Radicalism in the 1860s (New York: Viking Press, 1980).

14. ES B i E, 21, 291–2 (Novorossiiskii universitet); 'Kratkii otchet o sostoianii Imperatorskogo novorossisskogo universiteta v 1870–1871 akadimicheskogo goda', *Zapiski Imperatorskogo Novorossisskogo Universiteta*. God chetvertyi. Tom sedmoi (Odessa, 1871), 1–35 and 61–63.

15. Laura Engelstein, 'Combined Underdevelopment: Discipline and the Law in Late Imperial and Soviet Russia' (in AHR Forum), *The American Historical Review*, Vol. 98, No. 2. (Apr. 1993), 338–53.

16. BAR Kovalevskii, *Vospominaniia*, op. cit., ch. 3, 31–60 (Kharkov University, c. 1868); V. A. Posse, *Moi zhiznennyi put'* (Moscow, 1929), ch. 3 (StP University, 1880s); P. N. Miliukov, *Vospominaniia* (Moscow: Sovremennik, 1990), vol. 1, 102–41 (Moscow University, 1877–82). See, in general, Melissa Kirshcke Stockdale, *Paul Miliukov and the Quest for a Liberal Russia, 1880–1918* (Ithaca: Cornell, 1996), ch. 1.

17. St.P Institute of History, et. al., *Vlast' i nauka, uchenye i vlast', 1880-e-nachalo 1920-kh godov*. Proceedings of VI International Colloquium, summer 2001 (St Petersburg: Dmitrii Bulanin, 2003).

18. SZ II:148 ['O znachenii i vliianii universiteta na studentov'].

19. Leopold Haimson, *The Russian Marxists and the Origins of Bolshevism* (Cambridge, Mass: Harvard Univ. Press, 1955), ch. 1; Ivan Turgenev, *Fathers and Children* (1862).

20. SZ, II: 131–32, 141–42.

21. SZ, II: 140–5 ['O professorakh universiteta Grigorevich, Iagich i drugikh'].

22. BE 12: 714–16.

23. SZ II: 118–22 [o prebyvanie v Universitete].

24. SZ II: 120–55.

25. B. B. Glinskii, *Revoliutsionnyi period russkoi istorii (1861–1881 gg.)*. *Istoricheskie ocherki* [StP, 1913], vol. 1. Recent examples include Rebecca Friedman, *Masculinity, Autocracy and the Russian University, 1804–1863* (Houndmills, Basingstoke, Hampshire; New York: Palgrave Macmillan, 2005); Nikolai Chernyshevsky and Michael R. Katz (tr.), *What Is to Be Done?* (Ithaca, NY: Cornell University Press, 1989); Susan K. Morrissey, *Heralds of Revolution: Russian Students and the Mythologies of Radicalism*, op. cit.; Abbott Gleason, *Young Russia: The Genesis of Russian Radicalism in the 1860s*, op.cit.; and Barbara Engel, *Mothers and Daughters: Women of the Intelligentsia in Nineteenth Century Russia*, op. cit.

26. Adele Lindenmeyr, *Poverty Is Not a Vice: Charity, Society, and the State in Imperial Russia* (Princeton, NJ: Princeton University Press, 1996) and Joseph Bradley, *Voluntary Associations in Tsarist Russia: Science, Patriotism, and Civil Society* (Cambridge, Mass.: Harvard University Press, 2009).

27. SZ II: 120–24 [Ob Afanas'eve].

28. G. E. Afanas'ev, 'K konchine grafa S. Iu. Vitte', *Volny*, Mart 1915, No. 3: 97–100.

29. SZ II: 126–28 ['O Millere, studente'].

30. V. V. Kirkhner, 'K biografii S. Iu. Witte', *Volny*, April 1915, No. 4, 118.

31. SZ I: 90–93 [o generale Geimane].

32. Naryshkina-Vitte, *Zapiski devochki*, 94.

33. SZ III: 252 [O soobshchestve 'Sviataia Druzhina' i moem uchastii v nem].

34. G. E. Afanas'ev, 'K konchine grafa S. Iu. Vitte', op. cit.

35. BAR Witte, Box 1, Correspondence: R–S [Pimen Semniut to Witte, 23 June 1909]; SZ II: 213 [Ob osvobozhdenii ot nakazanii za Tiligul'skogo katastrofa, arrest" i otbytitie nakazaniia]; I. P. Belokonskii, 'K istorii politicheskikh ssylki 80-kh godov', *Katorga i ssylka* 31 (1927): 153; P. P. Semeniut, *Pervaia gosudarstvennaia duma, ee zhizn' i smert* (StP: M. M. Stasiulevich, 1907); *Bio-bibliograficheskii slovar': Deiateli revoliutsionnogo dvizheniia v Rossii* II, vyp. 1 (M: Vsesoiuznoe obshchestvo politicheskikh katorzhan i ssyl'no-poselentsev, 1929), 262 and *passim*.

36. Isabelle V. Hull, *The Entourage of Kaiser Wilhelm II, 1888–1918* (Cambridge; New York: Cambridge University Press, 1982); Donald Hall (ed.), *Muscular Christianity* (Cambridge: Cambridge Univ. Press, 1994); David Alderson, *Mansex Fine: Religion, Manliness and Imperialism in Nineteenth-Century British Culture* (Manchester, England; New York: Manchester University Press, 1998); Clements, Friedman, and Healey, *Russian Masculinities in History and Culture*, op. cit.

37. SZ I: 97 [O Chevchevadze] and II: 177–81 ['O rotmistre Kuzminskom'].

38. Anan'ich and Ganelin, 40 and *passim*.

39. RGIA f. 1622, op. 1, d. 448 l.1 [V. P. Meshcherskii to Witte, 19 May, copy].

40. ZGV: 13a-b ob./27–29 (Hamburg, June 1907).

41. SZ II: 124–126 ['O Iuzefoviche i Gesse, Dvortsovom Komandante'].

42. SZ II: 155–156 [Predpolozhenie sdelat'sia professorom].

43. Benedict Anderson, *Imagined Communities*, ch. 5; Dietrich Geyer, *Russian Imperialism*, op. cit., ch. 3; Misha Glenny, *The Balkan:. Nationalism, War, and the Great Powers, 1804–1909* (New York: Penguin, 1999).

44. R. Fadeev, *Mnenie o vostochnom voprose po povodu poslednikh retsenzii na 'Vooruzhenye sily Rossii* (StP: Departament udelov, 1870); SZ I: 48–51[Predlozhenie kn. Bariatinskogo o reorganizatsiia armii]. See also 'A. G.', 'Obzor literaturnoi deiatel'nosti R.A. Fadeeva', in Polnoe sobranie sochinenii, op. cit., vol. 1; Also Peter A. Zaionchkovskii and Gary M. Hamburg (ed. and tr.), P. A. Zaionchkovskii, *The Russian Autocracy in Crisis, 1878–1882* (Gulf Breeze, FL: Academic International Press, 1979); David McKenzie, *The Serbs and Russian Pan-Slavism, 1875–1878* [Ithaca, NY: Cornell University Press, 1967).

45. Fadeev, *Vostochnyi vopros*, 95 and *passim*.

46. SZ I: 32.

47. SZ II: 157.
48. Michael Freeman, *Railways and the Victorian Imagination* (New Haven, Conn.: Yale University Press, 1999); Stephen Kern, *The Culture of Time and Space 1880–1918* [Cambridge: Harvard University Press, 1983); David Haward Bain, *Empire Express: Building the First Transcontinental Railroad* (New York: Penguin, 1999); T. J. Stiles, *The First Tycoon: The Epic Life of Cornelius Vanderbilt* (New York: Alfred A. Knopf, 2009); Wolfgang Schivelbusch, *The Railway Journey: The Industrialization of Time and Space in the 19th Century* (Berkeley, Calif.: University of California Press, 1986).
49. Kislinski II, 7–10.
50. Kislinskii I: 121–145; II, 63–69; M. N. Baryshnikov, *Delovoi mir Rossii. Istoriko-biograficheskii spravochnik* (StP: Logos, 1998): 321.
51. SZ II: 155–63 [O grafom Bobrinskom i ego sovet postupit' na zheleznodorozhnuiu sluzhbu and O postuplenii na sluzhbu na Odesskuiu zh.d.].
52. Kislinskii I: 55–60, 69–78, 99–115; Alfred J. Rieber (ed.), *The Politics of Autocracy: Letters of Alexander II to Prince A. I. Bariatinskii, 1857–1864* (Paris, Mouton, 1966) and 'The Formation of La Grande Societe des Chemins de Fer Russes', *Jahrbucher fur Geschichte Osteuropas* 21 (1973), 3: 375–91.
53. Kislinskii II: 63–69 and 322–24; RGIA f. 560, op. 22, d. 168 [Dokladnye zapiski m-ra fin. I. A. Vyshnegradskogo Aleksanndru III ob umenshchenii defitsita po smete, 11 Aug. 1887 – 21 March 1892]; f. 268, op. 3–6 [Financial Division, Tariff Division, Personnel Division, Secret Division; Department of Railroad Affairs, MF], *passim*.
54. Kislinskii II: 63–69.
55. Kislinskii II: 105–06 and 309–10; f. 268, op. 3, d. 193 ['O rasshirenii russkoi zhelezno-dorozhnoi seti (1888–1891)'].
56. Kislinskii III: 13–14. A. F. Grinevskii, 'Obzor deiatel'nosti Obshchikh S"ezdov predstavitelei russkikh zheleznodorozhnykh dorog', in V. M. Verkhovskii (ed.), *Istoricheskii ocherk raznykh otraslei zheleznodorozhnogo dela i razvitiia finansovo-ekonomicheskoi storony zheleznykh dorog v Rossii po 1897 vkliuchitel'no* (StP: Min-vo putei soobshcheniia]: 1–15.
57. B. R. Mitchell, *European Historical Statistics 1750–1970* (New York: Columbia Univ. Press, 1978), 313–343; Kislinskii I: 69–78, 99–115; f. 268, op. 3, d. 193 ['O rasshirenii russkoi zhelezno-dorozhnoi seti (1888–1891)'].
58. SZ II: 161–211 *passim* [O postuplenii na sluzhbu na Odesskuiu zh. dorogu, O N. M. Chikhachev i predlozhenie sdelat' menia nachal'nikon dvizheniia dorogi, O polozhenii dorogi vo vremia Vostochnoi 1877 g. voiny, O proezde na voinu Imperatora Aleksandra II, O zheleznodorozhnom kongresse v Briussele]. On the civic world of post-emancipation Russia, see especially James von Geldern and Louise McReynolds (eds.), *Entertaining Tsarist Russia: Tales, Songs, Plays, Movies, Jokes, Ads, and Images from Russian Urban Life, 1779–1917* (Bloomington: Indiana University Press, 1998), parts III and IV.
59. SZ II: 163–165 [O Shterne].

60. Helmut Walser Smith, *The Continuities of German History: Nation, Religion, and Race across the Long Nineteenth Century* (Cambridge; New York: Cambridge University Press, 2008).

61. SZ II: 163–167, op. cit.; Benjamin Nathans, *Beyond the Pale: The Jewish Encounter with Late Imperial Russia.* (Berkeley: University of California Press, 2002).

62. BAR Witte, Box 1, Corr: A–G (Kn. A. I. Bariatinskii–N. M. Chikachev and reply, Jan–Feb. 1871); Anan'ich and Ganelin, op. cit., 9–20.

63. SZ II, 198–207 [O deiatel'nosti na Odesskoi doroge po perevozke voisk na teatr deistvii v voinu 1877 goda].

64. A. F. Grinevskii, 'Obzor deiatel'nosti Obshchikh S"ezdov predstavitelei russ-kikh zheleznodorozhnykh dorog', in V. M. Verkhovskii (ed.), *Istoricheskii ocherk raznykh otraslei zheleznodorozhnogo dela u razvitiia finansovo-ekonomicheskoi storony zheleznykh dorog v Rossii po 1897 vkliuchitel'no* (StP: Min-vo putei soobshcheniia): 1–15; SZ II: 207–11 [O zheleznodorozhnykh kongrese v Briussele].

65. A. F. Koni, *Sergei Iu'levich Vitte. Otryvochnye vospominaniia* (Moscow: Izd-vo Pravo i Zhizn', 1925), 6–9; SZ II: 211–17 [Ob osvobozhdenii ot nakazaniia za Tiligul'skuiu katastrofu, arrest i otbytie nakazaniia].

66. SZ II: 170–77; Richard Wortman, 'Rule by Sentiment: Alexander II's Journeys through the Russian Empire', *The American Historical Review*, Vol. 95, No. 3 (Jun., 1990), 745–71.

67. SZ II: 177–8; Anan'ich and Ganelin, op. cit., 13.

68. RGIA f. 1622, op. 1, d. 989, l.2.

69. Glenny, *The Balkans*, op. cit., 107–131.

70. RGIA f. 229, op. 1, d. 1102 ['S svedeniiami ob inostrannykh i polskikh urozhdennykh, sluzhashchikh na 16-ti zapadnykh i iugo-zapadnykh zhelez. dorogakh (20 Oct. 1876 – 9 Oct. 1878)], ll. 41–48 ob., 370 ob–377, 222–5, 388.

71. Konstantin Savitsky, 'Off to War [*Na voinu*], 1888', in *Paintings from the Russian Museum Collection* (Leningrad: Aurora Arts Publishers, 1975), plate 78.

72. SZ, II: 198–207 [O moei deiatel'nosti na Odesskoi dorogi po perevozki voisk na teatr deistvii v voinu 1877].

73. Glenny, 136–50.

74. f. 268, op. 3, d. 196, ll. 231–51 [acting MPS Witte to V. M. Vannovskii, 11 April 1892].

75. SZ II: 186–98 [Tiligul'skaia katastrofa].

76. Ibid., 211–17 [Ob osvobozhdenii ot nakazanii za telegul'skuiu katastrofu, areste i otbytii nakazanii].

77. Kislinskii II: 261–75.

78. SZ, II: 211–17.

79. The author expresses his thanks to Boris Vasil'evich Anan'ich for this insight and guided tour.

80. Francis W. Wcislo, *Reforming Rural Russia; State, Local Society, and National Politics, 1855–1914* (Princeton: Studies of the Harriman Institute and Princeton University Press, 1990), chs. 2–4.

81. Koni, *S.Iu. Vitte. Otryvochnye vospominaniia*, op. cit., 6–9; RGIA f. 268, op. 4, d. 115 [30 Nov. 1889–20 Dec. 1892], 'Ob obshchem tarife vsei seti rossiiskikh zheleznykh dorog," especially ll. 120–32.

82. Graf S. Iu. Vitte, 'Prichina ubytochnosti russkikh zheleznykh dorog. Doklad, prochitannyi 7 aprelia v institute inzhinerov putei soobshchenii', *Vestnik finansov, promyshlennosyti i torgovli*, 18 aprelia 1910 (no. 16).

83. SZ III: 222–23 ['O zheleznodorozhnykh koroliakh']; M. N. Baryshnikov, *Delovoi mir Rossii: Istoriko-biograficheskii spravochnik* (StP: Iskusstvo, 1998), *passim*.

84. *ESBE* II, 296; Baryshnikov, 122.

85. SZ III: 223 ['O Bliokhe i Kerbedze'].

86. Ibid., 224–31.

87. SZ II: 219–22 [O pervoi, zhenitbe] and III: 259–66 [O docheri pervoi zheny Soni i ee muzhe Meringe].

88. SZ III: 219–22 [Pereezd v Peterburg na mesto nachal'nika eksploatatsii Iugo-Zapadnykh zh.d.].

89. SZ II: 211–17, op. cit.

90. BAR, A. A. Spasskii-Odynets, *Vospominaniia* 4: 356–60.

91. SZ III: 240–44 [Ob uchastii v trudakh Komissii grafa Baranova].

92. SZ III: 244–45 [Pereezd v Kiev na dolzhnost' nachal'nika eksploatatsii Iugo-Zapadnykh zhel.-dorog].

93. Michael F. Hamm, *Kiev: A Portrait, 1800–1917* (Princeton, NJ: Princeton University Press, 1993).

94. SZ III: 279–95 [O podbore sotrudnikov vo vremia upravleniia Iugo-Zapadnymi zh. d.].

95. SZ III: 294–95.

96. SZ III: 308–20 [O Velikoi Kniagine Aleksandre Petrovne i Velikikh Kniaziakh Petre Nikolaeviche i Nikolai Nikolaeviche].

97. Wcislo, *Reforming Rural Russia*, chs. 2–3; Peter A. Zaionchkovsky and Gary M. Hamburg (ed. and tr.), *The Russian Autocracy in Crisis, 1878–1882* (Gulf Breeze, FL: Academic International Press, 1979); Wortman, *Scenarios of Power*, vol. 2, ch. 4; Richard Pipes, *The Degaev Affair: Terror and Treason in Tsarist Russia* (New Haven, Conn.: Yale University Press, 2003).

98. SZ III: 245–59 [O soobshchestve 'Sviataia Druzhina' i moem uchastii v nem].

99. R. Fadeev to Witte, 14 March 1881 ('Po povodu sviatoi druzhiny', Witte's handwritten title) [BAR Witte, Box 1 Corr: A–G]; Anan'ich and Ganelin, 19–33.

100. SZ III: 248.

101. SZ III: 245– 58, op.cit.

CHAPTER 3: DREAMING IN THE VICTORIAN 1880S

1. Sergei Witte, *Printsipy zheleznodorozhnykh tarifov po perevozke gruzov*, 3-e dop-oe izdanie (StP: Brokgauz i Efron, 1910): 80–1.
2. Kniaz' V. P.Meshcherskii, *Vospominaniia* (Moscow: Zakharov, 2001), 642–46.
3. SZ IV: 429 [O V. I. Kovalevskom].
4. SZ IX: 1019–20 [Pogrebenie Imperatora Aleksandra III and Moe predstavlenie Imperitritse Marii Fedorovne].
5. Ben Eklof, John Bushnell, and Larissa Zakharova (eds.), *Russia's Great Reforms, 1855–1881*, op.cit.
6. Richard Pipes, *Russia under the Old Regime* (London: Weidenfeld and Nicolson, 1974); Orlando Figes, *A People's Tragedy: The Russian Revolution, 1891–1924* (London: Jonathan Cape, 1996).
7. Andreas Kappeler, translation by Alfred Clayton, *The Russian Empire: A Multiethnic History* (Harlow, England: Pearson Education, 2001); Benjamin Nathans, *Beyond the Pale: The Jewish Encounter with Late Imperial Russia* (Berkeley; Los Angeles: University of California Press, 2002).
8. P. A. Zaionchkovskii, *Rossiiskoe samoderzhavie v kontse XIX stoletiia. Politicheskaia reaktsiia 80-kh-nachala 90-kh godov* (Moskva: Izd-vo "Mysl'", 1970). The most insightful view of this reign is Richard Wortman, *Scenarios of Power: Myth and Ceremony in Russian Monarchy*, vol. 2 (Princeton, NJ: Princeton University Press, 1995).
9. SZ VII: 776.
10. SZ VII:, 793–94.
11. Linda Colley, *Captives: The Story of Britain's Pursuit of Empire and How Its Soldiers and Sailors were Held Captive by the Dream of Global Supremacy, 1600–1850* (Pantheon, 2002) and Niall Ferguson, *Empire: The Rise and Demise of the British World Order and the Lessons for Global Power* (Basic Books, 2002).
12. RGIA f. 1622, op. 1, d. 503, 543, 549, 552, 554, 560, 562 and *passim*.
13. SZ VIII: 915–941 [O moem poezdke na Sever (Murmanskoe poberezh'e) and RGIA f. 1622, op. 1, ed.khr. 294, ll. 1–9 [Iz Arkhiva Gr. S.Iu. Vitte. Libava ili Murman?].
14. RGIA f. 560, op. 26, d. 55 [O poezdke ministra f-ov vo vostochnye gubernii, Aug.–Sept. 1896 and O poezdke min-a f-ov v iugo-vostochnye gubernii, Sept.–Oct. 1896] and d. 116 ['Perepiska min-va fin-ov po voprosu poezdki m-ra S. Iu. Vitte v Pribaltiiskii krai, July 1897']; f. 1622, op. 1,d. 711 ['Vsepoddanneishii doklad ministra finansov po poeszdke na dal'nii vostok'].
15. RGIA f. 268, op. 4, d. 177 ['O poezdke G-na M-a F-ov i Direktora D-ma zh.-d-nykh del v nashi Sredne-Aziatskie vladeniia [marshrut]'.
16. Sergei Vitte, *Printsipy zheleznodorozhnykh tarifov po perevozke gruzov* (StP, 1910; 3rd edition); SZ, IV, 335–38 ['Ob osnovanii gazety 'Kievskoe slovo' i

polemike s Pikhno i o knige 'Printispy zheleznodorozhnykh tarifov']; BAR
Witte, Box 1, Corr: A–G (A. I. Chuprov to Witte, 17 Feb. 1884).

17. Frederick List, *National System of Political Economy*. Translated from the German
by G. A. Matile. Including the Notes of the French Translation by Henri
Richelot. Stephen Colwell (ed.) (Philadelphia: J.B. Lippincott, 1856) and S.Iu.
Witte, *Natsional'naia Ekonomiia i Fridrikh List*, NP, ND (HB 165W45) and
Graf S. Iu. Witte. *Po povodu Natsionalizma. Natsional'naia ekonomiia i Fridrikh
List*, 2-e izdanie (St Petersburg: Brokgauz i Efron, 1912) and in general Esther
Kingston-Mann, *In Search of the West: Culture, Economics, and Problems of
Russian Development*, ch. 5 'Russian Historical Economics.'

18. *Printsipy*, 107–08.

19. Ibid., 139–51; Von Laue, *Sergei Witte*, op. cit., 50–54 is a very different view of
this text.

20. RGIA f. 268, op. 3, d. 1 93, Oct. 1888, 'O rasshirenii russkoi zhelezno-
dorozhnoi seti' (1888–1891).

21. Sergei Vitte, 'Predislovie k pervomu izdaniiu', Sept. 1883 in *Printsipy*, i–ii.

22. Ibid., 2–5.

23. Ibid., 8–15.

24. *Printsipy*, 18–21.

25. Ibid., 69–70.

26. Ibid., 80–81.

27. Ibid., 107–32.

28. Von Laue, *Sergei Witte*, 54–55; Anan'ich and Ganelin, op. cit, ch. 3; Wcislo,
Reforming Rural Russia, ch. 4; Esther Kingston-Mann, *In Search of the True West:
Culture, Economics, and Problems of Russian Development* (Princeton: Princeton
Univ. Press, 1999), ch. 5; Iu. Martov, et.al, *Obshchestvennoe dvizhenie v Rossii*,
op.cit, vol. 1, 'Ekonomicheskoe sostoianie strany i evoliutsiia khoziastvennykh
otnoshenii'.

29. *Printsipy*, 108–10.

30. *Printsipy*, 110.

31. Ibid., 110–11.

32. Esther Kingston-Mann, op. cit., *In Search of the True West: Culture, Economics, and
Problems of Russian Development* (Princeton: Princeton Univ. Press, 1999), ch. 5.

33. *Printsipy*, 110–12.

34. Ibid., 113; also Gustav Schmoller, *The Mercantile System and Its Historical
Significance from Studien uber die wirthschaftliche Politik Friedrichs des Grossen*
(London, Macmillan, 1897).

35. Ibid., 114.

36. Ibid., 114–15.

37. Ibid., 115–17.

38. Ibid., 117–18.

39. Ibid., 121–23.

40. Ibid., 123–24.

41. Anan'ich and Ganelin, ch. 3. See also V. L. Stepanov, *N. Kh. Bunge: Sud'ba reformatora* (Moscow and Institute of Russian History, RAN: Rosspen, 1998). In general Peter Gatrell, *The Tsarist Economy, 1850–1917* (New York: St Martin's Press, 1986); W. E. Mosse, *An Economic History of Russia* (London, New York: I.B. Tauris, 1992).

42. *Printsipy*, 126–27.

43. Ibid., 127–28.

44. Ibid., 127–29.

45. Ibid., 128.

46. Ibid., 128–30.

47. Ibid., 130–32.

48. List, *National System of Political Economy*, op. cit., v–xii; Witte, *Po povodu Natsionalizma* [1912], op. cit., 3–5 and 11–17. The original discussion of this document is Von Laue, *Sergei Witte*, 56–64.

49. Witte, *Po povodu*, 20.

50. Wcislo, *Reforming Rural Russia*, ch. 4.

51. Witte, *Po povodu*, p. 65.

52. Witte, *Po povodu*, 69–70.

53. Witte, *Po povodu*, 67–8; List, 70.

54. SZ III–IV: 245–433.

55. For example, V. I. Gurko, 'Chto est' i chego net' v 'Vospominaniia grafa S. Iu. Vitte', *Russkaia mysl'* 1922, no. 2; L. Kliachko (L'vov), *Povesti proshlogo* (Leningrad, 1929), 13–17; P. N. Miliukov, *Vospominaniia* (Moscow: Sovremennik, 1990), 321–22; V. Vonliarliarskii, *Moi vospominaniia*. 1852–1939 g.g. (Berlin: Russkoe natsional'noe isdatel'stvo, nd), ch. 8 and *passim*; E. V. Tarle, *Graf S.Iu. Vitte. Opyt' kharakteristiki vneshnei politiki* (Leningrad: Knizhnye novinki, 1927), 1–3; 73–76; Dominic Lieven, *Nicholas II: Twilight of the Empire* (New York: St Martin's Griffin, 1993), 73–76.

56. BAR, A. A. Spasskii, *Vospominaniia*, vol. 4, 356–60.

57. Anan'ich and Ganelin, 40–89 *passim* and Kniaz' Meshcherskii, *Vospominaniia* (Moscow: Zakharov, 2001), 643–46 and 656–60.

58. Meshcherskii, 643–44.

59. BAR Witte: 'Prisiaga brat'ev 2-go otdela'; SZ III: 257, 259 and generally 245–59 ['O soobshchestve "Sviatoi druzhiny" i moem uchastii v nem']; Sidney Harcave, *Count Sergei Witte and the Twilight of Imperial Russia: A Biography*: 25–28.

60. SZ III: 260–66 ['O docheri pervoi zheny Soni i ee muzhe Meringe'].

61. Louise McReynolds (tr. and ed.), 'Introduction', in *The Wrath of Dionysus: A Novel by Evdokia Nagrodskaia* (Bloomington, Ind.: Indiana University Press, 1997).

62. SZ III: 266–70 ['O Drentel'ne, gen. adiut'].

63. SZ III: 271, 270–74 ['O gen.-gub. Chertkove i ego zhene'].

64. Gay, *Schnitzler's Century*, esp. chs. 3, 9.

65. SZ III: 308–16 ['O Velikoi Kniagine Aleksandre Petrovne i Velik. Kniaziakh Petre Nikolaeviche i Nikolae Nikolaeviche']; see also 316–24.

66. BE 20 411.

67. SZ, III: 327.

68. SZ, III: 324–330 ['O Pikhno, D.I.'].

69. Vospominaniia V. I. Kovalevskogo, *Russkoe proshloe: Istoriko-dokumental'noi al'manakh* 1991 (no. 2), 64–65.

70. Ibid., 7–8.

71. SZ IV: 422–29 ['O V.I. Kovalevskom'].

72. SZ IV: 429.

73. SZ III, 275–76 ['O naznachenii menia upravlaiushchim Iugo-Zapadnymi dorogami'].

74. Kovalevskii, 59.

75. SZ III: 276–77.

76. Kovalevskii, 65.

77. SZ III: 277–79 ['O Vyshnegradskom, Ob A. I Putilove, O Barke'].

78. SZ III, 279–295 ['O podbore sotrudnikov vo vremia upravleniia Iu.Z. zh. d.'].

79. Ibid., 294–95.

80. SZ IV: 375.

81. RGIA f. 1622, op. 1, ed. khr. 1020, ll. 19–21 (S. Vitte to Aleksander Sprido-novich, Kiev, 24 XII 1880 g.g.; Vitte, 'Manufakturnoe krepostnichestvo', *Rus'* 3 (1885): 18–19; G. E. Afanas'ev, 'K konchine grafa S. Iu. Vitte, op. cit., 97–100; Anan'ich and Ganelin, chs. 2–3; RGIA f. 560 (Obshchaia kantseliariia ministra), 1893–1903, *passim*; Wcislo, *Reforming Rural Russia*, ch. 4.

82. SZ IV: 335–36 ['Ob osnovanii gazety 'Kievskoe slovo' i polemiki s Pikhno i o knigi "Printsipy zh.d. tarifov" '].

83. RGIA f. 560 (Obshchaia kantseliariia ministra), 1893–1903, *passim*; Wcislo, *Reforming Rural Russia*, ch. 5.

84. SZ, IV:, 332 ['O N.Kh. Bunge'] and 349 ['O rektore universiteta Renne-kampfe']. Bunge preceded Vyshnegradsky and Witte as Minister of Finances; his influence on the latter's program has been a subject of repeated speculation among economic historians. BAR Witte, Box 9, Delo 6 ['Zapiska, naidennaia v bumagakh N. Kh. Bunge'] is Bunge's undated and unmarked memorandum, preserved in Witte's personal papers, surveying imperial financial policy. See Stepanov, *N. Kh. Bunge*.b, op. cit., chs. 3–4 and Bunge, N.Kh. *The Years 1881–1894 in Russia: A Memorandum*, op. cit.

85. SZ IV: 337.

86. SZ IV: 349.

87. RGIA f. 1622, op. 1, d. 490–675 (undated letters of S.Iu. Witte to M. I. Witte), *passim*; also ZGV, *passim*.

88. SZ IV: 342–45 ['O professore Meringe i ego syne'].

89. B. V. Anan'ich, *Bankirskie doma v Rossii*, 1860–1914 (Leningrad: Nauka, 1991), 41, 46, 140, 146.

90. SZ IV: 394–6 ['O Brodskom, ego detiakh i brate']; Baryshnikov, op. cit, 57; Hamm, *Kiev*, op. cit., ch. 5.

91. SZ IV: 396–8 [O Pototskom i ego synoviakh]; BE 15, 512; Hamm, ch. 3.
92. Anan'ich, *Bankirskie doma*, 12–19.
93. SZ IV: 398–401 ['O Polotsove'].
94. SZ VII: 769–816 [O kharaktere i deiatel'nosti Imperatora Aleksandra III].
95. SZ VII: 769–76 [18 April 1911]; also Velikii kniaz' Aleksandr Mikhailovich, *Kniga vospominanii* (Moscow: Sovremennik, 1991), 41–52; Wortman, *Scenarios of Power*, vol. 2, chs. 5–6; Wcislo, *Reforming Rural Russia*, chs. 2–3; S. Iu. Witte, *Samoderzhavie i zemstvo: Konsidentsial'naia zapiska Ministra finansov Stats-Sekretaria S. Iu. Vitte* (1899) (Stuttgart, 1901).
96. SZ IV: 351–81.
97. SZ IV: 351–54 ('O priezde Imperatora Aleksandra III v Kiev'].
98. SZ IV: 355 [24 fev. 1911].
99. SZ IV: 363 ['O poezdke Imperatora Aleksandra III na manevry v Breste i Belostoke i svidanii s Imp. Vil'gelmom v bytnost' poslednogo naslednikom'].
100. Ibid., 360–64.
101. SZ, IV: 376–81 [O katastrofe Imperatorskogo poezdy v Borkakh i moem uchastii ekspertom v voprose o prichinakh katastrofy]; Wortman, *Scenarios of Power* II, 289–96; Meshcherskii, *Vospominaniia*, ch. L [1888. Krushenie tsarskogo poezda]; RGIA f. 239, op. 1 [Komitet po sooruzheniiu Khrama i Chasovni na meste sobytiia 17 oktiabria 1888 g.].
102. f. 268, op. 6, d. 1, ll. 27–28, 17 Nov. 1889.
103. A. F. Koni, *Sergei Iul'evich Vitte: Otryvochnye vospominaniia* (Moscow: Izd-vo Pravo i Zhizn', 1925), 10–18.
104. SZ, IV: 365–376 [O proezdakh Imperatora Aleksandra III po Iugo Zap. Zh. D. v kontse 80-kh godov].
105. SZ, IV: 369–70.
106. SZ, IV: 371–73.
107. SZ IV: 383–87 ['O moem naznachenii direktorom Departamena zh-d del'] and SZ IV: 418–21 [Ob uporiadochenii tarifnogo dela na russkikh zhel. dorogakh i moem uchastii v nem].
108. SZ IV: 388–89.
109. SZ IX: 1004–21 [Bolezn' i konchina IMPERATOPRA ALEKSANDRA III].
110. Naryshkina-Vitte, *Zapiski devochki*, 61.
111. SZ IX: 1020 [Moe predstavlenie Imp. Marii Fedorovne].
112. SZ VII: 776–77 [O kharaktere i deiatel'nosti Imperatora voobshche].
113. Ibid., 777–78.

CHAPTER 4: ST PETERSBURG, THE EMPIRE OF THE TSARS, AND IMPERIAL HORIZONS, 1889–1903

1. V. P. Lopukhin, 'Zapiski b. direktora departamenta ministerstva innostrannykh del, 1894–1917' OR RNL, f. 1000, op. 1, ed. khr. 765, l.2.
2. SZ VI: 579 [O kniagine Radzivill].

3. RGIA f. 560, op. 26, d. 66 [Konspekt programmy i obzora deiatel'nosti Ministerstva Finansov v 1892 g. i posleduiushchikh godakh predstavleno ministru finansov v 1896].

4. RGIA f. 1622, op. 1,d. 711, 'VD ministra po poeszdke na dal'nii vostok', f. 1622, op. 1, d. 711, ll. 1–2.

5. SZ VI: 588 ['O postroike Sibirskoi zheleznoi dorogi i moem uchastii v nei'].

6. Shilov, *Gosudarstvennye deiateli* (Vitte: 122–3).

7. f. 268 [DZhDD, MF], op. 3 (1880–1920), op. 4 (1889–1921), and 6 (1889–1919).

8. David Schimmelpenninck van der Oye, *Toward the Rising Sun: Russian Ideologies of Empire and the Path to War with Japan* (DeKalb, Ill.: Northern Illinois University Press, 2001); Mark Bassin, *Imperial Visions: Nationalist Imagination and Geographical Expansion in the Russian Far East, 1840–1865* (Cambridge, UK; New York: Cambridge University Press, 1999).

9. BAR Witte, Box 5 (Vosniknovenie...); f. 560, op. 27, d. 46 (10 Dec. 1892, 'Istoriia sooruzheniia Velikoi Sibirskoi zheleznoi dorogi'), and f. 560, op. 27 General Chancellory, Siberian Desk (1874–1913), *passim*; Steven G. Marks, *Road to Power: The Trans-Siberian Railroad and the Colonization of Asian Russia, 1850–1917* (Ithaca, NY: Cornell, 1991).

10. Wcislo, *Reforming Rural Russia*, chs. 3–4 and F. Vchislo, 'Vitte, samoderzhavie i imperiia: mechty kontsa XIX veka,' *Rossiia XXI: Obshchestvenno-politicheskii i nauchnyi zhurnal*, vol. 4 (Moscow: July-August 2001): 144–161.

11. Wcislo, *Reforming Rural Russia*, ch. 4. and 'Rereading Old Texts: Sergei Witte and the Industrialization of Russia', in McCaffrey, Susan P and Michael Melancon (eds.), *Russia in the European Context 1789–1914: A Member of the Family* (New York: Palgrave MacMillan, 2005), 71–84; RGIA f. 560, op. 26, f. 244, ll. 244–256 ['Kratkii istoricheskii ocherk stoletii deiatel'nosti Ministerstva Finansov. 1802–1902']; Sergei Witte, *Konspekt lektsii o narodnom i gosudarstvennom khoziastva* (St Petersburg, 1912).

12. For example, Anan'ich and Diakin, *Krizis samoderzhaviia v Rossii 1895–1917*, op. cit., ch. 1 and P. P. Maslov, 'Razvitie zemledeliia i polozhenie krest'ian do nachala XX veka', Martov, et al, *Obshchestvennoe dvizhenie*,op. cit., vol. 1, 1–38. An alternative view begins with Steven L. Hoch, 'On Good Numbers and Bad: Malthus, Population Trends and Peasant Standard of Living in Late Imperial Russia', *Slavic Review*, Vol. 53, No. 1 (Spring, 1994), 41–75 and 'The Banking Crisis, Peasant Reform, and Economic Development in Russia, 1857–1861', *The American Historical Review*, Vol. 96, No. 3 (Jun., 1991), 795–820; Elvira Wilbur, 'Was Russian Peasant Agriculture Really That Impoverished? New Evidence from a Case Study from the "Impoverished Center", at the End of the Nineteenth Century,' *Journal of Economic History*, vol. 43, no. 1 (March 1983), 137–44; James Y. Simms, Jr., The Crisis in Russian Agriculture at the End of the Nineteenth Century: A Different View', *Slavic Review*, Vol. 36, No. 3 (Sep., 1977), 377–98.

13. Theodore H. Von Laue, *Sergei Witte and the Industrialization of Russia* (New York: Studies of the Russian Institute, Columbia University and Columbia University Press, 1963); Anan'ich and Ganelin, *vitte*, ch. 2; Alexander Gerschenkron, *Economic Backwardness in Historical Perspective. A Book of Essays* (Cambridge: Belknap Press of Harvard University Press, 1962).

14. See especially Paul R. Gregory, *Before Command: An Economic History of Russia from Emancipation to the First Five-Year Plan* (Princeton, 1994), 7–31; Arcadius Kahan, edited by Roger Weiss. *Russian Economic History: The Nineteenth Century* (Chicago: University of Chicago Press, 1989); Peter Gatrell, *The Tsarist Economy, 1850–1917* (New York: St Martin's Press, 1986).

15. SZ X: 1241 [O vvedenii zolotoi valiuty v Rossii].

16. f. 563, op. 2, d. 355. Komitet finansov. Delo ob ispravlenii denezhnogo obrashcheniia (19, 27, 28 March and 12 April 1896). Zhurnal, ll. 45–54 ob.

17. Fedor Dostoevsky, *White Nights* (1848) and Andrei Bely, *Petersburg* (1916).

18. f. 40, op. 1, d. 44 (1892), l. 150 [30 Aug. 1892, 'Acting Minister of Finances Sergei Witte'].

19. Romanov, op. cit., 55.

20. BAR Box 1, Ermolov, A. S. to S.Iu. Vitte, 27 March 1893.

21. V. P. Lopukhin. Zapiski, op. cit., l. 12.

22. BAR Box 1, V. I. Kovalevskii–S.Iu. Vitte, 31 May 1910.

23. Dominic Lieven, *Russia's Rulers Under the Old Regime* (New Haven: Yale University Press, 1989).

24. Lotman, *Besedy* ['Liudi i chiny'], 18–45.

25. f. 1622, op. 1, d. 989, ll. 1–33.

26. f. 560, op. 38, d. 174, ll. 54–56 [Ob assignovanii 230,000 rublei dlia prisposobleniia fligelia Nikolaevskogo Dvortsa v S. Peterburge pod pomeshchenii De-ov Okladnykh Sborov, Zh-D Del, Redaktsii Vestnik Finansov i Arkhiv]; f. 560, op. 38, d. 172 and 173 (VD ministra za 1892 g., 1893 g], *passim*.

27. L. E. Shepelev in Vospominaniii V. I. Kovalevskogo, *Russkoe proshloe: Istoriko-dokumental'noi al'manakh* 1991 (no. 2), 18.

28. f. 1622, op. 1, f. 490–675 [S.Iu. Witte to M.I. Witte, correspondence].

29. f. 268, op. 6, d. 1 [VDZ ministra po tarifnomu otdelu za 1889] *passim*; f. 268, op. 4, dd. 9–10, DZhDD (April–Dec. 1889); f. 560, op. 22, d. 181, ll. 17–18 (Novoe vremia, 18930); f. 560, op. 38, d. 174, ll. 5–6 ob [O vydache byshemu izdateliu Birzhevykh Vedomostei Trubnikov 5000 R, 1894] and ll. 30–31 [Russkii Vestnik and Fedor Berg, 1894]; f. 1622, op. 1, d. 404, ll. 404, 406, 405 (F. Gravengof to S. Iu. Witte, 1893, 94; Moskovskie vedomosti).

30. Rieber, 'The Sedimentary Society', op. cit.

31. SZ VI: 569–579 (O general-adiutant Cherevin; O kniagine Radzivill).

32. BAR Bark, Petr L'vovich, Box 1 Memoirs, ch. 3, 38.

33. Wortman, *Scenarios of Power: Myth and Ceremony in Russian Monarchy*, op. cit.; A.Ia. Avrekh, *Tsarizm i tret'ei'iiun'skaia sistema* (Moskva, Nauka, 1966); Benedict Anderson, *Imagined Communities*, 18–22.

34. f. 560, op. 38, d. 173 [VD ministra, 1893], *passim*; f. 1622, op. 1, correspondence with M. I. Witte, *passim*.
35. SZ XV: 1989 ['Ob otstavke Durnovo i osobykh milostiakh Gosudaria k nemu'].
36. f. 1622, op. 1, ed. khr. 294, ll. 1–9 [Iz arkhiva Gr. S. Iu. Vitte. Libava ili Murman. Doklad po voprosu o voennom porte, June 1894]; SZ VIII: 915–41 [O moei poezdke na krainii sever] and X: 1232 [Moia poezdka po vostochnym guberniiam]; f. 560, op. 38, d. 177, ll. 59–61 [Ob okazanii denezhnogo posobiia khudozhniku Borisovu dlia soversheniia im poezdki na Dal'nem Severe']; f. 1622, op. 1, d. 711 [VD ministra po poezdke na dal'nyi vostok].
37. f. 1622, op. 1, d. 989, ll. 26–28 (Dec. 1890, scholarship at Novorossiisk University); f. 560, op. 38, d. 183, ll. 72 i ob [VD, 1903, library of St Petersburg Technological University]; SZ IX: 969–73 [O tserkovno prikhodskikh uchilishchakh]; f. 40, op. 1, d. 45, ll. 109–12 [VD ministra o podvedomstvennosti kommerchiskikh uchilishch, 1893], op. 1, d. 52 [VD ministra ob uchrezhdenii Tenishevskogo Instituta promyshlennykh znanii v S. Peterburge, 1900]; f. 560, op. 38, d. 173 [O nagrazhdenii t.s. Stasova, 1893]; f. 560, op. 26, d. 187 [O prazdnovanii stoletiia so dnia rozhdeniia A.S. Pushkina]; Koni, *Otryvochnye vospominanii*, 20–24.
38. BAR Witte, Box 10, delo 11 [Reskripty].
39. Wcislo, *Reforming Rural Russia*, ch. 4.
40. f. 268, op. 3, d. 16, ll. 346–369 [Zapiska po voprosu o finansovo-ekonomicheskom polozhenii Turkestanskogo kraia]; f. 40, op. 1, d. 45, ll. 76–77 (State Bank branch in Teheran, July 1893); f. 560, op. 22, d. 181, 12. Feb. 1893–14 Dec. 1896, correspondence. ll. 94–124.
41. SZ XII:1494–98 [O mirnoi konferentsii v Gaage]; Bernstein, *With Master Minds*, 44–49.
42. SZ VIII: 852–69 [O D.S. Sipiagin i V. K. Pleve, m-rakh vnut. Del].
43. f. 40, op. 1, d. 48, ll. 1–3 ['O sozyve v 1896 g. Torgovo-Promyshlennyi S'ezd']; f. 560, op. 27, d. 102 [Ob uchastii kommissii Sibirskoi zh. D. v Parizhskoi Vystavke 1900 g]; f. 560, op.26, d.253–54 [O prazdnovenii stoletnogo iubeleia MF].
44. SZ V: 558–565 [O vtoroi zhenitbe]; also S. M. Propper, 'Chto ne voshlo v gazemu. Vospominaniia glavnogo redaktora "Birzhevykh vedomostei"', in Anan'ich and Ganelin, 403–409.
45. SZ V: 559.
46. SZ V: 559–62.
47. SZ V: 562–65.
48. G. E. Afanasiev, 'K biografii gr. S.Iu. Vitte,' *Vol'ny* 1915 (No.6 June),115; Vonliarliarskii, *Moi vospominaniia*, 173.
49. f. 1622, op. 1, ed. khr. 961, l. 35 [Ukaz pravitel'stvuiushchemu senatu, 10 July 1896].
50. f.1622, op. 1 d. 978 [pis'ma vnuka k Vitte v kol. 22].

51. f. 1622, op. 1, d. 492–571 *passim*.

52. f. 560, op. 38, d. 172 (VD Vyshnegradskogo, 28 Feb 1892); f. 1622, op. 1, d. 402, ll. 1–2 [Vyshnegradskii to Witte, n.d. [∼1887]; f. 268 [DZhDD MF]; f. 560, op. 22, d. 171 [11 July–4 Oct. 1888: 'Dokladnye zapiski m-ra fin-ov I. A. Vyshnegradskogo Aleksandru III o padenii veksel'nogo i kreditnogo kursov, ob ozhidaemom urozhae ozimykh i iarovykh khlebov i o padenii tsen na khleb na russkom i zagranichnykh rynkakh']; SZ IV: 413–21 (3 March 1912) [Ob uporiadochenii tarifnogo dela na russkikh zhel. dorogakh i moem uchastii v nem].

53. f. 560, op. 22, d. 168, ll. 32–36ob [VD ministra ob umenshenii defitsita po rospisi 1892 goda].

54. f. 560, op. 38, d. 173 [O meropriiatiiakh po vvedeniiu kazennoi prodazhe vina v 4-x vostochnykh guberniiakh, June 1893].

55. f. 560, op. 22, d. 176 [Zapiska tov. Ministra F.G. Ternera o sostoianiia ekonomiki Rossii v 1892 g., Sept. 1892], ll. 1–16.

56. Yanni Kotsonis, '"Face-to-Face": The State, the Individual, and the Citizen in Russian Taxation, 1863–1917,' *Slavic Review*, Vol. 63, No. 2 (Summer, 2004), 221–46.

57. f. 560, op. 27, d. 46, Istoriia sooruzheniia Velikoi Sibirskoi zheleznoi dorogi.

58. Obshchaia kantseliariia ministra finansov, Sibirskii stol. f. 560 (1874–1913), inventarnaia opis' No. 27, Predislovie.

59. f. 268 (DZhDD, MF), op. 3, d. 193 (1888–1891), d. 194 (1891), d. 195 (1892) [O rasshirenii russkoi zh-d-noi seti], d. 516–19 (Northern Railroad, 1894–1907), d 665–669 (Black Sea Railroad, 1898–1906), d. 606–611 (Central Asia).

60. f. 560, op. 27, d. 46 (Feb. 1893); f. 268, op. 4, d. 115 (Ob obshchem tarife vsei seti rossiiskikh zheleznykh dorog); f. 268, op. 6, d. 6, ll.12–13 ob (Riazhsk-Morshansk, Sept. 1892), 16–18 (Orenburg, Nov. 1892) and d. 7, ll. 5–6 ob (Baltic, Feb. 1893), ll. 13–14 (Donetsk, May 1893), ll. 39–45 (Riga-Dvinsk, Dvinsk-Vitebsk, Orel-Vitebsk, Oct. 1893), ll. 47–56 (StP-Moscow, StP-Warsaw, Moscow-Nizhnii-Novgorod, Oct. 1893), and *passim*.

61. f. 40, op. 1, d. 44 (1892) and d. 45 (1893) Utverzhdennye vsepod. doklady m-ra f-ov po D-y TiM za 1892 g. and 1893 g., *passim*.

62. SZ VIII (26 April 1911): 884–900 [O pervom Torgovom dogovore s Germa-niiei i moem uchastii v vedenii peregovorov po nemu]; f. 560, op. 22, d. 181, ll: 17–18; f. 40, op. 1, d. 44 (1892) ll. 92–103 ob (Zhurnal o torgovom sblizheniem mezhdu Rossiei i Germaniei (May 1892); VD ministra po voprosu o torgovom soglashenii s Germaniei, 9 Oct. 1892, ll. 158–61. Korelin and Stepanov, *S.Iu. Vitte—finansist, politik, diplomat* [Moscow: Terra, 1998], 29–31.

63. SZ VIII: 900–902 [O mnenii Bismarka obo mne].

64. Utverzhdennye vsepod. doklady m-ra f-ov po D-y Torgovli i manufaktury za 1892 g. and 1893 g., *passim*.

65. Ibid, 23 June 1893, ll. 80–82 [Ob ustroistve v 1896 g. Vserossiiskoi Promysh-lennoi Vystavki v Nizhnem Novgorode].

66. Martov et al., *Obshchestvennoe dvizhenie*, op. cit., especially A. Ermanskii, 'Krupnaia burzhuaziia do 1905 goda,' vol. 1, 313–48.

67. Wcislo, *Reforming Rural Russia*, 127.

68. f. 560, op. 26, d. 66 'Konspekt programmy i obzora deiatel'nosti Ministerstva finansov v 1892 g i v posleduiushchikh godakh predstavlen ministru finansov v 1896.'

69. Ibid., ll. 1–2 ob.

70. Ibid., ll. 2 ob–5 ob.

71. Ibid., ll. 4–40b. Korelin and Stepanov, op. cit., 33–41.

72. Konspekt, ll. 50b–60b.

73. Ibid., ll. 6 ob–8; f. 40, op. 1, d. 44, ll. 92–103 ob and 158–61 (Germany), ll. 110–11 ob (Spain), ll. 153–57 ob (Serbia), ll. 172–74 ob (Egypt), d. 52, ll. 199–205 (USA) and f. 40, op. 1, *passim*.

74. Korelin and Stepanov, 31.

75. Konspekt, ll. 8–9.

76. Ibid., ll. 9–10.

77. Ibid., ll. 100b–11.

78. Ibid., ll. 110b–40b.

79. Ibid., ll. 14 ob–16.

80. Ibid., ll. 16–17.

81. Ibid., ll. 17–190b.

82. Anton Chekhov, *The Cherry Orchard* (1903).

83. Ibid., ll.200b–220b. Wcislo, *Reforming Rural Russia*, chs. 3–4.

84. Wcislo, *Reforming Rural Russia*, ch. 4 and Yanni Kotsonis. *Making Peasants Backward; Agricultural Cooperatives and the Agrarian Question in Russia, 1861–1914* (New York: St Martin's Press, 1999).

85. Konspekt, ll.190b–200b.

86. Ibid., l. 20 ob.

87. f.560, op. 38, d. 17 [O meropriiatiiakh po vvedeniiu kazennoi prodazhe vina v 4-x vostochnykh guberniiakh, vsepod. doklad, June 1893; SZ X: 1222–29.

88. Konspekt, ll. 23–25.

89. Ibid., ll.25–35; Yanni Kotsonis, '"Face-to-Face": The State, the Individual, and the Citizen in Russian Taxation, 1863–1917', *Slavic Review*, Vol. 63, No. 2 (Summer, 2004), 221–46; P. N. Miliukov, *Gosudarstvennoe khoziastvo Rossii v pervoi chetverti XVIII veka i reforma Petra Velikogo* (St Petersburg, 1892).

90. Konspekt, l. 25–25 ob.

91. Ibid., ll. 25 ob–35.

92. f. 560, op. 22, d. 201 ['Zapiska v.k. Al. Mikh. o neobkhodimosti usilenii russkogo flota na Tikhom okeane].

93. Konspekt, ll. 35–360b.

94. Theodore Von Laue, 'A Secret Memorandum of Sergei Witte on the Indus-
trialization of Imperial Russia', *The Journal of Modern History*, Vol. 26, No. 1
(Mar., 1954), 60–74 ['Report of the Minister of Finance to His Majesty on the
Necessity of Formulating and Thereafter Steadfastly Adhering to a Definite
Program of a Commercial and Industrial Policy of the Empire, March 1899'
(Library of Congress, 1931) and Wcislo, 'Rereading Old Texts', op. cit.

95. *Dnevniki Imperatora Nikolaia II* (K. F. Shatsillo (ed.). [TsGAOR SSSR and
Orbita: Moscow, 1991], 20/X/1894, 43. Hereafter *Dnevniki*.

96. SZ IX: 1004–1020 ['Bolezn' i konchina IMPERATORA ALEKSANDRA
III'].

97. MF Kantseliariia. Isprashivaemoe Vysochaichaishe soizvolenie na vnesenie v
Gosudarstvennyi Sovet predstavlenii. 19 October 1894. Livadia, ll. 68–69 ob.
and vsepod. doklady, ll. 57–60 ob. (6 Sept 1894), ll. 62–67 (30 Sept. 1894), ll.
66–67 (6 October 1894), and ll. 70–72 (nd, 20 October 1894).

98. V. N. Lamzdorf, *Dnevnik, 1894–1896* [Moscow: Mezhdunarodnye otnosheniia, 1991], 75–76.

99. SZ IX: 1017–19 [Mnenie o novom Imperatore moe, I. N. Durnovo, i
K.P. Pobedonostsev].

100. S. D. Sheremetev, *Memuary Grafa S. D. Sheremeteva*, 612 and 414–620 *passim*.

101. V. I. Gurko, *Cherty i siluety proshlogo* [Moscow: Novoe literaturnoe obozrenie, 2000], 28–29.

102. Lieven, Nicholas II, 29–30.

103. S. S. Oldenburg, *Last Tsar*, vol. 1, 35–38.

104. SZ IX: 1036 [O postornonnykh vliianiiakh na Imperatora Nikolaia II v
pervye gody tsarstvovanii].

105. SZ X: 1241–42 [Predubezhdenie protiv reformy v publike i u gosudarstvennykh deiatelei].

106. SZ IX: 1071–72 [O gen. Gurko, varshavskii general-gubernator i ego syno-
viakh].

107. SZ XI: 1295–97 [Ob otstavke ministra dvora gr. Vorontsova-Dashkova i
prichinakh k nei].

108. Lieven, 44–58.

109. Mark D. Steinberg and Vladimir M. Khrustalëv, *The Fall of the Romanovs:
Political Dreams and Personal Struggles in a Time of Revolution* (Russian docu-
ments translated by Elizabeth Tucker) (New Haven, Conn.: Yale University
Press, 1995); Edvard Radzinsky, *The Last Tsar: The Life and Death of Nicholas II*
(New York: Doubleday, 1992); Joseph T. Fuhrmann (ed.), *The Complete
Wartime Correspondence of Tsar Nicholas II and the Empress Alexandra: April 1914
– March 1917* (Westport, Conn.: Greenwood Press, 1999).

110. f. 560, op. 38, d. 178, ll. 84–84 ob [VD, 1898 g.]

111. SZ IX: 1013–14 [Privezenie tela c Nikolaevskogo vokz. v Petropavloskii
sobor].

112. ZGV: 74–75/44–5 (Hamburg, June 1907) and 188–189/112 ob. [Biarritz, Sept. 1907].

113. SZ VI: 582–88 [O postroike Sibirskoi zheleznoi dorogi i moem uchastii v nei].

114. SZ VIII, 942–43, 948–49 [O puteshestvii Imperatora Nikolaia II v bytnost' naslednikom na D. Vostok i ego vlechenie k nemu i uchastii v Komitet Sibirskoi zh.d] and Lieven, 37–39.

115. f. 560, op. 27, d. 122, ll.1–2 ob and 83 ob. [Zhurnal komiteta TSRR].

116. f. 560, op. 27, d. 46, ll. 224–25 and BAR, Box 5, Vozniknovenie Russko-iaponskoi Voiny, t. 1, ch. 1.

117. f. 560, op. 27, d. 46, ll. 118ff. and ll. 226–27 [Po voprosu ob utverzhdenie ustava Obshchestva KVZhD].

118. Schimmelpenninck, *Toward the Rising Sun*, op. cit., ch. 3, and B. A. Romanov, *Rossiia i Manchzhurii (1892–1906). Ocherki po istorii vneshnei politiki samoderzhaviia v epoke imperializma.* [Leningrad: Vestnik Leningrads-kogo gosudarstvennogo universiteta, 1928].

119. f. 560, op. 43, d. 55, l. 3 and *passim* [O russko-kitaiskom banke]; SZ X: 1148–53 and 1153–54 [O garantii Rossiei Kitaiskogo zaima and O Russko-Kitaiskom Banke].

120. Anan'ich and Ganelin, 79.

121. BAR P.L. Bark, Memoirs, ch. 4, 1–3.

122. f. 560, op. 27, d. 46, ll. 118 ff. [MF Chancellory, 11 Nov 1896, Ustav Obshchestvo KVZhD].

123. SZ X: 1156–59 [O priezde Li-Khun-Chan predstavitelem na Koronatsiiu].

124. SZ X: 1163–71 [O priezde Li-khun-chana v Peterburg a vedenie s nim peregovorov o provedenii Sibirskoi zh. d. cherez Manchzhuriiu].

125. f. 560, op. 27, d. 46, ll. 118 ff. [MF Chancellory, 11 Nov 1896, Ustava Obshchestvo KVZhD] and SZ X: 1155–1191 *passim*.

126. SZ IX: 1045–46 [O kharaktere i namereniiakh Gosudaria v pervye gody tsarstvovaniia].

127. SZ X: 1161. See also David M. McDonald, *United Government and Foreign Policy in Russia, 1900–1914* (Cambridge, Mass.: Harvard University Press, 1992) and Andrew Verner, *The Crisis of Russian Autocracy: Nicholas II and the 1905 Revolution* (Princeton, NJ: Princeton University Press, 1990).

128. SZ XI: 1304 [Ob ustanovlenie novogo poriadka isprosheniia kreditov po Min-u IMPERATORSKOGO Dvora i moem razgovore ob etom s Gosudaria].

129. f. 560, op. 22, d. 201, l.570b, 55 ob. [Zapiski vel. Kn. Aleksandra Mikhailo-vicha o neobkhodimosti usilenii russkogo flota na Tikhom okeane i otzyv na nee m-ra fin. S. Iu. Vitte].

130. BAR Witte, Box 1, Nicholas II to Witte, 24 Feb. 1898.

131. SZ XI: 1346–66 *passim* [O zaniatii Germaniei kitaiskogo porta Tsziao-Tszhou; Zasedanie pod predsedatel'stvom Gosudaria po povodu predlozheniiu Mur-av'eva o zaniatii Rossiei Port-Artura; Moi vozrazheniia protiv zaniatiia P. Artura i Da-lian-van; Reshenie Gosudaria zaniait' P.Artura i Da-lian-van];

f. 560, op. 38, d. 178 [Vsepod. doklady, 1898]: ll. 16–19 (appt of commercial agent in Tokyo, 6 March), ll. 23 i ob (construction of branch line, 13 March), ll. 24 i ob (Port Arthur concession, March 1898) and 31 (CER draft treaty, 8 May).

132. Shilov, 123.

133. *New York Times,* July 1899, *passim.*

134. f. 560, op. 27, d. 102, ll. 18–25, op. cit.; SZ XIII: 1564–1570 [Moia poezdka v Parizh na vystavku i zaezd v Konpengagen].

135. f. 560, op. 38, d. 180 [VD ministra, 1900), ll. 16, 36, 59.

136. Ibid., ll. 88–159, *passim.*

137. f. 560, op.38, d.181 [VD ministra za 1901], ll. 1–2 [Russian military construction in Manchuria,] 57 (Japanese ambassador protest in Beijing, February), 70–72 (threatened military occupation, March), ll. 125–29 (southern Manchurian railroad) and f. 560, op. 43, d. 57 [Perepiska m-ra f-ov S. Iu. Vitte s voennym ministrom i nachal'nikom Iuzhnogo otdeleniia o-va KVZhD o bokserskom dvizhenii i Kitai]; SZ XI: 1394–1419 [Bokserskoe vozstanie i okkupatsiia Manchzhurii Rossiei]. Also, McDonald, *United Government,* ch. 1.

138. f. 560, op. 38, d. 181, ll. 110–20 ob, 6 July 1901 [Ob okonchanie trudov kommissii dlia priniatiia mer k obezpecheniiu perevozki voisk na Dal'nyi Vostok].

139. f. 40 op. 1, d. 52, ll. 208 i ob. ('O dopushchenii nekotorykh lits k uchastiiu v uchrezhdenii 'Vostochno-Aziatskoi promyshlennaia kompaniia'); f. 560, op. 38, d. 182 and 183 (Manchurian Mining Co., 1902–03); f. 560, op. 29, d. 233 [Finansovo-ekonomicheskoe polozhenie Iaponii v 1893–1903 g]; f. 560, op. 26 d. 182, ll. 141–45 ob (commercial and economic significance of Dal'nyi, Aug. 1902).

140. f. 560, op. 38, d. 182, l. 138 (9 Aug. 1902).

141. f.560, op. 38, d. 182, l. 196 (VD, 7 Sept. 1902) 1902; f. 1622, op. 1, d. 711 [VD po poezdke na dal'nyi vostok]; f. 560, op. 29, d.243 [Perepiska poslannika v Tokio otnositel'no poezdke Vitte, Sept. 1902]; SZXIII: 1618–22 [Moia poezdka na Dal'nyi Vostok i moi doklad o poezdke].

142. BAR Witte, Box 10, Dela, No. 23, No-1-3 ['Neposredstvennaia Bezobrazovshchina']. McDonald, *United Government,* op. cit.; and ZGV, 6–95/1–58 [Frankfurt and Hamburg, June 1907].

143. Wcislo, *Reforming Rural Russia,* 135–165; S. Iu. Witte, *Samoderzhavie i zemstvo* (1899), op. cit.; BAR Witte Box 1, Correspondence N–P: 'Po povodu zemskoi zapiski' [letter of Aleksei Obolenskii to Witte, 14 Oct. 1899]; 'Otryvki iz vospominanii D. N. Liubimova, 1902–1904 gg,' *Istoricheskii arkhiv* no. 6 (1982); and Ryszard Kapuscinski, *The Emperor: Downfall of An Autocrat,* translated from the Polish by William R. Brand and Katarzyna Mroczkowska-Brand [San Diego: Harcourt Brace Jovanovich, 1983].

144. McDonald, *United Government*, chs. 1–3; ZGV, 6–95/1–58 [Frankfurt and Hamburg, June 1907]; SZ XIII: 1639–63 [Sobytiia, predshestvovavshie moemu ukhodu s posta M-ra Finansov].

145. A. F. Koni, *Otryvochnye vospominaniia*, op. cit., 27–28.

146. f. 1622 op. 1 d. 711 [VD ministra po poezdke na dal'nyi vostok].

147. SZ XIII: 1660–1663 [O prichinakh, posluzhivshikh prichinoi, pri edinstve vzgliadov, k moemu ukhodu s posta M-ra Finansov i prodolzhenie gr. Lamzdorfom upravleniia M-om Inostrannykh Del].

CHAPTER 5: MEMORIES OF REVOLUTIONARY RUSSIA, 1903–1912

1. SZ XIV: 1866.

2. ZGV: 321/216 [Sept. 1909, Biarritz].

3. ZGV: 201–3/120 ob–121 [Biarritz, Sept. 1907].

4. ZGV: 313/206 ob [September 1909, Biarritz].

5. ZGV: 487–7 [August 1912].

6. SZ XV: 1999–2000 14 February 1912 [O Vysochaishe vykhode k predstaviteliam G. Dumy i Soveta v Zimnem Dvortse 27 Aprelia 1906].

7. Abraham Ascher, *The Revolution of 1905*, 2 vols (Stanford, Calif.: Stanford University Press, 1988–1992); L. Martov, P. Maslov, A. Potresov (eds.), *Obshchestvennoe dvizhenie v Rossii v nachale XX-go veka*; Orlando Figes, *A People's Tragedy; A History of the Russian Revolution*, chs. 1–6; Anan'ich and Ganelin, 204–349; Jonathan D. Smele and Anthony Heywood, *The Russian Revolution of 1905: Centenary Perspectives* (London: Routledge, 2005).

8. SZ XV: 1998–2021.

9. SZ XV: 2015–21 [O poseshchenii Ekslebena, Vishi, i Gomburga; okhrana menia germanskoi politsiei i prichine k etomu] and 2024–29 [O poluchenii ot kn. Andronnikov ob opasnosti dlia menia vosvrashcheniia v Rossiiu].

10. BAR Witte, Box 10, Delo No. 18, Proshenie ob uvolnenii s posta Pred. Soveta ['Proshenie ob uvol'nenii s posta Pred.Soveta'], letters of Frederiks to Witte, 17 July 1906; Witte to Frederiks, 22 July 1906; Witte to Frederiks, 2 Sept. 1906; Witte to Frederiks, 10 Sept. 1906; Frederiks to Witte, 10 Sept. 1906. Also SZ XV: 2021–29 [O poluchenii mnoiu pis'ma Bar. Frederiksa o zhelatel'nosti Gosudaria moego nevozrashcheniia v Rossiiu a dalneishei perepiske po etomu povodu].

11. BAR Witte Box 10, Proshenie, Witte to Fredericks, 2 Sept. 1906, op. cit.

12. SZ XV–XVII *passim*, n.g SZ XVII: 2336–37 [O zaiavlenii Stolypina, chto edinstvennyi vrag, kotorogo on boitsia—eto ia]; f. 1622, op. 1, d. 375, ll. 1–2 and 376, ll. 1–2 [Witte and Stolypin correspondence, Sept. 1908] and d. 377, ll. 1–2 [letter of Stolypin to Witte, 11 Feb. 1909]; Wcislo, *Reforming Rural Russia*, chs. 5–8; Peter Waldron, *Between Two Revolutions: Stolypin and the Politics of Renewal in Russia* (London: UCL, 1998); Abraham Ascher,

P. A. Stolypin: The Search for Stability in Late Imperial Russia (Stanford, Calif.: Stanford University Press, 2001); V. S. Diakin, *Byl li shans u Stolypina? Sbornik statei* (Sankt-Peterburg: 'LISS', 2002); M. N. Lukianov, *Rossiiskii konservatizm i reforma 1907–1914.* Perm: Iz-vo Permskogo universiteta, 2001.

13. ZGV: 212–13 and 228/129 zh and ob. [Petersburg Jan. 1908].

14. ZGV: 213–20/128a–29b ob. (Spravka ob manifeste 17-go oktiabria 1905 goda) [St Petersburg, Jan. 1908].

15. ZGV: 208/124ob–25 [Biarritz, September-November 1907].

16. ZGV, 5/156 [June-Nov. 1907, Abroad]; Wcislo, 'A Reinterpretation of the Witte Memoirs', op. cit.

17. SZ XIII: 1653–1655 [Poslednyi moi doklad Gosudariu po Min-vu Fin-ov i predlozhenie Ego Velichestva mne posta Pred. K-ta M-ov] and ZGV: 6–15/1–76–7/1 i ob. [Frankfurt, June 1907]; Anan'ich and Ganelin, 134 and in general 127–228.

18. SZ XIII (Feb. 1912): 1696–1714 [O sooruzhenii pamiatnika Imperatoru Aleksandru III v S-Peterburge i moem uchastii v etom dele] and generally 1683–1745.

19. ZGV: SZ XIII (Feb. 1912): 1696–1714 [O sooruzhenii pamiatnika Imperatoru Aleksandru III v S-Peterburge i moem uchastii v etom dele]; SZ XII: 1461–77 [Osoboe soveshchanie o nuzhdakh sel'sko-khoz. promyshlennosti]; and generally SZ XIII: 1683–1745.

20. ZGV: 31–53/14–28ob. Hamburg, June 1907 SZ XIV: 1753–65 [Ob usilenii revoliutsionnykh proiavlenii v sviazi s neudachami voiny] and SZ XIV (5 Feb. 1912): 1756–58 [O merakh prinimaemykh Pleve k podavleniiu revoliutsionnoi proiavlenii (Zubatovshchina, pogromy)]; Wcislo, *Reforming Rural Russia*, ch. 4; also f. 560, op. 22, d.1 89, ll. 85–92 ob [Soobrazheniia po voprosu ob izmeneniia i dopolneniia nekotorykh deistvuiushchikh pravil o evreiakh, March 1896]; ZGV: 118–19/65–66 ob. [Catleret, Aug. 1907].

21. This enormous literature begins with a still classic essay, Sir Isaiah Berlin, 'The Marvelous Decade', in Isaiah Berlin, edited by Henry Hardy and Aileen Kelly, *Russian Thinkers* (New York: Viking Press, 1978).

22. For example, Joseph Bradley, *Voluntary Associations in Tsarist Russia: Science, Patriotism, and Civil Society* [Cambridge, Mass.: Harvard University Press, 2009); Melissa Kirschke Stockdale, *Paul Miliukov*, op. cit.; Susan Heuman, *Kistiakovsky: The Struggle for National and Constitutional Rights in the Last Years of Tsarism* (Cambridge, MA: Harvard University Press, 1998); Robert D. Crews, *For Prophet and Tsar: Islam and Empire in Russia and Central Asia* (Cambridge, Mass.: Harvard University Press, 2006).

23. ZGV: 118–19/65–66 ob.; SZ XIV (5 Feb. 1912): 1756–58 [O merakh prinimaemykh Pleve k podavleniiu revoliutsionnoi proiavlenii (Zubatovshhina, pogromy)].

24. ZGV: 32–34/14–15 ob. (Hamburg, June 1907).

25. Anan'ich and Ganelin, 127–228.

26. SZ XIV (5 Feb 1912): 1747–50 [Razgovor mezhdu Kuropatkin i mnoi pered ot'ezdom ego v armiiu]; 1752–54 [O glavnykh etapakh voiny]; ZGV: 141–42/ 83–84 [Biarritz, Sept. 1907].

27. ZGV: 139–40/83ob [Biarritz, Sept 1907].

28. SZ XIV: 1753–75 [Ob usilenii revoliutsionnykh proiavlenii v sviazi s neuda- chami voiny].

29. Zapiski, August 1907, 113/67.

30. Wcislo, *Reforming Rural Russia*, ch. 5; Anan'ich and Ganelin, 127–159; SZ XIV: 1776–86 [O proekte Ukaza, sostavlennom mnoiu i bar. Nol'de, vyzove menia Gosudarem pered podpisaniem Ukaza i iz"iatii iz proekta punkta o privleche- nii vybornykh v Gos. Sovet, 7 Feb 1912]; ZGV: 113/67 [Catleret, Aug. 1907].

31. SZ XIV: 1801 and 1795–1802 [O shestvii rabochikh dlia podachi petitsii Gosudariu 9 ianv. 1905 g.]

32. SZ XIV: 1802–1811 [Uchrezhdenie posta S-P Gen-Gub i naznachenie na nego gen. Trepova and Naznachenie Bulygina M-rom Vnut. Del]; ZGV: 124–130/ 720b–77 [Biarritz, Aug. 1907].

33. f. 1544, op. dopol. k XVI tomu Gos. Soveta, d. 3 [Delo po soveshchaniiu dlia obsuzhdeniia prednachertanii ukazannykh v Vysochaishem reskripte 18 fevra- lia 1905 g, chast' III)].

34. SZ XIV: 1842 [Mukdenskoe porazhenie].

35. SZ XIV: 1866 [O posylke flota iz Baltiiskogo moria po D. Vostok pod komandoi adm. Rozhdenstvenskogo i porazhenii v Tsushimskom prolive].

36. Herman Hagedorn (ed), *The Works of Theodore Roosevelt* (New York: C. Scribner's Sons, 1926), vol. 4, 1174, letter no. 3519; Washington, May 13, 1904.

37. Ibid., vol. 4, 1200; letter 3542 (Washington, June 1 1905).

38. Ibid., vol. 4, 1202–06 (Washington, June 5, 1905; to Henry Cabot Lodge 'Confidential') and 1221–1233 (Washington, June 16, 1905).

39. ZGV: 142–44/85–86 ob [Biarritz, Sept. 1907]; SZ XIV: 1873–98 [O nachale mirnykh peregovorakh s Iaponiei i nazhnachenii upolnomochennykh]; BAR Witte, Box 1: Correspondence R-S, Rutkovskii-Witte (nd; 14/27 July 1904, and 22 Feb/7 March 1905); Ananich and Ganelin, 188–190.

40. *The Works of Theodore Roosevelt*, vol. 4, 1262–63 [Oyster Bay, NY, July 7, 1905].

41. ZGV: 145–47/87–88 [Biarritz, Sept. 1907].

42. ZGV: 153–54/92–92 ob. [Biarritz, Sept. 1907]; Anan'ich and Ganelin, 188–90.

43. ZGV: 156/94–94 ob.; BAR Box 1, letter of Isaac Newton Seligman, Jacob H. S. Schiff, Adolph Lewisohn, Oscar S. Strauss, and Adolff Krauss to S. Iu. Witte, 5 Sept. 1905, NYC.

44. Bryan McGraw and Frank Wcislo, 'Witte and the American Press in 1905', Vanderbilt University Undergraduate Summer Research Project, 1992; see also Portsmouth Peace Treaty 1905–2005, http://portsmouthpeacetreaty.org/ index.cfm

45. SZ XV: 1939 [O poseshchenii mnoiu Kolumbiiskogo Universiteta v N'iu-Iorke].
46. ZGV: 158–159/94–96 [Biarritz, Sept. 1907]; SZ XV: 1904–07 [Poseshchenie mnoiu evreiskogo kvartala v N'iu-Iorke].
47. SZ XV: 1910, 1920–21, 1929–30, 1944–46, 1969 *passim* [Vospominaniia za vremia prebyvaniia v Amerike].
48. BAR Witte, Box 12, Dokumenty po portmutskomu dogovoru, Folder No. 3, 'Portmutskaia mirnaia konferentsiia 1905 goda. Otchet sekretaria konferentsii Plansona', 33–50.
49. BAR Witte, Box 12, Delo No. 29, No.8, telegram Witte to Kokovtsov, 28 July/10 August 1905, and Planson, *Otchet*, 40–41.
50. BAR Witte Box 12, No. 13, telegram Kokovtsev to Witte, 3/16 August 1905.
51. Planson, *Otchet*, 116–17.
52. BAR Witte, Box 12, Delo No. 29, telegrams Kokovtsov to Witte, 25, 27, 30 July, 4 August 1905.
53. Planson, *Otchet*, 135.
54. BAR Witte, Box 12, Delo. 29, telegram Witte to Kokovtsov, No. 24, 12 August.
55. Planson, *Otchet*, 128–29.
56. BAR Witte, Box 12, Delo No. 29, telegram Witte to Kokovtsov, 6/19 August 1905.
57. Planson, *Otchet*, 135–39 and 129–31 and BAR Witte Box 12, Delo No. 29, telegram Kokovtsov to Witte, 8/21 August 1905.
58. Planson, *Otchet*, 139–40.
59. Planson, *Otchet*, 146–47.
60. Planson, *Otchet*, 148–53.
61. Planson, *Otchet*, 155–59.
62. ZGV, Sept. 1907, 167–68/100 [Biarritz, Sept. 1907].
63. Planson, *Otchet*, 162–65; ZGV, 169/100 i ob [Biarritz, Sept. 1907]; SZ XV: 1924–27 [O podpisanii mirnogo dogovora i blagodarstvennom bogosluzhenii po etomu sluchaiu].
64. f. 1622, op. 1, d. 391, l.1 S. Sheremetev to M. I. Witte, Mikhailovskoe, 19 Aug. 1905; also d. 392, l.1.
65. SZ XV: 1924.
66. *Dnevniki*, 275 (17 Aug. 1905) and 276 (25 August 1905).
67. SZ XV: 1973 [O pervom moem predstavlenii Gosudariu po vosvrashchenii iz Ameriki i pozhalovanii mne grafskogo dostoinstva]; *Dnevniki*, 280 [16 Sept 1905 Friday and 17 Sept 1905. Saturday].
68. f. 1544, op. dopol. k XVI tomu Gos. Soveta, d. 3, ll. 300–39 [Memoriia Soveta ministrov po delu o poriadke osushchestvlenii Vysochaishikh predukazanii, vozveshchennykh v Reskripte 18 fevralia 1905 g., 1 July 1905] and *passim*.
69. Witte appointed to Solskii conference, 21–23 Sept. 1905 (f. 1544 op. dopol k XVI tom, d. 4, ll. 465–66 and *passim* and d. 22. See MacDonald, *United*

Government, ch. 4; Wcislo, *Reforming Rural Russia*, ch. 5; Verner, *The Crisis of Autocracy*; Anan'ich and Ganelin, 204–24.

70. ZGV: 201–03/120 ob–121 [Biarritz, Sept. 1907].
71. ZGV: 321/216 [Biarritz Sept. 1909]; *Dnevniki*: 284 [Sunday, 9 Oct. 1905].
72. 'Dokladnaia zapiska gr. Vitte Nikolaiu II', f. 1622, op. 1 d. 109, ll. 1–2; ZGV: 209–39/126–39 ob [Petersburg, Jan. 1908]; *Dnevniki*, 9, 14, 15, 17 October 1905, 284–5; Verner, *The Crisis of Russian Autocracy*, ch. 7.
73. Dokladnaia zapiska, ll. 1–2.
74. 'Spravka o Manifeste 17 Oktiabria 1905 g.', in ZGV: 214–15/129a [St Petersburg, January 1908].
75. *Dnevniki*, 284 [12 October 1905]; ZGV: 486–87 [Biarritz, August 1912].
76. BAR Witte, Box 1, telegram, Nicholas II to Witte, 13 Oct. 1905, Peterhof.
77. *Dnevniki*, 284 [Friday, 14 October 1905 and Saturday, 15 October 1905]; 'Zapiska N. I. Vuicha' and 'Zapiska Kn. N. D. Obolenskogo', in ZGV: 221/129a i ob. and 225/129e [January 1908].
78. ZGV: 228/132–33 [St Petersburg, 1908] and Zapiska kniazia N.D. Obolenskogo in ZGV: 228.
79. Verner, 233–45; Anan'ich and Ganelin, 220–21; ZGV: 215–16/129 b, 221/129g ob–129 d, 225–29/129 e ob–129 zh [Spravka o Manifeste, Zapiska N. I. Vuicha, Zapiska N. D. Obolenskogo] and 236/136 [St Petersburg, 1908]; *Dnevniki*, 284 [15 October 1905].
80. ZGV: 234–35/134 ob.–136 [St Petersburg, 1908].
81. *Dnevniki*, 17 October 1905, 284.
82. Verner, 241–42.
83. ZGV: 240/139ob [Vichy, August 1908].
84. P. A. Zaionchkovskii, *Rossiiskoe samoderzhavie v kontse XIX stoletiia. Politicheskaia reaktsiia 80-kh-nachala 90-kh godov* (Moskva: Izd-vo 'Mysl', 1970) and A. A. Avrekh, *Tsarizm i tret'eiiunskaia sistema* (Moskva, Nauka, 1966).
85. ZGV: 240–41/139ob–140 [Vichy, August 1908].
86. ZGV: 242–44/141–141 ob [Vichy, August 1908].
87. ZGV: 242–43/141 ob.–142.
88. ZGV: 244–46/143 ob–144 ob. [Vichy, August 1908].
89. B. V. Anan'ich, V. S. Diakin, et al., *Krizis samoderzhaviia v Rossii, 1895–1917* [Leningrad: 'Nauka', Leningradskoe otd-nie, 1984].
90. ZGV: 244–6/143 ob–144 ob. [Vichy, August 1908].
91. Ibid.
92. Ibid.
93. ZGV: 272/167 ob [Biarritz, Aug. 1909].
94. ZGV: 500–02; *Dnevniki*, 310 [15 April 1906]; BAR Witte, Box 1, Nicholas to Witte, 15 April 1906.
95. SZ XV (14 February 1912): 1999–2000 [O Vysochaishe vykhode k predstaviteliam G. Dumy i Soveta v Zimnem Dvortse 27 Aprelia 1906].
96. ZGV: 282–92/175–87 [Vichy, Aug 1909].

97. Wcislo, *Reforming Rural Russia*, 187–92.
98. ZGV: 500–502 [Biarritz, 25 August 1912].
99. Anan'ich and Ganelin, 329 and 312–34 *passim*; ZGV: 419–22 [Biarritz, Aug. 1911].
100. ZGV: 317–21/213 ob.–215 [Biarritz, Sept. 1909].
101. ZGV: 364/2480b–250 [Vichy, July 1910].
102. ZGV: 501–02 [Biarritz, Aug. 1912].
103. BAR Witte, Box 1, Nicholas to Witte, 15 April 1906.
104. ZGV: 503–04 [Biarritz, Aug. 1912].
105. Anan'ich and Ganelin, 231–348; Howard Mehlinger and John Thompson, *Count Witte and the Tsarist Government in the 1905 Revolution* (Bloomington: Indiana University Press, 1972); Wcislo, *Reforming Rural Russia*, ch. 5.
106. f. 1276, op. 2, d. 4, 'Vsepoddaneishii doklad Grafa Vitte, 23 aprelia 1906 g.' and 'Programma voprosov, vnosymykh na razsmotrenie Gos. Dumy'.
107. McDonald, *United Government*, op. cit and R. Sh. Ganelin, *Rossiiskoe samoderzhavie v 1905 godu. Reformy i revoliutsiia* (Sankt-Peterburg: 'Nauka', S-Peterburgskoe otd-nie, 1991).
108. f. 1622, op. 1, d. 961 [Papka s raznymi dokumentami, zametkami i t.d.] and ZGV: 306–33/1990b–228 passim. [Biarritz, Sept. 1909].
109. ZGV: 309/203.
110. Koni, 33.
111. BAR Witte, Box 12, Delo No.35, Ob osnovnykh zakonov [Memoriia Soveta ministrov 10, 12, 14, 18 i 19 marta 1906 g.] and f. 1544, 1905 g, op. dopol. K XVI t., d. 23 [Gos. Kantseliariia. Delo po peresmotru Osnovnykh Gosudarstvennykh Zakonov, ch. I-aia]).
112. BAR Witte, Box 12, Delo No.38, Ob osnovnykh zakonakh, No.10.
113. f. 1622, op. 1, d. 437, l.1.
114. *Entsiklopedicheskii slovar'*, 7th ed., vol. 10, 371–72 ('Vitte, S. Iu.') [Moscow: A and I. Granat, 1850–1926].
115. Herman Bernstein, *Celebrities of Our Times: Interviews by Herman Bernstein* (New York: Joseph Lawren, 1924), 17–19.

CONCLUSION: FROM THE ALEXANDER NEVSKY LAVRA, 1915

1. f. 1622, op. 1, d. 567, ll. 1–2.
2. ZGV: 499 [August 1912].
3. BAR Witte, Box 1, Correspondence: H–L [V.I. Kovalevskii to S. Iu. Witte, 31 May 1910].
4. Herman Bernstein, *With Master Minds. Interviews*, 46–47.
5. E. J. Dillon, *The Eclipse of Russia*, 274.
6. Leopold Haimson, 'The Problem of Social Stability in Urban Russia', in Michael Cherniavsky (ed.), *The Structure of Russian History* (New York:

Random House, 1970), and *Russia's Revolutionary Experience, 1905–1917* (New York: Columbia University Press, 2005).

7. f. 268, op. 3, d. 193 (June–Oct 1888), esp. ll. 560b–90b.

8. f. 1622, op. 1, ed. khr.292, ll. 1–4, 'Notarial'noe dukhovnoe zaveshchanie gr. M.I. Vitte, 21 May 1915.

9. Orlando Figes, *People's Tragedy*, 529.

10. Anan'ich and Ganelin: 390–91.

11. ZGV: 331–363 (Biarritz, 25 August 1912).

12. BAR Bark, Vospominaniia, ch. 4, 30–33 and ch. 6, 4–21.

13. Paul Gregory, *Before Command: An Economic History of Russia from Emancipation to the First Five-Year Plan*, op. cit.

14. Herman Bernstein, *With Master Minds*, June 1911: 48–49.

15. BAR Bark, Vospominaniia, ch. 10, 1–8.

16. f. 563, op. 2, d. 502. [1 March 1913, Zhurnal Komiteta finansov o sostoianii denezhnykh rynkov].

17. BAR Bark, *Vospominaniia*, XI, 4–5; f. 563, op. 2, d. 523, ll. 1–ob [Delo o zakliuchenii soglasheniia s Frantsuzskim Bankon (Banque de France), 30 Dec. 1914].

18. 4 March 1915, Zasedaniia Komiteta ministrov o skonchavshemsia Gr. Vitte, f. 563, op. 2, d. 525, l.5; also f. 563, op. 2, d. 504, ll. 17–21. [Ob obezpechenii pravil'noi oplaty po nashim zaimam za granitsei i o merakh podkrepleniia sredstv Gos-ogo Kazneichestva v vidu voennykh deistvii] 22 Aug. 1914.

19. Peter Holquist, "Information Is the Alpha and Omega of Our Work": Bolshevik Surveillance in Its Pan-European Context', *The Journal of Modern History*, Vol. 69, No. 3 (Sep. 1997), 415–50; Kotsonis, *Making Peasant Backwards*, op. cit.

20. *Vestnik finansov, promyshlennosti i torgovli*, 1914–1916, *passim*.

21. ZGV: 331–346 mss (Biarritz, 25 avgusta 1912 g.).

22. E. J. Dillon, *The Eclipse of Russia* (London, Toronto: J. M. Dent, 1918), 44–45.

23. A. F. Koni, *Otryvochnye vospominaniia*, 35–38.

Bibliography

PRIMARY SOURCES

**Bakhmeteff Archive of Russian and European Culture, Special Collections,
Columbia University Libraries, Columbia University, New York City**
Petr L'vovich Bark Papers
  Memoirs
Maksim M. Kovalevskii Papers
  My Life. Memoirs of Maksim Maksimovich Kovalevskii
Aleksei Aleksandrovich Spasskii-Odynets Papers
  Memoirs
Sergei Iul'evich Witte Papers, Boxes 1–11
  Vospominaniia (razskazy v stenograficheskoi zapisi) Grafa Sergeia Iul'evicha
Vitte. Parts I–XVII. 1911–12.
  Zapisi Grafa Vitte, 1907–1912.
Vozniknovenie Russko-Iaponskoi Voiny. Obzor predshestvovavshie voin sobytii,
sostavlennyi pod lichnym rukovodstvom i na osnovanii dokumentov lichnogo
arkhiva Grafa S. Iu. Vitte, 3 vols, St Petersburg, 1907.
  Dokumenty po portmutskomu dogovoru
  Correspondence

Manuscript Division, Russian National Library, St Petersburg
f. 1000, op. 1, ed. khr. 765. Lopukhin, V. P, 'Zapiski b. direktora departamenta
  ministerstva innostrannykh del, 1894–1917'

Russian State Historical Archive, St Petersburg
Fond 40, Department of Commerce and Manufacturing, Ministry of Finances
Fond 199 Council of the Minister of Ways of Communication
Fond 229, Chancellery of the Minister of Ways of Communication
Fond 237 Inspectorate of Imperial Trains, Ministry of Ways of Communication
Fond 239 Committee for Construction of a Church and a Shrine on the Site of the
  Events of 17 October 1888
Fond 241 Designees from the Ministry of Ways of Communication for the
  Adoption of Measures Against the Spread of the Cholera Epidemic, 1892
Fond 268 Department of Railroad Affairs, Ministry of Finances
Fond 272 General Congresses of Representatives of Russian Railroads for Tariff
  Issues

Fond 560 General Chancellery of the Minister of Finances, Ministry of Finances
Fond 563 Committee of Finances
Fond 564 Editorial Board of Periodical Publications, Ministry of Finances
Fond 573 Department of Direct Taxes, Ministry of Finances
Fond 575 Main Administration of Indirect Taxes and Crown Sale of Alcohol,
    Ministry of Finances
Fond 1276 Council of Ministers
Fond 1327 Special Files for Elections to the State Duma and State Council
Fond 1544 State Council
Fond 727 Personal Papers of E. Iu. Nol'de
Fond 864 Personal Papers of V. I. Kovalevskii
Fond 966 Personal Papers of V. N. Kokovtsev
Fond 1622 Personal Papers of S. Iu. Witte

Published Writings of S. Iu. Witte
Konspekt lektsii o narodnom i gosudarstvennom khoziastva. Saint Petersburg, 1912.
'Manufakturnoe krepostnichestvo', *Rus'* 3 (1885).
Natsional'naia Ekonomika i Fridrikh List [Kiev: Kievskoe slovo, 1889].
Po Povodu natsionalizma. Natsional'naia Ekonomika i Fridrikh List, 2-e izdanie [St Peters-
    burg, Brokgauz i Efron, 1912].
Printsipy zheleznodorozhnykh tarifov po perevozke gruzov. 3-e izdanie. [St Petersburg:
    Brokgauz i Efron, 1910].
Prichiny ubytochnosti russkikh zheleznykh dorog. Doklad, prochitannykh 7 apre-
    lia v institute inzhenerov putei soobshchenii. Vestnik Finansov, Promyshlennost,
    i Torgovli. No. 6, 18 April 1910.
*Samoderzhavie i zemstvo. Konfidentsial'naia zapiska Ministra finansov Stats-
    Sekretaria S. Iu. Vitte* (1899) [Stuttgart, 1901].
Zapiska po krest'ianskomu delu [St Petersburg, 1905].

Encyclopedias and Print Media
Bol'shaia entsiklopedia
Entsiklopedichesii slovar', Brokhauz i Efron
Russkii Biograficheskii Slovar'
Russkoe bogatstvo
Russkoe gosudarstvo
Vestnik evropy
Vestnik finansov, promyshlennosti i torgovli

Other Published Primary Sources
Afanas'ev, G. E. 'K konchine grafa S. Iu. Vitte', *Volny*, Mart 1915, No. 3: 97–100.
Anan'ich, B.V., R. Sh. Ganelin (eds.) and B.V. Anan'ich, F. Vchislo et. al. (editorial
    collegium), *Iz arkhiva S. Iu. Vitte. Vospominaniia.* 3 vols. [St Petersburg: Dmitrii
    Bulanin, 2003].

Bernstein, Herman. *With Master Minds. Interviews:* New York: Universal Series Publishing, 1913.

——*Celebrities of Our Times: Interviews.* New York, Joseph Lawren, 1924.

Bogdanovich, A. V. *Tri poslednykh samoderzhets: Dnevki A. V. Bogdanovicha.* Moscow, 1924.

Bok, M. P. P. A. *Stolypin: Vospominaniia o moem ottse.* Moscow: Novosti, 1992.

Bolotov, Andrei T. *Zapiski Andreia Timofeevicha Bolotova.* Vol. 1–2. Moscow: 1851.

Brodsky, Joseph. *Less Than One: Selected Essays.* New York: Farrar, Straus & Giroux, 1986.

Broido Vera. *Daughter of Revolution: A Russian Girlhood Remembered.* London: Constable, 1998.

Bunge, N.Kh. *The Years 1881–1894 in Russia: A Memorandum Found in the Papers of N.Kh. Bunge.* A Translation and Commentary by George E. Snow. Philadelphia: American Philosophical Society, 1981.

Chernyshevsky, Nikolai. *What Is to Be Done?* Trans. Michael R. Katz. Ithaca, NY: Cornell University Press, 1989.

Chuprov, A. I. *Rechi i stati.* Vol. 1–3. Moscow: Izd. M. i S. Sabashnikovykh, 1909–1911.

Clyman, Toby W. and Judith Vowles, (eds.), *Russia Through Women's Eyes: Autobiographies from Tsarist Russia.* New Haven: Yale University Press, 1996.

Dillon, E. J. *The Eclipse of Russia.* London & Toronto: J. M. Dent & Sons, Ltd., 1918.

Dnevniki Imperatora Nikolaia II (K. F. Shatsillo (ed.). TsGAOR SSSR and Orbita: Moscow, 1991.

Dnevniki Imperatritsy Marii Fedorovny (1914–1920, 1923). Kudrina, Iu. V, ed. Moscow: Vagrius, 2005.

Engel'gardt, A. N. *Iz derevni. 12 pisem 1872–1887.* Moscow: Mysl', 1987.

Engel, Barbara Alpern and Clifford Rosenthal (eds. and trs.). *Five Sisters: Women Against the Tsar.* New York: Knopf; distributed by Random House, 1975.

Fadeev, A. M. Vospominaniia Andreia Mikhailovicha Fadeeva (Nadezhda Andreevna Fadeeva, ed.), *Russkii arkhiv* 1891, no. 3: 289–329; 385–424; 465–94; 1891, no. 5: 14–60, 105–64, 229–57, 424–522.

Fadeev, R. A. *Sobranie sochinenii R. A. Fadeeva,* 3 vols. S.-Peterburg: V. V. Komarova, 1889–1890.

F(adeev)-a, N. A. 'Vospominaniia o Rostislave Fadeeve', in *Sobranie sochinenii R.A. Fadeeva,* vol. 1. StP: V. V. Komarov, 1889.

Feoktistov, E. M. *Vospominaniia za kulisami politiki i literatury.* Ed. Marc Raeff. Cambridge: Oriental Research Partners, 1975.

Fitslyon, Kyril and Tatiana Browning. *Before the Revolution: A View of Russia Under the Last Czar.* Woodstock, NY: The Overlook Press, 1978.

Gordin, Ia. A. i B. P. Milovidov, (eds.). *Osada Kavkaza. Vospominaniia uchastnikov kavkazskoi voiny XIX veka.* St Petersburg: Izdatel'stvo zhurnala Zvezda, 2000.

Gurko, V. I. *Cherty i siluety proshlogo. Pravitel'stvo i obshchestvennost' v tsarstvovanie Nikolaia II v isobrazhenii sovremennika.* Moscow: Novoe literaturnoe obozrenie, 2000.

——*Tsar' i tsaritsa.* Paris: Vozrozhdenie, 1927.

——'Chto est' i chego net v "Vospominanii grafa S. Iu. Vitte." ' *Russkaia letopis'*, no. 2 (1922).

Haimson, Leopold H. and Ziva Galili y Garcia and Richard Wortman. *The Making of Three Russian Revolutionaries: Voices from the Menshevik Past.* Cambridge: Cambridge University Press, 1987.

Hagedorn, Herman (ed). *The Works of Theodore Roosevelt.* 20 vols. New York: C. Scribner's Sons, 1926.

Kirkhner, V. V. 'Towards a Biography of S. Iu. Witte', *Volny*, April 1915, No. 4, 118.

Kokovtsev, V. N. *Iz moego proshlogo. Vospominaniia 1903–1919 gg.* Vol. 1-2. Moscow: Nauka, 1992.

Komitet ministrov, Kantseliariia. *Zhurnaly Komitet Ministrov po ispoleneniiu Ukaza 12 dekabria 1904 g.* St Petersburg, 1905.

Koni, A. F. *Sergei Iu'levich Vitte: Otryvochnye vospominaniia.* Moscow: Izad-vo Pravo i Zhizn', 1925.

Kovalevskii, V. I. (ed.). *Rossiia v kontse XIX veka.* St Petersburg: Ministerstvo finansov. Brokgauz'-Efron' 1900. The Hague: Mouton, 1969.

Kryzhanovskii, S. E. *Vospominaniia.* Berlin, 1938.

Lamzdorf, V. N. *Dnevnik 1894–1896.* Moscow: Mezhdunarodnye otnosheniia, 1991.

List, Frederick. *National System of Political Economy.* Trans. G. A. Matile. Philadelphia: J. B. Lipincott, 1856.

Liubimov, D. N. 'Otryvki iz vospominanii D. N. Liubimova, 1902–1904 gg', *Istoricheskii arkhiv* no. 6 (1982).

Maklakov, Vasilii. *Vtoraia gosudarstvennaia Duma. 20 fevralia – 2 iiunia 1907 goda.* Moscow: Tsentrpoligraf, 2006.

Meshcherskii, Kniaz' V. P. *Kniaz' Meshcherskii: Vospominaniia.* Moscow: Zakharov, 2001.

Miliukov, P. N. 'Vitte, S. Iu.' *Entsiklopedicheskii slovar*, 7th ed., vol. 10, 343–72. Moscow: A and I. Granat, 1850–1926.

——*Vospominaniia. 2 vols.* Moscow: Sovremennik, 1990.

Mosolov, A. A. *Pri dvore poslednego Rossiiskogo imperatora.* Moscow: Chastnaia firma Ankor, 1993.

Murchison, Roderick, Impey, Sir. *The Geology of Russia in Europe and the Ural Mountains.* London: J. Murray, 1845.

Nagrodskaia, Evdokia. *The Wrath of Dionysus.* Trans. Ed. Louise McReynolds. Bloomington. Indiana University Press,1997.

Naryshkina-Vitte, Vera. *Zapiski devochki.* Brussels: Izdanie avtora, 1922.

Nef, M. K. *Lichnye memuary E. P. Blavatskoi.* Moscow: Rossiiskoe Teosovskoe Obshchestvo, 1993.

Nikitenko, Aleksandr. *Up from Serfdom: My Childhood and Youth in Russia, 1804–1924.* Trans. Helen Saltz Jacobson. New Haven: Yale University, 2001.

Ol'denburg, S. S. *Last Tsar. Nicholas II: His Reign and His Russia,* 4 Vols. Academic International press, 1977.

Ometev, Boris and John Stuart. *St. Petersburg: Portrait of an Imperial City.* New York: The Vendome Press, 1990.

Paleologue, Maurice. *Tsarskaia Rossiia vo vremia mirovoi voiny.* Moscow: Mezhdunarodnye otnosheniia, 1991.

Peterburg. Khudozhestvennaia zhizn'. 1900–1916 fotoletopis'. St Petersburg: Iskusstvo-SPB, 2001.

Pyliaev, M. I. *Staryi Peterburg'.* St Petersburg: Tipografiia A. S. Suvorina, 1889.

Riqueti, Honore G. *Memoirs of the Courts of Berlin and St. Petersburg.* New York: P. F. Collier & Son Publishers, 1910.

Rittikh, A. *Russkii voennyi byt v deistvitel'nosti i mechtakh.* St Petersburg: 1893.

Sheremetev, grafa S. D. *Memuary grafa S. D. Sheremeteva.* Moscow: Izdatel'stvo Indrik, 2001.

Russkie memuary. *Arnadna Tyrkova-Vil'iams. Vospominaniia. To, chego bol'zhe ne budet.* Moscow: Slovo, 1998.

Samarin, Iu. F. *'Predislovie',* in *Sobranie sochinenii A. S. Khomiakova.* Moscow, 1867: reprinted in A. S. Khomiakov, Tserkov Odna. Izdateltel'stvo Prep. Iova Pochaevskago. Montreal, 1975.

Schmoller, Gustav. *The Mercantile System and Its Historical Significance from Studien uber die wirthschaftliche Politik Friedrichs des Grossen.* London, Macmillan, 1897.

Semenikov, V. P., ed. *Za kulisami tsarizma (Arkhiv tibetskogo vracha Badmaeva).* Leningrad: 1925.

Semeniut, P. P. *Pervaia gosudarstvennaia duma, ee zhizn' i smert'.* St Petersburg: M. M. Stasiulevich, 1907.

Shepelev, L. E., 'Vospominaniia V. I. Kovalevskogo'. *Russkoe proshlo: Istoriko-dokumental'noi al'manakh* 1991 (no. 2).

Sinyavsky, Andrei. *Goodnight! A Novel by Avrahm Tertz.* Translated and with an Introduction by Richard Lourie. New York and London: Penguin Books, 1989, 1991.

Sovet ministrov. *Osobye zhurnaly.* St Petersburg, 1906–17.

Struve, P. B. *Rossiia rodina chuzhbina.* St Petersburg: Izdatel'stvo Russkogo Kristianskogo gumanitarnogo instituta, 2000.

Suvorin, A. S. and N. A. Roskinoi et al. (eds.). *Dnevnik Alekseia Sergeevicha Suvorina.* Moscow: Izdatel'stvo nezavisimaia gazeta, 2000.

Tarle, E. V. *Graf S.Iu. Vitte. Opyt' kharakteristiki vneshnei politiki.* Leningrad: Knizhnye novinki, 1927.

Tertz, Abram. *Goodnight!* New York: Penguin, 1991.

Tikhomirov', L. A. *Monarkhicheskaia gosudarstvennost'*. St Petersburg: Rossiiskii imperskii soiuz'-orden, 1992.

Tiutcheva, Anna. *Anna Tiutcheva vospominaniia*. Moscow: Zakharov, 2000.

Tolstoi, I. I. *Dnevnik 1906–1916*. St Petersburg: Fond regional'nogo razvitiia Sankt-Peterburga, Evropeiskii Dom, Evropeiskii Universitet v Sankt-Peterburge, 1997.

Tomei, Christine D. (ed.). *Russian Women Writers* (2 vols). New York: Garland, 1999.

Verkhovskii, V. M. (ed.). *Istoricheskii ocherk raznykh otraslei zheleznodorozhnogo dela i razvitiia finansovo-ekonomicheskoi storony zheleznykh dorog v Rossii po 1897 vkliuchitel'no*. St Petersburg: MPS, 1901.

Vinogradova, A., ed. *Velikii kniaz' Aleksandr Mikhailovich. Vospominaniia*. Moscow: Sovremennik, 1991.

Zapiski Imperatorskogo Novorossisskogo Universiteta. God chetvertyi. Tom sedmoi. Odessa, 1871.

SECONDARY SOURCES

A Portrait of Tsarist Russia: Unknown Photographs from the Soviet Archives. New York: Pantheon Books, 1989.

Adams, Bruce F. *The Politics of Punishment: Prison Reform in Russia 1863–1917*. Dekalb, IL: Northern Illinois University Press, 1996.

Anan'ich, B. V. and V. S. Diakin (eds.). *Krizis samoderzhaviia v Rossii 1895–1917*. Leningrad: 'Nauka' (Akademiia Nauk SSSR. Institut istorii SSSR, Leningradskoe otdelenie), 1984.

Anan'ich, B. V. et al. (eds.). *Aleksandr Vtoroi. Vospominaniia. Dnevniki*. St Petersburg: Pushkinskii fond, 1995.

Anan'ich, B. V. and R. Sh. Ganelin. *Sergei Iul'evich Vitte i ego vremia*. St Petersburg: Dmitrii Bulanin, 1999.

Anderson, Benedict. *Imagined Communities*. 6th ed. New York: Verso, 1995.

Ascher, Abraham. *P. A. Stolypin: The Search for Stability in Late Imperial Russia*. Stanford, Calif.: Stanford University Press, 2001.

——— *The Revolution of 1905*, 2 vols. Stanford, Calif.: Stanford University Press, 1988–1992.

Babel, Isaac and Nathalie Babel (ed.). and Peter Constantine (tr.). *The Complete Works of Isaac Babel*. New York, London: W.W. Norton, 2002.

Baryshnikov, M. H. *Delovoi mir Rossii. Istoriko-biograficheskii spravochnik*. St Petersburg: Iskusstvo-SPB, Logos, 1998.

Bayly, C. A. *The Birth of the Modern World: 1780–1914*. New York: Wiley-Blackwell, 2003.

Belokonskii, I. P. 'K istorii politicheskoi ssylki 80-kh godov'. *Katorga i ssylka*, 31 (1927), 142–57.

Berlin, Isaiah, Henry Hardy and Aileen Kelly (eds.). *Russian Thinkers*. New York: Viking Press, 1978.

Berman, Marshall. *All That Is Solid Melts Into Air: The Experience of Modernity*. New York: Simon and Schuster, 1982.

Bethea, David M. *The Shape of Apocalypse in Modern Russian Fiction*. Princeton, NJ: Princeton University Press, 1989.

Blanch, Lesley. *The Sabres of Paradise*. London: John Murray, 1960.

Blight, David. *Race and Reunion: The Civil War in American Memory*. Cambridge, Mass.: Belknap Press of Harvard University Press, 2001.

Bonnell, Victoria E., Richard Biernacki, and Lynn Hunt. *Beyond the Cultural Turn: New Directions in the Study of Society and Culture*. Berkeley: University of California Press, 1999.

Bradley, Joseph. *Voluntary Associations in Tsarist Russi:. Science, Patriotism, and Civil Society*. Cambridge, Mass.: Harvard University Press, 2009.

Breyfogle, Nicholas B. *Heretics and Colonizers: Forging Russia's Empire in the South Caucasus*. Ithaca, NY: Cornell University Press, 2005.

Brumfield, William C., Boris V. Anan'ich, and Yuri A. Petrov, eds. *Commerce in Russian Urban Culture 1861–1914*. Washington: Woodrow Wilson Center Press, 2001.

Burbank, Jane, Mark von Hagen, and Anatolyi Remnev (eds.). *Russian Empire: Space, People, Power, 1700–1930*. Bloomington: Indiana University Press, 2007.

Cannadine, David. *Ornamentalism: How the British Saw Their Empire*. London: Allen Lane, 2001.

Cavender, Mary W. *Nests of the Gentry: Family, Estate, and Local Loyalties in Provincial Russia*. Newark: University of Delaware Press, 2007.

Chaudhuri, Nupur and Margaret Strobel (eds.). *Western Women and Imperialism: Complicity and Resistance*. Bloomington: Indiana University Press, 1992.

Chatterjee, Partha. *Nationalist Thought and the Colonial World*. Minneapolis: University of Minnesota Press, 1986.

Chernow, Ron. *Titan: The Life of John D. Rockefeller, Sr.* New York: Vintage Books, 1999.

Clendinnen, Inga. *Ambivalent Conquests: Maya and Spaniard in Yucatan, 1517–1570*. New York: Cambridge University Press, 1987.

Crawford, Katherine. *Perilous Performances: Gender and Regency in Early Modern France*. Cambridge, Mass: Harvard University Press, 2004.

Crews, Robert D. *For Prophet and Tsar: Islam and Empire in Russia and Central Asia*. Cambridge, Mass.: Harvard University Press, 2006.

Custine, Marquis de. *Empire of the Czar: A Journey Through Eternal Russia*. New York: Anchor Books, 1989.

Davies, David B. 'At the Heart of Slavery'. *New York Review of Books* 43.16 (1996): 51–54.

Davis, Natalie Z. and Arlette Farge (eds.). *A History of Women in the West: Renaissance and Enlightenment Paradoxes*. Cambridge, MA: The Belknap Press of Harvard University Press, 1993.

Davis, Natalie Zemon. *The Return of Martin Guerre*. Cambridge, Mass.: Harvard University Press, 1983.

De Madariaga, Isabel. *Catherine the Great: A Short History*. New Haven: Yale University Press, 1990.

Dennett, Tyler. *Roosevelt and the Russo-Japanese War*. Gloucester, MA: Peter Smith Pub Inc, 1958.

Diakin, V. S. *Byl li shans u Stolypina? Sbornik statei*. Sankt-Peterburg: 'LISS', 2002.

Diamond, Jared. *Collapse: How Societies Choose to Fail or Succeed*. New York: Viking, 2005.

Eidel'man, N. (ed.). *Iz potaennoi istorii Rossii XVIII–XIX vekov*. Moscow: Vysshaia shkola, 1993.

Eklof, Ben, John Bushnell, and Larissa Zakharova (eds.). *Russia's Great Reforms, 1855–1881*. Bloomington: Indiana University Press, 1994.

Eley, Geoff and Ronald G. Suny (eds.). *Becoming National*. New York: Oxford University, 1996.

Emmons, Terrence. *The Russian Landed Gentry and the Peasant Emancipation of 1861*. London: Cambridge University Press, 1968.

Engel, Barbara Alpern. *Mothers and Daughters: Women of the Intelligentsia in Nineteenth-Century Russia*. New York: Cambridge University Press, 1983.

——and Clifford Rosenthal (eds. and trs.). *Five Sisters: Women Against the Tsar.* New York: Knopf; distributed by Random House, 1975.

Englestein, Laura. *Keys to Happiness: Sex and the Search for Modernity in fin-de-siecle Russia*. Ithaca, NY: Cornell University Press, 1992.

——*Castration and the Heavenly Kingdom: A Russian Folktale*. Ithaca, NY: Cornell University Press, 1999.

——and Stephanie Sandler (eds.), *Self and Story in Russian History*. Ithaca: Cornell University Press, 2000.

Fennell, John. *A History of the Russian Church to 1448*. New York: Longman Publishing, 1995.

Ferguson, Nial. *Empire: The Rise and Demise of the British World Order and the Lessons for Global Power*. London: Allen Lane, 2002; New York: Basic Books, 2003.

Figes, Orlando. *A People's Tragedy: A History of the Russian Revolution*. New York: Penguin Books USA, 1997.

——*Natasha's Dance: A Cultural History of Russia*. New York: Picador, 2002.

Finkel, Caroline. *Osman's Dream: The Story of the Ottoman Empire 1300–1923*. New York: Basic Books, 2005.

Fraisse, Genevieve and Michelle Perrot (eds.). *A History of Women in the West: Emerging Feminism from Revolution to World War*. Cambridge, MA: The Belknap Press of Harvard University Press, 1993.

Frank, Stephen P. *Crime, Cultural Conflict, and Justice in Rural Russia, 1856–1914*. Berkeley: University of California Press, 1999. Electronic.

Frank, Stephen P. and Mark Steinberg. *Cultures in Flux: Lower-Class Values, Practices, and Resistance in Late Imperial Russia.* Princeton, NJ: Princeton University Press, 1994.

Friedman, Rebecca. *Masculinity, Autocracy and the Russian University, 1804–1863.* Houndmills, Basingstoke, Hampshire; New York: Palgrave Macmillan, 2005.

Gammer, Moshe. *Muslim Resistance to the Tsar: Shamil and the Conquest of Chechnia and Daghestan.* London, Portland, Or.: F. Cass, 1994.

Ganelin, R.Sh. *Rossiiskoe samoderzhavie v 1905 godu. Reformy i revoliutsiia.* Sankt-Peterburg: 'Nauka', S-Peterburgskoe otd-nie, 1991.

Gatrell, Peter. *Russia's First World War: A Social and Economic History.* New York: Longman, 2005.

——*The Tsarist Economy, 1850–1917.* New York: St Martin's Press, 1986.

——*A Whole Empire Walking: Refugees in Russia during World War I.* Bloomington, Indiana University Press, 1999.

Gay, Peter. *Modernism: The Lure of Heresy. From Baudelaire to Beckett and Beyond.* New York: W.W. Norton and Company, 2008.

—— *Shnitzler's Century: The Making of Middle-Class Culture 1815–1914.* New York: W.W. Norton and Company, 2002.

Geertz, Clifford. *Local Knowledge: Further Essays in Interpretive Anthropology.* New York: Basic Books Inc., 1983.

Geertz, Clifford. *The Interpretations of Culture*: New Haven: Yale University Press, 1968.

Geifman, Anna. *Entangled in Terror: The Azef Affaire and the Russian Revolution.* Wilmington, DE: Scholarly Resources Inc., 2000.

Gellner, Ernest. *Nations and Nationalism.* Ithaca, NY: Cornell University Press, 1983.

Geraci, Robert P. and Michael Khodarkovsky (eds.). *Of Religion and Empire: Missions, Conversion, and Tolerance in Tsarist Russia.* Ithaca, NY: Cornell University Press, 2001.

Geraci, Robert P. *Window on the East: National and Imperial Identities in Late Tsarist Russia.* Ithaca: Cornell University Press, 2001.

Gerschenkron, Alexander. *Continuity in History and Other Essays.* Cambridge, MA: The Belknap Press of Harvard University Press, 1968.

Geyer, Dietrich and Bruce Little (tr.). *Russian Imperialism: The Interaction of Domestic and Foreign Policy 1860–1914.* Leamington Spa: Berg, 1987.

Gaier, D., and R. Sh. Ganelin, V. S. Diakin (eds.). *Reformy ili Revoliutsiia. Rossia 1861–1917.* St. Petersburg: Nauka, 1992.

Gleason, Abbott. *Young Russia: The Genesis of Russian Radicalism in the 1860s.* New York: Viking Press, 1980.

Glenny, Misha. *The Balkans: Nationalism, and the Great Powers, 1804–1999.* New York: Penguin Books, 1999.

Glinskii, B. B. *Revoliutsinonnyi period russkoi istorii (1861–1881 gg.) Istoricheskie ocherki.* 2 vols. St Petersburg: 1913.

Glinskii, B. B. ed. *Prolog russko-iaponskoi voiny. Materialy iz arkhiva grafa S. Iu. Vitte.* St Peterburg: 1916.

Glushchenko, Evgenii. *Geroi Imperii. Portrety rossiiskikh kolonial'nykh deiatelei.* Moscow: XXI vek – Soglasie, 2001.

Golovachev, A. A. *Istoriia zhenleznodorozhnogo dela v Rossii.* 1881.

Goscilo, Helena and Beth Holmgren, eds. *Russia Women Culture.* Bloomington: Indiana University Press, 1996.

Green, Liah. *Nationalism: Five Roads to Modernity.* Cambridge, MA: Harvard University Press, 1992.

Gregory, Paul R. *Before Command: An Economic History of Russia from Emancipation to the First Five-Year Plan.* Princeton, NJ: Princeton University Press, 1994.

Gross, Jan T. *Neighbors: The Destruction of the Jewish Community in Jedwabne, Poland.* Princeton, NJ: Princeton University Press, 2001.

Haimson, Leopold H. *Russia's Revolutionary Experience, 1905–1917.* New York: Columbia University Press, 2005.

—— 'The Problem of Social Stability in Urban Russia', in *The Structure of Russian History,* edited by Michael Cherniavsky. New York: Random House, 1970.

—— *The Russian Marxists and the Origins of Bolshevism.* Cambridge, Mass: Harvard Univ. Press, 1955.

Hamm, Michael F. *Kiev. A Portrait, 1800–1917.* Princeton, NJ: Princeton University Press, 1993.

Harcave, Sidney. *Count Sergei Witte and the Twilight of Imperial Russia: A Biography.* Armonk, NY: M.E. Sharpe, 2004.

Herlihy, Patricia. *Odessa: A History, 1794–1914.* Cambridge: Harvard University Press and Harvard Ukrainian Research Institute, 1986.

Heuman, Susan. *Kistiakovsky: The Struggle for National and Constitutional Rights in the Last Years of Tsarism.* Cambridge, MA: Harvard University Press, 1998.

Hirsch, Francine. *Empire of Nations: Ethnographic Knowledge and the Making of the Soviet Union.* Ithaca, NY: Cornell University Press, 2005.

Hobsbawn, Eric J. *Nations and Nationalism since 1780: Programme, Myth Reality.* Cambridge: Cambridge University Press, 1992.

—— *The Age of Capital: 1848–1875.* New York: Vintage Books, 1996.

—— *The Age of Empire: 1875–1914.* New York: Pantheon Books, 1987.

Hobson, J. A. *Imperialism. A Study.* London: George Allen & Unwin, 1902.

Hoffmann, David L. and Yanni Kotsonis. *Russian Modernity: Politics, Knowledge, Practices.* New York: St Martin's Press, 2000.

Hogan, Heather. *Forging Revolution: Metalworkers, Managers, and the State in St. Petersburg, 1890–1914.* Bloomington and Indianapolis: Indiana University Press, 1993.

Holquist, Peter. *Making War, Forging Revolution: Russia's Continuum of Crisis, 1914–1921.* Cambridge, MA: Harvard University Press, 2002.

—— ' "Information Is the Alpha and Omega of Our Work": Bolshevik Surveillance in Its Pan-European Context'. *The Journal of Modern History*, Vol. 69, No. 3 (Sep. 1997), 415–50.

Hosking, Geoffrey. *Russia: People and Empire*. Cambridge, MA: Harvard University Press, 1997.

Ianzhul, I. I. *Istoricheskii ocherk razvitia frabrichno-zavodskoi promyshlennosti.*

Ignatieff, Michael. *The Russian Album*. New York: Elisabeth Sifton Books. Viking, 1987.

Ignat'ev, A. B. S. *Iu. Vitte-Diplomat*. Moscow: Mezhdunarodnoe otnoshenie, 1989.

Jahn, Hubertus F. *Patriotic Culture in Russia during World War I*. Ithaca, NY: Cornell University Press, 1995.

Jaszi, Oscar. *The Dissolution of the Hapsburg Monarchy*. Chicago: University of Chicago Press, 1929.

Kabuzan, V. M. *Izmeneniia v razmeshchenii naseleniia Rossii v XVIII – pervoi polovine XIX v*. Moscow: Nauka, 1971.

Kahan, Arcadius. *Russian Economic History: The Nineteenth Century*. Ed. Roger Weiss. Chicago: University of Chicago Press, 1989.

Kappeler, Andreas. *The Russian Empire*. Trans. Ed. Alfred Clayton. Harlow: Pearson Education Limited, 2001.

Kapuscinski, Ryszard. *The Emperor: Downfall of An Autocrat*. Translated from the Polish by William R. Brand and Katarzyna Mroczkowska-Brand. San Diego: Harcourt Brace Jovanovich, 1983.

Kelly, Catriona. *Anthology of Russian Women's Writing, 1777–1992*. Oxford: University Press, 1994.

—— *A History of Russian Women's Writing*. Oxford: Oxford University Press, 1994.

—— *Children's World: Growing Up in Russia, 1890–1991*. New Haven, Conn.: London: Yale University Press, 2007.

Khodarkovsky, Michael. *Russia's Steppe Frontier: The Making of a Colonial Empire, 1500–1800*. Bloomington: Indiana University Press, 2002.

King, Charles. *The Black Sea: A History*. Oxford: Oxford University Press, 2004.

—— *The Ghost of Freedom: A History of the Caucasus*. Oxford; New York: Oxford University Press, 2008.

Kingston-Mann, Esther. *In Search of the True West: Culture, Economics, and Problems of Russian Development*. Princeton, NJ: Princeton University Press, 1999.

Kirimli, Hakan. *National Movement and National Identity among the Crimean Tartars (1905–1916)*. Leiden: Brill, 1996.

Kislinskii, N. A. and A. N. Kulomzin. *Nasha zheleznodorozhnaia politika po dokumentam arkhiva Komiteta ministrov*. St Petersburg: Komitet ministrov, 1902. 4 vols.

Kivelson, Valerie A. *Autocracy in the Provinces: The Muscovite Gentry and Political Culture in the Seventeenth Century*. Stanford, Calif.: Stanford University Press, 1996.

Kliachko (L'vov), L. *Povesti proshlogo*. Leningrad, 1929.

Kliuchevsky, V. O. and Marshall S. Shatz (ed. and tr.), *A Course in Russian History: The Time of Catherine the Great.* Armonk, NY: M.E. Sharpe, 1997.

Kliuchevskii, V. O. *Istoricheskie portrety. Deiateli istoricheskoi mysli.* Moscow: Izda-tel'stvo Pravda, 1990.

——*Neopublikovanye proizvedeniia.* Moscow: Nauka (Akademiia nauk SSSR Arkhiv Akademii Nauk SSSR), 1983.

Kolchin, Peter. *Unfree Labor: American Slavery and Russian Serfdom.* Cambridge: Harvard Univ Press, 1987.

Korelin, A. and S. Stepanov. *S. Iu. Vitte – finansist, politik, diplomat.* Moscow: Terra-knizhnyi klub, 1998.

Kotsonis, Yanni. *Making Peasants Backward: Agricultural Cooperatives and the Agrarian Question in Russia, 1861–1914.* New York: St Martin's Press, 1999.

——'"Face-to-Face": The State, the Individual, and the Citizen in Russian Taxa-tion, 1863-1917', *Slavic Review*, Vol. 63, No. 2 (Summer, 2004), 221–46.

Landes, David S. *The Wealth and Poverty of Nations: Why Some Are So Rich and Some So Poor.* New York: W.W. Norton and Company, Inc., 1999.

Laqueur, Walter. *Black Hundred: The Rise of the Extreme Right in Russia.* New York: Harper Collins Publishers, 1993.

Layton, Susan. *Russian Literature and Empire: The Conquest of the Caucasus from Pushkin to Tolstoy.* Cambridge: Cambridge University Press, 1994.

Ledkovsky, Marina, Charlotte Rosenthal, and Mary Zirin. *Dictionary of Russian Women Writers.* Westport, CT: Greenwood Press, 1994.

LeDonne, John. *The Russian Empire and the World, 1700–1917. The Geopolitics of Expansion and Containment.* New York: Oxford University Press, 1997.

Levine, Philippa (ed.). *Gender and Empire.* Oxford; New York: Oxford University Press, 2004.

Lieven, Dominic. *Empire: The Russian Empire and Its Rivals.* London: John Murray, 2000.

—— *Nicholas II. Twilight of the Empire.* New York: St. Martin's Griffen, 1993.

Lincoln, W. Bruce.

——*Between Heaven and Hell.* New York: Viking Adult, 1998.

——*The Great Reforms: Autocracy, Bureaucracy, and the Politics of Change in Imperial Russia.* Dekalb, IL: Northern Illinois University Press, 1990.

——*Sunlight at Midnight. St. Petersburg and the Rise of the Modern Russia.* New York: Basic Books, 2000.

——*Nicholas I.* Bloomington: Indiana University Press, 1978.

Lindenmeyr, Adele. *Poverty Is Not a Vice: Charity, Society, and the State in Imperial Russia.* Princeton, NJ: Princeton University Press, 1996.

Lotman, Iu. L. *Besedy po russkoi kul'ture. Byt i traditsii russkogo dvorianstva (XVIII–nachalo XIX veka).* St Petersburg: Iskusstvo-SPB, 1994.

Lukianov, M. N. *Rossiiskii konservatizm i reforma 1907–1914.* Perm: Iz-vo Permskogo universiteta, 2001.

McCaffray, Susan P. and Michael Melancon (eds.). *Russia in the European Context, 1789–1914: A Member of the Family*. New York: Palgrave Macmillan, 2005.

McClintock, Anne. *Imperial Leather: Race, Gender, and Sexuality in the Colonial Context*. New York: Routledge, 1995.

McDaniel, Tim. *The Agony of the Russian Idea*. Princeton, NJ: Princeton University Press, 1996.

McDonald, David M. *United Government and Foreign Policy in Russia, 1900–1914*. Cambridge, Mass.: Harvard University Press, 1992.

Macmillan, Margaret. *Paris 1919: Six Months That Changed the World*. New York: Random House, 2001.

McReynolds, Louise. *The News under Russia's Old Regime: The Development of a Mass-Circulation Press*. Princeton, NJ: Princeton University Press, 1991.

——*Russia at Play: Leisure Activities at the End of the Tsarist Era*. Ithaca: Cornell University Press, 2003.

Marrese, Michelle Lamarche. *A Woman's Kingdom: Noblewomen and the Control of Property in Russia, 1700–1861*. Ithaca, London: Cornell University Press, 2002.

Marker, Gary and Rachel May (eds. and trs.). *Days of a Russian Noblewoman: The Memories of Anna Labzina, 1758–1821*. DeKalb, Ill.: Northern Illinois University Press, 2001.

Marks, Steven. *Road to Power: The Trans-Siberian Railroad and the Colonization of Asian Russia, 1850–1917*. Ithaca, NY: Cornell University Press, 1991.

Marples, David. *Motherland: Russia in the Twentieth Century*. London: Pearson Educational Ltd., 2002.

Marsh, Rosalind. *Gender and Russian Literature: New Perspectives*. Cambridge: Cambridge University Press, 1996.

Martin, Alexander M. *Romantics, Reformers, Reactionaries: Russian Conservative Thought and Politics in the Reign of Alexander I*. DeKalb, Ill.: Northern Illinois University Press, 1997.

Martov, L. et al. *Obshchestvennoe dvizhenie v Rossii v nachale XX-go vieka*. Vol. 1–4. St Petersburg: Tipografia t-va 'Obshchestvennaia pol'za', 1909–1914.

Mayer, Arno J. *The Persistence of the Old Regime: Europe to the Great War*. New York: Pantheon Books, 1981.

Mehlinger, Howard and John Thompson. *Count Witte and the Tsarist Government in the 1905 Revolution*. Bloomington: Indiana University Press, 1972.

Miliukov, P. N. *Gosudarstvennoe khoziastvo Rossii v pervoi chetverti XVIII veka i reforma Petra Velikogo*. St Petersburg, 1892.

Mironov, B. N. *Sotsial'naia istoriia Rossii perioda imperii: XVIII-nachalo XX v. Genezis lichnosti, demokraticheskoi sem'i, grazhdanskogo obshchestva i pravovogo gosudarstva*. 2 vols. St-Petersburg: D. Bulanin, 1999.

Morris, Edmund. *Theodore Rex*. New York: Modern Library, 2002.

Morrissey, Susan K. *Heralds of Revolution: Russian Students and the Mythologies of Radicalism*. New York: Oxford University Press, 1998.

Mosse, W. E. *An Economic History of Russia*. London, New York: I.B. Tauris, 1992.

Nathans, Benjamin. *Beyond the Pale: The Jewish Encounter with Late Imperial Russia.* Berkeley: University of California Press, 2002.

Novick, Peter. *That Noble Dream: The 'Objectivity Question' and the American Historical Profession.* New York: Cambridge University Press, 1988.

Owen, Thomas C. *Capitalism and Politics in Russia: A Social History of the Moscow Merchants, 1855–1905.* Cambridge: Cambridge University Press, 1981.

Pallot, Judith. *Land Reform in Russia 1906–1917: Peasant Responses to Stolypin's Project of Rural Transformation.* New York: Oxford University Press, 1999.

Perrie, Maureen. *Pretenders and Popular Monarchism in Early Modern Russia: The False Tsars of the Time of Troubles.* Cambridge: Cambridge University Press, 1995. Press.

Perrot, Michelle, et al. (eds.). *A History of Private Life: From the Fires of Revolution to the Great War.* Trans Arthur Goldhammer. Cambridge, MA: The Belknap Press of Harvard University Press, 1990.

Pipes, Richard. *The Degaev Affair: Terror and Treason in Tsarist Russia.* New Haven, Conn.: Yale University Press, 2003.

Polunov, Alexander, Thomas C. Owen and Larissa G. Zakharova (eds.), and Marshall S. Shatz (tr.). *Russia in the Nineteenth Century. Autocracy, Reform, and Social Change, 1814–1914.* Armonk, NY: M.E. Sharpe, 2005.

Pompeev, Iu. A. *Istoriia i filosofiia otechestvennogo predprinimatel'stva.* St. Petersburg: Sankt-Peterburgskii gosudarstvennyi universitet kul'tury i iskusstv, 2002.

Porter, Theodore M. *The Rise of Statistical Thinking.* Princeton, NJ: Princeton University Press, 1995.

Prebel'skii et.al., *Dom Romanovykh. Biograficheskie svedeniia o chlenakh tsarstvovavshego doma, ikh predkakh i rodstvennikakh.* St Petersburg, 1992.

Presniakov, A. E. and Judith C. Zacek (ed. and tr.). *Emperor Nicholas I of Russia: The Apogee of Autocracy, 1825–1855.* Gulf Breeze, Fla.: Academic International Press, 1974.

Raeff, Mark. *Russia Abroad: A Cultural History of the Russian Emigration 1919–1939 (Rossiia za rubezhom. Istoriia kyl'tury russkoi emigratsii 1919–1939).* New York: Oxford University Press, 1990; Moscow: Progress-Akademnia, 1994.

——*The Well-Ordered Police State: Social and Institutional Change through Law in the Germanies and Russia, 1600–1800.* New Haven: Yale University Press, 1983.

Radzinskii, Edvard. *Rasputin.* Moscow: Isdatel'stvo Vagrius, 2000.

Randolph, John. *The House in the Garden: The Bakunin Family and the Romance of Russian Idealism.* Ithaca, NY: Cornell University Press, 2007.

Rieber, Alfred J. 'The Sedimentary Society', in E. W. Clowes et.al., *Between Tsar and People: Educated Society and the Quest for Public identity in Late Imperial Russia.* Princeton: Princeton University Press, 1991.

Romanov, B. A. *Rossiia i Manchzhurii (1892–1906). Ocherki po istorii vneshnei politiki samoderzhaviia v epoke imperializma.* Leningrad: Vestnik Leningradskogo gosudarstvennogo universiteta, 1928.

——*Vitte kak diplomat (1895–1903 gg.)*. Leningrad: Vestnik Leningradskogo gosudarstvennogo universiteta, 1946.

——*Ocherki diplomaticheskoi istorii russko-iaponskoi voiny*, 1895–1907. Leningrad: Vestnik Leningradskogo gosudarstvennogo universiteta, 1955.

——'Retsenziia. Graf S.Iu. Vitte. Vospominaniia Tsaarstvovaniia Nikolaia II [M-P, 1923]'. *Kniga i revoliutsiia. Ezhemesiachnyi kritiko-bibliograficheskii zhurnal* 1923 [No.2 (26)]: 54–56.

Roosevelt, Priscilla. *Life on the Russian Country Estate: A Social and Cultural History.* New Haven: Yale University Press, 1995.

Rosen, Roger. *The Georgian Republic: An Independent Tradition.* Chicago: Passport Books, 1992.

Rosenthal, Bernice G. (ed.). *The Occult in Russian and Soviet Culture.* Ithaca, NY: Cornell University Press, 1997.

Rushdie, Salman. *Step Across This Line: Collected Nonfiction 1999–2002.* New York: Random House, 2002.

Said, Edward W. (ed.). *Reflections on Exile and Other Essays.* Cambridge, MA: Harvard University Press, 2000.

Sanborn, Joshua A. *Drafting the Russian Nation: Military Conscription, Total War, and Mass Politics, 1905–1925.* Dekalb, IL: Northern Illinois University Press, 2003.

Sanders, Thomas, Ernest Tucker and Gary Hamburg (eds.). *Russian-Muslim Confrontation in the Caucasus: Alternative Visions of the Conflict between Imam Shamil and the Russians, 1830–1859.* London, New York: Routledge Curzon, 2004.

Sankt-Peterburgskii Institut Istorii RAN. *Vlast' i Nauka, Uchenye i vlast' 1880-e – nachale 1920-x godov. Materialy mezhdunarodnogo nauchnogo kollkviuma.* St. Petersburg: Izdatel'stvo 'Dmitrii Bulanin', 2003.

Schama, Simon. *The Embarrassment of Riches: An Interpretation of Dutch Culture in the Golden Age.* Berkeley: University of California Press, 1988.

——*Dead Certainties: Unwarranted Speculations.* New York: Knopf, 1991.

Schimmelpenninck van der Oye, David. *Toward the Rising Sun: Russian Ideologies of Empire and the Path to War with Japan.* DeKalb, Ill.: Northern Illinois University Press, 2001.

Scott, James C. *Seeing Like a State: How Certain Schemes to Improve the Human Condition Have Failed.* New Haven: Yale University Press, 1998.

Seregny, Scott J. *Russian Teachers and Peasant Revolution: The Politics of Education in 1905.* Bloomington: Indiana University Press, 1989.

Seton-Watson, Hugh. *Nations and States. An Enquiry into the Origins of Nations and the Politics of Nationalism.* New York: Westview Press, 1977.

Shelokhaev, V. V. et. al. *Politicheskie partii Rossii. Konets XIX – pervaia tret' XX veka.* Moscow: Rosspen, 1996.

Shepelev, L. E. (ed.). *Tsarism i burzhuarziia vo vtoroi polovine XIX veka.* Leningrad: 'Nauka' (Akademiia nauk SSSR, Leningradskoe otdelenie), 1981.

——*Chinovnyi Mir Rossii.* St Petersburg: Iskusstvo-SLB, 1999.

Shilov, D. N. *Gosudarstvennye deiateli rossiiskoi imperii 1802–1917. Biobibliograficheskii spravochnik.* St Petersburg: Evropeiskii universitet v Sankt-Peterburge, 2001.

Shishov, A. V. *Vitte. Finansovyi genii poslednikh romanovykh.* Moscow: BECHE, 2004.

Slezkine, Yuri. *The Jewish Century.* Princeton, NJ: Princeton University Press, 2004.

Smele, Jonathan D. and Anthony Heywood. *The Russian Revolution of 1905: Centenary Perspectives.* London: Routledge, 2005.

Smirnov, N. N. (ed.). *Rossia i pervaia mirovaia vouna.* St Petersburg: Sankt-peterburgskii filial instituta rossiiskoi istorii RAN, 1999.

Smith Anthony D. *The Ethnic Origins of Nations.* New York: Wiley-Blackwell, 1986.

Smith, Donald E. *India as a Secular State.* Princeton, NJ: Princeton University Press, 1963.

Smith, Helmut Walser. *The Continuities of German History: Nation, Religion, and Race across the Long Nineteenth Century.* Cambridge; New York: Cambridge University Press, 2008.

Sohrabi, Nader. 'Historicizing Revolution: Constitutional Revolutions in the Ottoman Empire, Iran, and Russia, 1905–08', *The American Journal of Sociology.* (1995) 100.6: 1383–1447.

Solov'ev, S. M. *Izbrannye trudy Zapiski.* Moscow: Izdatel'stvo Moskovskogo universiteta, 1983.

Solov'ev, V. S. *Sovremennaia zhritsa izidy. Moe znakomstvo s E. P. Blavatskoi i 'teosoficheskim obshchestvom' (Epizod 'fin de siecle')* St Petersburg: Moscow: Respublika, 1994; 1904.

Steinberg, Mark D. *Moral Communities: The Culture of Class Relations in the Russian Printing Industry, 1867–1907.* Berkeley: University of California Press, 1992.

Stepanov, V. L. *N. Kh. Bunge. Sud'ba reformatora.* Moscow and Institute of Russian History, RAN: Rosspen, 1998.

Stockdale, Melissa K. *Paul Miliukov and the Quest for a Liberal Russia, 1880–1918.* Ithaca, NY: Cornell University Press, 1996.

Sunderland, Williard. *Taming the Wild Field: Colonization and Empire on the Russian Steppe.* Ithaca, NY: Cornell University Press, 2006.

Suny, Ronald Grigor. *The Making of the Georgian Nation.* Bloomington: Indiana Univ. Press and Hoover Institution Press, Studies of Nationalities in the USSR, 1988.

Tsion, I. F. *Sergei Iul'evich Vitte v publikatsiiakh (k 150-letiiu so dnia rozhdeniia).* Moscow: Institut Ekonomiki Rossiiskoi Akademii Nauk. Tsentr informatsii, 1999.

Ulrich, Laurel T. *A Midwife's Tale: The Life of Martha Ballard, Based on Her Diary, 1785–1812.* New York: Vintage, 1990.

Verbitskaia, Anastasya. *Keys to Happiness.* Trans. Beth Homgren and Helena Goscilo. Bloomington: Indiana University Press, 1999.

Verhoeven, Claudia. *The Odd Man Karakozov: Imperial Russia, Modernity, and the Birth of Terrorism*. Ithaca: Cornell University Press, 2009.

Verner, Andrew M. *The Crisis of Russian Autocracy: Nicholas II and the 1905 Revolution*. Princeton, NJ: Princeton University Press, 1990.

Vitte, S. Iu. Sidorova, A. L. et al. (eds.). *S. Iu. Vitte Vospominaniia. Tom 1 (1849–1894) Detstvo. Tsarstvovaniia Aleksandra II I Aleksandra III. Tom 2 (1894–Oktiabr' 1905) Tsarstvovanie Nikolaia II. Tom 3 (17 oktiabria 1905–1911)* Moscow: Izdatel'stvo sotsial'no-ekonomicheskoi literatury, 1960.

von Geldern, James and Louise McReynolds (eds.). *Entertaining Tsarist Russia: Tales, Songs, Plays, Movies, Jokes, Ads, and Images from Russian Urban Life, 1779–1917*. Bloomington: Indiana University Press, 1998.

Von Laue, Theodore. *Sergei Witte and the Industrialization of Russia*. New York: Studies of the Russian Institute and Columbia University Press, 1963.

——'A Secret Memorandum of Sergei Witte on the Industrialization of Imperial Russia', *The Journal of Modern History*. Vol. 26, No. 1 (Mar., 1954), 60–74.

Waldron, Peter. *The End of Imperial Russia, 1855–1917*. New York: St Martin's Press. 1997.

——*Between Two Revolutions: Stolypin and the Politics of Renewal in Russia*. DeKalb, IL: Northern Illinois University Press, 1998.

Ware, Timothy. *The Orthodox Church*. New York: Penguin Books, 1993.

Wcislo, Francis W. *Reforming Rural Russia: State, Local Society, and National Politics, 1855–1914*. Princeton: Studies of the Harriman Institute and Princeton University Press, 1990.

——'Witte, Memory, and the 1905 Revolution: A Reinterpretation of the Witte Memoirs'. *Revolutionary Russia*, vol. 8, no.2 (December 1995: 166–78).

——'Sergei Witte and His Times. A Historiographical Note', *Kritika. Explorations in Russian and Eurasian History*. New Series, Volume 5, Number 4 (Fall 2004): 749–58.

——'Vitte, samoderzhavie i imperiia: mechty kontsa XIX veka', *Rossiia XXI. Obshchestvenno-politicheskii i nauchnyi zhurnal*, vol. 4 (Moscow: July-August 2001: 144–61).

Weber, Max. *The Russian Revolutions*. Trans. Wells, Gordon C. and Peter Baehr. Ithaca, NY: Cornell University Press, 1995.

Weinberg, Robert. *The Revolution of 1905 in Odessa: Blood on the Steps*. Bloomington: Indiana University Press, 1993.

Werth, Paul W. *At the Margins of Orthodoxy: Mission, Governance, and Confessional Politics in Russia's Volga-Kama Region, 1827–1905*. Ithaca, NY: Cornell University Press, 2002.

Westwood, J. N. *A History of Russian Railways*. London: Allen & Unwin, 1964.

Williams, F. and Laura Chrisman (eds.). *Colonial Discourse and Post-Colonial Theory: A Reader*. New York: Columbia University Press, 1994.

Wortman, Richard S. *Scenarios of Power: Myth and Ceremony in Russian Monarchy*. 2 vols. Princeton, NJ: Princeton University Press, 1995.

Wortman, Richard S. 'Rule by Sentiment: Alexander II's Journeys through the Russian Empire'. *The American Historical Review*. Vol. 95, No. 3 (Jun., 1990), 745–71.

Wynn, Charters. *Workers, Strikes, and Pogroms: The Donbass-Dnepr Bend in Late Imperial Russia, 1870–1905*. Princeton, NJ: Princeton University Press, 1992.

Zaionchkovskii, P. A. *Pravitel'stvennii apparat samoderzhavnoi rossii v XIX veke*. Moskva: Mysl', 1978.

Zaionchkovsky, Peter A. and Gary M. Hamburg (ed. and tr.), *The Russian Autocracy in Crisis, 1878–1882*. Gulf Breeze, FL: Academic International Press, 1979.

Zurcher, Erik J. *Turkey. A Modern History*. London: I.B. Tauris & Co. Ltd, 2004.

Index